# Organizations as Knowledge Systems

# Organizations as Knowledge Systems

## Knowledge, Learning and Dynamic Capabilities

Edited by

Haridimos Tsoukas

and

Nikolaos Mylonopoulos

palgrave
macmillan

First published 2004 by
PALGRAVE MACMILLAN
Houndmills, Basingstoke, Hampshire RG21 6XS and
175 Fifth Avenue, New York, N.Y. 10010
Companies and representatives throughout the world

PALGRAVE MACMILLAN is the global academic imprint of the Palgrave
Macmillan division of St. Martin's Press, LLC and of Palgrave Macmillan Ltd.
Macmillan® is a registered trademark in the United States, United Kingdom
and other countries. Palgrave is a registered trademark in the European
Union and other countries.

ISBN 1–4039–1140–1

This book is printed on paper suitable for recycling and made from fully
managed and sustained forest sources.

A catalogue record for this book is available from the British Library.

Library of Congress Cataloging-in-Publication Data
European Conference on Organizational Knowledge, Learning, and
Capabilities (3rd: 2002: Athens, Greece)
Organizations as knowledge systems: Knowledge, learning, and dynamic
capabilities/edited by Haridimos Tsoukas and Nikolaos Mylonopoulos.
        p. cm.
Based on the Third European Conference on Organizational Knowledge,
Learning, and Capabilities in Athens, April 2002.
    Includes bibliographical references and index.
    ISBN 1–4039–1140–1 (cloth)
        1. Organizational learning – Congresses. 2. Intellectual capital –
Congresses. 3. Learning, Psychology of – Social aspects – Congresses.
4. Knowledge management–Congresses. 5. Organizational change–
Congresses. I. Tsoukas, Haridimos. II. Mylonopoulos, Nikolaos. III. Title.
HD58.82.E87 2002
302.3'5—dc21                                                    2003056339

10  9  8  7  6  5  4  3  2  1
13 12 11 10 09 08 07 06 05 04

Printed and bound in Great Britain by
Antony Rowe Ltd, Chippenham and Eastbourne

*To our parents*

*Fotini and Constantine (HT)*
*Alexandros and Eleni (NM)*

# Contents

# Notes on the Contributors

**Vasiliki Anyfioti** studied mechanical engineering in Greece followed by an MBA at INSEAD in 1998. She started her career in an engineering consultancy and continued in Roland Berger Strategy Consultants as project manager. Recently she moved to the drinks company William Grant & Sons as Business Development Manager for several European markets.

**Chris Argyris** is the James Bryant Conant Professor Emeritus, Harvard University. His books include *Overcoming Organizational Defenses* (1990), *Knowledge for Action* (1993), *Flawed Advice* (2000), *Theory in Practice* (1994) and *Organizational Learning II* (1996), both with Donald Schön, and *Action Science* (1985), with Diana Smith and Robert Putnam.

**Peter van Baalen** is Associate Professor in the Department of Decision and Information Sciences of the Rotterdam School of Management (Erasmus University, Rotterdam). His main fields of research interests are knowledge management, e-communities, e-learning, and management education. In these areas he wrote and edited a number of books and articles in national and international journals.

**Helen Blair** researched and taught HRM in the film and television industries at the University of Nottingham and Royal Holloway, and is now a human resource consultant with the BBC.

**Niels-Ingvar Boer** is a PhD candidate in the Department of Decision and Information Sciences of the Erasmus University Rotterdam. Currently he is working at the Ministry of the Interior and Kingdom Relations, at the Office of the State Secretary, dealing with strategic knowledge development. His research interests include social relations within knowledge networks, knowledge-sharing processes and organizational change.

**Irma Bogenrieder** trained at the Market Research Institute Interview, Amsterdam, and is Assistant Professor, Organizational Design and Organizational Processes, Rotterdam School of Management, Erasmus University Rotterdam, 1986. Her current research focuses on structures and processes for learning in organizations, and on co-ordination and learning.

**John Seely Brown** is a visiting scholar at the Annenberg Center at the University of Southern California. He was the Chief Scientist of Xerox Corporation until April 2002 and also the director of the Xerox Palo Alto Research Center (PARC) – a position he held for twelve years. His personal research interests include organizational and individual learning, digital culture, ubiquitous computing, and web service architectures.

**Maria Daskalaki** received her BA from the American College of Greece in Psychology, her MA from Lancaster University in Organisational Analysis and Behaviour and completed her PhD on Organisational Studies at Royal Holloway, University of London. She is currently a Senior Lecturer in HRM at Kingston Business School, UK, and Academic Liaison Director for Kingston University. Her research interests include social networks and organizational behaviour, organizational language and culture and knowledge and learning in organizations.

**Timothy Devinney** is Professor of Strategy at the Australian Graduate School of Management and Director of the Centre for Corporate Change. He has published six books and more than fifty articles in leading journals. He has broad research interests ranging from economics to strategy and organizational behaviour to statistical measurement. He has a PhD in economics from the University of Chicago.

**Soumitra Dutta** is the Roland Berger Professor of Business and Technology and Dean of Executive Education at INSEAD. He is the author of *The Global Information Technology Report* (2003), *The Bright Stuff* (2002) and *Embracing the Net* (2001). His current research is on business innovation with a particular focus on ebusiness.

**Theodore Evgeniou** is Assistant Professor of Information Systems in the Technology Management department of INSEAD. He holds two BSs, a MEng. and a PhD in Computer Science from MIT. His current research interests are in the areas of developing and implementing information-based strategies, as well as data mining and business intelligence, both developing technologies in these fields and studying their strategic impact on business.

**Stephen Gourlay** is Director of Doctoral Training at Kingston Business School, UK, responsible for the research methods training programme for the PhD and DBA students. He is a member of the School of Human Resource Management, and was previously director of the executive master's programme in Strategic Human Resource Management. He has been interested in knowledge management and learning for several years.

**Stefan Haefliger** studied economics at the University of St Gallen, Switzerland, and the Université Catholique de Louvain, Belgium. He works as a research associate at the Institute of Management at the University of St Gallen. His research focuses on the sociology of collective action and models of open source software development.

**Marleen Huysman** is Associate Professor in the Department of Business Administration, Vrije Universiteit, Amsterdam. Her research is focused on organizational learning and knowledge sharing within and between organizations. She has published articles in various international journals, and written and co-edited various books on this topic.

**Georg von Krogh** has been a Professor of Management at the University of St Gallen since 1994 and is also a Director of its Institute of Management. Dr von Krogh has published on such topics as the knowledge- and resource-based views of the firm, knowledge creation and technological innovation, as well as competitive strategy and organizational growth. He is currently exploring models of technological innovation and their effectiveness, in particular the characteristics of and conditions for open source software development.

**Kuldeep Kumar** is the Ryder Eminent Scholar and Professor of Information Systems at the Alvah H. Chapman Graduate School of Business, Florida International University. He is also the Professor of Information Systems Research at Erasmus University. His research interests include coordination of global work and outsourcing, component-based systems, and learning communities.

**Arie Y. Lewin** is Professor of Business Administration and Sociology and IBM Research Fellow at the Fuqua School of Business, Duke University. He is the Director of the Center for International Business Education and Research (CIBER). Professor Lewin has recently been named the Editor-in-Chief of the *Journal of International Business Studies*. He was founding Editor-in-Chief of *Organization Science* (1989–98). Professor Lewin is author or editor of several books and his research articles have appeared or are forthcoming in many different journals.

**Silvia Massini** is Lecturer in Economics and Technology Management at the Manchester School of Management of UMIST. Previously she was a researcher at CNR (Rome) and Warwick Business School (Coventry), and visiting fellow at SPRU (Sussex) and CRIC (Manchester). Her research spans the areas of the economics of innovation and technological change, the management of technology and organisational aspects of technological change. She has published in journals such as *Small Business Economics, European Management Journal, Research Policy* and the *Journal of Evolutionary Economics,* and contributed to a number of book chapters.

**David Midgley** is Professor and Head of Marketing at INSEAD. He has over 70 publications and is the author of three major reports on international competitiveness and management skills. His research areas include the diffusion of innovations, competitive strategy, global marketing and e-business issues.

**Nikolaos Mylonopoulos** is Assistant Professor of Information Systems at ALBA (Athens Laboratory of Business Administration), Greece. He has taught at Loughborough University Business School, Warwick Business School, Birkbeck College, the Athens University of Economics and Business and the Bordeaux School of Management, France. His work in information systems and electronic business has been published in international journals, he has served as guest editor for leading journals and is co-editor of the *International Journal of Information Technology Education.*

**Bart Nooteboom** has been operations research analyst, Shell International, The Hague and London, 1969–74; senior researcher, Research Institute for Small and Medium Sized Business, the Netherlands, 1974–87; Professor, first of Industrial Marketing and then of Industrial Organization, Faculty of Management and Organization, Groningen University, the Netherlands, 1987–99; Professor of Organizational Dynamics, Rotterdam School of Management, Erasmus University Rotterdam, 1999. His current research focuses on learning within and between organizations, alliances and networks, trust, and on governance and learning.

**Christos Pitelis** is Director of the Centre for International Business and Management (CIBAM) at the Judge Institute of Management, Cambridge Business School, and Director of Studies in Economics at Queens College, Cambridge University. He has published and consulted extensively on the areas of international business and industrial strategy, and is the editor of *The Collected Papers of Edith Penrose.*

**Christine Soo** is Assistant Professor of Strategy at the University of Western Australia. Her research areas include organizational learning, innovation, knowledge management and inter-organizational collaborations. She has a PhD from the Australian Graduate School of Management.

**Lesley Treleaven** is Senior Lecturer in the School of Management, University of Western Sydney, where she leads the Information Systems Knowledge Management Research Group. Her current research interests are in critical studies of organizations, employing Foucauldian discourse analysis and collaborative action research investigating new organizational capabilities for knowledge creation and knowledge sharing.

**Haridimos Tsoukas** is the George D. Mavros Research Professor of Organization and Management at ALBA and Professor of Organization Studies at Warwick Business School, University of Warwick. He has research and teaching interests in the areas of organizational behaviour and the management of change. He has taught at Manchester Business School, Warwick Business School, and the University of Cyprus. His research has been published in several leading academic journals and he has edited four books, including *The Oxford Handbook of Organization Theory*. He is Editor-in-Chief of *Organization Studies* and editorial board member of several leading journals.

# Foreword: Towards a Respectful Organization

*John Seely Brown*

In management fields, knowledge seems to be everywhere – the topic of every talk, the solution to every problem, the heart of every corporate mantra, and the topic of almost all workshops, conferences and proceedings. Five years ago, we all worried about 'information overload'. Now perhaps it is 'knowledge overload' that should worry us.

And yet, jaded by knowledge in all its guises, I found the Third European Conference on Organizational Knowledge, Learning and Capabilities in Athens, April 2002, on which this book is based, both invigorating and enlightening. It seemed to me that, running beneath the surface of the talks, discussions and the papers published here, there was something quite distinct. For once the participants did not try to appropriate knowledge for their own purposes. Rather, they treated it with what I can only describe as profound respect – respect for its complexities, subtleties, and difficulties. Truly respecting knowledge, it became evident as the conference went on, also involves respecting the people who embody that knowledge, the knowers. And it involves respecting the practices that manifest that knowledge, or the knowing. The knowledge that you will read about in these pages is not something to be expropriated or engineered. It is very much something to be respected.

Indeed, that word *respect* stayed with me throughout the conference, particularly in an intense dinner discussion with Chris Argyris following his keynote address. Our topic was 'double-loop learning', that absolutely fundamental insight with which Argyris and Schön revolutionized the field. Why, Chris wanted to know, after twenty-five years of discussions of the concept, were there still so few (if any) examples of corporations successfully engaging in double-loop learning? Why had so few failed to become 'Model II' learning organizations? And what would it take to change things?

Of course, one of the difficulties of addressing this question is finding the right level on which to approach it. Do we look at the individual – so often the hero or the villain of the story, the creative entrepreneur, or the stupid or cussed colleague, resistant to change? Do we look at the organization as a whole – the collective that, however large and diverse, is often assumed to share a common body of knowledge? Or do we look at something in between?

Inevitably, having analysed organizational behaviour for so long from the perspective of the community of practice, I tend to answer 'something in between' – and to believe that double-loop learning often does occur in organizations at the level of communities of practice, but that at the level of the organization as a whole, it is harder to understand and more likely to be discouraged than promoted. For double-loop learning is inherently disruptive and organizations dislike disruption.

In managing their internal division of labour, organizations inevitably produce what Karen Knorr Cetina (1999) has aptly called distinct 'epistemic cultures', each with distinct assumptions about such epistemic issues as evidence, reliability, trust, and truth. And while organizations know well how to deal with divisions of labour, they are usually less adept at dealing with divisions of knowledge. The former are approached principally as matters of co-ordination and they are controlled by establishing business processes. The latter tend more to require negotiation-in-practice, and when that breaks down to call for explicit negotiation. Processes, furthermore, are well suited to single-loop learning; they are less adept at, even resistant to, the double-loop kind.

Here lies a fundamental inevitable tension inherent in organization. On the one hand we have the division of labour, co-ordinated primarily through command-and-control mechanisms. On the other, we have a division of knowledge growing out of that division of labour which leads to divergence and calls for continuous intercommunal negotiation. But – and this is often difficult for those who see their job as resolving tensions to understand – this tension is not necessarily a bad thing. Indeed, approached in the right way it can be extremely valuable. For I don't want to suggest that communities of practice somehow magically 'grow' double-loop learning. There is, I find myself repeatedly having to say, no magic to communities of practice. Indeed, because a great deal of their collective learning comes to communities through their tacit negotiations in practice, they can be thoroughly unreflective. But, in the organizational context, this inherent development of knowing-in-practice has a great deal of potential because as communities, despite their changing knowing-in-practice, they have to co-ordinate with other communities who are themselves changing in response to their own practice-based knowledge and knowledge-based practices.

The demands of practice, that is, continually push organizations out of synch as communities follow different imperatives of their own. Continuous misalignment between different communities of practice within an organization, however, usually goes unnoticed in part because of the slack inherent in even the most tight business process, and in part because the inter-communal acts of reconciliation that bring them back into synch are often themselves imperceptible. (And in part, it must be added, because the demands of process often simply force communities back into line whatever the insights implicit in their changing practice.)

But, occasionally, the communities involved cannot reconcile themselves to one another so easily, the boundary objects with which they work no longer smooth over cracks. When this happens, anger, contempt, frustration, and blame are all common occurrences. Then whatever has been learned is easily lost. But the same abrasiveness that produces these destructive outcomes, handled properly, can also, as Dorothy Leonard-Barton (1995) reminds us, be creative. The failure of established processes, when it doesn't get wasted in finger-pointing, can force communities to contemplate their own assumptions, to become collectively reflective practitioners, and to engage in intra-community double-loop learning as a precondition for inter-community reconciliation.

So the central challenge for organizations, particularly in a rapidly changing environment, is to make sure that the abrasiveness that arises out of the division of knowledge is neither wholly subdued by process, nor lost to contempt and organizational infighting. Which is why I believe that respect is critically important to creative organizations. Responding to change in their practices, communities tend to fall out of alignment with those with whom they must work and thus become increasingly unintelligible to one another. The only thing that can enable the fruitful process of reconciliation through negotiation, other than a coercive process, is trust and respect.

Let me now try to illustrate this process using an example from my own experiences at Xerox Palo Alto Research Center (PARC).

## Divisions of knowledge

PARC, which I used to direct, is famous on the one hand for all of its great inventions and, on the other, for its equally great inability to take these inventions to market, at least through the Xerox channels. On reflection, I believe that lack of respect was one of the central reasons for its failure. Coming up through the pure research side of Xerox, I naturally shared the beliefs of my research colleagues. Simply said – we were geniuses and the engineering and marketing sides of Xerox were idiots. And, similarly, they viewed us as having our heads buried in a silicon sandbox and, perhaps, being a bit arrogant.

But experience undermined this arrogance and slowly taught me that the amount of creative problem solving and sense making required to take an invention to market, to turn the invention into a real innovation, were at least as great as what went into the invention itself. PARC researchers could have learned volumes from working with business development folks. Moreover, what we would have learned would have reflected critically on our own practice, illuminating not only the embedded assumptions of other communities, but of our own as well. The potential for abrasions between these two quite different communities of practice was undoubtedly significant, but with the right approach, on both sides, it could have been made creative rather than contemptuous. But since the communities did not respect one another the chance of useful exchange between the two was minimal. The intercommunity boundary was thoroughly sticky.

Let me take as an example a piece of research that led to a radically new kind of printing technology. As an example of radical innovation at work, this was research at its best. The technological breakthrough that enabled this new kind of printing technology was produced by a community of practice in our research centre that comprised physicists, material scientists, digital designers, computer scientists and lab technicians, most of whom had worked together or worked next door to each other for years. The design involved mems (micro mechanical electrical systems) devices and a scheme for digitally focussing acoustic waves that depended on surface tension of the inks to form the underlying 'explosive' or propelling mechanism. Unfortunately, surface tension has a mind of its own, so we also had to use digital logic to compensate for any misfirings and slight midcourse corrections that the pico-litre packets of ink might need as they set out to precisely hit their targets, all at a million times a second.

Tradeoffs were the name of the game. When some directional problems proved too hard to correct through materials science, the logic designers and computer scientists would jump in and add, to their already complex algorithms, more complexity to handle each new situation. There was always creative tension (and abrasion) between the different skills and responsibilities within our own small community of practice. But each researcher knew what he could do with his techniques and just how hard it would be for the others to compensate for it not being done. Designs were constantly being changed, skills combined, new analytical models built to cut down on the number of experiments that needed to be tried and so on. At times the physicists would turn to helping the algorithm folks and vice versa. In all there was a shared sense of dependability, trust, and respect within the group.

Under these conditions, the creation and circulation of knowledge was almost inseparable. A great deal of work was a form of negotiation in practice requiring very little explicit direction. Think, by analogy, of the way people take turns in a conversation. In such, no one has to say, 'Now it is my turn to speak.' Rather, turns are arranged 'on the fly' with very little attention to how it all happens. Communication and co-ordination occurred primarily in practice itself, rather than as separate and distinct activities. Trust was implicit and seldom articulated. But, on a more explicit level, we would ask each other hard questions. Was there really an absolute limit to how far that parameter could be pushed? Was the model really right? And so on. As such, we were becoming reflective practitioners simply because we really didn't know if our failure to achieve some goal was because of the lack of our techniques or because of limits to the underlying physics. Listening with humility was key. What was the backtalk of the situation actually telling us? Fundamental assumptions weren't being unearthed by yelling (physically or meta-physically) at each other but by challenging each other and responding to those challenges.

## Across the great divide

Everything seemed very different when it came to selling the idea to the engineers who would have to turn our prototype into a product. What they were offered looked like an inkjet but, based as it was on ultrasonic sound to propel the ink drops, it was, despite the apparent similarity, in fact profoundly new. None the less, after a great deal of extra testing to ensure its robustness, we finally approached the Chief Engineer, extolling its virtues and assuring him this technology was robust enough to serve as a product platform.

I remember all too well the exchange that unfolded. 'Tell me, John,' he said, 'just when was the last product you personally developed.' 'Never did,' I replied. 'OK, when was the last time you were in a manu-facturing plant?' 'Years ago,' I said. And so the questioning went on. Finally he said quite bluntly, 'Why should I believe in any of your judge-ments about the manufacturability of this product? You know virtually nothing about our manufacturing practices or our set of sensibilities. You are not from our community at all. You are an alien. Yes you have fancy data and fancy equations, but those abstractions don't talk to us.'

The trust, reciprocity, and respect, on which the group had depended quite as much as the individual's scientific skills, were now completely missing. Our sensibilities were worlds apart. Our practices were so different that the same words meant completely different things to each other. Even our prototype, while thoroughly significant for us, was so far from being a meaningful artifact in his world that it could not function as a useful boundary object between our two communities of practice. And in the place of these links, there was no trust or respect to bridge the gap.

Perhaps with the bitter experience of earlier breakdowns between the labs and the engineers, this time we worked to develop a working relationship. Over the next month we worked with his engineers to learn their point of view. We learned their language, their data analysis tools, their stress techniques and so on. We certainly learned more about manufacturing than we should have, but in the process we gained insight into their worldview, into what worked for them, into what they took as evidence and where they looked for reliability. They weren't being jerks – my initial characterization of them. Indeed, their suspicious reaction was quite understandable given past experience. There was no reason for them to accept our judgements about their world, the world of manufacturability. And, perhaps more critically, there was insufficient respect between the two groups for our insight to be taken on trust.

We did not only learn about the engineers in this process. We learned a great deal about ourselves and our own assumptions. It was not until we clashed at the boundaries of our two communities of practice, and clashed around a boundary object *qua* physical prototype, that we started to find a way to challenge our own beliefs about what the manufacturability and life expectancy of the envisioned product was apt to be. Slowly we began to understand enough about their practices that we could start to see why we were not answering their concerns. At which point, we could start to construct a bridge between the two and creativity could escape the boundaries of a particular community and flow into the organization as a whole.

## Organizational implications

This was just one small step towards creating a respectful organization but, from this experience, I began to sense just how hard it is to listen with humility and yet just how important that skill is if we are to transform radical inventions into radical innovations. Of course, a story does not make a theory but I hope it helps orient us towards appreciating just how important it is to be aware of the epistemic violence we can unconsciously do and how we can use the clashes between diverse communities of practice to help us become aware of our own implicit assumptions.

## Acknowledgement

I am deeply indebted to my colleague Paul Duguid for his insightful thoughts and his tireless help in crafting this foreword.

## References

Knorr Cetina, K. (1999) *Epistemic Cultures*, Cambridge, Ma: Harvard University Press.

Leonard-Barton, D. (1995) *Wellsprings of Knowledge*, Boston, Ma: Harvard Business School Press.

# Introduction: What does it Mean to View Organizations as Knowledge Systems?

*Haridimos Tsoukas and Nikolaos Mylonopoulos*

## The re-discovery of knowledge

Next time you receive your bank statement take a look at it. Probably the electricity and phone bills were directly debited, and the mortgage paid with a standing order. Perhaps you wrote a cheque for two tickets to the opera, and charged the cookery books you bought down town to your account. Suppose now that I look at all your bank statements for the past year. Can I tell what sort of person you are? Someone who always pays their bills on time? Someone who loves music and cooking? Probably. I have information about some of your financial transactions and, through them, I learn about your patterns of consumption. But do I get to know you?

Answering this straightforward question is not as simple as it might at first appear. All the terms of the question beg more questions: Who am I? Who are you? What does 'to know' mean? Suppose I am a banker considering your application for a loan. Your bank statements show that you pay bills on time, you have not encumbered yourself with excessive loans, your spending patterns are reasonable. I infer that, most likely, you are financially trustworthy, a safe bet. But my inference is not contained in the information I have in front of me. I need to work it out. Thus the question 'Who am I?' is crucial since the perspective I adopt and the kind of action I undertake depend on my institutional identity as a banker – a sensationalist journalist searching for a 'story', or a suspicious partner, would look at the same information differently.

Your bank statement represents a tiny portion of your set of actions during the past month. Even if I had records of all those actions, I would still be unable to answer the question 'Who are you?', for I would be unable to judge the *significance* of your recorded actions. You may have

1

become a member of your local tennis club, which might make me think that you are a sporty person. But, by talking to you, I realize that it is not so much your love of tennis that brought you to the club as your need to make new friends. Only if I know what *matters* to you, can I begin to know you better.

Your bank statement or, more generally, any record representing particular actions, may provide someone else with information, but not necessarily with knowledge. Although both of these terms are often used interchangeably, they are not identical. Philosophers such as Toulmin (1990), MacIntyre (1985) and Feyerabend (1999), among others, have described how the meaning of knowledge has changed radically in the last three centuries. Until the Middle Ages knowledge was conceived in essentially classical Greek (particularly Aristotelian) terms: knowledge was primarily self-knowledge and the search for the virtuous life; it did not so much imply the exercise of the individual cognitive faculty as the ability to participate effectively in a larger collective; it was context-dependent and infused with values. By contrast, with the mechanization and secularization of the world during the modern age, knowledge acquired a strongly utilitarian meaning. It gradually became identified with abstraction and the ability to obtain results; it no longer incorporated ultimate values but acquired descriptive neutrality.

Whereas in Aristotelian thinking individuals and objects were defined in terms of characteristic purposes, or roles they were expected to fulfil, in modern thinking they are described in abstract terms, dissociated from any evaluative criteria. Modern thinking has split apart evaluative and factual statements, which for the pre-moderns formed a unity (MacIntyre, 1985; Tsoukas and Cummings, 1997). For example, in Aristotelian thinking, the concept of a 'knife' cannot be defined independently of the concept of a *good* knife. Because we know that a knife is a tool for cutting things (that is to say, we know what it is *for*) we can draw the conclusion that a sharp knife is a good knife. A factual statement ('sharp knife') is also an evaluative statement ('a good knife').

Similarly, from such factual statements as 'He has more customers than any other carpenter in town', and 'He repeatedly wins prizes for his artifacts', we can draw the evaluative conclusion that 'He is a good carpenter'. We can do this because to think of people as carpenters (or teachers, farmers, managers, and so on) is to think of them as having certain purposes by virtue of their roles (MacIntyre, 1985). In such a mode of thinking, individuals and objects are not defined merely 'factually' (that is, as abstract entities), but socially – as being embedded in particular social practices and contexts, and this is what enables evaluative and factual statements to merge. From the Greek classical period until the late Middle Ages, knowledge was seen, at least throughout what is now termed the Western world, not as the exercise of an individual cognitive faculty (that is, information processing) but as a category of being.

Drucker (1993) has argued that one of the key events that reflected the changing meaning of knowledge in the eighteenth century was the publication of *Encyclopédie* in France (edited by Diderot and d'Alembert between 1751 and 1772). For the first time knowledge ceased to reside into the heads of certain authoritative individuals. It was extracted from social practices and contexts, taking instead the form of a manual, which contained generic statements – information – describing how the world works. In Drucker's words, '[the *Encyclopédie*] converted experience into knowledge, apprenticeship into textbook, secrecy into methodology, doing into applied knowledge' (Drucker, 1993). On the basis of such abstract, objective, codified, results-oriented, publicly available knowledge, modern individuals would be able to control their destiny in a way that had never been possible before. More than anything else, knowledge was power to change the world.

This conception of knowledge is reflected in the current use of the term 'information'. In late modern societies, 'information' denotes a set of abstract, de-contextualized items, subject to human manipulation, allegedly representing the world as it is (Tsoukas, 1997). The impressive development of Information and Communication Technologies (ICTs) has helped further to transform the earlier (ancient-cum-medieval) meaning of knowledge. The electronic storage, processing and retrieval, and the instant communication of information, manifested most impressively in the Internet, have made it so tempting for us late moderns to view *all* knowledge in terms of information. This leads to *information reductionism*: we believe we get to know the world through layers of abstract representations about the world.

If, however, all knowledge is viewed as information, if 'to know' means having information on the variation of certain indicators thought to capture the phenomenon at hand, our knowledge of the phenomenon itself risks becoming problematic. The quality of a social practice such as teaching, for example, belongs to a dimension different from that of its manifestations in the form of certain indicators. Just as a cube belongs to a dimension different from that of its sides and the angle from which each side is seen at any point in time, so the quality of teaching is not the sum of its appearances. It is something that is presented through them all and through other possible appearances as well. We recognize quality when we see it – we *infer* it – but quality itself is not contained in any of the formal statements describing it, usually in the form of procedures and indicators.

Not only is the identity of a phenomenon different from its manifold representations – for example, the quality of teaching differs from indicators of quality; trustworthiness differs from the payment of debts – but the representations themselves are only a part of all the representations that could be brought into existence. Our information about a phenomenon is clearly constrained by the available measurement and observation instruments (both human and technological). A bank statement is a particular description of some of one's actions, but it is by no means the only one available. There are several other aspects of one's life that are not captured through a bank statement. Even those aspects that *are* captured could be presented differently – who knows, one day our names and addresses may not be enough for a bank and our DNA profiles might also be printed. Our descriptions of the world are inherently incomplete. There always are more ways of thinking about the world than those in use at any point in time.

More generally, the presence of a phenomenon is surrounded by *absence* – what we know about it at any point in time, what is available, is a subset of what *could* be (see Argyris in this volume). Any phenomenon can be represented through other forms that may have not yet been stated or invented – indeed this is what is assumed by, say, efforts to continuously improve quality. In other words, phenomena are surrounded by the horizon of the potential and the absent. What we have available is a finite representation of something, never a complete one. As Sokolowski (2000: 28) observes, 'The horizon of the potential and the absent surrounds the actual presences of things. The thing can always be presented in more ways than we already know; the thing will always hold more appearances in reserve.'

The information representing a phenomenon and the phenomenon itself are not identical – the map is not the territory (Weick, 1990). Any phenomenon is given in a mixture of presence and absence – what is and what might be – and is thus inherently richer than information, which focusses on presence by revealing what is or has been. Notice that if all knowledge is reduced to information, the distinction between presence and absence is lost. Our notion of knowledge is impoverished, since to have knowledge of something is, among other things, to be aware of its *potential* – to have a sense of what it may become, whereas to have information is to be confined to the past, to what *has* been. The need to focus on potential – on how things could be different – is well understood by Argyris (in this volume), who criticizes organizational scholars for excessively focussing on the status quo: describing organizations as they are, instead of discussing how they might be. If we are interested in effecting real organizational change, we need to move beyond the Newtonian regulative ideal of describing organizations as completely as possible towards formulating testable normative theories.

This is not to say that the 'absent' is somehow objectively available 'out there', waiting to be discovered by the persistent researcher. There may be certain objective properties that simply escape our current information set but, importantly, since social phenomena are continuously reconstituted by human interpretation and action, their potential informational properties are indeterminate. Thus, the information read into the bank statement by the banker, the journalist or the partner does not exist without those individuals and their respective contexts, in the first instance.

As well as ignoring the meaning-full character of knowledge and collapsing a phenomenon to its manifestations, information reductionism misses the distinction between 'knowing that' and 'knowing how' (Ryle, 1949). 'Knowing that' is a set of propositions and statements about an object of study. Your bank manager knows *that* last month you bought two tickets for the opera. 'Knowing how', however, is a practical matter, a skill. Knowing *how* to buy tickets for the opera, trivial as it may sound, is a practical skill that is not (and cannot be) recorded into your bank statement. 'Knowing how' – practical knowledge – is not transferable in the way that 'knowing that' is. I may read plenty of books on how to behave at a tea ceremony in Japan but it is only by actually taking part at such a ceremony that I will really pick up the necessary social skills (Kondo, 1990). 'Knowing that' is the spectator's knowledge; 'knowing how' is the agent's knowledge.

We learn practical skills not by accumulating information *in abstracto*, but by participating with others in common activities. As Reed (1996) notes, we learn skills not through matching our separate individual representations but rather by *fitting in* our set of experiences with those of others, in the context of common undertakings. Knowing is not a purely cognitive activity, it is bodily too: our whole being takes part in learning a process (Dreyfus and Dreyfus, 1986; Polanyi, 1962). Much of the knowledge we thus learn is tacit and cannot be fully articulated as a set of instructions (as 'knowing that'). Individuals are not mere processors of information; far more than that, they are members of social practices whose knowledge derives, to a large extent, from such membership (Tsoukas, 1996, 2003). Individuals increase their knowledge by learning how to appreciate the *significance* of the patterns of events and actions they are concerned with.

For the bank manager, for example, to know how to assess your loan application, he needs to have learned to judge the significance of certain patterns of relevant information, and this presupposes his active participation into the bankers' community of practice (Spender, 1989). Knowing how to act within a domain of action is learning to make competent use of the categories and the distinctions constituting that domain. One learns how to act only because one has been taught by the more experienced members of a community of practice to apply the key categories of the practice in certain contexts (Cook and Yanow, 1996; Schön, 1991). We often make use of information in the context of *collective* domains of action – companies, schools, hospitals, and so on (Tsoukas and Vladimirou, 2001).

Information in the social world does not consist solely of free-floating items, representations that can exist independently of people. Whatever information is about, it is necessarily partial; it presupposes a particular perspective of looking at an activity and it requires interpretation. Both the *perspective* and the *interpretation* are not pieces of information; they are implicit and require a developed interpretive ability to choose them. Such ability is learned in the context of a particular domain of action with others. It is, to a large extent, tacit. Adopting a sharper perspective and applying a more in-depth interpretation (that is making better judgements of significance) is what distinguishes the expert from the novice.

Information is knowing *about* something – knowing about events, happenings, and transactions. Knowledge is knowing *of* something – appreciating the significance of patterns of events, happenings, and transactions. Information has extension – it can be accumulated, processed and extracted. Knowledge has depth – it involves the application of certain collectively sustained criteria in a particular domain of action. For information to lead to knowledge, we need to rediscover some of the classical and medieval connotations of knowledge: that it is essentially *social*, it is infused with *values*, and it is *personal* (Brown and Duguid, 2000).

We need also to realize that the desire to *know* presupposes *ac-knowledge-ment* of that which is to be known: the knowable is no mere *ob-ject*, something standing against the knower. Rather the knower needs to acknowledge the knowable, to develop what Bergson (1946) called 'intellectual sympathy' with the object to be known.

The development of expertise presupposes an 'intellectual sympathy' with one's endeavour. As novices we become experts by identifying with the activities we are engaged in; by 'assimilating' the tools, be they intellectual and/or physical, through which we make sense of the world.

As we learn to use a tool, any tool, we gradually become unaware of how we use it to achieve results – our knowledge becomes tacit, ineffable. We refine our ability to get things done by 'dwelling in' the tools through which we get things done. We know more than we can tell (Polanyi, 1962; Tsoukas, 2003).

## Organizations as knowledge systems: key issues and questions

Insisting on the distinction between information and knowledge and attributing to the latter an irreducibly social, value-laden and personal character has important implications for the way in which we view organizations. That organizations use, among other things, information to convert inputs into outputs has been widely accepted in management studies, especially by theorists espousing functionalist and systems' models of organizations. To go one step further, however, and take the view that organizations are *knowledge* systems requires further elucidation.

Viewing an organization, especially a firm, as a knowledge system focusses our attention not just on the kinds and amounts of information potentially stored in the formal organizational memory (made possible, clearly, by today's powerful ICTs) and on the consequent possibilities for searching for patterns in data warehouses (for example, through data mining) but, more broadly and more subtly, on how organizational members' work-related experiences are turned into publicly accessible knowledge (Smoliar, 2003; Tsoukas, 2002). We are thus enabled to ask questions about how information is elicited, interpreted and applied by organizational members in the particular circumstances confronting them, within the context of working with others; and how new usable knowledge comes about as a result of individuals applying what they know in ever-changing open-ended contexts.

Viewing organizations as knowledge systems makes us realize that the locus of individual understanding is not so much in the head as in *situated practice*: the individual understands and acts in the world through drawing on sets of socially defined values, beliefs and cognitive categories within particular material and social cirumstances (Brown and Duguid, 2000; Winograd and Flores, 1987; Eden and Ackerman, 1998; Suchman, 1987). Such a perspective views individuals not merely as information-processors (the human analogues of a computer) but as situated practical thinkers. An experienced photocopy repair technician, for example, does not form fully explicit representations of his tasks in an a-contextual manner. His ability to act comes from his habitual practical engagement in a social practice – *repairing* photocopiers – not by his abstract representation of his task in his mind (Orr, 1996). The world for him is 'ready-to-hand' (Heidegger, 1962) and it is so through the particular social practice into which he engages. The social practice (for example repairing photocopiers, teaching, navigating, writing software, etc.), not the cognizing subject, is the ultimate foundation of intelligibility. As Winograd and Flores (1987: 33) point out, summarizing Heidegger's view, 'a person is not an individual subject or ego, but a manifestation of *Dasein* within a space of possibilities, situated within a world and within a tradition'.

It has been argued above that 'knowledge' is different from 'information' in that the former is laden with judgements about *significance*. To take this further, following Bell (1999), it can be argued that the differentiating criterion is the extent to which each of these concepts reflects human involvement with the reality at hand. Whereas 'data' are given items and events (minimal involvement) in an ordered sequence, 'information' is a context-based arrangement of items whereby relations between them are shown (medium involvement), and 'knowledge' is the judgement of the significance of events and items derived from a particular context and/or theory (maximum involvement) (Bell, 1999: lxi–lxiv).

Thus, to have knowledge of something is to be able to make a judgement about the significance of events, problems, issues, and items, which comes from a particular context and/or theory – think, for example, of a medical diagnosis or an engineering recommendation (Hunter, 1991; Polanyi, 1962). Although it is individuals who make such judgements, the latter are made possible by the existence of pools of generalized knowledge (theories), produced and sustained by communities of peers (for example doctors, engineers, photocopy technicians, flute makers) upon which individuals draw in the course of their action (Brown and Duguid, 1991; Cook and Brown, 1999; Eden and Ackerman, 1998: 74; Spender, 1989). Organizational knowledge, therefore, can be defined as the ability members of an organization have developed to make *judgements* within a *collective domain of action*, based on an appreciation of *context* and/or set of *generalizations* (Tsoukas and Vladimirou, 2001: 979).

Thus, viewing an organization as a knowledge-based system implies that we are simultaneously concerned with the following three issues: (a) how individuals exercise their judgements and create new knowledge in the course of their work and/or of interaction with other people; (b) how collective domains of action are sustained and particular values and beliefs within them become institutionalized; and (c) how particular sets of generalizations – abstract categories such as 'a faulty photocopier'

(Orr, 1996), 'a clunky flute' (Cook and Brown, 1999), 'a pathological lung' (Polanyi, 1962: 101), and abstract statements of the if–then type – are selected, institutionalized and modified. Inversely, it is equally intriguing to explore how organizations forget what they know; when and why individuals avoid exercising their judgement; and if there are limits to the information-processing and learning capacity of the organization.

From these issues, several questions emerge. How is new knowledge created in organizations, both in conditions of direct and mediated social interaction? What are the conditions ensuring maximum knowledge creation? What are the most effective ways for sharing knowledge? What are the obstacles to knowledge sharing, within and across communities of practice, and how can they be best overcome? What sort of organizational processes facilitate or hinder the exercise of individual judgement? What is the influence of institutionalized values on how individuals exercise their judgement? How are institutionalized values and generalizations modified as a result of individuals applying them in open-ended contexts?

It should be clear by now that to view organizations, especially firms, as knowledge systems implies, among other things, the underscoring of the crucial role of *collective understandings* and *interpretations* that emerge in firms over time (see Treleaven in this volume). To be precise, it may be preferable to talk about *self*-understandings and *self*-interpretations, since firms' actions are guided by how firms perceive themselves and their environments (Morgan, 1997). As economic sociologists have long argued, for firms to exist at all, human and material resources must be combined in such a way that their integration generates more value than their individual utilization (Whitley, 1987). This implies that managers have delegated authority over the integration of resources so that managers can make a difference to the resources being combined and transformed (Barnard, 1966). The crucial element is not so much the resources a firm uses as what it does with them – the *services* rendered by a firm's resources (Penrose, 1959), which depend on how resources are interpreted and acted upon (see Pitelis in this volume). It is in that sense that the most important resource is knowledge: in as much as it is knowledge – the collective self-understandings that have emerged over time – that enables management to make distinct uses of organizational resources by devising distinctive value-creating strategies, organizational knowledge – the ability to collectively make 'better' judgements of significance than others – is what makes the difference. As Cockburn *et al.* (2000: 1124) aptly remark, commenting on Porter's five forces framework and the resource-based view of the firm, despite their differences in analytical focus and theoretical orientation, both perspectives 'share two assumptions: that competitive advantage arises through earlier or more favourable access to resources, markets, or organizational opportunities; and that exploiting such opportunities reflects some degree of *active interpretation of internal and external environmental signals by managers'* (emphasis added).

Organizations differ in terms of how they choose to use their resources and, by implication, in terms of the services they derive from them. Distinctiveness, in this view – a certain way of doing things – is an inherent feature of every organization (Kay, 1995; Pitelis, 2002, and in this volume; Tsoukas, 1996). As Lewin and Massini (in this volume), among others, point out, developing a distinctive way of utilizing resources depends on the formal and informal processes of communication and learning that are in place, through which organizational members are, in principle, enabled to draw upon accumulated organizational knowledge (that is routines) and experience, as well as upon externally supplied information, in order to carry out their tasks in a co-ordinated fashion (Grant, 1996, 2002). Doing so, and reflecting on how this is done, are the stimuli for inventing new ways of using resources. Viewing, therefore, an organization as a knowledge system draws our attention to both the organizational routines individuals draw upon to carry out their tasks *and* to the inherently creative potential of human action, which stems from the activation of routines in open-ended contexts (Cook and Brown, 1999; Spender, 1996; Tsoukas and Chia, 2002; Tsoukas, 2002).

Viewed from a knowledge-based perspective, Weber's classic description of formal organization (bureaucracy) is, in effect, a description of a knowledge hierarchy: the higher one moves up the organizational ladder, the more one deals with abstractions (decontextualized representations) (Barnard, 1966) and the more macroscopic knowledge of the organization one develops (Jaques, 1998). In formal organizations, how senior management teams (often referred to as 'top teams') view their firms and their environments; the cognitive structure that underlies their thinking; and how, and to what extent, individual managerial cognitions converge through interaction to make a collective knowledge representation, with what effects, have been, and still are, very interesting issues to explore (Eden and Ackerman, 1998; Eden and Spender, 1998; Huff and Jenkins, 2002). For example, Tripsas and Gavetti (2000) have shown, through their analysis of the difficulties Polaroid has had in coping with the shift from analogue to digital imaging technologies (in which, interestingly, the company had invested a lot of time before they became widely used in the industry), how managerial cognitive representations crucially shape organizational capabilities and contribute to inertia.

Following on from the above, several questions arise: how do collective managerial knowledge maps develop and change? What other non-cognitive factors, such as emotions, self-perceptions, personal background, and organizational politics, shape managerial cognitions, how, with what effects? Why are some top management teams better than others in responding with foresight to changes in their environment? How do geographically dispersed teams develop a sense of collective knowledge through mediated interaction, with what effects?

Several scholars have noted that Weber's description of formal organization is rather limited in today's advanced capitalist economies (Heckscher and Donnellon, 1994; Hirschhorn, 1997): while how top teams interact, reason, and cognitively represent their firms and their environments is still extremely interesting and important for the development of corporate strategy, the increasing reliance of economic activity on scientific knowledge and research makes the idea of a knowledge hierarchy difficult to sustain (Bell, 1999; Drucker, 1993). Such a challenge to the Weberian notion of organization has led some researchers to further argue that, from a knowledge-based perspective, *all* organizational activities are infused with knowledge anyway (Moingeon and Edmondson, 1996; Tsoukas, 1996; Tsoukas and Vladimirou, 2001) and, if this is recognized, the question of how knowledge and learning are facilitated and managed in an organization become legitimate and important concerns of management. Moreover, acknowledging the centrality of knowledge to organizational functioning, opens up a raft of new questions concerning the processes through which workers' task-related knowledge was de-legitimated and marginalized for the most part of the twentieth century, due to the historical dominance of mechanistic forms of organization and management (Thompson *et al.*, 2001: 929).

What a knowledge-based perspective of organizations does is to enable us to appreciate the fact that all organizational work necessarily involves knowledge (be it highly specialized scientific knowledge or generally available lay knowledge) and, moreover, that the knowledge an organizational member possesses does not so much consist of a finite set of pieces of information as of a constantly developing set of generalizations, collective understandings and experiences. As Spender (1996: 46) argues, 'this approach legitimates the knowledge and learning of the rest of the firm's employees and shows that the firm's learning is unlikely to be as effective as it might be if it is managed top-down by instructing subordinates on what and how to invent or observe about the environment. Customers' ideas and the ideas of those that interact directly with customers, become important.'

Systematically pooling individual experiences and, whenever possible, codifying and sharing them; enabling employees to share, reflect on, and learn from their experiences (codified or not); and dynamically updating the stock of knowledge upon which individuals draw, have been defining features of organizational knowledge and knowledge management. Clearly, this set of processes is even more important in knowledge-intensive firms – the business organizations that heavily depend on highly specialized, 'theoretical' knowledge for their functioning. While all organizations may be seen as knowledge systems, those that rely on expensive 'theoretical' knowledge (Bell, 1999) have every incentive to be the frontrunners in developing sophisticated systems for managing their knowledge assets.

From the above it follows that a knowledge-based perspective of the firm sees the latter not as an inert information store in which a large but finite amount of explicitly articulated information resides, but as a set of dynamic *social interactions* (both internal and with the outside world), through which individuals potentially develop and refine their knowledge sets and skills, aided by dynamic organizational information systems, and enabled to act towards organizational purposes by drawing on institutionalized values and beliefs. A very interesting question to explore is how people in a knowledge-intensive firm are organized, managed, and developed to help the firm achieve a sustainable knowledge-based competitive advantage.

Indeed, from a resource-based view of the firm, the challenge for knowledge-intensive firms is how to render their human resources valuable, rare, inimitable, and non-substitutable (Barney, 1991). This implies that the organization must ensure that it hires those people with the highest abilities, who continue to maintain and exhibit them throughout their careers; trains them to acquire firm-specific skills; and organizes and manages them in such a way as to maximize social and organizational capital. This is easier said than done. Whereas a highly analysable task is amenable to an explicit articulation of the steps the employee needs to go through, this is not so in a knowledge-intensive task. A software writer, for example, needs to exercise her intuition and judgement and undertake initiative to complete her task effectively, in a way that cannot be algorithmically described; rather her method of work is picked up indirectly through socialization in the community of her peers (Wenger, 1998). To be executed effectively, knowledge-intensive tasks rely on collective, semi-autonomous forms of work organization in a way that analysable tasks do not. Knowledge-intensive tasks are also difficult when it comes to evaluation and performance assessment. To be more precise, the community of peers appears to be the most appropriate one to carry out task evaluations, which raises interesting questions regarding the role of management in this process. How is performance appraisal to be conducted? What are appropriate forms of compensation? How is management control sustained? What is the role of leadership? Or, more generally, how should knowledge workers be organized and managed?

One might be easily tempted to see organizations as mechanistic knowledge systems, wherein the Weberian hierarchical structure is obsolete and more networked formal mechanisms are needed. Although this is a valid perspective in so far as it enables us to engineer the formal structures and computer-based information systems that are necessary, one should not overlook the intensely *organic* character of knowledge creation and sharing and use. Mechanistic structures and systems are important enablers, but they are by themselves sterile. Knowledge thrives when it is cultivated, cross-polinated, contaminated, fertilized. This is why acculturation is of such significance in the effective use of organizational knowledge.

To sum up, viewing organizations as knowledge systems highlights the crucial role of human interpretation, communication, and skills in generating effective organizational action. It also underlines the *dynamic* character of such processes since they unfold in time, in contexts of *social interaction*. A knowledge-based view of the firm enables us to move beyond the individual to explore the broader social basis – the social practices, forms of interaction, routines, and the work organization – upon which individual knowledge and action draw.

More than any other time in the history of management, what reflective practitioners have known all along is now widely acknowledged: intangible resources are crucial in giving a firm the basis of sustainable competitive advantage – how managers share their knowledge of their companies and their environments matters; how organizational members are organized to develop their knowledge and skills is crucial; how, and the extent to which, individuals are willing to re-arrange and re-order what they know is important for the emergence of new knowledge and innovation.

The ever-increasing reliance of economic activities in advanced capitalist economies on 'theoretical' knowledge and information, as well as the importance of innovation in conditions of 'hyper-competition' (Ilinitch, Lewin and D'Aveni, 1998), 'high-velocity markets' (Brown and Eisenhardt, 1998), shrinking product lifecycles and technological discontinuities, have made firms across a number of industries increasingly reliant upon finding effective ways to manage their knowledge assets.

Research into these topics is likely to be more illuminating if it draws on a number of perspectives and theories than if a singular perspective is adopted (Beech *et al.*, 2002). And this is one more additional benefit of a knowledge-based perspective of the firm: given that 'knowledge' is a concept that has historically crossed a variety of disciplines, it is more fruitfully explored if insights from a number of different approaches are incorporated into our explanatory accounts. For example, a micro-sociologist, especially an ethnomethodologist, interested in organiza-tional knowledge will have a lot to say about how individuals are socialized into certain sets of understandings and beliefs as well as how taken-for-granted routines are established and applied (Boden, 1994). Similarly, phenomenologists, pragmatists and hermeneutical philoso-phers have long examined the different kinds of knowledge that are involved in social life and how they are interwoven with different forms of action (Schutz, 1970; Joas, 1996). Social and cognitive psychologists have long dealt with the nuts and bolts of human cognition (Harre, 2002; Hutchins, 1995; Rogoff and Lave, 1999; Varela *et al.*, 1991), and some economists made knowledge a constitutive aspect of economic activity (Dosi *et al.*, 1998; Hayek, 1945, 1989; Foss and Loasby, 1998; Loasby, 1999; Pitelis, 2002). More recently, developments in complexity theory and evolutionary theory have focussed, respectively, on how knowledge emerges in complex adaptive systems (Axelrod and Cohen, 2000; Stacey *et al.*, 2000) and how knowledge, viewed as a collection of memes, is generated, selected and retained (Dennett, 1996). Drawing selectively on the above perspectives and seeking to synthesize coher-ently insights from several of them is, we believe, the way forward.

'Knowledge' is as complex a notion as it is old and the more angles we bring to it the more likely it is that we will make better sense of it. Just as new organizational knowledge is created out of human interac-tions (Nonaka and Takeuchi, 1995; Tsoukas, 2001), so new insights into organizational knowledge are likely to be created through the interac-tion of researchers with different backgrounds and conceptual frames. A knowledge-based perspective of organizations gives us the opportunity to overcome traditional barriers between different perspectives and dis-ciplines, and opens the way for conceptual innovation through imagi-native and coherent syntheses.

## Overview of the book

Most essays in this volume are derived from the Third European Conference on Organizational Knowledge, Learning, and Capabilities, which was hosted by ALBA (Athens Laboratory of Business Administration), in April 2002, in Athens. The conference topic reflected the increasing emphasis that has been placed in the last ten years or so on seeing organizations as knowledge systems: bundles of dynamic knowledge assets, the effective management of which affords business organizations competitive advantage (Choo and Bontis, 2002). The organizational capability to communicate, share, learn, and develop knowledge was a core theme of the conference, which, to a large degree, is manifested in the esssays included here.

Part I ('Organizational Knowing and Learning') examines some key issues in organizational learning, focussing on what makes organizational learning possible (or impossible). Chris Argyris ('Double-Loop Learning and Implementable Validity') addresses the defensive routines that are active in both the organizations that become the focus of academic research *and* the scholarly community whose members conduct organizational research. Discussing several examples of organizational defensive routines, Argyris points out that the scholars conducting relevant studies unknowingly 'collude' with practitioners in ways that inhibit double-loop organizational learning. We know why organizations develop defensive routines and adopt single-loop learning solutions to their problems, but why do we scholars do that as well? According to Argyris the reason is that scholars adopt an outdated naturalistic epistemology: they seek to produce valid, generalizable knowledge, where validity is assessed solely by deriving hypotheses and testing them in the empirical world. The problem with this is that, while the concepts of 'internal' and 'external validity' are useful and well accepted in social science, they are of little use when scholars aim to generate *actionable* knowledge. Knowledge claims may have internal and external validity, and yet be lacking in implementability. For the latter to be enhanced, scholars need to stop focussing on the universe as is (that is, describing the status quo) and start defining alternative organizational arrangements while specifying, at the same time, causal theories that explain current dysfunctionalities and suggest ways of reaching alternative organizational states. As long as this is not done, organizational research risks reinforcing single-loop learning in organizations at the expense of radically rethinking and changing organizational dysfunctionalities.

Irma Bogenrieder and Bart Nooteboom ('The Emergence of Learning Communities: A Theoretical Analysis') examine the emergence of learning communities that engage in knowledge exploration. Exploitation of knowledge takes place within an established frame of work practice and presupposes a sense of shared identity between community members. Exploration, by contrast, takes place outside established norms and seeks to invent new or modified ones. In order to elaborate an in-depth account of the structure and learning processes in organizations and communities, the authors develop a theoretical framework based on the notion of scripts. On the basis of this model they demonstrate different levels of exploratory learning and subsequent change and adaptation within the community. At the lowest level of exploration, actors adjust only the individual validation rules that constrain their action in relation to their immediate peers at work. At the intermediate level of exploration, actors extend or reinvent their individual behavioural scripts; this may entail reconfiguration of the linkages and the construction of work organization at community level. At the highest level of exploration, the whole organizational script architecture is reconfigured; this entails extensive adaptation, both individual and collective. The authors extend their analysis to address the different kinds of communication rules that are necessary to bridge the cognitive diversity that is necessary for innovation, and to reconstruct the relevant shared beliefs at different levels of exploratory thinking.

Marleen Huysman ('Communities of Practice: Facilitating Social Learning while Frustrating Organizational Learning') questions the presumed positive relationship between communities of practice (COPs) and organizational learning. Traditionally, she argues, COPs have been seen as the most promising vehicle to support organizational learning. While this is often true, it is not invariably the case. We need a more nuanced understanding of the process of organizational learning, Huysman remarks, which will allow the possibility of COPs obstructing organizational learning. If we see organizational learning as a process of institutionalization, namely as a process consisting of three moments – externalization, objectification, and internalization – COPs are most useful in the first and the third moments, but not necessarily in the second. For learning to become *organizational* learning, local tacit knowledge (typically the knowledge that exists and is generated in COPs) needs to be objectified – to be accepted and shared throughout the organization. Yet this process of objectification may be hindered by COPs. In fact, as Huysman argues, although COPs are well suited to support learning in organizations, they do tend to obstruct organizational learning. Local knowledge that is generated and communicated in COPs tends to be 'sticky' and may not be politically acceptable to the dominant organizational coalition, hence it may stay local without it being diffused and accepted by the entire organization. Yet for organizational learning to take place, objectification needs to be strengthened.

Stephen Gourlay ('Knowing as Semiosis: Steps Towards a Reconceptualization of Tacit Knowledge') aims to offer a coherent account of tacit knowledge in a way that overcomes the flaws and contradictions of accounts currently on offer in management studies. Reviewing the relevant literature, he points out a lack of agreement as to what the term exactly means and notes a few problems with current conceptualizations. Gourlay argues that Polanyi, the inventor of the term, has been largely misunderstood, but his focus on *knowing* points a way out of the conceptual difficulties. Drawing on Dewey and Bentley's treatment of knowing as a 'sign-process' (or semiosis), Gourlay advances an intriguing account of tacit knowledge. A sign-process is a spectrum consisting of signal, designation, and symbol. The move from left to right denotes learning through bodily action, through learning by using ordinary language, to learning through the use of specialized symbolic language. Tacit knowing is 'signal' referring to knowing conducted through bodily and sub-verbal means. This model is both evolutionary and developmental. It is evolutionary in the sense that it refers to a range of life forms, from protozoa to mathematics. It is developmental in the sense that we all begin by only being capable of 'tacit' or 'bodily' knowing which then develops into more symbolic forms. Non-verbal modes of knowing persist alongside the verbal and linguistic modes of signing, as children develop into adults. The same happens in the development of professional expertise. Viewed in this manner, a sign-process provides the link between tacit and explicit knowledge – it is not a question of one or the other, or even of turning the former to the latter, but of both forms of knowing persisting side by side since they are both essential to skilled action.

Part II ('Sharing and Managing Distributed Knowledge') focusses on how distributed knowledge is shared and managed. Stefan Haefliger and Georg von Krogh ('Knowledge Creation in Open Source Software Development') address the conundrum presented by Open Source software communities. These communities perform a knowledge-intensive job producing some of the most valuable knowledge assets of the information economy, in the absence of the social cues of co-presence, or the shared understanding of face-to-face exchange. Knowledge sharing, through the processes of socialization, externalization, combination and internalization, provides the basis for individual and collective knowledge creation. Haefliger and von Krogh take particular issue with the process of socialization, or the direct exchange of tacit knowledge.

They draw on signal theory and the concept of microcommunities to show how electronic communities of individuals, without any prior common history, who hardly ever meet face to face, develop their own reference context and locate important communication cues elsewhere. It is interesting to note that two individuals from very diverse cultural backgrounds would find it difficult to communicate tacit knowledge in a face-to-face encounter. By contrast, the homogenizing nature of the Internet attenuates the differences (including prejudices) and focusses the attention of participants on pursuing their common goal (develop a given piece of software). Open Source programmers ascribe contextual cues to meta-activities (patterns of online conduct), to references to a common background (shared metaphors and language) and to code patterns (the 'character' of a piece of software code). A related question is how a highly distributed community that relies entirely on the intrinsic motivation of its members co-ordinates the production of such complex work. The authors draw on earlier work on knowledge activism to show how knowledge activists engage in various kinds of behaviours in order to mobilize (but not direct) collective action under the four modes of knowledge sharing.

Niels-Ingvar Boer, Peter J. van Baalen and Kuldeep Kumar ('The Implications of Different Models of Social Relations for Understanding Knowledge Sharing') focus on the motivational aspects of knowledge sharing. By drawing on relation models theory they explore the feasibility and characteristics of knowledge sharing in the context of different webs of social relations. The social relations models theory postulates that any social relation can be analytically decomposed into four atomic invariant models, namely community sharing, authority ranking, equality matching and market pricing. These four models can be combined in arbitrarily complex forms and need to be interpreted within a given cultural context. The authors argue that the social relation model in use determines the perception of knowledge and the motivations for sharing it. For example, in community-sharing relations knowledge is a common resource and sharing is motivated by intimacy and a sense of altruism, whereas in market-pricing relations, knowledge is a commodity and will be exchanged if the price (perhaps non-pecuniary) is right. Knowledge sharing is obstructed when there is some conflict in the perception and application of the social relation model in use. Such conflicts may take three forms. First, actors in a relation may behave on the basis of the same model but employ different acculturation criteria for the limits of common identity, hierarchical ordering, valid reciprocation tokens or utility valuations. Second, actors may attempt to share knowledge by applying different models of social relations altogether. For example, someone may attempt to exercise authority where reciprocation is expected. Third, organizational structures and information systems may not be aligned with the dominant models of social relations. For example, an attempt to introduce a community-oriented intranet application in an authoritarian culture where employer–employee relations are of the market-pricing kind, is bound to fail. The authors conclude by proposing a research programme to empirically validate the role of social relations models in knowledge sharing.

Analysing organizational change from a knowledge-based perspective brings out the complexities in getting individuals to share common objectives and knowledge in change management projects. Lesley Treleaven ('A Knowledge-Sharing Approach to Organizational Change: A Critical Discourse Analysis') presents empirical findings from a study of an Australian university in which academics were invited by the university executive to participate in a process of knowledge sharing to propose the establishment of new schools. However, such a process of sharing knowledge failed. Treleaven explores the reasons for this failure by drawing on Foucauldian discourse analysis. She points out that the different proposals were situated within multiple competing discourses, operating at three levels of analysis: the system of higher education in Australia; the University under focus; and the University's School of Management. The resulting tensions and contradictions were not effectively addressed and, consequently, knowledge sharing failed. Echoing what we said in the first section of this introduction, Treleaven points out that knowledge sharing is not just the exchange of information, but something more fundamental, involving values and beliefs, which, unless they are addressed, are bound to disrupt the process of knowledge sharing. In other words, in order for knowledge sharing to be effective, organizational members need to reach mutual understanding and establish a common interpretive framework through exploring their diverse values, beliefs and assumptions. Unless a broadly common language is established (something that is particularly important for professional bureaucracies such as universities, in which power tends to be diffuse), there isn't much that can be shared – communication will be disrupted by definitional difficulties, competing values, and defensive postures.

Maria Daskalaki and Helen Blair ('Knowing as an Activity: Implications for the Film Industry and Semi-Permanent Work Groups') turn their attention to the special case of temporary project organizations and, through a case study in the film industry, explore the processes of knowledge sharing, creation and learning in such environments. At the outset, temporary project teams appear to defy some of the mainstream theory on knowledge: long-term competitive advantage, commitment, shared values and leadership are either not applicable or enacted differently in organizations that do not have a sense of permanence and lasting identity. The question that naturally arises is how temporary organizations manage knowledge. Filmmaking is a highly complex activity involving the intensive co-ordination of a relatively large number of specialists, organized in functional groups. These groups serve the purpose of the necessary division of labour but, unlike 'fixed' departments in firms, they have no spatial or formal (that is contractual) boundary. According to Daskalaki and Blair, what makes this system work is individual contacts, personal trust and a system of reputation. Individual performance is motivated by the perceived importance of maintaining personal and group reputation within the industry's social network. In this environment, an individual production project is a learning episode for individuals and their groups. Individuals and groups come together to enact the rituals, norms and language of the industry, to contribute their personal expert knowledge and to co-create new knowledge. At the end of the project, teams are disbanded until their members get together again (or in a different group composition) in another production. The authors draw on activity theory to demonstrate the functioning of this fluid organizational structure. Knowing is seen as a shared activity which is developed and enacted by dispersed semi-permanent social relations. Although these relations are informal and transient, knowledge persists together with the necessary trust, reputation and norms that enable the perpetual formation and performance of production projects.

Part III ('Organizational Knowledge and Dynamic Capabilities') focusses on how a knowledge-based perspective of firms helps us better understand the nature of dynamic capabilities firms develop. Noticing that only a few firms initiate technological changes that diffuse through the population of firms, Arie Lewin and Silvia Massini ('Knowledge Creation and Organizational Capabilities of Innovating and Imitating Firms') focus on *innovating* and *imitating* firms and their capabilities for knowledge creation, adopting a neo-evolutionary economics framework. Their argument is that these two types of firm differ in the configuration of routines and dynamic capabilities for managing the level of adaptive tension and for managing variation, selection and retention processes. Innovating firms are more likely to establish their innovation aspirations by comparisons with other firms that define the technological frontier, whereas imitating firms are more likely to establish their innovation aspirations at the level of the population average. Furthermore, the absorptive capacity of innovating firms includes both internal and external mechanisms whereby there are well developed routines for assimilating, reflecting on, and integrating internally generated knowledge *and* for exchanging and sharing information with partners, suppliers and customers. By contrast, the absorptive capacity of imitating firms is limited to adopting codified and mature knowledge. Taking an evolutionary knowledge-based view of business organizations, Lewin and Massini explicitly link the knowledge firms generate and the learning processes in which they engage at a micro-level with the routines and dynamic capabilities firms develop at a meso-level and, ultimately, with the population of firms at the macro-level. Although, as the authors themselves acknowledge, more work is required for these three levels of analysis to coherently fit together, their account makes an excellent start and provides us with a lot of thought-provoking material.

Christos Pitelis ('Edith Penrose's Organizational Theory of the Firm: Contract, Conflict, Knowledge and Management') revisits Penrose's theory of the growth of the firm and assesses her contribution to organizational economics. Pitelis' argument is that Penrose's focus on the 'insides' of the firm, notably its internal (especially managerial) resources, the role of intra-firm learning that generates endogenously innovation and growth, and the dynamic interaction between the internal and the external environment of firms that shapes their 'productive opportunities', makes hers the only economics-based organizational theory of the firm. Pitelis makes the point that it is intra-firm knowledge generation that affords firms the ability to reduce transaction costs – internally generated knowledge is logically prior to reducing transaction costs. However, for all the significant insights into intra-firm knowledge, Penrose's theory eschews discussing either conflict within firms or socio-psychological determinants of intra-firm 'contracts'. Yet, as Pitelis argues, her theory is readily amenable to the introduction of such ideas and can serve as a basis for building a knowledge-based theory of the firm that draws on the social sciences as well as economics. Furthermore, Penrose's focus on the relentless pursuit of productivity and innovation as well as on management's problem-solving capabilities can be seen as providing the means of addressing both the issues of intra-firm conflict, and the establishment of shared morals, vision, values, culture and beliefs. In this context, while belonging in the 'swollen middle', Penrose's theory can serve view this middle not as a 'third way' but a dialectic synthesis between 'conflict-induced strategy' and 'value-induced contract'.

Christine W. Soo, Timothy M. Devinney and David F. Midgley ('The Role of Knowledge Quality in Firm Performance') present empirical evidence of the antecedents of knowledge quality and its impact on firm innovation and financial performance. The authors turn their attention to the properties of performance-enhancing knowledge, by defining knowledge quality in terms of its usefulness and innovativeness. Two of the determinants of knowledge quality are formal and informal networks (internal or external) as sources of knowledge acquisition. The other determinant included in their model is the extent to which the firm is prepared to identify, assimilate and generate value out of knowledge (absorptive capacity). Their analysis is based on data from 317 companies across a broad range of sectors and firm sizes. Interestingly, formal networking does not contribute directly to knowledge quality, whereas informal networking does. Similarly, 'fellow colleagues' is rated the highest in terms of the most frequent, most useful and most innovative source of knowledge, suggesting that knowledge sharing is primarily a personal and informal social activity. The other interesting finding is that knowledge quality does not directly affect the financial performance of organizations. It determines innovative performance, which, in turn, determines financial performance. In other words, encouraging the accumulation of knowledge resources within the organization will not lead to the automatic generation of any added value unless these resources are converted into action. For example, a company will not create a competitive advantage by investing in innovative R&D alone; crucially, it must be able to turn its inventions into marketable products. Similarly, hiring the most intelligent people will not make a company automatically successful unless these people are led, motivated and generally managed appropriately.

Vasiliki Anyfioti, Soumitra Dutta and Theodore Evgeniou ('Making Sense of Customer Relationship Management Strategies in a Technology-Driven World') focus on two dominant trends in business organizations, namely the increasing interactivity of customers with companies and the growing interconnectivity and networking between actors in the value chain. Companies today interact with their customers through a growing number of physical and electronic channels, while recording and amassing in large databases every piece of information pertaining to this interaction. As a result of the availability of such volumes of detailed information, companies are able to offer highly customized services. The authors cite examples to argue that this trend goes beyond simple customization to the co-creation of products and services by combining the knowledge resources of the firm with those of the customer.

Simultaneously, companies engage in multidimensional partnerships that overcome the linear structure of the classic value chain. By cross-tabulating those two trends, the authors propose the Customer Integration and Market Integration Matrix. The positioning of a company on this framework reflects the depth and breadth of the CRM strategy followed as well as the variety and effectiveness of the CRM tools used. This matrix is a management decision-making tool that can be used either as an assessment or a prescriptive framework. While this chapter does not seek to conceptually elaborate on the mechanisms through which product co-creation and economic agents' interactions across the supply chain occur, and why, it does usefully emphasize that the opportunities afforded by CRM strategies and systems today are enabled by and depend upon the ability of the organization to identify, capture and manage a wealth of knowledge resources. A key success factor for any CRM initiative, the authors argue, is the organizational capability to process and act upon the vast amount of information that CRM systems accumulate. Beyond significant investments in IT, this requires broader organizational readiness to assimilate the information and embrace the changes (in products, processes and structures) that will emerge.

The contributions to this volume advance our understanding of organizations as knowledge systems by elaborating on the processes of organizational knowing and learning, of managing organizational knowledge, and the extent to which such processes become institutionalized routines that contribute to the development of dynamic capabilities in firms over time. While there is clearly a lot of work to be done before we can have fully-fledged, empirically testable knowledge-based theories of business organizations, these essays do point the way forward by offering a wealth of concepts and empirical material to help us better understand the role of knowledge in organizations.

## References

Axelrod, R. and Cohen, M.D. (2000) *Harnessing Complexity*. New York: Basic Books.
Barnard, C. (1966) *The Functions of the Executive*. Cambridge MA: Harvard, University Press.
Barney, J. (1991) Firm resources and sustained competitive advantage, *Journal of Management*, 17: 99–120.
Beech, N., MacIntosh, R., MacLean, D., Shepherd, J. and Stokes, J. (2002) Exploring constraints on developing knowledge: on the need for conflict, *Management Learning*, 33: 459–76.
Bell, D. (1999) The axial age of technology foreword: 1999. In D. Bell, *The Coming of the Post-Industrial Society*. New York: Basic Books, Special Anniversary Edition, pp. ix–lxxxv.

Bergson, H. (1946) *The Creative Mind*. New York: Carol Publishing Group.

Boden, D. (1994) *The Business of Talk*. Cambridge: Polity Press.

Brown, J.S. and Duguid, P. (1991) Organizational learning and communities-of-practice: toward a unified view of working, learning and innovation, *Organization Science*, 2(1): 40–57.

Brown, J.S. and Duguid, P. (2000) *The Social Life of Information*. Boston: Harvard Business School Press.

Brown, S.L. and Eisenhardt, K.M. (1998) *Competing on the Edge*. Boston: Harvard Business School Press.

Choo, C.W. and Bontis, N. (2002) (eds) *The Strategic Management of Intellectual Capital and Organizational Knowledge*. Oxford: Oxford University Press.

Cockburn, I.M., Henderson, R.M. and Stern, S. (2000) Untangling the origins of competitive advantage, *Strategic Management Journal*, 21: 1123–46.

Cook, S.D. and Brown, J.S. (1999) Bridging epistemologies: the generative dance between organizational knowledge and organizational knowing, *Organization Science*, 10: 381–400.

Cook, S.D. and Yanow, D. (1996) Culture and organizational learning. In M.D. Cohen and L.S. Sproull (eds), *Organizational Learning*. Thousand Oaks, CA: Sage, pp. 430–59.

Dennett, D. (1996) *Darwin's Dangerous Idea*. New York: Simon & Schuster.

Dosi, G., Teece, D.J. and Chytry, J. (1998) *Technology, Organization, and Competitiveness*. Oxford: Oxford University Press.

Dreyfus, H.L. and Dreyfus, S.E. (1986) *Mind over Machine*. New York: Free Press.

Drucker, P. (1993) *Post-Capitalist Society*. Oxford: Butterworth/Heinemann.

Eden, C. and Ackerman, F. (1998) *Making Strategy*. London: Sage.

Eden, C. and Spender, J.-C. (1998) *Managerial and Organizational Cognition*. London: Sage.

Feyerabend, P. (1999) *Conquest of Abundance*. Chicago: University of Chicago Press.

Foss, N. and Loasby, B.J. (1998) *Economic Organization, Capabilities and Co-ordination*. London: Routledge.

Grant, R. (1996) Toward a knowledge-based theory of the firm, *Strategic Management Journal*, 17 (Special Winter Issue): 109–22.

Grant, R. (2002) The knowledge-based view of the firm. In C.W. Choo and N. Bontis (eds), *The Strategic Management of Intellectual Capital and Organizational Knowledge*. Oxford: Oxford University Press, pp. 133–48.

Harre, R. (2002) *Cognitive Science*. London: Sage.

Hayek, F.A. (1945) The use of knowledge in society, *American Economic Review*, 35: 519–30.

Hayek, F.A. (1989) The pretence of knowledge, *American Economic Review*, 79: 3–7.

Heckscher, C. and Donnellon, A. (1994) *The Post-Bureaucratic Organization*. Thousand Oaks, CA: Sage.

Heidegger, M. (1962) *Being and Time*. New York: Harper & Row.

Hirschhorn, L. (1997) *Reworking Authority*. Cambridge, MA: MIT Press.

Huff, A.S. and Jenkins, M. (2002) *Mapping Strategic Knowledge*. London: Sage.

Hunter, K.M. (1991) *Doctors' Stories*. Princeton: Princeton University Press.

Hutchins, E. (1995) *Cognition in the Wild*. Cambridge, MA: MIT Press.

Ilinitch, A.Y., Lewin, A.Y. and D'Aveni, R. (1998) *Managing in Times of Disorder*. Thousand Oaks, CA: Sage.

Jaques, E. (1998) *Requisite Organization*. London: Cason Hall.

Joas, H. (1996) *The Creativity of Action*. Cambridge: Polity Press.

Kay, J. (1995) *Foundations of Corporate Success*. Oxford: Oxford University Press.

Kondo, D. (1990) *Crafting Selves*. Chicago: University of Chicago Press.

Kreiner, K. (1999) Knowledge and mind, *Advances in Management Cognition and Organizational Information Processing*, 6: 1–29.

Loasby, B.J. (1999) *Knowledge, Institutions and Evolution in Economics*. London: Routledge.

MacIntyre, A. (1985) *After Virtue*. London: Duckworth (2nd edn).

Moingeon, B. and Edmondson, A. (1996) *Organizational Learning and Competitive Advantage*. London: Sage.

Morgan, G. (1997) *Images of Organization*. Thousand Oaks, CA: Sage (2nd edn).

Nonaka, I. and Takeuchi, H. (1995) *The Knowledge-Creating Company*. New York: Oxford University Press.

Orr, J.E. (1996) *Talking about Machines*. Ithaca, New York: ILR Press/Cornell University Press.

Penrose, E. (1959) *The Theory of the Growth of the Firm*. New York: Wiley.

Pitelis, C. (ed.) (2002) *The Growth of the Firm*. Oxford: Oxford University Press.

Polanyi, M. (1962) *Personal Knowledge*. Chicago, IL: University of Chicago Press.

Reed, E.S. (1996) *The Necessity of Experience*. New Haven: Yale University Press.

Rogoff, B. and Lave, J. (1999) *Everyday Cognition*. Cambridge, MA: Harvard University Press.

Ryle, G. (1949) *The Concept of Mind*. Chicago: University of Chicago Press.

Schön, D. (1991) *Educating the Reflective Practitioner*. San Francisco: Jossey-Bass.

Schutz, A. (1970) *On Phenomenology and Social Relations*, edited by H.R. Wagner. Chicago: University of Chicago Press.

Smoliar, S. (2003) Putting relations back in Customer Relations Management, Unpublished paper.

Solokowski, R. (2000) *Introduction to Phenomenology*. Cambridge: Cambridge University Press.

Spender, J.-C. (1989) *Industry Recipes*. Oxford: Blackwell.

Spender, J.-C. (1996) Making knowledge the basis of a dynamic theory of the firm, *Strategic Management Journal*, 17 (Special Winter Issue): 45–62.

Stacey, R., Griffin, D. and Shaw, P. (2000) *Complexity and Management*. London: Routledge.

Suchman, L.A. (1987) *Plans and Situated Actions*. Cambridge: Cambridge University Press.

Thompson, P., Warhurst, C. and Callaghan, G. (2001) Ignorant theory and knowledgeable workers: interrogating the connections between knowledge, skills and services, *Journal of Management Studies*, 38: 923–42.

Toulmin, S. (1990) *Cosmopolis*. Chicago: University of Chicago Press.

Tripsas, M. and Gavetti, G. (2000) Capabilities, cognition, and inertia: evidence from digital imaging, *Strategic Management Journal*, 21: 1147–62.

Tsoukas, H. (1996) The firm as a distributed knowledge system: a constructionist approach, *Strategic Management Journal*, 17 (Special Winter Issue): 11–25.

Tsoukas, H. (1997) The tyranny of light: the temptations and the paradoxes of the information society *Futures*, 29(9): 827–44.

Tsoukas, H. (2001) Where does new organizational knowledge come from? Keynote address at the International Conference on Managing Knowledge: Conversations and Critiques, Leicester University, UK, 10–11 April.

Tsoukas, H. (2002) Introduction: knowledge-based perspectives on organizations: situated knowledge, novelty and communities of practice, *Management Learning*, 33: 419–26.

Tsoukas, H. (2003) Do we really understand tacit knowledge? *The Blackwell Handbook of Organizational Learning and Knowledge Management*. Oxford: Blackwell, pp. 410–27.

Tsoukas, H. and Chia, R. (2002) On organizational becoming: rethinking organizational change, *Organization Science*, 13: 567–82.

Tsoukas, H. and Cummings, S. (1997) Marginalization and recovery: the emergence of Aristotelian themes in organization studies, *Organization Studies*, 18: 655–83.

Tsoukas, H. and Vladimirou, E. (2001) What is organizational knowledge? *Journal of Management Studies*, 38: 973–93.

Varela, F.J., Thompson, E., and Rosch, E. (1991) *The Embodied Mind*. Cambridge, MA: MIT Press.

Von Krogh, G., Ichijo, K. and Nonaka, I. (2000) *Enabling Knowledge Creation*. New York: Oxford University Press.

Weick, K. (1990) Introduction: cartographic myths in organizations. In A.S. Huff (ed.), *Mapping Strategic Thought*. Chichester: J. Wiley, pp. 1–10.

Weick, K. (1995) *Sensemaking in Organizations*. Thousand Oaks, CA: Sage.

Weick, K.E. (1979) *The Social Psychology of Organizing*. Reading, MA: Addison-Wesley (2nd edn).

Weick, K.E. (1998) Improvisation as a mindset of organizational analysis, *Organization Science*, 9(5): 543–55.

Wenger, E. (1998) *Communities of Practice*. Cambridge: Cambridge University Press.

Whitley, R. (1987) Taking firms seriously as economic actors: towards a sociology of firm behaviour, *Organization Studies*, 8: 125–47.

Winograd, T. and Flores, F. (1987) *Understanding Computers and Cognition*. Reading, MA: Addison-Wesley.

# Part I

# Organizational Knowing and Learning

# 1
# Double-Loop Learning and Implementable Validity

*Chris Argyris*

This chapter has two main objectives. The first is to suggest that a greater emphasis on double-loop learning and implementable validity represents a next important focus of research if the field of organizational learning is to become more scientifically robust and provide greater assistance to practitioners. The second objective is to propose that the widespread ideas about theory and research methods that scholars use, when implemented correctly, will inhibit the progress to achieving this objective. I plan to focus on the defensive routines of the scholarly community of practice.

## The meaning of double-loop learning

Learning is defined as the detection and correction of error. Error is any mismatch between intentions and implementation. Learning occurs when these features are connected to effective action. The evidence for learning is that we can *implement* what we claim to have learned.

Learning may be characterized as either single-loop or double-loop. Single-loop learning occurs when the correction of the error is accomplished by not changing the underlying values and policies as practised. Double-loop learning occurs when the correction of the error is accomplished after changing the actual underlying values and practices.

The vast majority of empirical research on organizational learning is single-loop (see, for example, Argyris, 1980, 1993, 2000; Argyris and Schön, 1996). This emphasis is to be expected. One of the most fundamental features of managing organizations is to define routines and then expect to implement them (Nelson and Winter, 1982). Implementing routines is a single-loop activity.

There are several reasons why double-loop learning is important in organizations:

1. Routines are intended to reduce the necessity for double-loop change (Christensen and Overdorf, 2000). This predisposes employees to become desensitized to inner contradictions that routines often develop. Overcoming this desensitization requires double-loop learning.
2. The research emphasis upon single-loop learning leads to scholarship that is in the service of the status quo. Such limits unnecessarily constrain the progress of inquiry in producing new knowledge.
3. Combining points 1 and 2, above, leads scholars and practitioners to create and reward mindsets that inhibit the exploration of non-trivial changes within organizations, including those that are derivable from their own research (Argyris and Schön, 1996).

Here are some recent examples:

### Example 1: Intel's practitioners

In a recent study of strategy processes in Intel, Burgelman (2002) found that middle managers wanted Intel to move from memory products to the development and production of microprocessors. They strove to communicate their views to the top executives, but failed to get their message across. They explained their failure by asserting to themselves that top management was incapable of being influenced.

Later, when Burgelman told Andrew Grove this story, he did not believe it. To his credit, he interviewed the relevant managers and learned that the story was true.

Grove reacted by reiterating and explaining company policies and practices, emphasizing in particular the importance of open and honest communication around business/technical issues. He did not encourage discussion about leadership or followership behaviours and styles because he believed such discussions would not be fruitful.

Some of the key Intel policies and practices about leadership and performance were:

1. Hire very bright people who know the technology and science relevant to their tasks. Moreover, they should be dedicated to and competent in being at the intellectual forefront of their technical/scientific domain.
2. Hire individuals who have a lot of energy to work very hard and who are dedicated to the governing values of Intel.

3. Manage individuals' performance by focussing on the details of their performance.
4. Reward individuals' performances by using strict, quantitative procedures that are credible and transparent.
5. Manage the actions of individuals by focussing on content and not style.
6. Allocate scarce organizational resources by using strict, quantitative models that are credible and transparent.
7. Hire executives who have the courage of their convictions. The rule is do what is right, not what you are ordered to do.
8. Hire executives capable of crafting positions that are rigorously sound and implementable. Executives should be good at making clear distinctions and not soft-money claims.

Grove's leadership style included these features:

1. Advocate your position; make evaluations or attributions in ways that are clear, explicit, and in the service of winning the argument. Sell and persuade. For example, be very detail-driven, see issues as black and white, and expect clear-cut choices. Nothing mushy, like, 'it seems that', and 'perhaps'. If individuals get into an argument, listen in order to get their inconsistencies and gaps, point them out, and expect them to resolve them or 'I will'. Or, synthesize the views in a coherent whole that is consistent with those views.
2. Advocate courage, honesty, and trust in ways that inhibit these features. If this self-defeating behaviour is revealed, blame it on the actions of others. For example, deal with lack of courage and mistrust by espousing the opposite and do so in ways that make it difficult for others to uncover the inconsistency. If inconsistency is revealed, explain it by 'I am forced to do this by others' actions.'
3. Use rules of effective leadership that keep you in unilateral control. For example, do not trust people to keep their promises, therefore monitor their actions frequently. Claim that the follow-up is not in the service of unilateral control as much as it is holding others responsible for their promises. Solidify and 'vectorize'. Vectorize means establish a direction, a point of application and a strong magnitude of continual energy and commitments. Grove emphasized that Job 1 (microprocessors) was *the* focus. Strive to educate those who appear to disagree. If education does not work, then remove those who are not co-operative or who will delay progress.

4. Be demanding but fair. Demanding means very high standards and very hard work. Fair means subjecting what he advocates and what he criticizes to test as long as they are about substance. Exclude discussion of leadership style and seek organizational mechanisms by which to bypass style problems.

5. Send mixed messages about effective leadership; act as if they are not mixed. Make these features undiscussable, and make the undiscussability undiscussable.

Grove's theory-in-use about leading people may be summarized by a motto he uses. 'Let chaos reign, then rein in chaos.'

The managers developed ways to deal with Grove that were every bit as unilateral as Grove's methods. They were also covered-up. Based on Burgelman's description, the executives may be said to use the following strategy:

1. Sense Grove's mood.

2. Remember, if he is confused he gets tough. He bulldozes everything in his way. He tells anyone who is in his way to get lost – to get out of the way.

3. Remember, once he has made up his mind, it is difficult to change it. If he does change his mind, he often does it without acknowledging the fact.

4. Remember, Grove is unaware of his actions. Or if he becomes aware, he will likely blame the reasons for his actions as being outside his way of leading.

5. Keep these rules in mind when you craft your conversations with him. Do so by acting as if you are not using these rules.

We have a situation where:

(a) Top management and middle managers espouse openness and trust.

(b) Top management behaves in ways that are inconsistent with what they espouse. They are unaware of their inconsistencies while producing them.

(c) Middle managers also behave in ways that are inconsistent with the espoused theory. However, many are aware of the inconsistency. They blame the top for coercing them to act inconsistently.

(d) All this is undiscussable and uninfluencable. In order for this strategy to work, it is necessary to make the undiscussability and uninfluencability also undiscussable, and to cover up that this is happening.

Single-loop learning occurs when Grove pleads for openness, and when he creates financial and promotional awards to support such actions. Double-loop learning would occur if the focus was on the causes of the inconsistencies, of the undiscussability, of the cover-up and how these factors inhibited the double-loop learning that would have moved the company faster towards microprocessors.

The same dynamics occurred several years later, when Intel moved from microprocessors to a new product. They attempted to minimize the possibility that existing organizational defensive routines may reoccur by creating a 'separate' company. That is a single-loop solution. There were no changes in the governing values.

### The scholars studying Intel

How do we explain that Burgelman knew all this and decided not to focus directly upon the self-reinforcing anti-double-loop learning activities that he documented? When asked, he responded that he did not believe that progress would be made by adopting such a focus. He also recognized that such a stance could produce a self-fulfilling prophecy. Burgelman, the scholar, has the same doubts as do Intel's top and middle management. He does not test the validity of the claim that such an inquiry is not worthwhile. Nor does Jim March, who holds a similar position (Argyris, 1996). His position is the same one that Grove took as CEO. Thus we have scholars 'colluding' with practitioners in ways that inhibit, and in some cases actually prohibit, double-loop learning.

These findings are reflected in our literature (Argyris, 1980, 1993, 2000; Argyris and Schön, 1996). The question arises, why do scholars who espouse an unbridled seeking of truth act in ways to limit such inquiries based on personal, untested, and untestable claims?

### Example 2

Van de Ven and Polley (1992) carried out a rigorous study of the development of a new product and the marketing strategy required to bring it to market. After a systematic and primarily quantitative description, we learn that the entire project failed. The authors developed generalizations about organizational learning to explain the failures that were in keeping with their empirical findings.

The authors concluded their report with a qualitative description of what happened during the many meetings that they had observed. They provided many illustrations of miscommunication, politics, coverups, and other organizational defensive routines (Argyris, 1990). The defensive routines were key to the failure of implementation. However, they were not integrated into the theory of learning that Van de Ven and Polley had presented. If they had been, this would have helped to create a more generalizable and valid theory of organizational learning.

## Example 3

Nielson and Nørjberg (2001) conducted a systematic study intended to re-design a model for evaluating the maturity of the IT practice in organizations. They showed that defensive routines within organizations played a crucial role in inhibiting the effective implementation of the IT model. However, they did not conduct research on how to overcome the organizational defensive routines.

## Example 4

Peters (2001) identified key organizational factors that inhibit the implementation of effective leadership in organizations. They include that leaders are faced with too few choices, time is fragmented, bad news is normally hidden, and major choices take months or years to emerge. Peters then identified 'silver linings' for each. For example, the one-option strategy is acceptable because it usually reflects senior leaders' previously expressed preferences, each fragment can be used to signal the leaders' preferences, using the good news given them eventually reinforces their own values and priorities and, over time, consistent choices will accumulate into consequences.

It is not clear how these 'silver linings' actually emerge. Nor is it clear if dark linings do not accompany them. What is clear is that the solutions are examples of single-loop learning in that they are designed to work within the constraints of the status quo. There is no attempt to advise leaders how to change organizations so that the 'sad facts' are reduced and that the 'silver linings' are not simply a guaranteed reinforcer of organizational defensive routines.

## Example 5

A review of the current themes and practices about leadership, learning, change, and commitment indicates that much of the advice espoused is consistent with double-loop learning. Yet the implementation is single-loop. The professionals who provide the advice appear to be unaware of this discrepancy. When they are helped to become aware they blame others or the systems, and ignore their own responsibility for the situation (Argyris, 2000).

For example, an analysis of transcripts depicting change professionals' attempts to produce double-loop changes shows that they fail to do so. As a result the line executives become disenchanted, which causes the professionals to adopt the very same sorts of defensive actions that they advise against using. The line managers soon distance themselves from the 'soft stuff', which frustrates the change professionals, and causes them to escalate their actions in even more counterproductive ways (Argyris, 2000).

To sum up, scholars recognize the importance of the counterproductive impact on learning of organizational defensive routines. They do not provide theories or empirical research on how to reduce them. Practitioners, who espouse double-loop learning, are unable to implement it and are unaware of their own limitations. When failure occurs the predisposition is to blame others (for example, line or organizational structures and policies).

## The meaning of implementable validity

Scholars see their task as to produce valid, generalizable knowledge where validity is assessed by deriving hypotheses and testing them in the empirical world. Campbell and Stanley (1963) wrote a highly influential book on how to accomplish the above.

Campbell and Stanley argue that field research that is quasi-experimental can be conducted in ways that meet the criteria for validity. They specify two kinds of validity: internal and external. Briefly, internal validity is about making as certain as possible that the theories and the research methods used do not produce unrecognized gaps and inconsistencies that make it difficult to assess the validity of the claim being made. External validity is about the relevance of the findings in settings external to the ones in which they were produced.

These requirements are necessary but not sufficient if one intends to produce knowledge about effective action. For example, we saw above that the concept of organizational defensive routines has high external validity. Yet knowledge was not produced as to how to implement the advice the researchers gave to reduce them. Organizational defensive routines have high external validity and low implementable validity.

This has scientific and practical implications. With regard to the latter, human beings are not able to implement the actions they seek to produce. As to the former, the opportunity to test robustly the scientific claims about the impact of organizational defensive routines upon learning is missed.

Implementation occurs as a result of human beings taking action. Action is behaviour with meaning. Meaning is represented by the intentions of the actors. Human beings must use their mind/brain to bring about implementation. What does the mind/brain require if it is to accomplish this function correctly? Cognitive neuro-scientists are providing the features necessary to act (Churchland, 2000; Simon, 1969). Among the features they identify the following.

## Action and the mind/brain

1. Actions are produced by human beings using their mind/brain.
2. Actions are produced by designs stored in the mind/brain and can be retrieved, that specify the behaviours and the procedures required to implement whatever consequences that are intended.
3. The designs for action are causal. They specify *If A then B*.
4. Producing causal designs requires skills. Skills, in turn, are developed by practice. Practice, in turn, produces the designs used to take action.

## Effective action

Human beings have theories of action programmed in their heads, that they use to design and to implement what they intend to be effective action. Some of the most prominent features of these theories-in-use are (Argyris and Schön, 1996):

1. Human beings hold master designs/programs about how to produce effective consequences. These programs are causal. They specify the actions required to produce the consequences that they intend.
2. Human beings hold two types of designs. These are the designs that they espouse and the designs that they actually use when they act.
3. There is a systematic discrepancy between the espoused designs, and the designs-in-use (typically identified, in the literature, as theories-in-use). The number and scope of the discrepancies increase, as the issues being dealt with are embarrassing or threatening.
4. Individuals are unaware of these discrepancies while they are producing them. If they become aware, their automatic response is to explain away their errors by blaming someone else or some larger social system. The same individuals are able to observe accurately any inconsistencies that others produce and hold them responsible for doing so.
5. Human beings hold the same theories-in-use. Culture, gender, race, age, wealth, education, and type of organization make no difference. Espoused theories vary but they do not produce action.
6. The theory-in-use has been modelled. It has been described extensively and hence I will not dwell on it (Argyris, 1982, 1987,

**Model I**
**Theory-in-use**

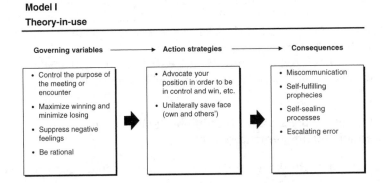

*Figure 1.1*   Model I theory-in-use

1990, 1993, 2000; Argyris and Schön, 1974, 1996). The theory-in-use is called Model I (Figure 1.1). Simply put, Model I is a theory-in-use that values unilateral control, winning not losing, and suppressing negative feelings. Model I leads to defensive behaviour such as skilled unawareness and skilled incompetence. Andy Grove's leadership is consistent with Model I.

Model I causes organizational defensive routines that, in turn, feed-back to reinforce it. An example of an organizational defensive routine found frequently in organizations is mixed messages.

1. Mary, you run the department, but check with Charley.
2. Bill, be creative, but be careful.

The theory-in-use that human beings use to produce mixed messages goes something like this:

1. Produce a message that is mixed.
2. Act as if it is not mixed.
3. Make the first two undiscussable.
4. Make the undiscussability undiscussable.

The result is an ultra-stable state. Human beings and their organizations appear as if they are 'hard-wired' to prevent double-loop learning. One is reminded of Lawrence Kubie's (1958) definition of neurotic behaviour – namely, actions that are compulsively repetitive and not open to examination and correction. Fromm (1955) reached similar conclusions about society.

Interestingly, the features of the ultra-stable state are similar to the features of routines. Both resist double-loop changes. So we have human beings who may be asked to make double-loop changes in the routines, yet who lack the necessary skills to do so.

In the next section of this chapter we return to the theme of how scholarly researchers ignore or inhibit double-loop learning.

## Theories scholars create that inhibit double-loop learning and implementable validity

A common norm about research is that scholars should seek to describe their chosen universe as completely as possible, typically in the form of generalizations that are testable.

Focussing on describing the universe 'as is' limits the description to the status quo. Descriptions of the universe, as is, are inherently incomplete because they do not tell us how the universe is likely to react if it undergoes dramatic changes. Describing the status quo will not provide such knowledge.

What is needed: first, organizational theories that define organizations that are different from the ones in good currency. Second, causal theories of how to get from here to there. Third, we cannot specify how to get from here to there without first specifying how the patterns were created in the first place. If, for example, we describe inter-departmental rivalries, low trust, cover-up, and cover-up of the cover-up, we must answer the question: how did the human beings create these in the first place?

Theories about new forms of organization are normative. They are based on subjective cultural values. They are not objective. In order to test theories, we derive hypotheses and test them in the empirical world. Such hypotheses are causal in the sense that they claim if we behave in such-and-such a manner, the following will occur. All causal hypotheses when implemented prescribe the actions to be taken, hence they are prescriptive. Hence we need normative theories about effective action and prescriptive theories as to how they are to be implemented and tested. These tests should be implementable in everyday life situations by scholars or practitioners.

All these ideas are illustrated in the Intel case. The company was structured and managed by normative propositions. The propositions were subjective in that they conformed to top and middle management's views. The everyday tests of the validity of these propositions were based on how well they were implemented. Those who created the rules carried out the implementation. In doing so, they used self-serving, self-referential logic.

The logic used to create the propositions was the logic used to test their validity. There was no room for double-loop learning.

## Making knowledge actionable

The majority of the studies that Donald Schön and I reviewed about organizational learning were based on studying variance among variables. The difficulty with the knowledge produced in these circumstances, is that it was not actionable.

For example, a curvilinear relationship is specified between two variables. The human mind can produce a curvilinear relationship in order to understand and explain. However, the mind cannot produce a curvilinear relationship when it acts.

The first reason that such knowledge is not implementable is that it does not specify the causal designs required to act. The second reason is that such a generalization is very rich with variables and their relationships. Typically, scholars make many observations over time to produce these generalizations. Even if causality were not required, it is not possible for the human mind, given its limited capacity for information processes, to produce the relationship in such a way that it is timely for effective action in a given situation.

In order to produce effective action, it is necessary to begin with knowledge that is generalizable. This knowledge alerts the actors as to what actions are likely to be required to implement. However, the actual implementation occurs in a specific context. Theories of effective action therefore require propositions that are generalizable *and* applicable in the unique context. For example, a general theory of organizational defensive routines should be useable to engage the defensive routines in a specific context.

## Empirical methodologies that inhibit and limit valid and implementable knowledge about double-loop learning

Elsewhere, I have argued that the theory-in-use of empirical research methodologies is consistent with Model I (Argyris, 1980, 1993, 2000; Argyris and Schön, 1996). For example, the researchers are largely in unilateral control over the 'subjects'. They hide important knowledge from the subjects in the service of internal validity. They control the subjects' time perspective. They control the nature of the feedback to the subjects during and after their participation. They cover-up that they are doing so. They make these features both undiscussable and incapable of being influenced.

There are two consequences that follow from this: first, propositions that have been developed through adherence to the Model I theories-in-use, regardless of their substantive claims, will lead to propositions that are consistent with, and limited to, the status quo. I quote four examples from my book (Argyris, 1980):

1. From some of the most sophisticated research on mass communications the following advice could be found. If you are trying to convince an audience about choosing an option or stance, and if you consider the audience to be composed of human beings who are not so bright, describe only one alternative. If the audience is considered 'bright', describe several alternatives. Imagine what would happen if those communicating to a 'dumb' audience were to state that they are providing them with one alternative because science recommends that they deal with not-so-bright audiences in this way.

2. Scholars recommended to activists who were against the Vietnam War how to lie and spin in order to get their foot in the door, and to convince the listener of the injustice of the war, and to cover-up that this was their intention.

3. Scholars quoting reactance theory advised individuals on how to manipulate people into buying window shades that were often unneeded and in many cases would not fit the windows for which they were being bought. Most of the buyers were poor.

4. Scholars using reinforcement learning theory advised executives how to reward their subordinates in ways that required the use of reinforcement schedules that were covered-up. These schedules would work if the subordinates behaved as dutifully as did the animals in the experiments where the results were originally produced (Argyris, 1980).

The second consequence is that if someone tries to implement such propositions, be they scholars or practitioners, they will find that they must use Model I actions to do so. For example:

In a careful, systematic experimental study, Barker, Dembo and Lewin (1941) reported that frustration leads to regression. They also reported that mild frustration leads to creativity. Let us picture a leader who wishes to use this knowledge to enhance her groups' creativity. How would she go about implementing this knowledge?

Would she tell her group members that she intends to frustrate them mildly in order to enhance their creativity? How would she assess when mild frustration is produced and when it was exceeded? How would she stop it when the frustration became too high?

Consider also the situation of the group members. How would they react to learning about her strategy? How would they react to periodic attempts to measure their frustrations? What kinds of measures would they be? If they were intrusive, would that not be a major act of manipulation and cover-up? If so, both parties would be acting in ways that support mistrust.

The argument so far is:

1. Theories about organizational learning and the research methods used to test them are consistent with Model I and with scholarly community norms of organizational defensive routines.
2. The resulting generalizations, if they were implemented in the everyday world, would require that the implementors act consistently with Model I, with organizational defensive routines, and act as if they are not doing so.

## Concluding statement

I should like to begin my concluding statement by describing the most frequent claims scholars make when I question them about double-loop learning and implementable validity.

| They claim | My response |
|---|---|
| There is interest in double-loop learning. Witness concepts like surprise and competency traps. | Yes, we find many scholars cite the importance of double-loop learning, yet few study it. |
| The research on learning is in its infancy. As knowledge accumulates, it will deal with research on double-loop learning and implementable validity. | Theories that focus on describing the status quo and research methods that are consistent with Model I, no matter how cumulative, will not lead to actionable knowledge about double-loop learning. |
| Produce credible evidence that double-loop problems exist and scholars will begin to study them. | Burgelman and March (to cite but two) state that double-loop problems exist. They also state that they are not correctable. They do not seek to test their claim. |
| What is needed is more sophisticated quantitative research. | Numbers are abstractions that, at best, focus on espoused theories. |
| Be patient. Progress will occur. | My three reviews of the literature since 1980 do not support this claim. The claim may act as a defence by scholars that inhibits progress. |

## Intervention

Next, I turn to the central role of intervention in producing knowledge about double-loop learning that has implementable validity. Lewin and his colleagues illustrated an early form of this strategy that was a combination of ethnography and social psychology. Argyris (1970), Jaques (1951), and Likert (1961) have each developed different views of intervention.

Argyris and Schön (1996) represent a view that uses intervention in the service of learning in organizations that is based on what is called Model II (Figure 1.2) theory-in-use. Detailed descriptions have been published that describe the interventions using Model II. They describe double-loop changes at the individual, interpersonal, group, inter-group and organizational levels. The interventions last from one day through eleven years (Argyris, 1982, 1985, 1987, 1990, 1993, 2000; Argyris, Putnam and Smith, 1985; Argyris and Schön, 1996).

Although it is beyond the scope of this chapter to describe these interventions, I should like to describe a few of their fundamental characteristics.

In all the interventions we *begin* by helping the participants become aware of the degree to which their theory-in-use approximates Model I (or some other). There are two reasons for this strategy.

1. Any interventions that focus on double-loop changes require individuals who are competent in problem-solving and interacting with

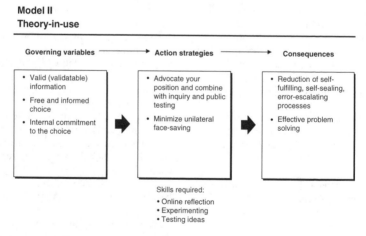

*Figure 1.2*   Model II theory-in-use

each other using governing values of producing valid or validatable information, creating informed choice, being causally responsible for their actions, and learning to detect and correct errors. Model I theory-in-use, as we have seen, is not suited to these values. We have developed a model that is consistent with these values. Model II (Figure 1.2), if it becomes an operative theory-in-use, decreases the counterproductive consequences of Model I, including the ultra-stable state of defences at all levels of the organization and throughout its different units. Participants intending to move toward Model II type organizations require Model II competencies and skills. Otherwise people will revert to Model I when the going gets rough.

For example, Perry (1984) describes an experiment to make a new plant more participative. After the early starts, the participants had to engage such issues as their competence to be participative as well as their commitment to accept personal responsibility for their errors. The team managing the intervention dealt with these difficulties by creating measurements, which would make performance responsibilities transparent. It was not long before the matrices became so complicated that they created a new top-down, 'I gotcha' culture. As one professional told me, *we soon realized that we were creating a world similar to the one Frederick Taylor made famous – a world that we were against.*

2. This leads us to the second reason. Ackoff (1999) has designed a new organizational structure intended to make organizations better at learning and at performing. He calls this new structure the circular organization. A core feature of this structure is a 'democratic hierarchy'.

The underlying governing values of democratic hierarchy are consistent with Model II. It is our prediction that progress would be made as long as the issues were single-loop. The moment double-loop issues arise (for example, sharing power, changing reporting relationships, holding people accountable with instruments that they design) we would predict difficulties. Ackoff (personal communication) confirms this prediction. Indeed, he put me in touch with two other intervention attempts at new structural arrangements consistent with the circular organization. In both cases, the interventionists warned that defences do arise, even when the CEO is an ardent champion and his immediate reports espouse genuine commitment (Goggin, 1974; Halal, 1996).

There is an important implication of these interventions. To the extent that structural arrangements (such as structures and compensation plans, etc.) are designed that represent non-trivial changes, they should not be implementable without the implementers having Model II skills and the capabilities to overcome defensive routines.

In the final analysis, when interventions are made to implement double-loop changes, the actions will include individual and organizational learning. Double-loop learning and effective implementation are tightly linked.

## References

Ackoff, Russell L. (1999) *Re-Creating the Corporation*. New York: Oxford University Press.

Argyris, C. (1970) *Intervention Theory and Method: A Behavioral Science View*, Reading, MA: Addison-Wesley.

Argyris, C. (1996) Unrecognized defenses of scholars: impact on theory and research, *Organization Science*, 7(1): 79–87.

Argyris, Chris (1980) *Inner Contradictions of Rigorous Research*. San Diego, CA: Academic Press.

Argyris, Chris (1982) *Reasoning, Learning, and Action: Individual and Organizational*. San Francisco, CA: Jossey-Bass.

Argyris, Chris (1985) *Strategy, Change, and Defensive Routines*. Boston, MA: Putnam.

Argyris, Chris (1987) Reasoning, action strategies and defensive routines: the case of organizational dynamics practitioners, in R.N. Woodman and W.A. Passmore (eds), *Research in Organizational Change and Development*, Vol. 1, Greenwich, CT: JAI Press, pp. 89–128.

Argyris, Chris (1990) *Overcoming Organizational Defenses: Facilitating Organizational Learning*. Needham, MA: Allyn & Bacon.

Argyris, Chris (1993) *Knowledge for Action*. San Francisco, CA: Jossey-Bass.

Argyris, Chris (2000) *Flawed Advice and the Management Trap*. New York: Academic Press.

Argyris, Chris (2002) Double loop learning, teaching and research, *Academy of Management Learning and Education*, 1: 206–18.

Argyris, C., Putnam, R. and Smith, D. (1985) *Action Science: Concepts, Methods, and Skills for Research and Intervention*. San Francisco, CA: Jossey-Bass.

Argyris, C. and Schön, D. (1974) *Theory in Practice: Increasing Professional Effectiveness*. San Francisco: Jossey-Bass.

Argyris, C. and Schön, D. (1996) *Organizational Learning II*. Reading, MA: Addison-Wesley.

Barker, R., Dembo T. and Lewin, K. (1941) Frustration and regression, *Studies in Child Welfare*, University of Iowa Press.

Burgelman, R.A. (2002) *Strategy is Destiny*. New York: The Free Press.

Campbell, D.T. and Stanley, J.C. (1963) *Experimental and Quasi-Experimental Design for Research*. Skokie, IL: Rand-McNally.

Cartwright, D. (1950) *Field Theory and Social Science*, ed. Kurt Lewin. New York: Harper.

Christensen, Clayton M. and Overdorf, Michael (2000) Meeting the challenge of disruptive change, *Harvard Business Review*, March–April, pp. 66–76.

Churchland, P.M. (2000) *The Engine of Reason, the Seat of the Soul*. Cambridge, MA: MIT Press.

Coggin, William C. (1974) How the multidimensional structure works at Dow Corning, *Harvard Business Review*, 52 (January–February): 54–65.

Ezzamel, M., Willimott, H. and Worthington, F. (2001) Power, control and resistance in 'the factory that time forgot', *Journal of Management Studies*, 38(8): 1053–80.

Fromm, E. (1955) *The Sane Society*. New York: Holt, Rinehart & Winston.

Halal, William E. (1996) *The New Management: Democracy and Enterprise are Transforming Organizations*. San Francisco, CA: Berrett-Kochler.

Jacques, Elliot (1951) *The Changing Culture of a Factory*. London: Tavistock/Heinemann.

Kubie, Lawrence S. (1958) *Neurotic Distortions of the Creative Process*. Lawrence, KS: University of Kansas Press.

Lewin, Kurt (1935) *A Dynamic Theory of Personality*. New York: McGraw-Hill.

Likert, Rensis (1961) *New Patterns of Management*. New York: McGraw-Hill.

Nelson, Richard and Winter, S.G. (1982) *An Evolutionary Theory of Change*. Cambridge, MA: Belknap Press of Harvard University Press.

Nielson, Peter Axel and Nørjberg, Jacob (2001) Assessing software processes: low maturity or sensible practice, *Scandinavian Journal of Information Systems*, 13: 51–67.

Perry, Barbara (1984) *Enfield: A High Performance System*. Bedford, MA: Digital Educational Services and Publishing.

Peters, Thomas J. (2001) Leadership: sad facts and silver linings, *Harvard Business Review*, 79(11): 121–8.

Simon, H.A. (1969) *The Science of the Artificial*. Cambridge, MA: MIT Press.

Ven, Andrew Van de and Polley, D. (1992) Learning while innovating, *Organizational Science*, 3(1): 93–115.

White, R.W. (1959) 'Motivation recommended: the concept of competence', *Psychological Review*, 66: 297–333.

# 2
# The Emergence of Learning Communities: A Theoretical Analysis

*Irma Bogenrieder and Bart Nooteboom*

## Introduction

A central issue in theories of organizational learning concerns the relation between knowledge of individuals and knowledge on the level of an organization (Cohen, 1991; Cook and Yanow, 1993; Weick and Westley, 1996). Communities form an intermediate level for learning between an organization as a whole and individual people. There, knowledge links between individuals are achieved and common knowledge is acquired. The central purpose of this chapter is to further analyse this process, in communities. One question to be explained is what types of communities there are (Bogenrieder and Nooteboom, 2002).

In their account of 'communities of practice', Brown and Duguid (1996: 60) employ an 'activity theory' of knowledge (see for example Blackler, 1995), in which action and learning are intertwined, and they view 'learning as a bridge between working and innovation'. They employ the notion of 'canonical' and 'non-canonical' or 'procedural' (Cohen and Bacdayan, 1996) knowledge. Canonical knowledge entails decontextualized, codified and formalized rules for operation. Inevitably, such rules cannot cover the richness and the variability of practical contexts. It is by context-dependent deviations from canonical rules, with the ensuing need for improvisation and experimentation (Brown and Duguid employ Levy-Strauss' concept of *bricolage*), that learning arises, in interaction between members of the community. This is based on 'storytelling', to capture and share context-bound experience, to guide experimentation. As a result, communities emerge from shared work practice rather than being designed *ex ante*. Wenger and Snyder (2000: 139, 140) characterize a community of practice as a 'group of people informally bound together by shared expertise and passion for a joint enterprise'.

In the literature on learning, a distinction is made between first- and second-order learning (Hedberg, Nystrom and Starbuck, 1976; Fiol and Lyles, 1985) or, equivalently, between 'single loop and double loop' learning (Argyris and Schön, 1978). The first is learning to do existing things better (more efficiently) and the second is learning to do new things (from a new perspective). This is also connected with the notion of 'parametric' change (Langlois and Robertson, 1995) as opposed to 'architectural' change (Henderson and Clark, 1990). The Austrian economist Hayek distinguished between two kinds of 'spontaneous order': the first kind entailed the operation of rules; the second kind entailed the change of those rules.

Holland (1975) and March (1991) distinguished between 'exploitation' and 'exploration'. The first entails the efficient use of existing competencies and the second the development of new ones. Exploitation requires the maintenance of existing identity, knowledge and practices, with a certain amount of control and co-ordination, in a 'dominant design'. Exploration requires their change, with a loosening of control and co-ordination. First-order learning entails improved exploitation, and second-order learning entails successful exploration. Exploitation corresponds with the notions of first-order learning, parametric change, and the operation of rules. Exploration corresponds with second-order learning, architectural change and the change of rules. Throughout this chapter we will employ the notions of exploitation and exploration.

While the distinction between exploitation and exploration is conceptually useful, in the process of learning the two kinds of learning do not stand apart from each other. Exploitation is based on exploration, and vice versa. We exploit what we have explored, and it is on the basis of exploitation that we explore. As Brown and Duguid argued, learning forms the bridge between practice and innovation. Keeping this in mind, there is nevertheless a distinction in the required processes for exploration and exploitation. Distinctions are identified on several dimensions. Processes for exploitation take place within a group's identity, whereas in exploration identity is yet to be developed. Identity also refers to the existence of norms of behaviour that constitute a shared basis for co-ordination. This is one of the important characteristics of a community (Komito, 1998). In exploration, shared norms cannot be assumed *ex ante*. They develop in the course of co-operation. Furthermore, exploitation is associated with having a shared frame of reference (Boland and Tenkasi, 1995). Changes take place within this common frame of reference. In exploration, a common frame of reference has yet to be developed by constructing shared meanings. Thus, as explorative processes cannot rely on shared commonalities (identity, frame of reference, norms of mutuality) different processes are required in order to achieve co-operation. Nevertheless, groups can be primarily aimed at exploitation, which may then yield exploration, or at exploration, which should in due course yield exploitation.

The extent to which the two can be combined in time and place depends on how 'systemic' or 'stand-alone' (Langlois and Robertson, 1995) tasks are. In highly systemic tasks, there are many linkages between elements (individual actions), with tight and durable constraint on them, to ensure mutual fit. An example would be a refinery. Here, there is little scope for local change. In stand-alone activities, there is scope for local change. An example is a consultancy, with highly autonomous professionals who can vary their practice without disrupting that of others. Of course, there the question is how they can share their knowledge, to avoid the re-invention of wheels, for the sake of efficient exploitation. Brown and Duguid (2001) suggest the concept of networks of practice in order to explain how knowledge is shared between professionals with the same practice but in different organizations. As consultants may adopt different practices within the same organization, learning is more bound to the relevant community of practitioners although this community might be outside the 'own' organization.

We proceed as follows. First, we discuss theoretical foundations. We introduce some notions of learning groups as they already exist. Next we summarize the theory of knowledge and learning we use, and we give a conceptualization of the multi-level problem, concerning the connection between the level of individuals and the level of collective action. Next, we give a detailed analysis of how communities for exploration might work as a system of distributed cognition. The focus is on how to establish sufficient commonality of understanding and communication, while utilizing diversity of knowledge. In an elaboration of this, we discuss types of co-operation and the function of communication processes.

## Learning communities

From the accounts of Brown and Duguid and Wenger and Snyder, communities of practice appear to be aimed primarily at exploitation, in 'shared expertise' for a 'joint enterprise', which may then form the basis for (some) exploration. Shared work practice constitutes a common identity and frame of reference (Brown and Duguid, 2001). As learning takes place within this common identity it resembles exploitation. 'Epistemic communities' (Steinmüller, 2000; Haas, 1992; Cowan, David and Foray, 2000) are commonly defined as groups or networks of people who perform exploratory learning. The assumption of shared beliefs appears in the following definition of an epistemic community/exploratory community (Haas, 1992: 3), which distinguishes various dimensions in shared beliefs:

> An epistemic community is a network of professionals with recognized expertise and competence in a particular domain and an authoritative claim to policy relevant knowledge within that domain or issue-area ... Although an epistemic community may consist of professionals from a variety of disciplines and backgrounds, they have (1) a shared set of normative and principled beliefs, which provide a value based rationale for the social action of community members; (2) shared causal beliefs, which are derived from their analysis of practices leading or contributing to a central set of problems in their domain and which then serve as the basis for elucidating the multiple linkages between possible policy actions and desired outcomes; (3) shared notions of validity – that is intersubjective, internally defined criteria for weighing and validating knowledge in the domain of their expertise; and (4) a common policy enterprise – that is, a set of common practices associated with a set of problems to which professional competence is directed, presumably out of the conviction that human welfare will be enhanced as a consequence.

Although the author develops this definition as a political scientist, which is especially visible in (4), the definition is also applicable to communities in business. Here, full cognitive identity is not required, just identity in certain aspects (1 to 4). More roughly, Haas distinguishes two central dimensions of shared belief that he considers to be necessary for co-operation: shared beliefs about social behaviour (what is right and wrong) and shared beliefs concerning the criteria for validation of knowledge. However, this already covers a broad range of identification. In our view, most shared beliefs should be considered as the (end-)result of an interaction process and cannot be assumed as a necessary condition at its beginning.

Epistemic communities engage in transdisciplinary and/or transfunctional activities, at the interstices between the various disciplines. In contrast with communities of practice, they are not organized around a common discipline or practice but around a common topic or problem. Exploratory learning is not only understood as exploring existing options for problem solution but also as building something new out of diversity of individual knowledge related to the topic. Exploratory learning requires diversity of knowledge, which may be combined into something new, in Schumpeterian 'novel combinations'. The conditions under which this happens form the subject of this chapter.

There is little literature on the emergence of shared beliefs. Is it a process of self-selection between the members, where members are attracted to each other on the basis of applying the same epistemic criteria? Social identity theory would suggest this approach. This theory states that people prefer to work together with similar others, having similar values, preferences, and interests (Schneider and Northcraft, 1999). Or should shared beliefs be conceived as 'only' the result of negotiation processes, on the basis of existing beliefs? In this case, some essential questions are left unanswered. First, in these approaches 'shared beliefs' between the participants are assumed without explaining the origins. Second, the assumption of shared beliefs seems to go too far. Why, and to what extent, should people share causal and normative beliefs? From a pragmatic perspective, they may have widely varying causal beliefs and norms of behaviour as long as their actions stick together well enough to yield useful results. What, exactly, is meant by validity? Here again we would like to take a more pragmatic approach: ideas and actions are valid when they fit in collective action. Third, sharing beliefs may hamper exploration.

For this chapter, we prefer to use the term 'communities of exploitation' (or 'exploitative communities'), aimed primarily, or initially, at exploitation, and 'communities of exploration' (or 'exploratory communities') rather than 'epistemic communities'. It is not clear whether 'epistemic' knowledge is understood to include only codified or declarative knowledge, or also more tacit, procedural knowledge. In exploration one can expect an emphasis on tacit and procedural knowledge, but it can also be based on codified, declarative knowledge. Conversely, in exploitation, practice is based at least partly on codified, declarative knowledge, as well as on more tacit, procedural knowledge. We agree with Brown and Duguid that canonical rules are seldom sufficient to capture the richness and variability of practice, but such knowledge can form the basis for instruction, which is then expanded and enriched in practice, with context-specific procedural knowledge. We do not want to commit ourselves a priori to any difference, between exploitation and exploration, in emphasis on practice, in 'procedural knowledge', or emphasis on 'epistemic' knowledge.

According to the activity theory of knowledge that we employ, as others do, exploration is based on communicative practice. While communities of practice are focussed on exploitation, they may break out into exploration. If epistemic communities are focussed on exploration, they may 'consolidate' into exploitation (Nooteboom, 2000).

## Learning, diversity and cognitive distance

To proceed, we first specify our activity theory of knowledge. In research in psychology (Doise and Mugny, 1984), in organizational decision-making (Eisenhardt, Kathway and Bourgeois, 1997; Fiol, 1996), and in organizational innovation (Nooteboom, 2000; Kanter, 1988), diversity of knowledge or functional diversity (Schneider and Northcraft, 1999) is considered a necessary condition for exploratory learning. Diversity is needed for Schumpeterian novel combinations to emerge. Innovation is thus perceived as the combination and re-integration of already existing, diverse parts of knowledge into something new. Thus, diversity of knowledge is a necessary condition for exploratory learning but not a sufficient one. Next to diversity, the learning community must be able to develop a co-operative practice without already relying on shared beliefs or a shared identity.

We adopt a social constructivist perspective of knowledge. It is based, among other things, on the 'symbolic interactionism' of G.H. Mead, and was introduced to the organizational literature by Weick (1979, 1995), with his notions of 'enactment' and 'sensemaking'. According to this view: '(People) construct, arrange, single out and demolish many "objective" features ... unrandomize variables, insert vestiges of orderliness, and literally create their own constructs' (Weick, 1979). We view knowledge as structured on the basis of mental models, frames, schemata or scripts (Johnson-Laird, 1983; Abelson, 1976) or categories (Nooteboom, 1992, 2000). These notions are equivalent and refer to mental constructs by which we order our perceived world.

From our view of knowledge it follows that to the extent that people have developed their knowledge in different environments, and have not been in communication with each other, cognition (in the wide sense of perception, interpretation and evaluation) will differ: there will be greater or lesser 'cognitive distance' (Nooteboom, 1992, 2000). Cognitive distance yields both an opportunity and a problem. The opportunity is that contact with others gives us a possibility to escape from the myopia of our personal cognitive construction, by profiting from the different insights of others, based on different experience. A problem, however, is that the greater the cognitive distance, the more difficult it is to cross it, that is to understand the actions and expressions of a partner. The difference between cognitive variety and cognitive distance is as follows: variety refers to how many different individual systems of mental scripts there are, and distance refers to the degree of the difference between any two of them.

## Scripts, transactive memory and absorptive capacity

To make the theory more concrete, we employ the notion of scripts, which we apply to individuals as well as organizations (Gioia and Poole, 1984; Nooteboom, 2000). The notion of an organizational script may be seen as an elaboration of the notion of an organizational routine, proposed by Nelson and Winter (1982). Originally, the notion of scripts was proposed on the level of personal mental constructs (Abelson, 1976; Shank and Abelson, 1977).

A script is an ordered structure of sequential and/or parallel component activities called 'nodes' in the script. On an organizational level, in organizational rather than mental scripts, nodes refer to local 'communities'. On the level of communities, studied here, nodes in a community script refer to (potential) activities of individuals. Nodes entail 'repertoires' of action, in the form of a set of 'subscripts', from which people contribute to the community script. In this setting, individual 'capability' corresponds with a subscript, which includes knowledge and skills. Thus a 'repertoire' is a set of capabilities/subscripts.

In a script, there are direct connections or 'linkages' between nodes when their activities are dependent in any way. The linkages that a node has with other nodes define its 'role' in the community. Neighbouring nodes, that is nodes with direct connections of dependence, exert demands on each other, which yield constraints on their connections. These constraints define boundaries of the 'task' of a node. In other words, a role entails a set of linkages and corresponding tasks. The notion of constraints is our specification of the notion of 'validation criteria'. The process of 'validation' entails the determination of such constraints on linkages. Each node entails one or more subscripts (which together constitute a repertoire of capabilities) for the activities that are contributed, in the node, to the community script. On the level of a node, exploratory learning entails a change of subscripts (capabilities). Within communities, this entails individual learning. Such change is constrained by the constraints on linkages, which provide the boundary conditions of task performance. In systemic activities, there are dense connections between nodes, with tight constraints. In stand-alone systems, there are sparse connections, with ample, wide constraints, yielding scope for local change of repertoires.

People have mental representations of their own subscripts, and of at least part of the collective script (at least the identity of neighbouring nodes). That constitutes part of their 'knowledge'. Concerning other nodes, they need to know at least the constraints on connections with neighbours, for example their needs and expectations, in so far as they affect the linkage. They may or may not need to know about the repertoires of scripts in other nodes. We will return to that later. Individuals have mental representations of a collective script that may be very incomplete, including only the linkages that concern them directly. If they have a representation of the repertoire of subscripts of another node, it may be incomplete and incorrect.

This yields a specification of cognitive and structural 'connectedness' within a group, and the notion of an organization as a 'distributed cognitive system' (Hutchins and Klausen, 1996; Tsoukas, 1996). It also serves to incorporate the notion of 'transactive memory', originally developed for close dyads (Wegner, Giuliano and Hertel, 1985; Wegner, Erber and Raymond, 1991; Wegner, 1995). This notion is defined as follows (Wegner, Giuliano and Hertel, 1985: 256):

(1) an organized store of knowledge that is contained entirely in the individual memory systems of the group members, and (2) a set of knowledge-relevant transactive processes that occur among group members. Stated more colloquially, we envision transactive memory to be a combination of individual minds and communication between them.

The authors suggest 'a set of communication processes whereby two minds can work as one' (Wegner, Giuliano and Hertel, 1985: 263). In transactive memory, various levels of knowledge are assumed – as we also do in the notion of a script. There is 'lower order' knowledge: that is, detailed, specialized knowledge embodied in the subscripts of individual repertoires of knowledge and skills. This can be paraphrased by the individual's statement 'I know x'. This can include 'know-that' and 'know-how', which can be both tacit and codified, up to a point. Another type of knowledge is 'location knowledge': knowledge about who knows what. The paraphrase here is 'I know that you know x ...'. Wegner *et al.* assume that location knowledge should be shared between 'minds'/individuals, in collective transactive memory. This can be paraphrased as: 'I know that you know that I know that you know x ...' Shared location knowledge yields the basis for intersubjectivity to develop in a system of distributed cognition (Hutchins and Klausen, 1996).

As indicated, we propose that 'lower-order knowledge' corresponds with mental representations of subscripts in nodes. Shared location knowledge corresponds with knowledge about roles and tasks. We believe that with these distinctions we have a useful framework to conceptualize exploratory learning. It yields a more rigorous specification of Weick and Robert's definition of a collective structure:

> They [people] construct their actions (contribute) while envisaging a social system of joint actions (represent), and interrelate the constructed action with the system that is envisaged (subordinate). (Weick and Roberts, 1993: 360)

In our specification, the individual's contribution is conceived as depending (1) on the perceived role that one has in the collective script ('represent'); (2) on the tasks that this role entails ('contribute'); and (3) accepting the constraints on actions that this entails ('subordinate').

This elaborates the notion of absorptive capacity (Cohen and Levinthal, 1990): one can absorb what one can fit into a relevant mental script. Scripts create but also limit absorptive capacity. Mutual absorptive capacity between people entails that they can understand each others' actions, and take appropriate action from their repertoires. Collective absorptive capacity constitutes the ability of the community to absorb events into the collective script. An important question is how that works: how is this related to roles, tasks, repertoires and mental representations that people have of them? Is it clear what nodes are involved; whose role it is to absorb the event? And what does this mean for the whole architecture?

## Levels of exploration

So far, using the notion of a script, we have specified the necessary components in a distributed cognitive system, and we have given a preliminary analysis of how a distributed cognitive system may work. We now employ the notion of script in order to conceptualize exploration. We can now identify different kinds or 'levels' of exploration, as follows:

1. Change that preserves existing architecture, existing linkages (roles) and constraints on linkages (tasks):

    1a: with new selections, within nodes, from existing individual repertoires of subscripts (existing capabilities);

    1b: with new capabilities, i.e. new subscripts in individual repertoires, in individual learning, or new participants with different repertoires. At this level of exploration, new staff would have to satisfy existing roles and tasks, by socialization and instruction.

2. Change that preserves existing architecture and existing linkages (roles), with new repertoires (subscripts), from individual learning or new staff, which require change of constraints (tasks), i.e. new validation:

   2a: only local change of constraints for individual nodes (isolated tasks);

   2b: change of constraints (tasks) throughout the architecture.

3. Architectural change with existing nodes and repertoires, in new linkages (roles). Generally, new linkages will entail new constraints (validation).

4. New architecture of old and new nodes, including new capabilities (repertoires), with new linkages (roles) and new constraints (tasks).

To illustrate the framework, let us ask which type of exploration occurs in varying project teams of specialists. If different specialists enter with different capabilities (repertoires of subscripts) but in fixed roles with fixed tasks, we have type 1b. If they have different capabilities, and they are given new tasks, but in the same roles, we have type 2a if there is a change only in their individual tasks, and 2b when tasks change across the whole team. The other way round leads to the same result. If in a situation with changes in constraints members would not respond with changes in their repertoire, this would lead to a problem in the cooperation. If they enter with existing subscripts in new roles, in a new team structure, we have type 3. If there is a new team structure, with new roles and development of new subscripts (capabilities), we have type 4. The script concept also indicates that a certain level of exploration also implies changes on lower levels. Thus, a combination where there is a change in architecture but not in constraints and repertoires is not plausible as changes in architecture have consequences on constraints and repertoires.

A survey of changes for different levels of exploration is given in Table 2.1.

This framework can be seen as a refinement, in terms of scripts, of the work of Henderson and Clark (1990), who recognized similar types of innovation: change that preserves both elements and architecture (1), change of elements in a given architecture (2), change of architecture of existing elements (3), and new architecture with new elements (4).

*Table 2.1*   Types of change

| Change | Type of exploration | | | | | |
|---|---|---|---|---|---|---|
| | *1a* | *1b* | *2a* | *2b* | *3* | *4* |
| Validation criteria | no | no | local | collective | collective | collective |
| Repertoires of subscripts | no | yes | yes | yes | no | yes |
| Script architecture | no | no | no | no | yes | yes |

A central idea now is that in order to maintain exploitation as much as possible during exploration, organizations will proceed from less to more radical forms of change (Nooteboom, 2000). One does not engage in further change until both the promise (potential) and need for such change has become manifest. When new repertoires (capabilities) are developed, in the first approach they need to submit to constraints imposed on existing linkages (existing tasks). This can severely constrain the utilization of the potential of new capabilities, which can exert pressure to revise constraints (tasks) while preserving the architecture of linkages (roles). First one will try to constrain such change to local adaptations. If even wider changes of constraints are not enough, pressure arises for a change of architecture to yield scope for a full utilization of new repertoires (Nooteboom, 2000).

We will now use this framework to analyse communication processes in communities for different levels of exploration. First we turn to the literature for some examples, and then we try to explicate communication processes.

## Examples

To get some empirical sense of how exploration and transactive knowledge work, let us consider some examples. The first is taken from Weick and Roberts (1993: 370):

This bos'n, who is responsible for the smooth functioning of deck operations, gets up an hour early each day just to think about the kind of environment he will create on the deck that day, given the schedule of operations. This thinking is individual mind at work, but it also illustrates how collective mind is represented in the head of one person. The bos'n is dealing with collective mind when he represents the capabilities and weaknesses of imagined crewmembers' responses in his thinking, when he tailors sequences of activities so that improvisation and flexible response are activated as an expected part of the day's adaptive response.

Here, the crewmembers know that the bos'n knows about their skills and this is something that the bos'n knows. On top of this – and this is the contribution of Weick and Roberts – there is an internalization of distributed cognition by the individual. The individual contributes while subordinating his contribution to collective action. He does this on the basis of his mental representation of the collective script, or parts thereof. In this particular case, crew members did not need to know their colleagues' repertoires. The bos'n knows, and on the basis of that knowledge (re)constructs the architecture of co-ordination to fit operational needs. In other words, in this case there is no need for everyone to have full location knowledge. Crew members need to know the architecture of the collective script only in so far as it regards their individual actions.

It appears that the situation here is one of limited exploration, in variations within an existing script, with different selections from existing repertoires (exploration type 1a). Perhaps it could also be seen as exploration with novel configurations (sequences) from existing repertoires (exploration type 3), by a central co-ordinator (the bos'n). The more radical type of exploration (type 4), with a change of both individual repertoires and collective architecture, under the direction of a central co-ordinator, is much more problematic. How can the central co-ordinator know not only what all participants know but also what they could learn, in mutual interaction?

Another example is the following: an organization involved in research on technology for 'alternative' (durable) energy generation, had various departments with specialized expertise. The organization was a distributed cognitive system. When a new technology needed to be invented for saving energy, co-operation between the departments was weak. Moreover, there were different expectations of the success of a new technology. This organization used a certain technique (Matheson: The smart organization, HBS Press) in order to create a shared understanding of both the possible contribution of the various departments and their expectations of future success. This yielded a map similar to mental maps often supported by computer simulation (Vennix, 1996). In terms of transactive memory, the use of this technique and its publication within the group had two effects: the departments learned about the distribution of knowledge and their possible contributions (relative to estimated success) and this location knowledge was now shared.

The possible contributions also give insight in the roles that the various departments identified for themselves. As expectations about the success of the new technology differed, this may also have consequences for the task that a department intends to contribute.

Here, the assumption is that existing repertoires, in the different departments, can yield the desired result. Thus, exploration is of type 3. The difference with the previous case is that here there is no central co-ordinator who knows what everyone knows, and shared location knowledge had to be developed, in a collective mapping procedure. If, however, such repertoires have to be changed, in exploration type 4, the question arises who has to learn what, in a change of repertoire, and what novel architecture such individual learning might yield. We were not able to observe the mechanics how such changes in exploration type 4 take place due to the end of our contacts with this organization.

## Construction of shared beliefs

So far, we have argued that it goes too far to assume that there are shared beliefs *ex ante*, concerning norms of conduct, causal structures, validity and common enterprise. We argued that in exploration these are mostly not given *ex ante*, but arise from communicative interaction. We are looking for the communication rules needed for that. We proposed that an important part of such communication rules consists of transactive knowledge, in particular location knowledge. Subsequently, we saw that for some types of exploration it is not necessary that everyone knows what everyone knows. Depending on the type of exploration, location knowledge may itself be distributed rather than shared by all. To proceed, we now look in more detail at who has to know what, under what types of exploration, and what the implications are for communicative interaction.

For pure exploitation, and exploration that preserves the architecture and constraints on linkages (exploration type 1), it is not necessary for everyone to know what everyone knows. All one needs to know is who one's existing neighbours are (one's role), and existing constraints imposed on linkages with them (constraints on one's tasks). As we suggested before, from a pragmatic perspective such constraints correspond with the notion of 'validity'. Actions in nodes are valid if they satisfy constraints on linkages with other nodes in the collective script. The process of validation, then, leads to the establishment of new constraints. These new constraints make a reconstruction of tasks necessary. In exploration type 1, that is not needed. In terms of shared beliefs, everyone needs to share beliefs only on existing criteria of validity (the constraints), only with existing neighbours in the collective script. No causal beliefs are needed concerning the repertoires of even neighbouring nodes, as long as they satisfy existing constraints. Here, people are transacting rather than interacting. No development of new shared beliefs is needed. In exploration type 1b it may be a little different. In this type, individuals learn, that is extend their repertoires, or new individuals come in, and neighbours may need to know something about this in order to adapt. A potential problem here is that new options arise from individual learning, whose use may require adaptation of constraints in linkages with one's neighbours. Then, we move to a higher level of exploration.

This yields exploration type 2a, with new repertoires that require only local adaptation of constraints, that is new validation. For this, one needs to know the repertoires of neighbouring nodes, in so far as needed to conduct new validation (new constraints), in mutual interaction. This requires not only that one knows what neighbours know, but also that one has sufficient understanding of that for mutual adaptation. That requires a certain mutual absorptive and communicative capacity. In terms of shared beliefs, this entails the development of some shared causal beliefs, concerning repertoires of action, in so far as necessary for validation, but only between neighbours. A new element here, on a 'meta-level', is the possible need to establish shared beliefs on norms of behaviour for interaction and adaptation, according to which validation can take place. This may, however, be local, with mutual adaptation between neighbours. Some locally shared beliefs are also needed on the limits one needs to observe, with regard to 'collective enterprise', so that no wider adaptations are needed, elsewhere in the collective script. A potential problem remains: what if as a result of mutual adaptation neighbours, in turn, need to adapt constraints with their neighbours, resulting in a more pervasive change of constraints, in a collective validation process?

This yields exploration type 2b. This requires mutually consistent validation in multiple connections (across many roles). This requires either some central agent to co-ordinate multiple validation, or discussion with all other participants. The first may be the case in the first example we discussed in the previous section (the bos'n as a central co-ordinating agent). The second appears to be the case in the second example (joint development of a new method for saving energy). Here, there is a need to develop collective knowledge of repertoires (location and content knowledge), for which there need to be shared causal beliefs, but only limited, in so far as needed for collective validation. One also needs collective beliefs on norms for interaction, and on the overall architecture of the collective script. A potential problem remains: what if in the existing architecture no overall consistent validation can be achieved, and the architecture of the collective script needs to be changed to achieve coherence?

This yields exploration type 3, with architectural innovation with existing nodes and their repertoires, with new linkages. As in type 2a, there needs to be collective knowledge, in every node, or in a central pool of knowledge, of the location and content of all individual repertoires, and norms for the conduct of mutual adjustment. However, more extensive new knowledge of individual repertoires and procedures is needed, because mutual adjustment goes beyond existing neighbours, to allow for novel linkages. While in existing linkages norms of interaction have stabilized, this may have created an 'in-group' ethic and feeling that now have to be loosened to allow for 'out-group' linkages. Also, a new collective enterprise has to be developed, in a new collective script. How is that to be established? Does it follow from an experimental design from a central authority, or in a process of self-organization? Especially in the latter case, to guide the process of architectural change, shared aims and norms have to be developed. A potential problem here is that to enable a newly emerging script, repertoires in nodes have to be adapted to allow for the new linkages that it requires. In other words, it may require individual learning, or the introduction of new staff with new knowledge.

This yields exploration type 4, with a change of both individual knowledge, in new repertoires, and the development of a new collective script. Here we have a 'chicken-and-egg' situation. Existing repertoires may need to be adapted, but one can identify potential linkages, for a new script, only on the basis of existing repertoires. So, an iterative process of mutual adaptation may be needed. This requires iteratively adapted knowledge on the collective script, aims of collective enterprise, norms of interactive conduct, and individual repertoires. This iterative process indicates, precisely, the relation between individual learning (change of subscripts, on the basis of mutual adaptation) and collective learning (formation of a new collective script). In this process, people need to communicate their own repertoires of scripts to others, absorb what they communicate about theirs, they may need to adapt their individual repertoires, and they need to adapt their mental scripts concerning collective script architecture. New norms for conduct have to be developed, iteratively, and new shared views of collective enterprise.

The differences are summarized in Table 2.2.

*Table 2.2* Construction of new shared beliefs

| Type of belief | Type of exploration | | | | | |
|---|---|---|---|---|---|---|
| | 1a | 1b | 2a | 2b | 3 | 4 |
| Validation criteria | no | no | local | collective | collective | collective |
| Location of knowledge | no | local | local | collective | collective | collective |
| Content of knowledge (causal beliefs) | no limited | local limited | local limited | collective | collective extensive | collective iterative |
| Norms of conduct | no | no | local limited | collective limited | collective extensive | collective iterative |
| Collective enterprise | no | no | no | no | collective | collective extensive |

## Communication rules

Schall (1983: 56) proposed that:

> Communication rules have been variously defined but, in general, they are considered to be tacit understandings (generally unwritten and unspoken) about appropriate ways to interact (communicate) with others in given roles and situations, they are choices, not laws (though they constrain choice through normative, practical, or logical force), and they allow interactors to interpret behaviour in similar ways (to share meanings).

What communication rules are needed to develop what shared beliefs? Table 2.2 shows that depending on the level of exploration, rules of communication are needed on the following subjects:

1. The identity of nodes in a collective script: who's who?
2. The repertoires of subscripts within nodes (capabilities): who knows what?
3. The connections between nodes, in an existing architecture (role and task): location knowledge.
4. Type 1 exploration: the constraints on linkages, in an existing architecture (task): validation criteria.
5. Type 2 exploration: norms of interactive conduct concerning changing constraints on linkages (task).
6. Type 3 exploration: norms of interactive conduct concerning reconfiguration of roles (architecture).
7. Type 4 exploration: aims of collective enterprise concerning changes in architecture.

The first three types of communication rules are meant to identify the characteristics of a specific exploratory community. These characteristics were developed from the notion of a script that was transferred to an exploratory community. Location knowledge can be translated in an exploratory community as 'You know that I know that you know x' and as far as tasks are concerned: 'You know that I do x'.

As we go to higher levels of exploration (from point 4 onwards), fewer 'tacit understandings' can be taken for granted, since more and more existing beliefs and 'appropriate ways to interact' are up for change. As a result, communication rules shift to 'higher', more abstract levels of norms of interactive conduct, to guide the changes of lower level rules. Changes in architecture are embedded in shared aims of the collective enterprise.

In type 4 exploration, what is new, compared to type 3, is that communication rules no longer include individual repertoires of action, since they also are now up for change, in individual learning, or in the entry of new players with different repertoires. Norms or guidelines are now needed for both collective enterprise, to guide new script formation and the direction of individual learning, and for interaction in joint learning. The latter goes beyond new role formation on the basis of existing repertoires. Here, there is a need to adapt absorptive and communicative capacity. This is likely to entail an iterative process, in which beliefs concerning collective enterprise interact with the results of interactive individual learning. In other words, communication rules consist of shared perceptions of strategic goals, and cultural norms for communicating on individual learning, and adjusting absorptive and communicative capacities.

On several levels, the question arises: where do the new rules come from? Are they dictated 'from above', or do they arise from interaction, in 'self-organization'?

## Conclusion

Communities form an important intermediate level in organizational learning. Communities of exploration are characterized by the use of diverse knowledge. The central question that this chapter tried to answer is how co-operation can take place under the condition of cognitive distance within a community. Several conditions have been identified:

1. A community should be viewed as a collective structure of co-ordinated interaction, and not as a purely transactional network.

2. The concept of transactive memory adds that such a collective structure is characterized by shared location knowledge.
3. Communication rules serve to integrate cognitive diversity on a collective level.
4. Communication rules within an exploratory community are highly tacit.
5. There are different communication rules for different levels of exploration. As we move to higher levels of exploration, communication rules shift to higher levels of abstraction.
6. On lower levels of exploration, one can make more use of existing shared beliefs, concerning tasks, roles, distributed knowledge, norms of conduct, and collective enterprise. As we go to higher levels, new shared beliefs have to be developed, first concerning tasks and some norms of conduct, then roles and more extensive norms of conduct, and collective enterprise, then both collective enterprise and interactive learning, in an extension of repertoires for action.
7. The analysis develops the idea that to combine exploitation and exploration as long as possible, one will release and renew shared beliefs step by step, from lower to higher levels of exploration, as needs and opportunities emerge.

Our analysis has been structural and cognitive, and little attention has been paid to motivational issues. Under what conditions will people be willing to share knowledge, in view of 'psychological risk', in loss of reputation or 'face', or acceptance in a group, and possible risk concerning salary, career and internal competition for careers within the firm? (Edmonson, 1999). How can such risks be mitigated, and how does that depend on the content, purpose, and level of learning and exploration? And how does it depend on role structures? That is a different subject that could not be treated here, but is obviously of crucial importance.

## References

Abelson, R.P. (1976) Script processing in attitude formation and decision making. In J.S. Carroll and J.W. Payne (eds), *Cognition and Social Behavior*. Hillsdale, NJ: Lawrance Erlbaum, pp. 33–45.

Argyris, C. and Schön, D. (1978) *Organizational Learning*. Reading, MA: Addison-Wesley.

Blackler, F. (1995) Knowledge, knowledge work and organizations: an overview and interpretation, *Organization Studies*, 16(6): 1021–46.

Bogenrieder, I. and Nooteboom, B. (2002) *Learning groups: what types are there? A theoretical analysis and an empirical study in a consultancy firm*, Research paper, Rotterdam School of Management, Erasmus University, Rotterdam.

Boland, R.J. and Tenkasi, R.V. (1995) Perspective making and perspective taking in communities of knowing, *Organization Science*, 6(4): 350–72.

Brown, J.S. and Duguid, P. (1996) Organizational learning and communities-of-practice: toward a unified view of working, learning, and innovation. In M.D. Cohen and L.S. Sproull (eds), *Organizational Learning*. Thousand Oaks: Sage, pp. 58–82.

Brown, J.S. and Duguid, P. (2001) Knowledge and organization: a social-practice perspective, *Organization Science*, 12(2): 198–213.

Cohen, M.D. (1991) Individual learning and organizational routine, *Organization Science*, 2(1), reprinted in M.D. Cohen and L.S. Sproull (eds) (1996), *Organizational Learning*. London: Sage, pp. 188–229.

Cohen, M.D. and Bacdayan, P. (1996) Organizational routines are stored as procedural memory. In M.D. Cohen and L.S. Sproull (eds) (1996), *Organizational Learning*. London: Sage, pp. 403–30; first printed in *Organization Science*, 5(4) in 1994.

Cohen, M.D. and Levinthal, D.A. (1990) Absorptive capacity: a new perspective on learning and innovation, *Administrative Science Quarterly*, 35: 128–52.

Cook, S.D.N. and Yanow, P. (1993) Culture and organizational learning, *Journal of Management Enquiry*, 2(4); reprinted in M.D. Cohen and L.S. Sproull (eds) (1996), *Organizational Learning*. London: Sage, pp. 430–59.

Cowan, R., David, P.A. and Foray, D. (2000) The explicit economics of knowledge codification and tacitness, *Industrial and Corporate Change*, 9(2): 211–53.

David, P.A., Foray, D. and Steinmüller, W.E. (1999) The research network and the new economics of science. In A. Gambardella and F. Malerba (eds), *The Organization of Economic Innovation in Europe*. Cambridge: Cambridge University Press, pp. 303–42.

Edmondson, A. (1999) Psychological safety and learning behavior in work teams, *Administrative Science Quarterly*, 44: 350–83.

Eisenhardt, K., Kathway, J. and Bourgeois, L.J. (1997) Hoe directeuren een productieve ruzie uitvechten, *Holland Management Review*, 55: 43–50; originally published as: How management teams can have a good fight, *Harvard Business Review*, July–August, 1997.

Fiol, C.M. and Lyles, M.A. (1985) Organizational learning, *Academy of Management Review*, 10(4): 803–13.

Gioia, D.A. and Poole, P.P. (1984) Scripts in organizational behaviour, *Academy of Management Review*, 9(3): 449–59.

Haas, P.M. (1992) Introduction: epistemic communities and international policy co-ordination, *International Organization*, 46(1): 1–35.

Henderson, R.M. and Clark, K.B. (1990) Architectural innovation: the reconstruction of existing product technologies and the failure of established firms, *Administrative Science Quarterly*, 35: 9–30.

Hedberg, B.L.T., Nystrom, P.C. and Starbuck, W.H. (1976) Camping on seesaws: prescriptions for a self-designing organization, *Administrative Science Quarterly*, 21: 41–65.

Holland, J.H. (1975) *Adaptation in Natural and Artificial Systems*. Ann Arbor: University of Michigan Press.

Hutchins, E. and Klausen, T. (1996) Distributed cognition in an airline cockpit. In Y. Engeström and D. Middleton (eds), *Cognition and Communication at Work*. Cambridge: Cambridge University Press.

Johnson-Laird, P.N. (1983) *Mental Models*. Cambridge: Cambridge University Press.

Kanter, R.M. (1988) When a thousands flowers bloom: strucutural, collective and social conditions for innovation in organizations. In L.L. Cammings and B. Staw (eds), *Research in Organizational Behavior*. Vol. 10, Greenwich, CT: JAI Press.

Komito, L. (1998) The net as a foraging society: flexible communities, *The Information Society*, 14: 97–106.

Langlois, R.N. and Robertson, P.L. (1995) *Firms, Markets and Economic Change*. London: Routledge.

March, J. (1991) Exploration and exploitation in organizational learning, *Organization Science*, 2(1): 71–87.

Nelson R.R. and Winter, S. (1982) *An Evolutionary Theory of Economic Change*. Cambridge: Cambridge University Press.

Nooteboom, B. (1992) Towards a dynamic theory of transactions, *Journal of Evolutionary Economics*, 2: 281–99.

Nooteboom, B. (2000) *Learning and Innovation in Organizations and Economies*. Oxford: Oxford University Press.

Schall, M.S. (1983) A communication-rules approach to organizational culture, *Administrative Science Quarterly*, 28: 557–81.

Schneider, S.K. and Northcraft, G.B. (1999) Three social dilemmas of workforce diversity in organizations: a social identity perspective, *Human Relations*, 52(11): 1445–67.

Shank, R. and Abelson, R. (1977) *Scripts, Plans, Goals and Understanding*. Hillsdale, NJ: Lawrence Erlbaum.

Smircich, L. (1983) Organization as shared meaning. In L.R. Pondy, P.J. Frost, G. Morgan and T.C. Dandridge (eds), *Organizational Symbolism*. Greenwich, CT: JAI Press, pp. 55–65.

Steinmüller, W.E. (2000) Will new information and communication technologies improve the 'codification' of knowledge?, *Industrial and Corporate Change*, 9(2): 361–76.

Thompson, J.D. (1967) *Organizations in Action*. New York: McGraw-Hill.

Tsoukas, H. (1996) The firm as a distributed knowledge system: a constructionist approach, *Strategic Management Journal*, 17(Winter Special Issue): 11–25.

Vennix, J.A.M. (1996) *Group Model Building: Facilitating Team Learning Using System Dynamics*. New York: John Wiley.

Wegner, D.M. (1995) A computer network model of human transactive memory, *Social Cognition*, 13(3): 319–39.

Wegner, D.M., Giuliano, T. and Hertel, P. (1985) Cognitive interdependence in close relationships. In W. Ickes (ed.), *Compatible and Incompatible Relationships*. New York: Springer.

Wegner, D.M., Erber, R. and Raymond, P. (1991) Transactive memory in close relationships, *Journal of Personality and Social Psychology*, 61(6): 923–9.

Weick, K.F. (1979) *The Social Psychology of Organizing*. Reading, MA: Addison-Wesley.

Weick, K.F. (1991) The nontraditional quality of organizational learning, *Organization Science*, 2(1): 163–74.

Weick, K.F. (1995) *Sensemaking in Organizations*. Thousand Oaks, CA: Sage.

Weick, K.F. and Roberts, K.H. (1993) Collective mind in organizations: heedful interrelating on flight decks, *Administrative Science Quarterly*, 38: 357–81.

Weick, K.F. and F. Westley (1996) *Organizational Learning: Affirming an Oxymoron*. In S.R. Clegg, C. Hardy and W.R. Nord (eds), *Handbook of Organization Studies*. London: Sage, pp. 440–58.

Wenger, E.C. and Snyder, W.M. (2000) Communities of practice: the organizational frontier, *Harvard Business Review*, January–February, 139–45.

# 3
# Communities of Practice: Facilitating Social Learning while Frustrating Organizational Learning

*Marleen Huysman*

## Introducing organizational learning and communities of practice

Despite its almost fifty years of existence, the literature on organizational learning is still growing. Over the years, the topic has been approached from various angles. Some scholars have been mostly interested in learning processes as adaptation with typically organizational routines as its outcomes (for example Simon and March, 1958; March and Olsen, 1976; Cyert and March, 1963; Levitt and March, 1988). Others focus mainly on the cognitive rather than the behavioural aspects that typify the learning of organizations (for example Hedberg, 1981; Argyris and Schön, 1978). With the advent in the 1980s of Management Information Systems, IS scholars joined the organizational learning debate by introducing an information processing perspective to learning (for example Huber, 1991; Duncan and Weiss, 1979; Walsh and Ungson, 1991), stimulating people to think of ways to technically support learning processes and storage and retrieval of organizational knowledge bases. At the start of the 1990s, yet another perspective was introduced within the literature on organizational learning. This time the topic gained attention from ethnographers studying organizational behaviour. Based on theories derived from Vygotsky and Piaget, the idea was introduced that learning is essentially social. The learner as (peripheral) member of a community participates in actual practice and as such gradually learns how to think and act as a community member (Lave and Wenger, 1991). The focus on COPs as the core social unit where learning in organizations takes place, has gained almost total acceptance within the OL discipline. By participating together, communities emerge whose members have learned tacitly how to interpret knowledge, how to behave as an insider, etc.

The concept of communities of practice inspired many authors to think of it as a tool or social mechanism to support learning processes (for example Davenport and Prusak, 1998; Wenger, 1998; Boland and Tenkasi, 1995; Dougherty, 2001; Brown and Duguid, 1991). Probably the most often-cited article that relates learning with COP is Brown and Duguid's article in *Organization Science* (1991). Their argument is that COPs are social structures that are able to blend learning, working and innovating during day-to-day work activities. In his book *Communities of Practice: Learning, Meaning and Identity*, Etienne Wenger (1998) provides more theoretical depth while linking the two concepts. Central to his work is a 'social theory of learning'. Learning occurs through active participation in practices of communities while at the same time identities in relation to these communities are constructed. Learning thus refers both to action and belonging by members of (multiple) COPs. Wenger's work and the work of Brown and Duguid can be considered breakthroughs in later academic and practice-oriented debates about learning, knowledge, and management.

Communities contribute to this social learning as they provide the most suitable setting for learning to take shape. Collections of individuals bound by informal relationships share knowledge in action, and voluntary and informal learning happens. In general, the argument goes that COPs stimulate social learning by providing a suitable 'non-canonical', non-hierarchical, informal and flexible surrounding that is considered a fruitful breeding ground for learning.

After a decade of enthusiasm for COPs' role in promoting organizational learning, it might be time to become more critical about this mutual relationship. In fact, in this chapter we will argue that although we know a lot about COPs' contribution to learning *within* organizations, not much is known about their role in contributing to learning by organizations or 'organizational learning'.

Those who see learning as a social practice resulting in shared, situated knowledge usually consider the concept of organizational learning as learning *within* organizations. What is typical is that they tend to downplay the role of COPs in supporting *organizational* learning defined as the learning *by* organizations.

The distinction between learning within and learning by organizations is an important one. Learning by organizations refers to the process of institutionalization in which knowledge gains acceptance by members of the organization and is taken for granted. Organizational learning in that sense refers to the process in which shared knowledge becomes subsidiary knowledge (Polanyi, 1966). To understand what makes learning dinstinctly organizational, it helps to shift the attention from the product 'organization' to the process of 'organizing' (Weick, 1979). Organizing implies generalizing or institutionalizing knowledge. During organizing, institutionalized knowledge is used by individuals in their day-to-day activities while at the same time they create new and rearrange existing institutional knowledge. When this organizing process occurs at the level of the organization, we refer to organizational learning. Depending on various conditions, such as history, size, the multidisciplinarity of professions etc., this process of institutionalization can take years. When organizing processes occur at the level of the group or community, we refer to learning within organizations and focus on learning processes that take place within the context of an organization but do not necessarily influence the organization. This learning within organizations can be mainly individual learning, but can also have a more collective nature, which is the case with community learning.

We will argue that COPs' contribution to *support organizational learning* is much more complex in comparison to their often-praised role in supporting social *learning within organizations*. This distinction between learning within and learning by sheds a less optimistic light on the contribution of COPs. With the use of ideas on social construction and institutionalization of knowledge as well as Polanyi's ideas on focal and subsidiary awareness, more theoretical underpinnings will be given to the idea that COPs facilitate social learning but at the same time frustrate organizational learning.

## Organizational learning and learning within organizations

Despite the still-growing literature on organizational learning, there remains a need for more scientific understanding on how to explicate actual organizational learning processes (Thatchenkery, 1996). Perhaps the most important cause of this confusion lies in the combination 'organization' and 'learning' on top of the fact that both terms are highly conceptual. Because of the conceptual nature of these terms, it is difficult to see organizations as well as to see learning taking place (Yanow, 2000). Researchers have problems *seeing* organizations and likewise seeing the learning of organizations. If organizations cannot be observed, than it will be difficult to theorize about them, let alone about the process of organizational learning (Sandelands and Srivatsan, 1993; Yanow, 2000). Learning only becomes apparent after the fact, when something has been learned. Learning is usually approached as an 'achievement' verb, focussing on learning as changes or confirmation of existing knowledge (Sandelands and Drazin, 1989). This means that the same word 'learning' refers to both an outcome and a process, concealing rather than revealing the dynamics of learning. In combination with the problem of perceiving organizations (Sandelands and Srivatsan, 1993), this is probably one of the most important reasons that although scholars talk about OL, the practical illustrations deal with learning by individuals and groups. Many well-known OL researchers, such as March and Olsen and Argyris and Schön, treat organizational learning as individual learning within an organizational context (Weick and Westley, 1996). For example, Aryris and Schön as well as March and Olsen state that the organization learns that when individuals adapt their cognitions and behaviour to the feedback signals as environmental reactions to individual actions. Although March and Olsen acknowledge that organizational learning is usually not based on the outcome of individual learning ('audience learning'), they in fact refer to management learning as representatives of the organization. Supplementing top management as the visible representative of organization, is a tendency of many OL scholars (for example Senge, 1992) again mixing up organizational learning with learning within organizations.

Weick and Westley (1996), as well as Yanow (2000) and Cook and Yanow (1993), have tried to address this problem by introducing a cultural perspective on learning. They argue that by treating organizations as culture, we are better able to see learning happening. These and other scholars argue that communities of practice are a suitable perspective to open up our eyes for the cultural approach to learning. Based on cultural-interpretive research methods, learning is studied within, for example, communities of system analysts (Ciborra and Lanzara, 1994), maintenance engineers (Orr, 1996), midwives (Jordan, 1989), flight crews and ground staff (Weick and Roberts, 1993), claim processors (Wenger, 1998), IT consultants (Teigland and Wasko, 2000), flutemakers (Cook and Yanow, 1993), and technicians (Barley, 1996). The interpretive ethnographic methods try to reveal how the 'social world is constituted by the local production of meaningful action' (Suchman, 1987: 58). The focus is not so much on the outcome or the achievement of learning but on the process of learning as it has actually taken shape as part of the day-to-day activities of communities. In the course of their day-to-day interactions, people learn to become a practitioner, such as a photocopier repairman or an experienced midwife. Learning within these communities takes place through the communication of tacit knowledge. Or as Yanow (2000: 255) puts it 'in interaction with and through the actifacts, leaving their embodied meanings unspoken'. This learning is very much tacit. In terms of Polanyi, practitioners learn to become a community member while focussing on something else.

This cultural approach has contributed significantly to the debate on organizational learning. As mentioned earlier, this approach to organizational learning has put COPs as suitable vehicles for learning to the forefront. This can be considered a very welcome contribution. Because of its use of learning as a 'process verb' the approach provides more insight into *how* learning takes place. Further, it departs from the individual bias within the literature on organizational learning (Huysman, 2000a) by directing the attention on (tacit) learning of collectives and in specific on community learning. Combined, the approach provides a valuable framework to analyse the actual process of learning by communities. Its downside is, however, that although these and other scholars talk about 'organizational learning' they in fact continue the tradition within the OL literature by approaching OL as learning within organizations. In the rest of this chapter we will make the argument that in the case of community learning, group-level learning is facilitated but organizational learning is frustrated. This statement will be based on the theory of social construction and institutionalization of knowledge (Berger and Luckmann, 1966) combined with some ideas on focal and subsidiary knowledge introduced by Polanyi.

## A social constructivist approach to organizational learning

A social constructivist approach to OL will show that organizational learning is different from social (community) learning in that the former needs objectification of the outcome of the latter. Social constructivist approaches to organizational learning emphasize the process through which an organization constructs knowledge or reconstructs existing knowledge. Through knowledge sharing, individual knowledge may become shared knowledge. This shared knowledge might become taken-for-granted, tacit organizational knowledge that will – often as subsidiary knowledge – influence subsequent action. In other words: organizational learning can be looked upon as a process that occurs as a result of the actions of the organization's members, while these same actions are simultaneously influenced by collectively accepted knowledge. As a result of this duality between, on the one hand, the actions of individuals and, on the other, the deterministic or formative influences of existing organizational factors, organizational learning can be viewed as a process of institutionalization (Berger and Luckmann, 1966).

The term 'institutions' is used to describe social practices that are regularly and continuously repeated, are sanctioned and maintained by social norms and have a major significance in the social structure (Abercrombie *et al.*, 1984). Institutionalization is the process through which social practices become sufficiently regular and continuous as to be described as institutions. This concept is widely used in sociology, though often without precise specification. Different schools of sociology treat the concept of institutionalization in different ways. For example, functionalists tend to see institutions as fulfilling the needs of individuals or society (for example, Durkheim, 1978; Parsons, 1960) while phenomenologists may concentrate on the way in which people create or adapt institutions rather than merely respond to them (Berger and Luckmann, 1966; Schutz, 1971). Scott (1987) distinguishes different 'institutional schools': two dealing with the process of institutionalization and two with institutions as systems. Institutionalization can be conceived of as 'a process of instilling value'. Selznick, for example, argues that 'institutionalisation is to infuse with value beyond the technical requirement of the task at hand' (Selznick, 1957: 17) which may lead to an unplanned and unintended nature of institutions. Institutionalization can also be conceived of as 'a process of creating reality'. Social order is founded on a shared social reality, which is created by social interaction. In this chapter Selznick's conception of institutionalization is used. The process of institutionalization requires that 'types of behavior in types of situations are connected to types of actors' (Berger and Luckmann, 1966).

With organizational knowledge, reference is made to knowledge as in rules, procedures, strategies, activities, technologies, conditions, paradigms, terms of reference, etc. around which organizations are constructed and through which they operate (Levitt and March, 1988). Organizational knowledge refers to knowledge that is being generated, developed and transmitted by individuals and that individuals use when acting as organizational members. This is organizational knowledge in the weak sense (Tsoukas and Vladimirou, 2001). In a strong sense, knowledge becomes organizational when 'individuals draw and act upon a corpus of generalizations in the form of generic rules produced by the organization' (Tsoukas and Vladimirou, 2001: 979).

Berger and Luckmann (1966) describe the process of institutionalization as consisting of three phases or 'moments': 'externalization, objectification, and internalization'. These three moments refer to the two interpretations of institutionalization: constructing a social structure which members use to act upon. Externalizing refers to the process through which personal knowledge is exchanged with others.

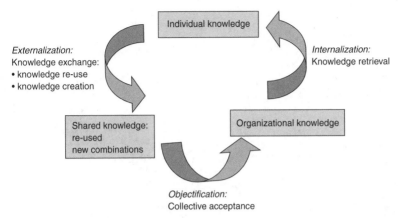

*Figure 3.1* Processes of institutionalization in relation to organizational learning

COPs seem to be well suited to support two of the three processes that make up organizational learning: internalization and externalization. In fact, COP writers that connect the concept with learning usually focus on these two processes (for example, Lave and Wenger, 1991; Brown and Duguid, 1991; Botkin, 1999). The question of whether COPs also contribute to learning at the level of the organization, depends on the role of COPs in supporting the process of objectification. In the following sections, we will discuss this relationship between COP and learning within and by organizations in more detail.

## Communities of practice and learning as institutionalization

In the rest of this chapter, an attempt is made to conceptually unravel the relationship between organizational learning and COP. This will be done by using a theoretical framework based on the notion of learning as the process of institutionalization.

Figure 3.2 illustrates the contribution of COP in supporting the process of learning as a process of institutionalizing knowledge.

COPs can be appropriate structures to support this process of internalization. Through internalization, individuals acquire organizational knowledge. It is through internalization that individuals become members of the organization. In fact, internalization means the process through which one becomes an 'insider'. A powerful way to support competence learning by newcomers is by letting people work together. There is a growing band of authors who argue that learning should be

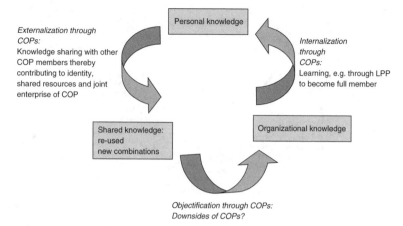

*Figure 3.2*   COPs' contribution to OL as institutionalization

considered as being inextricably bound up with working (for example, Brown and Duguid, 1991; Gherardi, 2000; Nicoloni and Meznar, 1995; Yanow, 2000). For example, Lave and Wenger (1991) introduced the concept of 'legitimate peripheral participation' as a method of learning by actively participating as opposed to learning outside the relevant task environment such as accumulating information from manuals.

Participating in COPs, or at least in their periphery, is often seen as one of the key mechanisms through which individuals socialize and learn 'collective knowledge'. Referring to Lave and Wenger, Brown and Duguid (1991: 50) put it as follows:

> Learners need legitimate access to the periphery of communication – to computer mail, to formal and informal meetings, to telephone conversations, etc. and, of course to war stories. They pick up invaluable know how – not just information but also manner and technique – from being on the periphery of competent practitioners going about their business.

Next to learning to become competent in a new organization, learning in COPs also happens for the purpose of knowledge re-use or knowledge renewal. This process of *externalization* supported by COPs is often seen as important to support knowledge sharing and knowledge management. Many organizations nowadays are experimenting with the concept of COP to enable the knowledge transfer between – often geographically dispersed – organizational members (Botkin, 1999; Leonard and Sensiper, 1998; Sole and Huysman, 2001). The idea is that by building or supporting COPs, people are more inclined to share knowledge with each other, which otherwise would either be lost or duplicated. It is in particular the communication of tacit knowledge for which COPs are believed to offer a suitable environment. Tacit knowledge in COPs is communicated through explicit knowledge. Communication within COPs is usually 'done' in interaction with and through artefacts, leaving their embodied meanings unspoken (Yanow, 2000: 255). A way to support the transfer of this knowledge in communities is for example by telling stories and swapping anecdotes (Sims, 2000) between old-timers and newcomers.

Just because knowledge is exchanged does not mean that the shared knowledge has already been collectively accepted. Shared knowledge only turns into organizational knowledge when the organization's members accept it as such. Collective acceptance as a process is, in other words, the link between individual learning and organizational learning.

This process of collective acceptance or objectification usually does not take place consciously and can be a long, drawn-out process. By collectively accepting local knowledge the collective – often gradually – starts to accept existing shared knowledge as being part of the organization. This process is not so much one of sharing knowledge but more one of sedimentation. Von Krogh *et al.* (2000) refers to this process in the context of knowledge creation as 'globalizing local knowledge'. For example, a group of technicians might have learned a new way of fixing a machine. This new operational knowledge remains local knowledge until it is accepted by the organization, for example – as expressed in organizational stories, in manuals and in the training of newcomers. This process of objectification usually takes much longer than is the case with the two other sub-institutionalization processes discussed above (Berger and Luckmann, 1966; Dixon, 2000; Douglas, 1987). Ignoring the importance of collective acceptance can be a serious obstacle to organizational learning. In fact, most organizations tend to ignore the outcomes of local learning processes or have problems collectively accepting these outcomes (Huysman and De Wit, 2002).

Below two general tendencies inherent to communities are discussed that might obstruct the objectification of local knowledge and therefore hinder learning by organizations. These are the tendency of COPs to be less visible and consequentially be ignored by management, and the tendency of COPs to be unconscious of their own (tacit) knowledge that has been learned over time. We will discuss these two negative tendencies below.

## COPs frustrating organizational learning

Tsoukas and Chia (2002) argued that although there are ongoing changes in organizations, this should not be taken to mean that organizations constantly change. The same argument applies to learning: although there is a lot of learning going on in organizations, this does not mean that the organization as a whole learns. A lot of learning within organizations remains unrecognized. Non-learning or inflexibility in an organization is often the result of managers not paying attention to learning processes that take place within communities (Brown and Duguid, 1991). During their day-to-day activities, COPs continuously create new knowledge as a solution to daily problems. They create new ways of working, give new interpretations to their situation and discuss existing practices. In other words, whereas internalization and externalization practices can be highly innovative, the problem often lies in inflexible objectifying processes, as local knowledge is often not transformed into new organizational knowledge.

More often than not, collective acceptance occurs when knowledge sharing processes are ratified through the endorsement of dominant coalitions within an organization (Simon and March, 1958). Dominant coalitions are formed by, for example, management, a critical mass, reference groups, old-timers, or charismatic personalities. Dominant coalitions can have a negative impact on the result of learning processes. For example, management – as an important member of a dominant coalition – might be oblivious to what is actually going on within the organization. 'Whether local changes are amplified and become institutionalised depends on the "structural context," created to a large extent ... by senior managers' (Tsoukas and Chia, 2002: 579). By not accepting existing knowledge as being important to the organization as a whole, management hinders the construction of organizational learning, as a result of which the learning process of the organization will eventually become out of step with the learning process of individuals within the organization (Brown and Duguid, 1991).

The next illustration provides an example of the power enjoyed by dominant coalitions, consisting of management and old-timers, who were able to frustrate the collective acceptance process and thus organizational learning as a whole.

A group of information system (IS) designers worked in the computer department of a large organization for a number of years. They all had records of long service within the company, where they had previously been employed as computer programmers. The company was using a number of routines that had been introduced by these employees over the years. For example, employees worked mainly on their own, there was little contact with the clients, almost every designer used his or her own particular style of IS design and there was a heavy bias towards technical details. The fact that their clients were unhappy with these routines was never explicitly discussed. This complacency was reinforced because the department enjoyed a monopoly position within the organization.

At the beginning of the 1990s, the demand for information systems doubled, which resulted in a drastic expansion in the number of personnel. Twenty new system designers were brought in from outside the organization; all of who had enjoyed a professional training in IS design and had often worked for a substantial length of time for software houses. These newcomers brought knowledge and skills with them that radically differed from the organization's existing in-house knowledge and skills. However, despite the fact that knowledge was exchanged, the existing collective routines and practices did not change. A critical mass consisting of 'old-timers' and management did not adapt to the new practices that most of them even did not recognize. Over time, the majority of the newcomers eventually adapted to the established routines. Although they realized that clients were unhappy with the methods and knowledge that were being used, they learned not to express their opinions in public and definitely not to report them to management (Huysman, 2000).

Consequently, despite the potential for the organization to learn new (IS designers') routines, inflexibility was the result. The community of old-timers formed such a powerful coalition that it hindered the transformation of newly shared knowledge into organizational knowledge.

Next to being not recognized by existing dominant coalitions such as management, organizational learning is hindered by the fact that COPs are often unaware of their own learning and, consequently, of the potential new knowledge that might be the result of this situated learning. Ciborra and Lanzara (1994), for example, describe the case of system designers at a computer company who were unaware of their innovative ways of working that developed over time. Because their personal activities are so much integrated in their day-to-day context, they became blind to changes in their 'formative context'. This subsidiary knowledge that community members share will only become recognized by the members when explicit focus on certain knowledge requires bringing this knowledge into focal awareness. It is only in such cases that tacitly shared knowledge of which COP members are not aware become explicit and might be communicated to others across the COP borders.

There are various ways to support the process of objectification so that knowledge becomes accepted by the organization as a whole.

Top management can support objectification through their explicit acknowledgement of the importance of COPs (Huysman and De Wit, 2002; Brown and Duguid, 1991, 2000; Cohen and Prusak, 2000). Recognizing the importance of communities and networks requires an awareness of where valuable communities are located and what holds them together (Wenger, 2000). According to Wenger, this requires a new set of responsibilities that are a long way from the technical emphasis of knowledge management. It requires an 'anthropological nose' (Wenger, 2000: 19). COPs cannot be managed nor structured, but instead calls for new – if you like 'soft' – management principles such as 'hospitality' (Ciborra, 1996) and 'doing no harm' (Cohen and Prusak, 2000). Objectification through more attentive managers requires that they are more capable of absorbing what is learned within communities. This means the need to understand communities' history, their interpretive codes, their practices, and so on (Tsoukas and Chia, 2002: 579). Creating such absorptive capacity among dominant coalitions is extremely difficult as the knowledge shared by community is highly tacit. To become aware (focally) of this knowledge that is often subsidiary to the members, managers need to dwell into the communities' praxis. In addition, a lot of the learning of COP is 'heuristic', requiring active membership as well. Heuristic knowledge is gained through improvisations while carrying out tasks and often resides in the stories told by community members (Brown and Duguid, 1991).

Supporting objectification from inside instead of outside is also a strategy to support organizational learning. Objectification can take place for example via the intervention of 'domain experts', people who are considered to be the *primus inter pares* among the community members. Most communities informally select one individual or a group of people to be the *primus inter pares* of the community. This person plays an important role in objectifying the knowledge that is shared between the communities. His or her acknowledgement of the knowledge as being relevant, innovative, useful and so on to the community will stimulate other members to use it. This corresponds with the idea of reference groups and significant others, concepts that were intro-duced a century ago by symbolic interactionists (Shibutani, 1955; Thomas, 1914). It is important that managers recognize these key peo-ple and take their knowledge seriously. If not, knowledge will only remain relevant to the community itself.

These key community members also need to have a stake outside their community to support the acceptance of the value and usability of the knowledge by other organizational participants. Thus, in order for community knowledge to cross boundaries and become accepted by a larger audience, knowledge brokers who are seen as being 'significant others' are needed (Wenger, 1998).

Next to a more natural role of senior members or experts, experts can also take part in a jury of people who peer-review the knowledge of their community members. Brown (2000) provides an example taken from Xerox, that illustrates how peer reviewing can help objectify community knowledge. Photocopier and printer repairmen at Xerox ('reps') use a web-based system called 'Eureka' as a way of accelerating their learning and structuring the community knowledge on how to act as a successful repairman. The system is based on actionable expert knowledge con-cerning printers and copiers. To transform reps' opinions and experi-ences into 'warranted beliefs', contributors had to submit their ideas for peer review, a process facilitated by the web. The peers would vet and refine the story, and connect it to others. As such, these experts helped to make sure that knowledge contained by Eureka is perceived as valu-able and reliable, while merely opinions and 'fantastic horror stories' were filtered out. Eureka is used as a tool to learn organizational knowl-edge and thus contributes to the process of organizational learning (Storck and Hill, 2000).

Highlighting the expert's role in COPs detracts the egalitarian image of COPs. However, when organizations are perceived as political arenas more than as friendly communities of communities, issues of power, structures and hierarchies cannot be ignored. Clearly, more research is needed to analyse the ambivalent role of COPs in supporting organiza-tional learning and in specific in supporting the collective acceptance of shared knowledge.

## Conclusions

A still-growing group of organizational practitioners and scholars per-ceive COPs to be the most promising vehicle to support organizational learning. Originally, this link between COPs and learning was introduced by ethnographic researchers who argued that during their day-to-day activity community members gradually learn the tacit knowledge that holds a community together. In general, the relationship is often perceived as positive, obvious and inherent. It is striking to note that the link between organizational learning and COPs is almost always taken for granted while the focus is on learning within organizations and not on learning by organizations, or 'organizational learning'. A social constructivist perspective on the relationship between learning and COP provides a different view than we are used to. In this chapter, we have tried to critically analyse this optimistic relationship by introducing a model that perceives learning as the process of institutionalization. Communities have different roles during this process. We agree with the 'communitarian' view that during the process of externalizing and internalizing knowledge, COPs might serve as suitable structures to support learning. This learning is, however, limited to social learning within organizations. It does not inform us about the learning that occurs at a higher-level of abstraction: organizational learning. For this higher-level learning to take place, local tacit knowledge – which is often the outcome of community learning – needs to be collectively accepted by organizational members. We have argued that this process of objectification is often hindered by COP. In other words, although COPs are well suited to support learning within organizations, they have a tendency to obstruct learning by organizations. Clearly, empirical research is needed to analyse these and other possibilities for communities to support organizational learning. We believe that the social constructivist perspective on organizational learning as discussed in this chapter, provides an interesting framework to do so.

## Note

1. The 'moments' of Berger and Luckmann correspond to a certain extent to Giddens' structuration theory (1984). Giddens is one of the most well-known contemporary sociologists who proposes a dialectical relationship between action and structure. Action and structure presuppose each other, instead of being mutually exclusive. Giddens is more explicit than Berger and Luckmann (1966) about the possible occurrence of the consequences of human action that are unknown or unintended.

## References

Abercrombie, N., Hill S., and Turner, B.S. (1984) *Dictionary of Sociology*. Harmondsworth: Penguin Books.

Argyris, C. and Schön, D. (1978) *Organizational Learning: a Theory of Action-Perspective*. Reading, MA: Addison-Wesley.

Barley, S. (1986) Technology as an occasion for structuring: evidence from observations of CT scanners and the social order of radiology departments, *Administrative Science Quarterly*, 31: 78–108.

Berger, P. and Luckmann, T. (1966) *The Social Construction of Knowledge*. London: Penguin Books.

Boland, R.J.J. and Tenkasi, R.V. (1995) Perspective making and perspective taking in communities of knowing, *Organization Science*, 6(4): 350–72.

Botkin, J. (1999) *Smart Business: How Knowledge Communities Can Revolutionize Your Company*. New York: Free Press.

Brown, J.S. (2000) Growing up digital: the web and the new learning ecology, *Change, the Magazine of Higher Learning*, March/April: 11–22.

Brown, J.S. and Duguid, P. (1991) Organizational learning and communities-of-practice: toward a unified view of working, leaning and innovation, *Organization Science*, 2(1): 40–57.

Ciborra, C.U. (ed.) (1996) *Groupware and Teamwork*. Chichester: John Wiley and Sons.

Ciborra, C.U. and Lanzara, G.F. (1994) Formative contexts and information technology, understanding the dynamics of innovation in organizations, *Accounting, Management and Information Technology*, 4(2): 61–86.

Cohen, D. and Prusak, L. (2000) *In Good Company: How Social Capital Makes Organizations Work*, Boston, MA: Harvard Business School Press.

Cook, S.D.N. and Yanow, D. (1993) Culture and organizational learning, *Journal of Management Inquiry*, 2(4): 373–90.

Cyert, R.M and March, J.G. (1963) *A Behavioral Theory of the Firm*, Englewood Cliffs, NJ: Prentice Hall.

Davenport, T.H. and Prusak, L. (1998) *Working Knowledge: How Organizations Manage What They Know*, Boston: Harvard Business School Press.

Dixon, N.M. (2000) *Common Knowledge*. Cambridge MA: Harvard Business School Press.

Dodgson, M. (1993) Organizational learning: a review of some literatures, *Organization Studies*, 14(3), 375–94.

Dougherty, D. (2001) Reimagining the differentiation and integration of work for sustained product innovation, *Organization Science*, 12(5): 612–31.

Douglas, M. (1987) *How Institutions Think*. London: Routledge and Kegan Paul.

Duncan, R.B. and Weiss, A. (1979) *Organizational Learning: Implications for Organizational Design Research in Organizational Behavior*. Greenwich, CT: JAI Press.

Durkheim, E. (1978) *On Institutional Analysis*. Chicago: Chicago University Press.

Gherardi, S. (2000) Practice-based theorizing on learning and knowing in organizations, *Organization*, 7(2): 211–23.

Giddens, A. (1984) *The Constitution of Society*. Cambridge: Polity Press.

Hedberg, B.L.T. (1981) How organizations learn and unlearn. In P.C. Nystrom and W.H. Starbuck (eds), *Handbook of Organization Design*, vol. 1. New York: Oxford University Press.

Huber, G.P. (1991) Organizational learning: the contributing processes and the literatures, *Organizational Science*, 2(1): 88–115.

Huysman, M.H. (2000a) Rethinking organizational learning, *Accountancy Management and Information Technology*, 10: 81–99.

Huysman, M.H. (2000b) Organizational learning or learning organizations, *European Journal of Work and Organizational Psychology*, 9(2): 133–45.

Huysman, M.H. and de Wit, D. (2002) *Knowledge Sharing in Practice*. Boston: Kluwer Academic.

Jordan, B. (1989) Cosmopolitical obstetrics: some insights from the training of traditional midwives, *Social Science and Medicine*, 28(9): 52–65.

Lave, J. and Wenger, E. (1991) *Situated Learning: Legitimate Peripheral Participation*. Cambridge: Cambridge University Press.

Leonard, D. and Sensiper, S. (1998) The Role of Tacit Knowledge in Group Innovation, *California Management Review*, 40(2): 112–32.

Levitt, B. and March, J.G. (1988) Organizational learning, *Annual Review Sociology*, 14: 319–40.

March, J.G. and Olsen, J.P. (1976) *Ambiguity and Choice in Organizations*, Bergen, Norway: Universitetsforlaget.

Nicolini, D. and Meznar, M.B. (1995) The social construction of organizational learning: conceptual and practical issues in the field, *Human Relations*, 48(7): 727–46.

Nonaka, I. and Takeuchi, H. (1995) *The Knowledge Creating Company: How Japanese Companies Create the Dynamics of Innovation*. New York: Oxford University Press.

Orr, J. (1996) *Talking about Machines: an Ethnography of a Modern Job*. New York: IRL Press.

Parsons, T. (1960) *Structure and Process in Modern Societies*. Glencoe, IL: The Free Press.

Pentland, B.T. (1995) Information systems and organizational learning: the social epistemology of organizational knowledge systems, *Accounting, Management and Information Technology*, 5: 1–21.

Polanyi, M. (1966) *The Tacit Dimension*. London: Routledge & Kegan Paul.

Putnam, R.D. (1993) The prosperous community: social capital and public life, *American Prospect*, 13: 35–42.

Sandelands, L. and Drazin, R. (1989) On the language of organizational theory, *Organization Studies*, 10: 457–78.

Sandelands, L. and Srivatsan, V. (1993) The problem of experience in the study of organizations, *Organization Studies*, 14.

Schutz, A. (1971) *Collected Papers*, vols 1 and 2. The Hague: Martinus Nijhoff.

Scott, W.R. (1987) The adolescence of institutional theory, *Administrative Science Quarterly*, 32: 493–511.

Selznick, P. (1957) *Readership in Administration*. New York: Harper & Row.

Senge, P. (1992) *The Fifth Discipline: The Art and Practice of the Learning Organization*. London: Random House.

Shibutani, T. (1955) Reference groups as perspectives, *American Journal of Sociology*, 60: 562–9.

Simon, H. and March, J. (1958) *Organization*. Wiley: New York.

Sims, D. (2000), Organizational learning as the development of stories. In M. Easterby-Smith, L. Araujo and J. Burgoyne (eds), *Organizational Learning and the Learning Organization: Developments in Theory and Practice*. Thousand Oaks, CA: Sage.

Sole, D. and Huysman, M. (2001) Knowledge, practice and the role of location: a community of practice perspective, *Trends in Communication*, 8: 27–35.

Spender, J.C. (1996) Making knowledge the basis of a dynamic strategy of the firm, *Strategic Management Journal*, 17: 45–62.

Star, S.L. (1992) The trojan door: organizations, work and the 'open black box', *Systems Practice*, 5: 395–410.

Storck, J. and Hill, P.A. (2000) Knowledge diffusion through 'strategic communities', *Sloan Management Review*, Winter: 63–74.

Szulanski, G. (1996) Exploring internal stickiness: impediments to the transfer of best practice within the firm, *Strategic Management Journal*, 17: 27–43.

Teigland, R. and Wasko, M. McLure (2000) Creative ties and ties that bind. Proceedings of the 21st Annual International Conference on Information Systems, December, Brisbane, Australia.

Thatchenkery, T.J. (1996) Organizational learning, language games and knowledge creation, Editorial note, *Journal of Organizational Change Management*, 9(1) 4–11.

Thomas, W.I. (1914) The Prussian–Polish Situation: an experiment in assimilation, *American Journal of Sociology*, 19: 624–39.

Tsoukas, H. and Chia, R. (2002) On organizational becoming: rethinking organizational change, *Organization Science*, 567–82.

Tsoukas, H. and Vladimirou, E. (2001) What is organizational knowledge?, *Journal of Management Studies*, 38: 973–93.

von Krogh, G., Ichijo, K. and Nonaka, I. (2000) *Enabling Knowledge Creation: How to Unlock the Mystery of Tacit Knowledge and Release the Power of Innovation.* Oxford and New York: Oxford University Press.

Walsh, J.P. and Ungson, G.R. (1991) Organizational memory, *Academy of Management Review*, 16(1): 57–91.

Weick, K. (1979) *The Social Psychology of Organizing*, 2nd edn. Reading, MA: Addison-Wesley.

Weick, K.E. and Roberts, K.H. (1993) Collective mind in organizations: heedful interrelating on flight desks, *Administrative Science Quarterly*, 38(3): 357–81.

Weick, K.E. and Westley, F. (1996). Organizational learning: affirming an oxymoron. In S.R. Clegg, C. Hardy and W.R. Nord (eds), *Handbook of Organization Studies*. Thousand Oaks, CA: Sage Publications.

Wenger, E. (1998) *Communities of Practice*. New York: Cambridge University Press.

Wenger, E. (2000) Communities of practice: the key to knowledge strategy. In E. Lesser (ed.), *Knowledge and Communities*, Boston: Butterworth Heinemann.

Yanow, D. (2000) Seeing organizational learning: a cultural view, *Organization*, 7(2): 247–68.

# 4

# Knowing as Semiosis: Steps Towards a Reconceptualization of 'Tacit Knowledge'

*Stephen Gourlay*

## Introduction

The importance of tacit knowledge in and for organizations is widely attested to. As Baumard (1999: 8, 22) wrote, tacit knowledge is the basis of expertise, it is critical to daily management activities, and is a firm's source of competitive advantage (see also Wagner and Sternberg, 1986; Lubit, 2001; Ambrosini and Bowman, 2001; Johannessen *et al.*, 2001; Berman *et al.*, 2002; Marwick, 2001). Nevertheless it appears that there are flaws in the argument for tacit knowledge, and that we lack agreement on what the phrase refers to, which bode ill for any attempts to manage it. This chapter will argue that Polanyi has largely been misunderstood, but that his focus on *knowing*, an activity, and Dewey and Bentley's (1949) treatment of knowing as semiosis opens the way for a potentially more coherent approach to tacit knowledge.

## Tacit knowledge – some problems

### The (flawed) argument for tacit knowledge

The observation that people can do things but cannot describe what they have done is commonplace. As Polanyi wrote on various occasions, people 'know more than they can tell'. The largely implicit argument for tacit knowledge derived from such observations runs as follows: if someone can do something they must possess the requisite knowledge, but since they cannot express it, this knowledge must be tacit, at least at that point, if not generally.[1]

There are two problems with this argument. First, the assumption that if people can do things, then they should be able to 'tell' is flawed. Children can do many things that they cannot 'tell' and Piaget (1977) conducted many studies to understand how they develop this ability. Hutchins (1995: 310–11) argued that experts cannot 'tell' because skilled performance is inseparable from context and although some skills are learned explicitly, and the representations used during training sufficed to orient the novice appropriately, those representations atrophy and are in any case not adequate to describe developed expertise.

A second difficulty concerns the distinction between know-how (often equated with tacit knowledge) and 'knowledge that' or propositional knowledge, equated with explicit knowledge (Whitehill, 1997; Willman, 1996; Nonaka and Takeuchi, 1995). Barbiero (n.d.) pointed out that Dretske (1988) challenged this distinction, arguing that knowing *how* to do something necessarily entails knowing *that* certain things are relevant to an action. Thus, Barbiero concluded, 'knowing-how would seem to be closely bound up with, if not dependent on, some variety of knowing-that'. Two forms of knowledge that are widely regarded as being distinct might not in fact be so.

## Tacit knowledge – some contradictions in use

In addition to these conceptual difficulties while there is widespread agreement that tacit knowledge is largely acquired through experience, and is contextual (for example Nonaka and Takeuchi, 1995; Herbig *et al.*, 2001; Eraut, 2000) in many other respects there are important differences and disagreements.

In keeping with regarding tacit knowledge as experiential and contextual most writers say that it is a personal form of knowledge. Others, however, say that it is also a property of groups (Baumard, 1999: 30–3; Szulanski, 1996: 31), is diffused throughout an organization (Berman *et al.*, 2002), is embedded in operations and found in test equipment (Grant and Gregory, 1997: 152–3, 156). Boisot's distinction between 'semi-tacit' knowledge in communities, and uncodifiable personal knowledge, seems an equivalent one (1995: 61–3, 145). More cautiously Choo (1998: 118–19) suggested that the existence of shared working practices and tacit understandings in groups indicates something *analogous* to, but not identical with, the tacit knowledge of individuals and that the relationship between these two phenomena remains unclear. Since 'personal' is used to mean private individual processes as opposed to social or collective ones it is logically impossible for the same thing (tacit knowledge) to be both personal and collective, let alone also 'embedded' in artefacts.

Further confusion arises over the question of where tacit knowledge can be found. If it is personal then it could well be described as 'embodied' (Scharmer, 2000: 36; Grant and Gregory, 1997: 156) or 'embedded' in people (Argote and Ingram, 2000: 153); as skills (Ambrosini and Bowman, 2001: 814) existing only in peoples' hands and minds (Stenmark, 2000). But Howells (1996: 94) claimed, without any citations, 'It is widely accepted that tacit knowledge is…*disembodied* know-how…' (my italics). Again, it is difficult to imagine how the same thing could be both embodied, and disembodied, or embodied/embedded in people *and* 'embedded' in operations and equipment, suggesting different phenomena are being referred to by the same name.

Important differences are also apparent over the question of codifying tacit knowledge, something many argue is very important if it is to be managed (for example, Herbig *et al.*, 2001; Johannessen *et al.*, 2001; Boiral, 2002; Saviotti, 1998). While few argue that codification is not possible (for example Stenmark, 2000) or that tacit knowledge cannot be communicated (von Krogh and Roos, 1995: 50–1), others simply state that codification is difficult, subject in varying degrees to limits about which we are largely unclear (Eraut, 2000: 134–5; Wagner and Sternberg, 1986; Johannessen *et al.*, 2001; Nonaka and Takeuchi, 1995). Difficult does not mean impossible, and Wagner and Sternberg treat tacit knowledge as if it could all be codified, given the right tools (Wagner, 1987, 1991; Sternberg, 1999; see also Johannessen *et al.*, 2001). While most of these authors implicitly treat tacit knowledge as homogeneous (all either can, or cannot, be codified), others distinguish in various ways between codifiable and non-codifiable forms (Janik, 1988; Grant and Gregory, 1997: 152–3; Boiral, 2001; Ambrosini and Bowman, 2001; Collins, 2001; Baumard, 1999; Boisot, 1995).

Grant and Gregory (1996: 152–3), focussing on tacit knowledge in technology transfer, suggested that codifiability is dependent on factors such as task pace, the opportunities for task pace to be varied, and whether or not task performance contexts can be standardized. These factors themselves vary with the lifecycle of a technology, and further difficulties arise as factors interact, such as when both standardization and high task speed occur together with maturity.

Janik drew on examples and case studies to argue that the phrase 'tacit knowledge' was used in two distinct senses. On the one hand it referred to 'aspects of human experience which are *wholly* knowable self-reflectively…but by their very nature are incapable of *precise* articulation' (Janik, 1988: 54–8) and on the other to aspects that could be codified. The latter includes, for example, trade secrets, things overlooked, such as craft knowledge and skills, and the general presuppositions that we all hold in everyday life. In principle, Janik argued, these could all be made explicit. On the other hand, we cannot express in words purely sensuous experiences such as the smell of coffee or the sound of a musical instrument (Janik, 1988). Similarly, following Wittgenstein, the 'open-textured character of rule-following behaviour' (Janik, 1988: 54–8) precludes us from fully specifying rules for an action without falling into the infinite regress of requiring yet more rules to interpret the original ones. Rule-following, like sensuous experiences, rests on doing, practice, or activity (Janik, 1988: 57–8).

Collins, whose research into tacit knowledge in scientific work was also inspired by Wittgenstein (Collins, 1974: 184; 2001), suggested there are three broad models of tacit knowledge. The first or motor-skills model is exemplified by riding a bicycle or any other such skilled activity while the second is the rules-regress model. Advances in neural net computing made it possible to incorporate both these types into a computer program and thus make them explicit (Collins, 2001: 111–17). Stenmark (2000) reported on efforts to make experts' rule-following practices tangible using advanced computing techniques.

Collins uniquely distinguished a third model of tacit knowledge which he called the 'forms of life' approach. People are unaware of the social basis of their certainties and thus, he argued, if the true sources of our beliefs are necessarily hidden from us then our beliefs are based on tacit understandings. Computers cannot capture this since they cannot participate in human society; it is thus inherently beyond codification (Collins, 2001: 110–11). This may be a claim about presuppositions, which Janik argued can be codified, or it may be the observation that any system's fundamental principles cannot be observed from inside the system.

So far as obstacles to codification are concerned, there are several important differences. Baumard (1999: 2, 23, 59) suggested that motivation is a key factor inhibiting codification while for Boisot (1995: 61–3) and Boiral (2002) the distinction appears to mirror that between personal (uncodifiable) and public (codifiable) forms or sites of 'tacit knowledge'. For motivation to be a hindrance, however, presupposes awareness. If someone does not recognize the special nature of their craft knowledge or that they take certain presuppositions for granted, the initial problem is that of awareness on the part either of the knower, or of others (see also Eraut, 2000). While Baumard, Janik and Collins all appear to concur in regarding some 'tacit knowledge' as in some sense inherently uncodifiable, Collins would disagree with Janik over the codifiability of rules, although Stenmark's research arguably settles this issue in Collins' favour. Janik might dispute the claim that presuppositions are uncodifiable, and would be supported by Wagner and Sternberg.

Overall, it seems that 'tacit knowledge' is used to denote something that is personal, and collective, embodied/embedded, and disembodied, that can, and cannot be codified. Even where there is agreement that only some 'tacit knowledge' can be codified, authorities differ over the reasons for codification difficulties, and whether rules, and presuppositions, can or cannot be codified. All this confusion suggests a lack of clarity as to just what is meant by 'tacit knowledge.' This must hinder any attempts to investigate and understand it that must precede considering whether and if possible how to manage it.

## Polanyi, 'tacit knowledge' and tacit knowing

Although Polanyi probably coined the phrase 'tacit knowledge' he was certainly not the first to consider the notion (Barbiero, n.d.; Reed, 1997) but in view of his prominence, it is reasonable to turn to his work to seek conceptual clarification. While Janik and Collins, for example, found inspiration in Wittgenstein's later philosophy, Gill (1974) suggested that in this context Polanyi's and Wittgenstein's ideas are essentially similar.[2]

In the 1960s Polanyi elaborated on his earlier work (Polanyi, 1958/1962) in a series of papers (Polanyi, 1966, 1968, 1969a,b,c,d) few of which, except for *The Tacit Dimension* (Polanyi, 1966), have been considered in the context of knowledge management. These papers are important because they show clearly that he actually discussed a *process*, 'tacit knowing' and not some *thing*, 'tacit knowledge.' He made this quite clear, writing, 'Knowledge is an activity which would better be described as a process of knowing' (Polanyi, 1969a: 132), and, 'I shall always speak of "knowing," therefore, to cover both practical and theoretical knowledge' (Polanyi, 1966: 7; 1969a: 131, 133). The phrase 'tacit knowing' occurs approximately five times more often than 'tacit knowledge' in this series of papers.[3] Moreover, his description of 'tacit knowledge' makes it clear that he meant a process or activity, and not the completed results of an activity.

Polanyi based his 'logic' of tacit knowing on the part–whole model of perception (Polanyi, 1966: 7; 1969c: 138–9, 145). He argued that *gestalt* psychology had shown we have 'powers of perceiving coherence' that can make us see the 'thousand varied and changing clues' of a moving object 'jointly as one single unchanging object' (Polanyi, 1969c: 139).

Furthermore, just as these 'powers' integrate the clues or parts into the whole object, so

> a scientific discovery reduces our focal awareness of observations into a subsidiary awareness of them, by shifting our attention from them to their theoretical coherence. This act of integration, which we can identify both in the visual perception of objects and in the discovery of scientific theories is the tacit power we have been looking for. I shall call it tacit knowing. (Polanyi, 1969c: 140)

In addition to perception and scientific discovery, he claimed that implicit learning, learning physical skills, experts' pattern detection skills, mastery of tools, speech and language, reading, and the formation of class concepts (such as 'man') were all due to 'tacit knowing' (Polanyi, 1969c: 143; 1969a: 123–8; 1968: 30; 1966: 7; 1969d: 182–3; 1969b: 166–7). Tacit knowing, the 'power of perceiving coherence' among 'thousands of clues', is a 'fundamental power of the mind' whereby coherence is constructed and maintained by a 'mechanism of imagination-*cum*-intuition' (Polanyi, 1969c: 156; see also 1969d: 185, 191, 195ff.; 1968: 29, 32, 37).

Since tacit knowing is a process it is not surprising that he regarded it as being quite distinct from 'explicit knowledge' (Polanyi, 1969c: 144). He only used the phrase 'explicit knowledge' occasionally[4] and defined it as knowledge 'capable of being clearly stated', such as words, formulae, maps and graphs, and mathematical theory (Polanyi, 1966: 22; 1969d: 195). A letter, for example, was described as a 'piece of explicit knowledge' (Polanyi, 1969d: 195). Explicit knowledge is arrived at by a non-tacit process, 'explicit inference' (Polanyi, 1969d: 194), but is nevertheless dependent on tacit knowing. As is well known, he argued that knowledge of the mathematical formula for balancing on a bicycle was ineffectual for the rider unless known tacitly. Similarly, he argued that when a traveller described their experiences, 'this focal awareness of an experience was introduced subsidiarily into a communication which was a piece of explicit knowledge, the meaning of which was tacit' (Polanyi, 1969d: 195). Thus while: 'tacit knowledge can be possessed by itself, explicit knowledge must rely on being tacitly understood' (Polanyi, 1969c: 144). Hence his claim that all knowledge (that is knowing) is tacit, or rooted in tacit knowledge/knowing.

Polanyi initially rejected the notion that tacit knowing could be codified. In 1962, for example, he argued that if 'explicit rules' for 'intuitive actions' (that is tacit knowing) could be set out (implying they could not) they would have to describe both the parts on which perception of the whole relied, and the integrative relations by which successful perception occurred (Polanyi, 1969b, pp. 162–4). In *The Tacit Dimension* (1966) he conceded that it was possible to 'know' parts explicitly, and that the relations between them could also sometimes be stated. Such a process might even go beyond 'tacit integration' just as an engineer's understanding of a machine goes beyond that of a user, a physiologist's theoretical knowledge of our body is more revealing than our practical knowledge (Polanyi, 1966: 18–20) and linguists know the complex rules of language that are only known tacitly by speakers (Polanyi, 1969d: 204). While in 1967 he still maintained that the integration of parts depended on the 'tacit operation of the mind' (Polanyi, 1969d: 191) he later wrote that 'one can paraphrase the cognitive content of an integration' leaving only 'the sensory quality which conveys this content' as non-codifiable (Polanyi, 1968: 32).

There can be no doubt therefore that Polanyi was concerned to describe a *process* of knowing, and not a type of knowledge. It would be inconsistent with Polanyi's theory to suggest that 'tacit knowledge' could refer to the outcome of tacit knowing. For him, tacit knowing results in the perception of 'phenomenal qualities of external objects' and 'mental qualities' of 'feeling, action and thought' (Polanyi, 1969c: 153) and, more generally, the 'understanding of the comprehensive entity' constituted by the integrated parts (Polanyi, 1966: 13; 1969b: 162; 1968: 32). In other words, tacit knowing produces an effect in the knower, and not some thing. On the other hand 'tacit knowledge' could be used to refer to the parts of which any whole is comprised at the time of knowing that whole. This would be consistent with Polanyi's ideas since these parts are what is known tacitly. His theory would then support the view that all 'tacit knowledge' can be codified since he conceded that 'parts' can be described as well as (for him) the more important aspect, the integrative process.[5]

Accepting his model, however, would also entail accepting the part–whole hypothesis on which his theory rests. While the part–whole model may even be the dominant model of perception (see Latimer and Stevens, 1997; Turvey and Shaw, 1999) it is not without its critics. In its modern form it developed in the mid-nineteenth century (Reed, 1997) and was described in the 1860s in terms not differing much from Polanyi's (see Gregory, 1981: 362–6).[6] William James soon challenged the idea that perceptual wholes are constructed from parts unconsciously perceived (Dewey, 1938: 510) and the counter argument that perception *starts* from wholes, and that parts are only identified subsequently, has been made by others (Dewey, 1922; Bartlett, 1932; Mead, 1938; and Piaget – see Furth, 1969). Ecological psychology also disputes the part–wholes model and proposes an alternative (Turvey and Shaw, 1999; Burke, 1994), and since such perspectives appear to be consistent with the situated approach (see, for example, Clancey, 1997) we might be better advised to start elsewhere.

Polanyi's emphasis on *process* is, however, in tune with contemporary thought and can form a useful starting point. Moreover, he indirectly drew attention to an ambiguity in the word 'knowledge' (does it mean a process, or the results of a process?) that may well be a source of the difficulty in understanding his ideas, as well as in developing satisfactory theory for knowledge management.

In the next section a perspective on tacit knowledge/knowing will be described drawing not from ecological psychology but from suggestions made by Dewey and Bentley (1949), whose ideas have been seen as to some extent foreshadowing contemporary ecological and situated perspectives (Burke, 1994; Clancey, 1997).

## Knowledge/knowing as semiosis

In the 1940s Dewey and the polymath Arthur Bentley collaborated on a series of papers largely concerned with 'knowledge', and after struggling to arrive at a satisfactory definition (see Ratner and Altman, 1964) they concluded that:

> The word 'knowledge'... is a loose name... No. 1 on a list of 'vague words'... Only through prolonged factual inquiry... can the word 'knowledge' be given determinable status with respect to such questions as: (1) the range of its application to human or animal behaviors; (2) the types of its distribution between knowers, knowns, and the presumptive intermediaries; (3) the possible localizations implied for knowledge as present in space and time. (Dewey and Bentley, 1949: 48)[7]

They set out some postulates for the study of 'knowledge', outlined and developed parts of a new framework, and proposed a formal terminology without which they felt attempts to clarify understanding of 'knowledge' would fail. It is this framework that provides a useful conceptual base for 'tacit knowledge/knowing'.

Dewey and Bentley proposed to concern themselves 'directly with knowings and knowns' – things that could be observed in relation to the knowing process – and postulated that 'Knowings are behaviors' (Dewey and Bentley, 1949: 48, 74). Theirs was not a behaviourist model for they rejected Watsonian behaviourism (Dewey and Bentley, 1949: 77, 97). Behaviour simply meant 'the wide ranges of adaptive living ... including thereunder everything psychological and everything sociological in human beings', thus indicating a region of inquiry distinguishable from the physical and the physiological sciences (Dewey and Bentley, 1949: 65, 129–30). Behaviour entails 'sign' or 'sign-process', 'the characteristic behavioral process' that takes place 'only when organism and environment are in behavioral transaction' (Dewey and Bentley, 1949: 64, 71, 150–1). The concept of transaction is an important one, emphasizing the idea that organisms live 'not ... *in* ... but by means of an environment'. Organism and environment are observably an 'integration', not two separate things that come together (Dewey, 1938/1984: 32; Dewey and Bentley, 1949: 129–30).[8]

On this basis they described and developed a sign-process 'spectrum' which can be represented as shown in Figure 4.1.

Signal covered 'perceptions, manipulations, habituations' or the 'perceptual-manipulative' phase, designation referred to situations where 'organized language is employed as sign' while symbol indicated the 'mathematical regions' of sign. Within designation they further distinguished cue, characterization, and specification to mark degrees of increasing linguistic sophistication. Cue covered grunts and similar noises; characterization was the phase of everyday language while specification marked the development of scientific terminology (Dewey and Bentley, 1949: 71; chaps 6 and 10). They did not develop signal, or symbol. Sign or sign-process thus covers the entire range of 'behavioral activity' from the 'sensitive reactions of protozoa to the most complex symbolic procedures of mathematics' (Dewey and Bentley, 1949: 71) and from 'the bodily end to the symbolic' (Dewey in Ratner and Altman, 1964: 142).

It is interesting to note that Bruner (1966: 10–11) independently proposed that human beings represent their experience of the world in

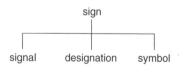

*Figure 4.1*   The sign-process spectrum

three ways – enactive, iconic, and symbolic. Enactive is learning through action, such as is involved in teaching someone to ride a bicycle. Iconic representation depends on visual or other sense organs and upon summarizing images by means of which we are able to detect patterns, while symbolic representation refers to words or language. It would appear that enactive and iconic representation can be regarded as aspects of signalling while Bruner's 'symbolic' covers designation and symbol.

Dewey and Bentley's framework can thus be understood on three different levels. First, as evolution, and second, as behaviour, as they clearly intended. In addition, following Bruner, we can treat Dewey and Bentley's scheme as a developmental one. The evolutionary level was indicated by Dewey and Bentley when they noted that the scheme united the 'reactions of protozoa' with mathematics. The idea that it also linked bodily 'knowing' and 'perceptual-manipulative' or 'sub-verbally operated' behaviour with 'linguistically operated object-discriminations' or systems of representations (Dewey and Bentley, 1949: 71, 91, 299; Bentley in Ratner and Altman, 1964: 123) clearly suggests ongoing behaviour. Both these levels, however, have clear parallels with a developmental perspective – children initially operate on the perceptual-manipulative level and only later on the symbolic both in general, and with respect to particular things they learn (Piaget, 1977) and there is evidence that adults may learn about novel things in similar ways (Granott, 1998).

'Signal' and 'tacit knowing' thus clearly refer to the same object – namely, 'knowing' conducted through 'bodily' and 'sub-verbal' ways and means. Designation, and symbol, on the other hand, clearly equate to 'explicit knowledge', or knowing through language at various levels of specificity. Dewey and Bentley's scheme thus allows us to see a 'sign' as providing the conceptual connecting link between 'tacit' and 'explicit' knowledge. In addition, knowing in all its forms is seen as activity that agents engage in (or 'behaviour' in their terms). The evolutionary perspective suggests that we could usefully regard 'tacit knowledge/knowing' as characteristic of all life forms, while the developmental approach reminds us that we all begin by only being capable of 'tacit' or 'bodily' knowing. As an aspect of contemporaneous activity/cognition, signal is also found in ongoing activity.

In the rest of this chapter I will consider the question of the link between sign-process and behaviour; explore the extent to which human behaviour involves non-verbal signing and discuss some implications of this framework for 'tacit knowledge'.

## Semiosis and behaviour

Had Dewey and Bentley been writing today they would probably have used the term 'semiosis' rather than 'sign-process'. In the late 1940s, however, they felt compelled to defend their interpretation of Peirce's notion of 'sign' against a contemporary reinterpretation that used the term 'semiotic' (Dewey, 1946; Dewey and Bentley, 1949: 259).[9] Is this shift towards behaviour, and knowing/knowledge as sign-process or semiosis justifiable?

Dewey and Bentley were certainly not alone in advancing this argument. Von Uexküll, a theoretical biologist writing in the first half of the twentieth century, viewed semiosis as a criterion of life (Sebeok, 1979: x). Kaplan (1964: 32) considered 'the use of signs' as the most generally applicable discriminant of 'behaviour' and Sebeok (1981: 136) claimed that semiosis 'is as much a critical attribute of all life as is the ability to metabolize' (see also Sebeok, 1979: viii). Leach (1976), a social anthropologist, also regarded semiosis as central to human societies as did Bruner (1990), a cognitive psychologist. Stamper and others (for example, Stamper, 1996) have applied a semiotic perspective to information systems and organizations. Scholars in many different disciplines thus accept that behaviour can usefully be regarded as entailing, or be modelled by, semiosis or sign-process.

## Non-verbal sign-processes in humans

Studies of child development clearly show the importance of non-verbal signing in early life. Gesture and pointing by infants, and between adult carers and infants, are important sources of language and linguistic competence (Clark, 1978). Turning to adults, Lyons (1972) noted that in everyday communication language is accompanied by nods, gestures, eye-movements, as well as intonation and Argyle (1972) provided a survey of such non-verbal signals. Leach (1972: 317) argued that 'non-speech' or 'meaningful action that is peripheral to speech action' is highly significant for human beings, and, moreover, that the distinction between speech and non-speech is an arbitrary one from the perspective of communication. Sebeok (1979: 44) cites research suggesting that human memory has two interconnected verbal and non-verbal components (see also Schooler and Engstler-Schooler, 1990: 37), and claimed that human beings have two 'repertoires of signs' at their disposal (Sebeok, 1994: 7). Nöth (1990) reviewed research and theories of non-verbal communication, indicating they can all be approached as forms of semiosis. In terms of *development* from child to adult non-verbal modes clearly persist alongside the verbal or linguistic modes of signing and knowing, and the view that human adults communicate through a wide and complex range and combination of verbal and non-verbal signs is widely supported by evidence from linguistics, social anthropology, social and cognitive psychology, communication studies, and semiotics.

Finally, we should also note the extensive research on implicit learning, our ability to learn without being aware of what we have learned as a result of which we are able to do without being able to 'tell' (Reber, 1993; Stadler and Frensch, 1998; Berry and Dienes, 1993). Early studies of implicit learning noted that subjects who had received an electric shock on viewing a set of nonsense syllables showed physiologically detectable symptoms of anticipating the shock when presented with the same syllables, but that they were not aware of preparing themselves (Reber, 1993: 17). Polanyi cited this example to show that psychological research supported his claims about tacit knowing (Polanyi, 1966: 7–8). It is clear therefore that implicit learning enables people to unconsciously make observations that are critical to their performance, a process which could be described within a semiotic framework.

## 'Tacit knowing' as non-verbal signing

Non-verbal signing is thus a key feature of human behaviour, complementing, perhaps even enhancing, the verbal 'explicit' dimension. Some examples of 'tacit knowledge' also appear clearly to involve non-verbal sign-processes.

Josefson (1988) reported two stories about nurses knowing more than they could tell.[10] In one example a nurse recounted how she had felt there was something wrong with a post-operative patient. A young inexperienced doctor called in on the nurse's insistence disagreed since in his opinion, according to the nurse's account, 'the patient's vital signs were normal'. The patient died later that day of complications 'that could not have been diagnosed by an examination of his vital signs' (Josefson, 1988: 27). We are not told why the 'vital signs' could not have yielded such information, nor what might have provided evidence. The second case involved an experienced nurse reflecting on her experiences as a trainee, faced with violent patients. She recalled that she noticed an older woman, a nursing auxiliary, 'was better able than others to induce calm in those around her'. She attached herself to the woman from whom she learned a great deal, although she never discussed how to deal with problematic situations with the older woman.

A study of meteorologists who produced local weather forecasts using 'traditional' non-computerized methods (Perby, 1988) showed that they typically began their shift by being briefed by outgoing colleagues. This provided a 'sign-post', as they expressed it, for their work. They would then draw a map by hand which required analysis and plotting of information from a wide range of sources, including personal observations. They talked about this activity as enabling them to 'see signs of other changes' (Perby, 1988: 42). Such maps were drawn at three-hour intervals during the shift, providing a means and opportunity for continuous reflection on and updating of understanding about the weather. The meteorologists felt that such skills took a long time to learn, and said that they did not know how they knew about the weather.

Both these reports can be seen as exemplifying unconscious, or semi-conscious, semiosis. Indeed, the nurses and forecasters seem to have been aware of this, although not in an analytically sophisticated way. Thus both the nurse and the doctor read the 'vital signs', but they drew different conclusions. Whether what each meant by 'vital signs' was the same, or different, or each attributed different significance to the same things, and hence differed in their diagnosis, must remain an open question. The forecasters also explicitly talked about looking for signs, interpreting phenomena for which they were particularly attuned to look for, and so on. In all instances the non-verbal and the verbal are both present – both forms of sign-process are apparently essential to the nurses' and meteorologists' practice.

The nurse example is particularly interesting on the one hand because Polanyi himself saw medical diagnosis as providing evidence for 'tacit knowing' (Polanyi, 1969a), and on the other because medical diagnosis is a paradigmatic case for semiosis (Sebeok, 1979, 1981; Nöth, 1990: 13). Polanyi, moreover, occasionally reported tacit knowing in semiotic terms. When he described the early studies of implicit learning involving an electric shock (Polanyi, 1966: 7–8), he remarked: 'When the sight of certain syllables makes us expect an electric shock, we may say that they *signify* the approach of a shock. This is their *meaning* to us' (Polanyi, 1966: 11, his italics).

What Collins has termed the motor-skills model of 'tacit knowledge' may also be expressed in semiotic terms. Taking a traditional example, riding a bicycle, aspects of this are likely to depend on skills acquired through development, such as maintaining balance, propelling oneself along using legs and feet, and so on. These skills have to be applied in what is initially a novel situation in which new sensations will be felt and some will come to be experienced as relevant to moving forward, to maintaining a balance, and so on, in the new context. In other words, the novice rider's attention will be drawn, through experience or via the assistance of a coach, to feelings or sensations to attend to.[11]

## Conclusion

For the present focus on tacit knowledge/knowing, Dewey and Bentley's framework suggests first that knowing without being aware can be regarded as a consequence of evolutionary and developmental processes (including in the latter things learnt explicitly but subsequently automatized). Ongoing knowing is inseparable from behaviour in general, and involves organism–environment transactions and semiosis whereby agents, on the basis of prior learning and their current behavioural orientation, notice and attribute significance to certain things in their field of observation.

There is no need to evoke the notion of elusive 'tacit powers', a mysterious 'force' reminiscent of vitalism in biology, harking back to the idea of the soul (Jacob, 1993; Reed, 1997), to explain the processes that concerned Polanyi. His 'tacit powers' are natural life-processes that have evolved, and which develop as each individual organism lives its life and which therefore do not require an explanation *on the level of behaviour* such as Polanyi sought to provide. Semiotics provides a way of conceptualizing these processes that emphasizes their unity. Whether it will prove useful to regard all forms of 'knowledge' in this light will require further investigation, but it does seem advantageous for some kinds of 'tacit knowledge'.

Motor-skills 'tacit knowledge' can also be accounted for in this way – each individual organism enters this world with a certain potential for motor activities which are largely developed in the earliest phases of life. In operation we soon cease to be conscious of what we are doing, but that does not mean we are not unconsciously aware of signs signifying press harder, hold back, and so on. When we attempt to acquire some novel motor skills, our awareness of at least new stresses is usually only too obvious.

'Intuition' of the kind exemplified by the nurses' stories can probably also be understood in terms of unconscious semiosis. Instead of assuming 'intuition' is some mysterious, unknowable process we could ask first whether or not the nurses were right more often than would be expected by chance. If they are, then we should assume they were making some kind of observation, and begin a process of investigating just which senses were at work, and what was being sensed that is interpreted as significant by the knower.

The nurses' stories also indicate that some knowledge may be 'hidden' because of the lack of awareness due to habit and custom. The low social standing of people like nurses leads others to disregard their knowledge, and they themselves to devalue their knowledge on the one hand, or mystify it on the other (see also Boiral, 2002). Wagner and Sternberg have pioneered a method to enable managers to reflect on aspects of their otherwise hidden knowledge and tacit assumptions. Collins' cases show, despite his insistence that 'forms of life' cannot be made explicit, that groups can discover their deep assumptions about their behaviour. Of course, in so far as there are *universal* 'forms of (human) life' we may well remain unaware of these unless we explicitly confront other 'forms of life', but then perhaps this is what animal ethologists have been doing all along.

We can also now understand *why* experience is critical for the acquisition of 'tacit knowledge' (if not for all forms of knowledge) – because the knowers have to identify for themselves what is attended to in the transactions in which they engage. Similarly, the claim that 'tacit knowledge' transfer requires 'personal contact' particularly with relative experts (see, for example, Lubit, 2001; Nonaka and Takeuchi, 1995) can be explained in terms of those experts' ability to provide examples, or to coach and otherwise direct the attention of novices. There is nothing more mysterious about the process of learning by doing in the company of others than this.

So far as the individual/collective dimension is concerned, it might seem that Dewey and Bentley's scheme focusses on the individual. However, this assumption would not do justice to their ideas. Their transactional approach implies that if one wanted to focus on an 'individual' the appropriate unit of analysis would be the individual–environment transaction(s), and not the individual in some kind of isolation. Since the 'environment' of humans includes community, human individuals are necessarily so highly socialized that the individual–social distinction often makes no sense when it comes to understanding behaviour. Ideas, attitudes and behaviour are thus naturally similar within groups, particularly when people overtly co-operate to achieve certain goals, or even when they work independently on similar activities within the same social context. The relationship between tacit knowledge/knowing, and what has been called 'tacit knowledge' at the collective level will, however, require further study as will the suggestion that 'tacit knowledge' can be 'embedded' in artefacts.

It also appears that virtually all that has been called 'tacit knowledge' can be described or codified, provided we do not require the codes to be directly understandable by human beings, or that every possible application of a rule will have to be specified (which would in any case take for infinity). Incomplete codification may be sufficient to orient novices' attention to the extent that they can develop adequate rules themselves through doing, as Hutchins and other situated cognitivists have suggested. At least we should hold to the hypothesis that all 'tacit knowledge' can be codified given adequate methods, until we consistently find something uncodifiable, rather than presuming *a priori* that codification is impossible since there is no longer any theoretical justification for the latter view.

This leaves us with Polanyi's 'mental qualities of feeling action and thought' that an individual experiences which are probably equivalent to Janik's uncodifiable smells and sounds (Janik, 1988, 1990; Prawitz, 1990). It does seem likely that even if subjective experiences can be described there is no way of discovering whether the description produces the same effect in the reader/listener that the experience had on the describer. Whether this kind of 'knowledge', if that it the right word to indicate such feelings, is important enough to require managing remains to be seen, but it too may require further study.

## Notes

1. The argument is rarely if ever spelt out in this way, but is implicit in most accounts of tacit knowledge.
2. It does not appear that Wittgenstein actually discussed the notion of 'tacit knowledge', but rather that readers have inferred this idea from some of his other often cryptic remarks. On Wittgenstein's ideas see, for example, Johannessen, 1988, 1992.
3. Content analysis of Polanyi, 1966, 1968, 1969a,b,c,d.
4. Nine times in Polanyi, 1966, 1968, 1969a,b,c,d.
5. This account differs from the standard view. See Tsoukas, 2003 for a more mainstream account.
6. That is, Helmholtz' notion of the cognitive unconscious. Polanyi was aware of Helmholtz, and acknowledged similarities between Helmholtz' ideas and his 'tacit integration' (see Polanyi, 1968, 1969b).
7. Epistemologists do not yet appear to have reached any firm conclusions despite the intervening period to judge by Klein's (1998) account.
8. The implications of this perspective for knowledge/knowing remain to be worked out but it complements notions of knowledge/knowing as situated in respect to activity – see Clancey (1997). Garrison (2001) provides a recent account of Dewey's transactionalism.

9. There are several schools of semiotics – Nöth (1990) provides a comprehensive review and account. Dewey and Bentley drew their ideas from C.S. Peirce.
10. Such stories appear to be common amongst nurses – see Herbig *et al.* (2001).
11. An anecdotal account unfortunately. It is possible that, for example, sports' science studies might provide an evidence-based account.

## References

Ambrosini, V. and Bowman, C. (2001) Tacit knowledge: some suggestions for operationalization, *Journal of Management Studies*, 38(6): 811–29.

Argote, L. and Ingram, P. (2000) Knowledge transfer: a basis for competitive advantage in firms, *Organizational Behavior and Human Decision Processes*, 82(1): 150–69.

Argyle, M. (1972) Non-verbal communication in human social interaction. In R.A. Hinde (ed.), *Non-Verbal Communication*. Cambridge: Cambridge University Press.

Barbiero, D. (n.d.) Tacit knowledge. In C. Eliasmith (ed.), *Dictionary of Philosophy of Mind* (http://artsci.wustl.edu/~philos/MindDict/tacitknowledge.html) (accessed 15 February 2002).

Bartlett, F.C. (1932) *Remembering: a Study in Experimental and Social Psychology*. Cambridge: Cambridge University Press.

Baumard, P. (1999) *Tacit Knowledge in Organizations*. London and Thousand Oaks, CA: Sage.

Berman, S.L., Down, J. and Hill, C.W.L. (2002) Tacit knowledge as a source of competitive advantage in the National Basketball Association, *Academy of Management Journal*, 45(1): 13–31.

Berry, D.C. and Dienes, Z. (1993) *Implicit Learning. Theoretical and Empirical Issues*. Hove and Hillsdale: Lawrence Erlbaum Associates.

Boiral, O. (2002) Tacit knowledge and environmental management, *Long Range Planning*, 35: 291–317.

Boisot, M.H. (1995) *Information Space: a Framework for Learning in Organizations, Institutions and Culture*. London and New York: Routledge.

Bruner, J.S. (1996) *Toward a Theory of Instruction*. Cambridge, MA: Belknap Press.

Bruner, J.S. (1990) *Acts of Meaning*. London: Harvard University Press.

Burke, T. (1994) *Dewey's New Logic. a Reply to Russell*. London and Chicago: Chicago University Press.

Choo, C.W. (1998) *The Knowing Organization*. New York and Oxford: Oxford University Press.

Clark, E. (1978) From gesture to word: on the natural history of deixis in language acquisition. In J. Bruner and A. Garton (eds), *Human Growth and Development*. Oxford: Clarendon Press.

Clancey, W.J. (1997) *Situated Cognition: On Human Knowledge and Computer Representations*. Cambridge: Cambridge University Press.

Collins, H.M. (1974) The TEA set: tacit knowledge and scientific networks, *Science Studies*, 4: 165–86.

Collins, H.M. (2001) What is tacit knowledge? In T.R. Schatzki, K. Knorr Cetina and E. von Savigny (eds), *The Practice Turn in Contemporary Theory*. London and New York: Routledge.

Dewey, J. (1930) *Human Nature and Conduct*. New York: Random House, originally published 1922.

Dewey, J. (1938/1986) *Logic: the Theory of Inquiry*. Carbondale and Edwardsville, IL: Southern Illinois University Press.

Dewey, J. (1946) Peirce's theory of linguistic signs, thought and meaning, *The Journal of Philosophy*, XLIII(4): 85–95.

Dewey, J. and Bentley, A.F. (1949) *Knowing and the Known*. Boston: The Beacon Press.

Dretske, F. (1988) *Explaining Behavior. Reasons in a World of Causes*. Cambridge, MA and London: MIT Press.

Eraut, M. (2000) Non-formal learning and tacit knowledge in professional work, *British Journal of Educational Psychology*, 70(1): 113–16.

Furth, H.G. (1969) *Piaget and Knowledge: Theoretical Foundations*. Englewood Cliffs, NJ: Prentice-Hall.

Garrison, J. (2001) An introduction to Dewey's Theory of Functional 'Trans-Action': an alternative paradigm for Activity Theory, *Mind, Culture, and Activity: An International Journal*, 8(4): 275–96.

Gill, J.H. (1974) Saying and showing: radical themes in Wittgenstein's *On Certainty, Religious Studies*, 10: 279–90.

Granott, N. (1998) We learn, therefore we develop: learning versus development – or developing learning?, Chapter 2 in M.C. Smith and T. Pourchot (eds), *Adult Learning and Development: Perspectives from Educational Psychology*. Mahwah, NJ and London: Lawrence Erlbaum Associates.

Grant, E.B. and Gregory, M.J. (1997) Tacit knowledge, the life cycle and international manufacturing transfer, *Technology Analysis & Strategic Management*, 9(2): 149–61.

Gregory, R.L. (1981) *Mind in Science*. London: Weidenfeld & Nicolson.

Herbig, B., Bussing, A. and Ewert, T. (2001) The role of tacit knowledge in the work context of nursing, *Journal of Advanced Nursing*, 34(5): 687–95.

Howells, J. (1996) Tacit knowledge, innovation and technology transfer, *Technology Analysis and Strategic Management*, 8: 91–105.

Hutchins, E. (1995) *Cognition in the Wild*. Cambridge, MA, and London: MIT Press.

Jacob, F. (1993) *The Logic of Life*. Princeton, NJ: Princeton University Press.

Janik, A. (1988) Tacit knowledge, working life and scientific method. In B. Göranzon and I. Josefson (eds), *Knowledge, Skill and Artificial Intelligence*. London and Berlin: Springer-Verlag.

Janik, A. (1990) Tacit knowledge, rule-following and learning. In B. Göranzon and M. Florin (eds), *Artificial Intelligence, Culture and Language: On Education and Work*. London: Springer-Verlag.

Johannessen, J.-A., Olaisen, J. and Olsen, B. (2001) Mismanagement of tacit knowledge: the importance of tacit knowledge, the danger of information technology, and what to do about it, *International Journal of Information Management*, 21: 3–20.

Johannessen, K.S. (1988) Rule following and tacit knowledge, *AI & Society*, 2: 287–301.

Johannessen, K.S. (1992) Rule-following, intransitive understanding and tacit knowledge. An investigation of the Wittgensteinian concept of practice as regards tacit knowing. In B. Göranzon and M. Florin (eds), *Skill and Education: Reflection and Experience*. London and Berlin: Springer-Verlag.

Josefson, I. (1988) The nurse as engineer – the theory of knowledge in research in the care sector. In B. Göranzon and I. Josefson (eds), *Knowledge, Skill and Artificial Intelligence*. London and Berlin: Springer-Verlag.

Kaplan, A. (1964) *The Conduct of Inquiry*. San Francisco: Chandler Publishing.

Klein, P.D. (1998) Knowledge, concept of. In E. Craig (ed.), *Routledge Encyclopaedia of Philosophy*. London and New York: Routledge.

Latimer, C. and Stevens, C. (1997) Some remarks on wholes, parts and their perception, *Psycholoquy*, 8(13) (Source: http://psychprints.ecs.soton.ac.uk/archive/00000549/ (8 January 2003)).

Leach, E. (1972) The influence of cultural context on non-verbal communication in man. In R.A. Hinde (ed.), *Non-Verbal Communication*. Cambridge: Cambridge University Press.

Leach, E. (1976) *Culture and Communication: the Logic by which Symbols are Connected*. Cambridge: Cambridge University Press.

Lubit, R. (2001) Tacit knowledge and knowledge management: the keys to sustainable competitive advantage, *Organizational Dynamics*, 29(3): 164–78.

Lyons, J. (1972) Human language. In R.A. Hinde (ed.), *Non-Verbal Communication*. Cambridge: Cambridge University Press.

Marwick, A.D. (2001) 'Knowledge management technology', *IBM Systems Journal*, 40(4): 814–30.

Mead, G.H. (1938) *The Philosophy of the Act*. Chicago and London: University of Chicago Press.

Nonaka, I. and Takeuchi, H. (1995) *The Knowledge-Creating Company*. New York and Oxford: Oxford University Press.

Nöth, W. (1990) *Handbook of Semiotics*. Bloomington, IN: Indiana University Press.

Perby, M.-L. (1988) Computerization and skill in local weather forecasting. In B. Göranzon and I. Josefson (eds), *Knowledge, Skill and Artificial Intelligence*. London and Berlin: Springer-Verlag.

Piaget, J. (1977) *The Grasp of Consciousness: Action and Concept in the Young Child*. London: Routledge & Kegan Paul.

Polanyi, M. (1958/1962) *Personal Knowledge: Towards a Post-Critical Philosophy*. Chicago and London: Chicago University Press.

Polanyi, M. (1966) *The Tacit Dimension*. London: Routledge and Kegan Paul.

Polanyi, M. (1968) Logic and psychology, *American Psychologist*. 23(1): 27–43.

Polanyi, M. (1969a) Knowing and being. In M. Grene (ed.), *Knowing and Being. Essays*. London: Routledge and Kegan Paul.

Polanyi, M. (1969b) Tacit knowing: its bearing on some problems of philosophy. In M. Grene (ed.), *Knowing and Being. Essays*. London: Routledge and Kegan Paul.

Polanyi, M. (1969c) The Logic of Tacit Inference. In M. Grene (ed.), *Knowing and Being. Essays*. London: Routledge and Kegan Paul.

Polanyi, M. (1969d) Sense-giving and sense-reading. In M. Grene (ed.), *Knowing and Being. Essays*. London: Routledge and Kegan Paul.

Prawitz, D. (1990) Tacit knowledge – an impediment for AI? In B. Göranzon and M. Florin (eds), *Artificial Intelligence, Culture and Language: On Education and Work*. London: Springer-Verlag.

Ratner, S. and Altman, J. (1964) *John Dewey and Arthur F. Bentley: a Philosophical Correspondence 1932–1951*. New Brunswick, NJ: Rutgers University Press.

Reber, A.S. (1993) *Implicit Learning and Tacit Knowledge: an Essay on the Cognitive Unconscious*. Cambridge: Cambridge University Press.

Reed, E.S. (1997) *From Soul to Mind: the Emergence of Psychology from Erasmus Darwin to William James*. New Haven and London: Yale University Press.

Saviotti, P.P. (1998) On the dynamics of appropriability, of tacit and of codified knowledge, *Research Policy*, 26: 843–56.

Scharmer, C.O. (2000) Organizing around not-yet-embodied knowledge. In G. von Krogh, I. Nonaka and T. Nichiguchi (eds), *Knowledge Creation: a Source of Value*. Basingstoke and London: Macmillan Press.

Schooler, J.W. and Engstler-Schooler, T.Y. (1990) Verbal overshadowing of visual memories: some things are better left unsaid, *Cognitive Psychology*, 22: 36–71.

Sebeok, T.A. (1979) *The Sign and its Masters*. Austin and London: University of Texas Press.

Sebeok, T.A. (1981) *The Play of Musement*. Bloomington, IN: Indiana University Press.

Sebeok, T.A. (1994) *Signs: an Introduction to Semiotics*. Toronto: University of Toronto Press.

Stadler, M.I. and Frensch, P.A. (1998) *Handbook of Implicit Learning*. London: Sage.

Stamper, R. (1996) Signs, information, norms and systems. In B. Holmqvist *et al.* (eds), *Signs of Work*. Berlin: Walter de Gruyter.

Stenmark, D. (2000) Turning tacit knowledge tangible, *Proceedings of the 33rd International Hawaii Conference on System Sciences (HICSS33)*, Maui, Hawaii (http://w3.adb.gu.se/~dixi/publ/DDOMLO1.pdf).

Sternberg, R.J. (1999) What do you know about tacit knowledge? Making the tacit become explicit. In R.J. Sternberg and J.A. Horvath (eds), *Tacit Knowledge in Professional Practice*. Mahwah, NJ and London: Lawrence Erlbaum Associates.

Szulanski, G. (1996) Exploring internal stickiness: impediments to the transfer of best practice within the firm, *Strategic Management Journal*, 17: 27–43.

Tsoukas, H. (2003) Do we really understand tacit knowledge? In M. Easterby-Smith and M.A. Lyles (eds), *Handbook of Organizational Learning and Knowledge*. Oxford: Blackwells.

Turvey, M.T. and Shaw, R.E. (1999) Ecological foundations of cognition I. Symmetry and specificity of animal-environment systems. In R. Núñez and W.J. Freeman (eds), *Reclaiming Cognition. the Primacy of Action Intention and Emotion*. Thorverton: Imprint Academic.

von Krogh, G. and Roos, J. (1995) *Organizational Epistemology*. London: Macmillan.

Wagner, R.K. (1987) Tacit knowledge in everyday intelligent behavior, *Journal of Personality and Social Psychology*, 52(6): 1236–47.

Wagner, R.K. (1991) Managerial problem solving. In R.J. Sternberg and P.A. Frensch (eds), *Complex Problem Solving: Principles and Mechanisms*. Hillsdale, NJ: Lawrence Erlbaum Associates.

Wagner, R.K. and Sternberg, R.J. (1986) Tacit knowledge and intelligence in the everyday world. In R.J. Sternberg and R.K. Wagner (eds), *Practical Intelligence: Nature and Origins of Competence in the Everyday World*. Cambridge: Cambridge University Press.

Whitehill, M. (1997) Knowledge-based strategy to deliver sustained competitive advantage, *Long Range Planning*, 30(4): 621–7.

Willman, P. (1996) Protecting know-how. (Safeguarding the information held by employees), *Business Strategy Review*, 7(1): 9–14.

# Part II

# Sharing and Managing Distributed Knowledge

# 5
# Knowledge Creation in Open Source Software Development

*Stefan Haefliger and Georg von Krogh*

## Introduction to Open Source

Open Source development projects are internet-based communities of computer programmers (von Hippel and von Krogh, 2003). Internet technology not only enables worldwide and almost cost-free distribution of software, but also enables a distributed production of software by users (von Hippel, 2001). The physical distance between the community members (programmers) prevents most face-to-face contact. This condition, together with the internet-based communication that is limited to written conversation and software code, provide the basis for our investigation. Using knowledge creation theory we discuss and analyse the Open Source software development process. How is new knowledge generated in Open Source projects? Who constitutes Open Source communities and how do people interact? Based on findings that indicate a direct sharing of tacit knowledge in Open Source communities (von Krogh, Spaeth and Lakhani, 2003), we propose how this may occur without co-location of the sharing parties. The knowledge creation process can be enabled by activities that take into account the emergent nature of Open Source projects. We address the question of what the role of a knowledge activist can be in Open Source and draw theoretical and practical implications.

In the early days at the pioneering labs at MIT and UC Berkeley in the US, before dedicated software companies existed, researchers programmed their machines themselves and shared their work. In 1971, Richard Stallman started working at the Artificial Intelligence (AI) lab at MIT, which was later referred to as a *hacker's*[1] *paradise*, until the early 1980s when software companies started to hire programmers away from the research labs. Stallman's community also disappeared around that time (Moody, 2001: 18). Frustrated but resolved to build a new community, he started to work on GNU ('GNU's Not Unix'), a free Unix-like operating system.[2] Over the years, the GNU operating system grew at a steady pace and Stallman received support from a growing number of users and volunteers. By 1990, it lacked one central element; its kernel.[3] The spread and popularity of the Internet in large parts of the world led to exponential growth not only in electronic communication in general and the application of software, but also in programming expertise and user involvement. During the early 1990s, the Finnish computer science student Linus Torvalds started programming and co-ordinating a global development effort for an operating system (kernel) that would later become known as Linux, and, in its capacity as a kernel, complement the GNU operating system. The development of Linux generated unprecedented participation and media coverage and subsequently received widespread public attention.[4] Open Source software development communities have produced such software as the operating system GNU/Linux or the server software Apache. In both cases, this free software attained market shares rivalling those of commercial players. Free or Open Source software comes with publicly available source code. This is the level of program code discernible by humans, whereas most commercially offered, 'packaged' software reaches the user in the form of machine or binary code only. However, the development of software by a group of like-minded individuals over the Internet is not necessarily an Open Source project. The term Open Source[5] was coined by a small number of acclaimed experts of Free software, such as Eric Raymond, marking the distinction between any software provided free of charge and Free software provided with the source code, thus being free in terms of unrestricted access and the individual right to improve and redistribute the code. The accompanying legal discussion deals with the handling of intellectual property in the context of Free software. The GNU General Public License (GPL), the first and most well known of a series of similar licences, complies with the Open Source definition and requires that anyone can modify or improve the software as long as their subsequent product is also distributed under the GPL. Thus, the GPL propagates and forces itself on later versions. Due to this contaminating effect it is sometimes termed *viral*. Under this protection, authors of free software should never have to compete with closed commercial software derived from their own work. The more fundamentalist view (with Richard Stallman being the most prominent advocate) rejects non-free (closed) software altogether, averring a strong general preference for free sharing and co-operation over the market exchange mechanism. Today, thousands of Open Source software development projects compete for skilled programmers and produce almost every imaginable software product, from office or communication tools to operating systems and games.[6]

The importance that Open Source software has attained reflects the impact that some of these programs exert on established firms and markets. For example, Apache dominates the server software market with a market share of roughly 60 per cent, ahead of Microsoft's 30 per cent.[7] Far from being a marginal phenomenon, Open Source software development thereby challenges researchers with explaining the motivation to innovate or the innovation processes itself (von Krogh and von Hippel, 2003).

The problem of motivation, as made explicit by Lerner and Tirole (2000), still poses a major puzzle for Open Source researchers. Two recent surveys (Wolf, Lakhani, Bates and DiBona, 2002: Ghosh, Glott, Krieger and Robles, 2002) have gathered questionnaires (over 600 and over 2700, respectively) assessing demographics and motivations. The findings reveal a large share of well-educated IT professionals among the programmers. A majority of programmers spends no more than ten hours a week on developing Open Source software (Ghosh *et al.*, 2002: 20). They are motivated by the creative activity of programming and the intellectual stimulation (Wolf *et al.*, 2002), the learning, knowledge exchange or skill enhancing possibilities (Wolf *et al.*, 2002: Ghogh *et al.*, 2002), or, what is often mentioned in various terms, fun or entertainment (Torvalds, 2001). An anthropological perspective, as put forth by Eric Raymond (1997, 1998), finds an own cultural context to the work (and life) of programmers.

Innovation process research, on the other hand, focuses on the co-ordination and the governance mechanisms inside the projects. How do developers communicate (Lakhani and von Hippel, 2001), and co-ordinate (Koch and Schneider, 2000)? How is the division of labour achieved (von Krogh, Spaeth and Lakhani, 2003), and how are resources attracted and allocated? The process research opens up a wide field for empirical studies and we are presently at the beginning of such endeavours. To understand how innovative products emerge from globally scattered communities, we need to analyse the process of learning within these communities. This chapter will shed light on some of the building blocks of knowledge creation within Open Source development communities.

Traditional knowledge creation theory (Nonaka, 1994; Nonaka and Takeuchi, 1995; von Krogh, Ijicho and Nonaka, 2000) and the knowledge-based theory of the firm (see Grant, 1996: Spender, 1996:

Porter Liebeskind, 1996) focus on the firm and the organization as a unit of analysis. Open Source communities could be viewed as organizations themselves. Their aims are not financial returns on investment (similar to charity organizations) and their member base is voluntary and not bound to legal contracts (similar to political pressure groups). The detailed process of software development in this context and the different contributors to Open Source software can illustrate how knowledge is successfully created in Open Source software development. We highlight each of the four modes of knowledge conversion (socialization, externalization, combination and internalization) and describe how knowledge activism can enable the process of knowledge creation.

## Open Source communities

The voluntary, emergent, and distributed nature of Open Source software development produces a number of obstacles to co-ordination, which are moderated in the circumstances of commercial software development. Unlike the co-ordination of work within a firm, co-ordination in Open Source communities is dominated by self-co-ordination, where communication is not used to delegate, and tasks are not assigned. A number of Internet-based tools build the technical basis for this development process; the concurrent versioning system (CVS), mailing lists, a hosting site providing downloads, and other tools such as bug databases, automatic snapshot generators or chatrooms. Program code is usually managed and exchanged via the CVS application. Well organized Open Source projects keep track of their code evolution from a centralized site. The CVS allows for multiple access to the code base and tracks all changes made to the code with a time stamp and author identification. The CVS also provides an exact reproduction of any previous state of the code, in case mistakes have made their way into the official version. The fact that there exists one official, centralized version of the software does not imply a knowledge monopoly since it can be downloaded or 'mirrored' (copied) to other locations, such as universities or private servers, to facilitate local downloading. The purpose of this central version is simply the co-ordination of work. Mailing lists, the tool for written conversation, distribute each e-mail sent to the list to all subscribers. Where a smaller project may manage with two or three independent lists, Linux manages hundreds of them.[8] The number of lists employed is connected to the traffic load, which can easily amount to hundreds of mails per day. The content varies systematically between the different lists. One major distinction often observed is between user support and active software development. With larger projects such as Linux, software modules have their independent mailing lists dealing only with the development of the particular module. Reasons for this are the complexity of certain modules and the workload, which resonates in the amount of communication needed to handle the development of this part of the software. Within mailing lists, content tends to be focused and technical, although personal remarks or even unrelated comments are frequent. According to *netiquette*, inappropriate statements or comments may be ignored or their author may be reprimanded. Mailing lists are the preferred communication tool for written conversation. A third essential tool is the host providing the current version for downloading. The host may be a professional provider of hosting services to Open Source projects (such as sourceforge.net), or larger projects running their own infrastructure on the net.

Based on these technologies, and with the legal protection of an Open Source license, contributors can share their code and collectively develop it in communities. These communities build around one project, manage their software (versions), and structure their communication and their organization. Before looking at this process and the roles of community members from a knowledge creation point of view, we first describe the role of the individual and differentiate the constituents within a development community.

For illustrative purposes, we consider the activities of a fictitious contributor to an Open Source project. As a skilled programmer who writes code on a regular basis, he allocates his limited time resources to a project in line with his preferences. However, before being able to contribute to the community, he has to learn about the details and current issues in the community and browse through the daily mail communication in order to be up to date. The costs associated with simply skimming through heavy traffic mail, in both time and effort, are considerable. When our programmer finds a suitable topic and an issue where he feels he may have something of value to add, he either posts or codes, or does both. Posting refers to a contribution in the form of a written comment to the mailing list. Discussions often involve dozens of contributors and the corresponding threads within the mailing list can carry on for days or weeks. His comments may add to a purely theoretical discussion, or relate to programming he has done and is about to share. Coding refers to the act of writing program code. He then, for various reasons, may choose to offer his code for submission. His code might add a new feature to the overall code or solve an existing problem. Submitting code means adding his patch[9] to the overall program code of the project. The process by which his code is included depends on his status as a programmer within the community.

The term meritocracy is used to describe the governance structure of Open Source development communities (Raymond, 1998). Four groups of people differing by their levels of involvement can be distinguished within the community (von Krogh, Spaeth and Lakhani, 2003). These groups vary from project to project, but generally the influence over the development of the code increases with involvement and achievement. The first group being the core developers, which are usually few people in number, takes on the majority of coding, plans the version releases, and decides on the inclusion of features or any issues determining the overall direction of the development. Among these developers, the founder of the project may even be granted more power (for example a right to veto certain developments). Again, this type of authority and the attribution of power implicitly follows a record of achievement. The second group consists of the developers with CVS access. The concurrent versioning system hosts the most current version of the program and allows multiple programmers to simultaneously change code. Thus, CVS access is synonymous with a privileged position to change the official code version. Technically, anyone could download and recreate this system and build a second competing version, but practically speaking the authority of the official version is rarely questioned. Access is granted to a relatively small circle of skilled programmers who have earned trust through their contributions and effort given to the project. The third group, the (regular) contributors, are the largest visible group of affiliates to the project. They either contribute code via a *gatekeeper*, who has CVS access and evaluates the submission, or they participate in the discussions. A presumably large but covert group is usually referred to as *lurkers*. Lurkers eavesdrop on mailing or discussion lists without posting (Nonnecke and Preece, 2000). This group helps to promote standards, reputation and 'recruiting', since nearly all developers started out by simply reading the mailing lists and trying the software.

Knowledge is thought to originate from individuals, and through their interaction the different constituents of a community create new collective knowledge. But the interaction among the project members is limited to a few channels, of which only two are public: mailing lists, code submissions (with signatures identifying the author of the code) and private e-mail or chat. The latter escapes the public eye but could be relevant for the sharing of knowledge and decision making. The discussion (mailing) lists are the prime locus of knowledge sharing. Using knowledge creation theory we will show how the four modes of knowledge conversion apply to Open Source software development. Open Source software development reveals an addition to established theory by showing that tacit knowledge can be shared despite developers hardly ever meeting in person. We formulate a rough, first proposition for explaining the phenomenon. The modes of knowledge conversion in an Open Source context then deliver the basis for the subsequent analysis of knowledge activism.

## Modes of knowledge conversion

Knowledge can be understood to be either explicit or tacit (Polanyi, 1966). Explicit knowledge is generally easy to document and thus found in text or image. Knowledge on how to install computer hardware, for example, is largely explicit. Knowledge on how to ride on inline skates, on the other hand, is experience related and tacit. In most practical examples, tacit and explicit knowledge are used in tandem. Cooking illustrates this well; a recipe, for instance, can only tell you so much about how to prepare a certain dish. In order to prepare it successfully, it takes specific experiences and knowledge on how to interpret and apply the recipe. There exist four possible modes to convert knowledge: from tacit to tacit, from tacit to explicit, from explicit to explicit and from explicit to tacit. The assumption that the sharing of knowledge leads to the creation of new knowledge epitomizes the model of knowledge creation (Nonaka, 1994). In the following we look at the four modes in greater detail.

### Socialization

The concept of socialization, the first mode of knowledge conversion, refers to the direct transfer of tacit knowledge. Established knowledge creation theory holds that shared experience plays a key role in the transfer of tacit knowledge. Socialization may require co-location of both parties (Nonaka and Konno, 1998) who in advance exchange cues about when and where to engage in knowledge sharing (von Krogh, 2002). Literature on distant learning and virtual reality (Dreyfus, 2000; Hoffman and Novak, 1997) holds contradicting views on whether, and to what extent, knowledge can be shared without face-to-face contact. Dreyfus rejects the possibility of learning over a distance beyond a certain level of intermediate expertise, whereas Hoffman and Novak argue that via mediated sensual experiences (from the telephone to virtual reality goggles and gloves) telepresence can emerge. We follow Hoffman and Novak when we find tacit knowledge sharing to be possible over a distance. However, we argue within the limited means of communication prevailing in our empirical phenomenon.

A master–apprentice relationship, exemplifying the concept of socialization, involves non-verbal communication such as observation and practice in order to convert tacit knowledge. However, when we look at Open Source software development communities, as described above, socialization can only occur through very limited channels, as the distance between developers impedes the direct sharing of experience through observation of what others do. Communication is limited to written language and program code. Under these circumstances, theory would predict no direct sharing of tacit knowledge. However, preliminary findings hint at a conversion of tacit knowledge within the community, which would correspond directly to the mode of socialization, since knowledge that has not been made explicit, such as the overall software architecture, appears collectively as a model of reference for a software architecture (von Krogh, Spaeth and Lakhani, 2003). There are two ways to explain this phenomenon. One involves a theory of signals intelligence and the other one rests on microcommunities of knowledge.

First, signs transmit perspectives containing tacit knowledge, for example about software complexity. With a continued involvement in the community, a contributor's skill to interpret these signs increases and tacit knowledge can be shared. From a knowledge creation theory perspective this process is functionally equivalent to socialization (signs may directly transfer tacit knowledge from one person to another). We briefly introduce Signal Detection Theory and then explain the three types of signs with brief illustrations. Evolving with the dawn of communication and radar, the psychophysics literature developed Signal Detection Theory, which is a framework to analyse the detection of unclear signals (Tanner and Swets, 1954) and later decision making in other fields (McMullen and Shepherd, 2002). '...people can learn what cues to look for, and that with additional effort they can acquire more (and more reliable) information' (McMullen and Shepherd, 2002: 7). Applied to knowledge creation, contributors can detect subtle signs from other contributors and interpret them.

There are three distinct types of signs or cues derived from conversations with developers and observation: meta-activities, references to a common background and code patterns. Their content is largely independent from the type of sign used and may vary from perspectives on software assessment (complexity, relevance to the project, larger purpose) to knowledge about programming techniques. For clarity we will only use software complexity as an example and illustrate how perspectives on software complexity can be transmitted through those signs. Meta-activities include the amount, quality or the timing of communication (or coding). Is a debate about one module intense or heated? How many code submissions and corrections does it take to get a feature to work? Do documentation efforts centre around one module? The answers to these questions, through individual interpretation, may convey a collective understanding of the obstacles associated with parts of the code and refer to the difficulty to program certain tasks. These matters are not only highly subjective, but also delicate due to political implications.[10] In essence, heated debates and a long and tedious way to the implementation of a certain module can diffuse a general understanding of how difficult this module is to code.

References to a common background are the second type of medium able to transmit implicit perspectives of community members. The assumption of a common background among culturally and geographically disperse contributors may seem questionable, but most programmers have been exposed to similar literature such as Eric Raymond's publications (1997, 1998) or commercial products such as Microsoft software or science fiction. The Jargon File (2002) calls science fiction fandom 'another voluntary subculture having a very heavy overlap with hackerdom; most hackers read SF [science fiction] and/or fantasy fiction avidly, and many go to "cons" (SF conventions) or are involved in fandom-connected activities such as the Society for Creative Anachronism. Some hacker jargon originated in SF fandom; see *defenestration, great-wall, cyberpunk, h, ha ha only serious, IMHO, mundane, neep-neep, Real Soon Now*. Additionally, the jargon terms *cowboy, cyberspace, de-rezz, go flatline, ice, phage, virus, wetware, wirehead*, and *worm* originated in SF stories.'[11] In written conversation, through mailing lists, literary forms such as the allusion or the metaphor can be used to communicate tacit knowledge. A well-known movie quote, for example, can easily be understood by many contributors, and thereby communicate, coming back to our example, the assessment of a module as complex.

Code patterns are structures or formations of program code used to perform a certain task in software. Programmers can learn by observing code and analysing how it is written, which algorithms are used, and how it is structured (as there might be several ways to implement one functionality). Code as such is externalized knowledge, its content is visible and its functionality can be objectively tested. However, the way in which code is structured and built conveys more (tacit) knowledge.

This tacit knowledge can be communicated only if the reader of code pays attention to the patterns. The analogy here is learning by observing practice (Brown and Duguid, 1991). Since the distribution of code is nearly cost free over the net, a contributor or lurker can have a close look at the code in different stages and observe its development. Scrutiny can reveal, following our example, differences in complexity across software modules. Taken together, these signs can transport tacit knowledge despite the fact that it has never been shared explicitly and the different members have never met in person.

The second explanation for tacit knowledge transfer within Open Source communities employs the concept of microcommunities, and assumes a very abstract level of communication due to common backgrounds and a history of common specialization. Microcommunities are defined as small groups of individuals within an organization engaging in knowledge creation (von Krogh, Nonaka and Ichijo, 1997). The foundation for the exchange of tacit knowledge within a microcommunity are close social ties emerging from face-to-face interaction, or in contrast Internet-based contacts generating the social ties in the Open Source context. If two or more contributors have been working on the same problem within a project, their common background increases and in parallel their exchange of knowledge becomes more efficient.[12] Due to the co-operation in one microcommunity, people develop a common understanding and common terms to deal with their particular problem (von Krogh, Spaeth and Lakhani, 2003). And, as the perspective on the task becomes collective and the specialized knowledge increases, they may be able to share knowledge faster and at a higher level of detail. The combination of common language and an exchange of code draws the group of involved insiders closer, and consequently outsiders may not be able to observe the knowledge transfer or follow its content. This perspective suggests the existence of special kinds of microcommunities within the Open Source development community. Members of a microcommunity tend to be core developers and contributors, who work on one module or feature. The group of core developers may be seen as a microcommunity within itself. Strictly speaking, the knowledge creation occurring within a microcommunity is not identical to the concept of socialization. Where socialization only refers to the direct sharing of tacit knowledge, a microcommunity integrates all process phases (socialization, externalization, combination and internalization) on a micro-level.

Anyone can observe the exchange of code patches as they happen in public, but an understanding of the context, within which the exchange makes sense, is limited to the involved few. Externalized knowledge can hardly be observed (and subsequently understood) from the outside in this curtate form of knowledge creation, nevertheless, explicit and tacit knowledge is being shared. For this reason, micro-communities are one insightful way of framing the phenomenon of tacit knowledge sharing in Open Source software development. Apart from the new knowledge emerging within the microcommunity, knowledge creation theory views the role of those specialized few as a trigger to knowledge creation in the overall organization (von Krogh, Nonaka and Ichijo, 1997). In Open Source, this aspect can be observed when a new feature, created by a microcommunity, spurs new coding to accommodate the new code or feature. The new knowledge inspires contributors to further changing and adapting the code towards the new options available due to the new feature.

### Externalization

Externalization of knowledge takes place through both media of communication: language and code. Aside from pure functionality, aesthetic preferences or even ethical convictions influence the judgement and use of code. Computer code is seen as a form of art (Knuth, 1969) or as formalized practice and an evolved set of tools (Arn, 2002). In both cases code may function as an indirect medium of communication just as any human artifact embodies knowledge and information in its characteristics and use. By writing and looking at code people can exchange knowledge and learn about the functionality of code, because code is externalized knowledge. Programmers regularly document their code by inserting comments next to the program code. This helps the reader of code to more readily navigate and grasp the purpose of the particular line of code. Additionally, documentation, technical manuals and declarations are often written as separate documents. The CVS provides another source of documentation or collective memory by keeping track of all version changes. In the mail discussions contributors freely express their thoughts and ideas. All these forms of written conversation and code make some tacit knowledge explicit and at the same time public. Anyone interested can download code and documentation, and can subscribe to the flow of the discussion in the mailing lists. As the development proceeds, the code base represents an externalization of shared tacit knowledge and reflects the shared experience accrued during the course of the project. Similarly, the frequently asked questions (FAQs) posted for newcomers develop into a common denominator of all contributors and externalize shared tacit knowledge.[13]

## Combination

The combination of freely available explicit knowledge can follow naturally as hundreds or even thousands of lurkers and contributors read the mailing lists and browse through the code, whereby only some of them understand the comments and the issues discussed. Existing ideas are categorized and evaluated. During this process new ideas emerge and new knowledge is created. A contributor may see a connection to work he has done earlier, compare the tasks, and contribute to the community his adapted work. The discussion about a new feature and how it could be implemented could trigger the idea of a solution with a reader who understood how the stated positions could be integrated. New people join the community and pick up ideas they reuse for their own purposes, add new features to the project, or improve existing code (von Krogh, Spaeth and Lakhani, 2003). Free software licences (such as the GPL) encourage and legally protect redistribution and combinations with existing code by imposing that any modifications must be openly available again.

## Internalization

Internalization resembles the traditional concept of learning and refers to the organizational act of interpretation and reconstruction of perspective (Nonaka, 1994). On the individual level this applies equally to a core developer and to a lurker; both can learn from knowledge that has been externalized and is publicly available. A question for future research points towards a possible differential in quality or speed of learning with increased involvement (von Hippel and von Krogh, 2003). Internalization of the existing code, of earlier discussions and of technical obstacles is a prerequisite for any newcomer. To become an active contributor, a sound knowledge of the project seems indispensable (von Krogh, Spaeth and Lakhani, 2003). Newcomers are explicitly referred to the project's FAQs, where general information and answers can accelerate their learning and enable them to contribute.

Thus far we have unfolded the process of knowledge creation in the context of Open Source software development communities. These communities emerge and develop into self-governed organizations. As opposed to firms, resources cannot be directed. Contributors choose not only their preferred Open Source project, but also within the project they choose a module or sub-component of the software to work on. Apart from a few core developers who work on multiple modules, most contributors specialize (von Krogh, Spaeth and Lakhani, 2003). Their choice corresponds to a resource self-allocation within the project.

Any effort to foster or increase knowledge creation activities must take this self-governed aspect into consideration. It seems difficult if not impossible to authoritatively assign tasks, thereby directing where knowledge creation should take place. Nor does it seem likely programmers will accept someone assigning working groups or microcommunities. Hence, the most appropriate knowledge enabler is the knowledge activist who mobilizes resources instead of directing them (von Krogh, Ichijo and Nonaka, 2000). In the next section we will consider the knowledge creation process from a knowledge activist's point of view. Our focus will be on the actions likely to positively impact the process.

## Knowledge activism

The sharing and creation of knowledge in organizations cannot be directly managed but must be indirectly enabled (von Krogh, Ichijo and Nonaka, 2000). Where the perspective of describing enablers in a business context is aimed at management, it takes on a more descriptive nature in our context. It would be premature to speak of management in Open Source, even though we do observe leaders who take great care to shape 'their' project according to their preferences. Any contributor could become a knowledge activist, but we usually observe project founders and core developers taking on the role of knowledge activists. Linus Torvalds and his style of running the Linux development efforts have been widely discussed (Moon and Sproull, 2000; Moody, 2001). The stakeholders in Open Source projects contribute code based on different motives than would stakeholders in firms. We do not yet know which powers management or leadership really possesses in Open Source, as long as the motivation for participation itself remains obscure. What we do observe, however, is helping behaviour (Lakhani and von Hippel, 2002) and norms prevalent within the hacker community (Raymond, 1997, 1998). Hence, we observe patterns of behaviour that resemble the enabling factors in a business context. In contrast, Open Source communities are self-governed in nature and resources cannot be allocated, since contributors will not take directions regarding what task to work on or with whom. Only a mobilizing, 'grass roots' activity can potentially impact an Open Source knowledge creation process. Figure 5.1 synthesizes the activities enabling knowledge creation during the process.

Socialization refers to the direct conversion of tacit knowledge between individuals. The question of how to foster socialization resonates more clearly when we remember the proposition drawing on Signal

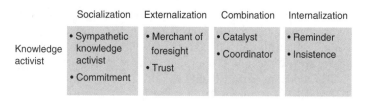

| | Socialization | Externalization | Combination | Internalization |
|---|---|---|---|---|
| Knowledge activist | • Sympathetic knowledge activist<br>• Commitment | • Merchant of foresight<br>• Trust | • Catalyst<br>• Coordinator | • Reminder<br>• Insistence |

*Figure 5.1*   Means of the knowledge activist to enable knowledge creation

Detection Theory: how can contributors learn to better interpret their peers' cues when the only channels of communication are computer-mediated? The answer opens a field of activity for the knowledge activist. In general, people must feel at home in a community and they should 'stop by often', in terms of time spent mentally with the project and reading through mails and contributing to the discussion. This will allow them to keep up to date with current events and know their peers' preferences better, and thus interact more effectively. Understanding of each others' arguments and cues may enable tacit knowledge sharing among programmers. A knowledge activist, who succeeds in seizing the community's attention and ultimately involving them with their expertise, can enable this process. When choosing her activities she should first show commitment for the community, and, second, appear as a sympathetic figure. In a purely computer-mediated communication context, non-verbal communication or cultural differences between community members are deflated and accents altogether eliminated. There are few a priori obstacles to portraying a certain image due to a high perceived similarity among members in this form of communication (Jarvenpaa and Leidner, 1998).

In many projects, programmers devote time and resources to sponta-neously responding to others' demands for help (Lakhani and von Hippel, 2002). When looking at joining behaviour, we observe that direct help is usually treated subsidiarily and newcomers are referred to the FAQs. The direct exchange of ideas is valued and, despite off-topic comments, a large part of the discussions can safely be considered pro-ductive. The idea of proactive commitment towards another person, such as help or encouragement or appreciation of others' work, is often seen in Open Source communities, where projects usually feature credit files containing the names of contributors. Linus Torvalds, for example, set up and personally maintained the credit files in Linux (Moon and Sproull, 2000). Although credit lists also serve other purposes such as reputation building, they are a visible symbol of appreciation for others' work. As such they are part of a commitment displayed towards contributors, which enables a free flow of knowledge among community members (Nonaka and Konno, 1998; von Krogh, Ichijo and Nonaka, 2000). Examples for helping behaviour and encouragement are usually too numerous to attribute to one person. Nevertheless, they enable knowledge creation and socialization.

The second role of a knowledge activist is the role as a sympathetic figure. Again, Linus Torvalds, being a famous example of a project leader and a generally sympathetic figure, was described as lacking self-confidence as a young man and 'frequently deflate[d] some expression of apparent arrogance with a self-deprecating and honest humility' (Moody, 2001: 38). Perhaps a likable image of a project leader does not turn contributors off by inducing negative feelings, as would arrogance or spite. Expressed positively, the sympathetic image leaves room for the projection of positive connotations and could inspire community members.

Knowledge activism ignites externalization of knowledge with new visions of the future. Described as 'merchants of foresight' (von Krogh, Ichijo and Nonaka, 2000: 157), knowledge activists inspire through visions of how the world and the project may look in the future. This does not imply any imposition, as it would be doomed from the outset if it were. Rather, a merchant of foresight recognizes the value of ideas and brings them to the forefront when they have been ignored. This activity could mean asking for details on an idea that has only been briefly mentioned, or encouraging a contribution by an individual whose expertise is already known. A prerequisite is continuous involvement; the knowledge activist has to avoid the trap of losing touch with current issues and needs to stay up do date on the details of the development process. Still, the even more important role of the knowledge activist is the building of trust within the community.

In knowledge creation theory, trust is regarded as a key requirement for people to externalize their tacit knowledge (Nonaka and Takeuchi, 1995). The knowledge activist can establish trust through his communication behaviour. But how does trust work in Open Source? Open Source communities assemble people with a limited to no common history of working together. The rather resilient trust established in temporary systems, where diversely skilled participants without a common history work on complex, non-routine tasks, has been described as swift trust (Meyerson, Weick and Kramer, 1996). Two key features in Open Source diverge from this construct: first, the lack of face-to-face interaction and, second, time limitation. According to Jarvenpaa and Leidner

(1998: 21), commitment (group-support and group well-being functions) and communication behaviour become important determinants of trust when face-to-face contact is not an option. This suggests for Open Source software development that trust can be established by applying commitment in communication. The lack of limitation to the time of interaction, implying that Open Source projects can exist as long as they receive sufficient support, relaxes an important constraint of the temporary system underlying swift trust. The open time horizon provides community members with a common future, an option that was deliberately absent from the experiments underlying the discovery of swift trust (Meyerson *et al.*, 1996). Excitement, support or enthusiasm can be expressed through mails, and a knowledge activist can enable trust and thereby induce community members to externalize their tacit knowledge. During the Linux development, a few particularly skilled and loyal programmers became known as Linus Torvalds's 'trusted lieutenants'; among them were, for example, Alan Cox or Ted Ts'o (Moody, 2001: 82). These long-term, trusting relationships featured prominently in the development process of Linux; namely contributing to the additional layer in the hierarchy that the trusted lieutenants represented (Raymond, 1997). A knowledge activist can enable the externalization of tacit knowledge by fostering trust and by taking on the role of a merchant of foresight.

The combination of explicit knowledge may be improved by a catalyst and co-ordination efforts. New perspectives on a certain issue may redirect the discussion in the community. Similar to the merchant of foresight, the catalyst cannot apply authority, but rather mobilizes contributors. A knowledge activist as a catalyst triggers new developments by providing impulses to the community. These impulses can ask for higher quality, propose new features or set time frames such as a release date. These impulses are heard only if they reflect the current state of discussion and if they are sound and realistic. Thus, the requirements for a knowledge activist are high when it comes to technical and social competence. He has to see space for new development opportunities and know the overall state of the project. Linus Torvalds never left doubt about who was in charge and who had the last word on the code (Moody, 2001: 59). At the same time, he was involved in all the major modules and programmed large parts of Linux himself, earning respect for his competence (Moody, 2001). The competence and the involvement in everyday development lies at the basis of his knowledge catalyst activities. One example for providing space for new opportunities and experimental development, and an important institutional innovation to Linux, was the introduction of the parallel release structure (Moon and Sproull, 2000: 12). To every new version of Linux there is the even more recent, 'experimental' version where new features can be tested and developers and lead users may report on bugs[14] and improvements, thus combining more knowledge. The regular version served those users who wanted to rely on a safe version containing established and tested features. Another activity may be co-ordinating work within the community. A knowledge activist can communicate needs and open issues and promote certain activities as being most helpful for the overall development. Thus, he may mobilize contributors to consider new tasks and combine their knowledge with what is already available or with other contributors' expertise.

Knowledge activism helps important issues to 'sink in' better (internalization). By repeating issues and bringing them up in the discussion regularly, the activity may trigger learning and knowledge creation. Insistence on learning can include the mention of lessons learned or reminding the community of mistakes or developments that have taken place when many current contributors were not yet aboard. Anyone in the community can be a knowledge activist but, as discussed above, the requirements include high social competence and a good knowledge of the existing code base. In order to acquire these skills, a knowledge activist must show commitment to the project. Hence, core developers, project leaders, or founders could take on the role of the knowledge activist.

## Conclusion

Open Source communities innovate under limitations in communication and face-to-face contact. Communication is web-based and computer-mediated and face-to-face contacts hardly ever occur. Yet knowledge is being created and we observe the production of new software. We described the role of mailing lists and the concurrent versioning system (CVS) in the co-ordination of work, and we introduced the people who constitute an Open Source software development community, their usual activities, and their levels of involvement. With this information, the knowledge creation process could be analysed in some detail. A particular difficulty for established knowledge creation theory, in a context of physical distance between actors, is the direct sharing of tacit knowledge. We propose that signs can transmit perspectives, and may integrate (and socialize) developers with a history of common specialization. As a possible enabler of the knowledge creation process in Open Source software development, we suggest an activist who mobilizes community members: the role of a knowledge activist in Open Source is the role of a motivator among equals. Any person with sufficient knowledge of the project and who understands the potential to increase knowledge creation can act as a knowledge activist. Thus, he can actively contribute to the innovation process, accelerate it, or improve the quality of the software. The practical implications should be fairly clear; promoting the well-being and group enthusiasm, the knowledge activist can enable knowledge sharing among the community members. He can envision future developments and promote trust to get people to externalize knowledge. For Open Source, as for other virtual teams, trust starts to develop with 'the first few keystrokes' (Jarvenpaa and Leidner, 1998: 21) As a co-ordinator, the knowledge activist leads people to combine and internalize knowledge.

Regarding the sharing of tacit knowledge we propose that signs transmitting knowledge can be interpreted and, hence, the knowledge is shared. To deepen the understanding of distance learning and tacit knowledge sharing, Open Source projects provide an optimal empirical setting since it can almost be ruled out that people will meet face-to-face. Thus, whenever congruence in tacit knowledge appears in different locations, and it has not before been made explicit, there is evidence for direct tacit knowledge sharing. To test the proposition itself, in-depth case studies should locate and describe particular examples of signs capable of transmitting tacit knowledge. Such an in-depth study should, at the same time, reveal the evolution of expertise covered by microcommunities, since they offer an alternative, complementing explanation for the creation of knowledge within Open Source software development communities.

We observe the production of high-quality and innovative software products by dispersed and global, virtual communities. This analysis of how communities create new knowledge, and which enabling factors may play a particularly important role in the process, may bear insights for any organization facing voluntary affiliates or geographic distribution of work such as decentralized teams.

## Notes

1. hacker *n.*: [originally, someone who makes furniture with an axe] 1. A person who enjoys exploring the details of programmable systems and how to stretch their capabilities, as opposed to most users, who prefer to learn only the minimum necessary. 2. One who programs enthusiastically (even obsessively) or who enjoys programming rather than just theorizing about

programming.... 8. [deprecated] A malicious meddler who tries to discover sensitive information by poking around. Hence 'password hacker', 'network hacker'. The correct term for this sense is cracker (The Jargon File 2002).

2. The history of GNU can be found at: http://www.gnu.org/gnu/gnu-history.html.

3. A kernel is the central element of a computer operating system that schedules the processing time for the different applications. In other words, it manages the system's resources.

4. The Linux Counter Project estimates 18 million Linux users today (http://counter.li.org/), having grown from one person in 1991.

5. For the exact wording refer to: http://www.opensource.org/docs/definition.php.

6. http://sourceforge.net/ (one of the largest OSSD websites) lists more than 50,000 Open Source projects.

7. See: http://www.netcraft.com/survey/.

8. http://www.linuxrx.com/Lists/Lists.perl counts more than 700 mailing lists (retrieved on 7 November 2002).

9. patch, 1. *n.* A temporary addition to a piece of code, usually as a quick-and-dirty remedy to an existing bug [see note 14] or misfeature. A patch may or may not work, and may or may not eventually be incorporated permanently into the program. (...) 2. vt. To insert a patch into a piece of code. (...) (Jargon File, 2002).

10. As a side note: these implications may explain why this type of knowledge is never made explicit.

11. The Jargon File (2002) contains entries explaining the meaning of each of these terms.

12. Similarly, but on the firm level, absorptive capacity accounts for lower costs of knowledge acquisition after prior investments in learning (Cohen and Levinthal, 1990).

13. The authors would like to thank Nikos Mylonopoulos for pointing this out.

14. A flaw in a computer program or more exactly: 'An unwanted and unintended property of a program or piece of hardware, esp. one that causes it to malfunction. Antonym of feature' (The Jargon File, 2002).

# References

Arn, Stefan (2002) Mehr Brückenbauer als Physiker: Das Software-Engineering aus der Sicht des Praktikers, *Neue Zürcher Zeitung*, 221, 91.

Brown, John Seely and Duguid, Paul (1991) Organizational learning and communities-of-practice: toward a unified view of working, learning, and innovation, *Organization Science*, 1: 40–57.

Cohen, W.M. and Levinthal, D.A. (1990) Absorptive capacity: a new perspective on learning and innovation, *Administrative Science Quarterly, Special Issue: Technology, Organizations, and Innovation*, 128–52.

Dalle, Jean-Michel and Jullien, Nicholas (2001) *Open Source vs. proprietary software.* Working paper. Retrieved on 31 October 2002: http://opensource.mit.edu/papers/dalle2.pdf.

Dreyfus, Hubert (2001) *On the Internet: Thinking in Action.* New York: Routledge.

Ghosh, Rishab A., Glott, Ruediger, Krieger, Bernhard and Robles, Gregorio (2002) *Free/Libre and Open Source software: Survey and study (FLOSS)*, Part 4: Survey of developers. Retrieved on 20 November 2002: http://www.infonomics.nl/FLOSS/report/.

Grant, Robert M. (1996) Toward a knowledge-based theory of the firm, *Strategic Management Journal, Special Issue: Knowledge and the Firm*, 109–22.

Hippel, Eric von (2001) Open Source shows the way: innovation by and for users – no manufacturer required!, *Sloan Management Review*, 4: 82–6.

Hippel, Eric von and von Krogh, Georg (2003) Exploring the Open Source software phenomenon: issues for organization science. Forthcoming in *Organization Science*. Retrieved on 21 November 2002: http://opensource.mit.edu/papers/hippelkrogh.pdf.

Hoffman, Donna L. and Novak, Thomas P. (1997) A new marketing paradigm for electronic commerce, *The Information Society*, 13: 43–54.

Jargon File (2002) *The on-line hacker Jargon File*, version 4.3.3, 20 SEP 2002. http://www.tuxedo.org/~esr/jargon/html/index.html.

Jarvenpaa, Sirkka L. and Leidner, Dorothy E. (1998) Communication and trust in global virtual teams, *Journal of Computer-Mediated Communication*, 3(4): 1–28. Retrieved on 20 November 2002: http://jcmc.huji.ac.il/vol3/issue4/jarvenpaa.html.

Knuth, Donald E. (1969) *The Art of Computer Programming*. Reading, MA: Addison-Wesley.

Koch, Stefan and Schneider, Georg (2000) *Results From Software Engineering Research Into Open Source Development Projects Using Public Data*. Retrieved on 10 November 2002: http://opensource.mit.edu/papers/koch-ossoftwareengineering.pdf.

Krogh, Georg von (2002) The communal resource and information systems, *Journal of Strategic Information Systems*, 11: 85–107.

Krogh, Georg von and von Hippel, Eric (2003) Open Source software: an introduction to the special issue. Forthcoming in: *Research Policy, Special Issue on Open Source Software Development*.

Krogh, Georg von, Ichijo, Kazuo and Nonaka, Ikujiro (2000) *Enabling Knowledge Creation*. New York: Oxford University Press.

Krogh, Georg von, Nonaka, Ikujiro and Ichijo, Kazuo (1997) Develop knowledge activists! *European Management Journal*, 5: 475–83.

Krogh, Georg von, Spaeth, Sebastian and Lakhani, Karim (2003) Innovation, joining scripts and specialization in Open Source software development. Forthcoming in: *Research Policy, Special Issue on Open Source Software Development*.

Lakhani, Karim and von Hippel, Eric (2002) How Open Source works: 'Free' user-to-user assistance. MIT Sloan: Working Paper. Forthcoming in *Research Policy*.

Lerner, Josh and Tirole, Jean (2000) *The Simple Economics of Open Source*. Cambridge, MA: NBER Working Paper 7600.

McMullen, Jeffery and Shepherd, Dean A. (2002) *Toward a Theory of Entrepreneurial Intention: Recognizing and Evaluating Opportunities*. University of Colorado at Boulder: unpublished working paper.

Meyerson, Debra, Weick, Karl E. and Kramer, Roderick M. (1996) Swift trust and temporary groups. In R.M. Kramer and T.R. Tyler (eds), *Trust in Organizations: Frontiers of Theory and Research*. Thousand Oaks, CA: Sage.

Moody, Glyn (2001) *Rebel Code*. Cambridge, MA: Perseus Publishing.

Moon, Jae Yun and Sproull, Lee (2000) Essence of distributed work: the case of the Linux kernel. *First Monday*, 5,11. Retrieved on 7 November 2002: http://www.firstmonday.dk/issues/issue5_11/moon/index.html.

Nonaka, Ikujiro (1994) A dynamic theory of organizational knowledge creation, *Organization Science*, 1: 14–37.

Nonaka, Ikujiro and Takeuchi, Hirotaka (1995) *The Knowledge-Creating Company: How Japanese Companies Create the Dynamics of Innovation*. New York: Oxford University Press.

Nonaka, Ikujiro and Konno, Noboru (1998) The concept of 'Ba': building a foundation for knowledge creation, *California Management Review*, 3: 40–54.

Nonnecke, Blair and Preece, Jenny (2000) Lurker demographics: counting the silent. *Proceedings of CHI 2000*. The Hague: ACM.

Polanyi, Michael (1966) *The Tacit Dimension*. London: Routledge and Kegan Paul.

Porter Liebeskind, Julia (1996) Knowledge, strategy, and the theory of the firm, *Strategic Management Journal, Special Issue: Knowledge and the Firm*, 93–107.

Raymond, Eric (1997) *The Cathedral and the Bazaar*. Retrieved on 2002 November 8: http://www.tuxedo.org/~esr/writings/cathedral-bazaar/cathedral-bazaar/.

Raymond, Eric (1998) Homesteading the Noospere. *First Monday* 3, 10, Retrieved on 20 October 2002: http://www.firstmonday.dk/issues/issue3_10/raymond/.

Spender, J.C. (1996) Making knowledge the basis of a dynamic theory of the firm, *Strategic Management Journal, Special Issue: Knowledge and the Firm*, 45–62.

Tanner, W.P.J. and Swets, J.A. (1954) A decision-making theory of visual detection, *Psychological Review*, 61, 401–9.

Torvalds, Linus (2001) Prologue. In Pekka Himanen, Linus Torvalds and Manuel Castells, *The Hacker Ethic and the Spirit of the Information Age*. London: Random House.

Wolf B., Lakhani, K. Bates, J. and DiBona, C. (2002), *The Boston Consulting Group Hacker Survey*. Retrieved on 20 October 2002: http://www.osdn.com/bcg/.

# 6

# The Implications of Different Models of Social Relations for Understanding Knowledge Sharing

*Niels-Ingvar Boer, Peter J. van Baalen and Kuldeep Kumar*

## Introduction

It is generally agreed upon that knowledge sharing is a crucial process within organizational settings, whether these are, for example, project teams, formal work groups or communities of practice. One might even argue that sharing knowledge is the *raison d'être* of such organizational settings. After all, due to the division of labour and accompanying fragmentation, specialization and distribution of knowledge, it becomes essential to integrate and thus share the diversity of complementary knowledge in order to produce complex products and services (Grant, 1996).

Many practitioners and academics assume that since knowledge sharing is crucial for achieving the collective outcome of organizational settings, people *will* share all the required knowledge. However, many companies and institutions have experienced that knowledge sharing is not obvious in practice, whether a codified strategy or a personalized strategy has been followed (Hansen, Nohria and Tierney, 1999).

A variety of conditions has been identified in the literature, trying to explain the lack or presence of knowledge sharing. It is assumed that when any of these conditions is not given into, knowledge sharing is unlikely to take place, or at least in an efficient or effective way. Among these conditions are characteristics of knowledge such as its tacitness (Boisot, 1998; Szulanski, 1996), characteristics of the sender such as one's workload (Huber, 1991), characteristics of the receiver such as one's absorptive capacity (Cohen and Levinthal, 1990; Lane and

Lubatkin, 1998), and characteristics of the organizational context such as the communication infrastructure (Moenaert, Caeldries, and Wauters, 2000) and the richness of the media (Daft and Lengel, 1984).

Rather than considering individual (including epistemological), organizational or technological conditions for sharing knowledge, this chapter addresses the motivational dimension of knowledge sharing by focussing on the relationships within which knowledge is being shared. With respect to motivations for sharing knowledge, the literature is preoccupied with a rather rational economic perspective on sharing knowledge. According to Davenport and Prusak (1998), knowledge should be shared according to the logic of markets. 'Many knowledge initiatives have been based on the utopian assumption that knowledge moves without friction or motivation force, that people will share knowledge with no concern for what they may gain or lose by doing so' (Davenport and Prusak, 1998). However, although the economic rationality is necessary, it is not sufficient for understanding why people (do not) share knowledge.

Business practice illustrates that in some situations knowledge is not being shared while it would be expected to take place according to the economic rationality (see Textboxes 1 and 2). For example, it seems very rational for organizations to develop knowledge repositories and to build intranets in order to share their 'best practices' so that their employees do not have to 'reinvent the wheel' over and over again. However, many intranets and knowledge repositories remain without content, since people do not contribute to it by sharing their knowledge (Ciborra and Patriotta, 1996).

Besides situations in which knowledge is not being shared while it would be expected to take place according to an economic rationality, the opposite also occurs. In some situations one would *not* expect to find people sharing knowledge, while it *does* take place. For example, people contributing to discussion groups on the Internet or developing Open Source software cannot be explained solely from a rational economic perspective (see Textbox 1). Sometimes people share knowledge even though they are not receiving any direct financial value in return (Raymond, 2001). Thus, motivations other than pure economic rationality exist that either promote or inhibit the process of knowledge sharing.

Alternative models for describing or prescribing the motivational and relational dimension of knowledge sharing have been proposed. For example, sociologists have interpreted work-related and scientific communication as gift giving (Blau, 1963; Hagstrom, 1965) and enrolling allies (Latour, 1987). Others have pointed to the importance

Textbox 1

---

**Developing best practices**

In an increasingly competitive environment, organizations need to operate as efficiently as possible, especially when they are dealing with repetitive work (e.g., doing similar consultancy assignments, processing insurance claims or developing software). Since these organizations employ people who all have acquired particular knowledge in practice, it seems rational to try to benefit from this knowledge, so that every employee can take advantage of prior experiences of their colleagues. It would be inefficient to let people 'reinvent the wheel' every time. Therefore organizations have tried to set up knowledge repositories that contain best practices and other knowledge that could be of interest for other employees. Rationally most people subscribe the usefulness of such knowledge systems. However, in practice many repositories remained 'empty' since the employees did not contribute to the accumulation of knowledge in the database.

**Open Source Software Development**

The success story of Open Source Software Development (OSSD) started with the creation and collective development of Linux in 1991. Collaborative, networked development was a new model of software development made possible by the Internet. The full power of this collaborative method can only be realized when the source code to software is freely shared among developers. The source code is copyrighted under the GNU Public License, meaning that software must be freely distributed with source code available, and anyone may freely modify that source code provided that any modifications they distribute are distributed with source code. OSSD breaks down the barriers between developers and users, and removes obstacles in developer-to-developer communication. Each new version of a software application (e.g. an operating system) is rapidly viewed and tested by thousands of programmers world wide, aptly demonstrating the adage that 'given enough eyeballs, all bugs are shallow'. In this way, OSSD can accelerate the software development process, increase the level of customization and makes the software more reliable. The question arises what makes thousands of developers around the world contribute to a particular source code? They are not motivated by economic motives to share their knowledge, since they do not receive any financial rewards for it.

---

of communities (Brown and Duguid, 1991; Wenger, 1998). Within social capital theory the social relations are emphasized rather than the market relations, or the hierarchical relations (Adler and Kwon, 2002). Most research is dominated by only one model of social relations, resulting in a fragmentary understanding of knowledge sharing.

The objective of this chapter is to illustrate how the relation models theory (Fiske, 1991), which postulates that human relations may be based largely on combinations of *four* relational models (communal sharing, authority ranking, equality matching and market pricing), can contribute to a better understanding of the dynamics of knowledge sharing within different organizational settings. By taking these four relational models into account as mechanisms behind knowledge sharing, rather than just one, it is asserted that the understanding of knowledge sharing might improve.

## Different models of social relations

Knowledge sharing is considered to be a fundamentally social phenomenon. 'Social behavior is inherently relational in nature: individual behavior assumes social meaning only in the context of human relations. The basic unit of analysis is therefore not individual behavior, but behavior-in-a-relational context' (Fiske, 1991). In line with the idea of structuration (Giddens, 1984), it can be stated that a relationship between people is established as soon as they share knowledge with one another and that a particular relationship between people consequently influences the way knowledge is being shared. Knowledge can be shared between people interacting face-to-face, or mediated by technology, both synchronous and asynchronous. 'It is not necessary that the "other persons" be present or even exist – nor, if they do exist, that they actually perceive the action or perceive it as it was intended. A social relationship exists when any person acts under the implicit assumption that they are interacting with reference to imputedly shared meanings' (Fiske, 1991).

The relation models theory of Fiske (1991, 1992) claims that people are fundamentally sociable. They generally organize their social life in terms of their relations with other people. In general people seek to create, sustain, and repair social relationships because the relationships themselves are subjectively imperative, intrinsically satisfying, and significant. The relation models theory integrates the work of the major social theorists and builds on a synthesis of empirical studies across the social sciences, including anthropological fieldwork. From an exhaustive review of the major thinking on relationships in sociology (such as Blau, 1964; Buber, 1987; Durkheim, 1966; Tönnies, 1988; Weber, 1975), social anthropology (such as Malinowski, 1961; Polanyi, 1957; Salins, 1965; Udy, 1959) and social psychology (such as Clark and Mills, 1979; Krech and Crutchfield, 1965; Leary, 1957; Piaget, 1973), Fiske argues for the existence of four fundamental forms of human relationships: communal sharing, authority ranking, equality matching and market pricing. These four structures are manifestations of elementary mental models (schemata). Table 6.1 summarizes some of the major postulations

*Table 6.1* Postulations of relation models theory

---

- People are fundamentally sociable; they generally organize their social life in terms of their relations with other people.
- People use just four relational models (*communal sharing, authority ranking, equality matching* and *market pricing*) to generate, understand, co-ordinate and evaluate these social relationships; the four social structures are manifestations of elementary mental models (schemata).
- These models are autonomous, distinct structures, not dimensions; there is no continuum of intermediate forms.
- People find each of the models of relationships intrinsically satisfying for its own sake. There is typically an extremely high degree of consensus among interacting actors about what model is, and should be operative.
- People believe that they should adhere to the models, and insist that others conform to the four models as well.
- Social conflicts often occur when people are perceived to be profoundly violating the elementary relationships.
- The residual cases not governed by any of these four models are *asocial interactions*, in which people use other people purely as a means to some ulterior end, or *null interactions*, in which people ignore each other's conceptions, goals and standards entirely.
- People commonly string the relational models together and nest them hierarchically in various phases of an interaction or in distinct activities of an organization.
- Relations and operations that are socially significant in one relational structure may not be meaningful in certain others.
- People in different societies commonly use different models and combinations of models in any given domain or context. Cultural implementation rules (rules that stipulate when each model applies and rules that stipulate how to execute each model) are essential for the realization of any model in practice (domain, degree).
- The four models do not all work equally well in every domain, and each is dysfunctional for some purposes in some contexts.

---

*Source*: Derived from Fiske (1992).

of the relation models theory. Each of the relational models is now briefly described.

*Communal sharing* relationships (CS) are based upon a conception of some bounded group of people as equivalent and undifferentiated. In this kind of relationship, the members of a group or dyad treat each other as being identical, focussing on commonalities and disregarding distinct individual identities. People in a CS relationship often think of themselves as sharing some common substance, and hence think that it is natural to be relatively kind and altruistic to people of their own kind. Close kinship ties usually involve a major CS component, as does intense love; ethical and national identities and even minimal groups are more attenuated forms of CS. When people are thinking in terms of equivalence relations, they tend to regard the equivalence class to which they themselves belong as better than others, and to favour it.

*Authority ranking* relationships (AR) are based on a model of asymmetry among people who are linearly ordered along some hierarchical social dimension. People higher in rank have prestige, prerogatives, and privileges that their inferiors lack, but subordinates are often entitled to protection and pastoral care. Authorities often control some aspects of their subordinates' actions. Relationships between people of different ranks in the military are predominantly governed by this model, as are relations across generations and between genders in many traditional societies. Although, in principle, in any society or situation, people could be ranked in different hierarchies according to innumerable different status-relevant features, in practice, people tend to reduce these factors to a single linear ordering. When people are thinking in terms of such linearly ordered structures, they treat higher ranks as better.

*Equality matching* relationships (EM) are based on a model of even balance and one-for-one correspondence, as in turn taking, egalitarian distributive justice, in-kind reciprocity, tit-for-tat retaliation, eye-for-an-eye revenge, or compensation by equal replacement. People are primarily concerned about whether an EM relationship is balanced, and keep track of how far out of balance it is. The idea is that each person is entitled to the same amount as each other person in the relationship, and that the direction and magnitude of an imbalance are meaningful. Colleagues who are not intimate often interact on this basis: they know how far from equality they are, and what they would need to do to even things up. People value equality and strongly prefer having at least as much as their partners in an EM relationship.

*Market pricing* relationships (MP) are based on a model of proportionality in social relationships and people attend to ratios and rates. People in an MP relationship usually reduce all the relevant features and components under consideration to a singular value or utility metric that allows the comparison of many qualitatively and quantitatively diverse factors. People organize their interactions with reference to ratios of this metric, so that what matters is how a person stands in proportion to others. Proportions are continuous, and can take any value. The most prominent examples of interactions governed by MP are those that are oriented towards prices, wages, commissions, rents, interest rates, tithes, taxes and all other relationships organized in terms of cost–benefit ratios and rational calculations of efficiency or expected utility.

The four described relational models all imply a social relationship between people. If there is no truly social relationship, Fiske speaks about *null interaction*, in which people ignore each other's conceptions, goals and standards entirely. Obviously, any given person has no social relationship at all with most of the people on earth. Furthermore, using the same toilet, and drinking at the same coffee machine are not social relationships ipso facto. People sometimes may simply disregard the existence of other people as social partners, acting towards others as if they were merely animate organisms, or taking no account of them at all. On the other hand, people may have a social relationship without ever encountering each other face to face or even communicating directly (Anderson and O'Gorman, 1983).

Fiske furthermore distinguishes *asocial interactions*, in which people use other people purely as a means to some ulterior end. In asocial relations one party treats the other merely as an object, a means to an end, and the other submits out of fear, pain, hunger, or the like. Although the relation models theory does not include these asocial relationships, they play an important role in understanding why people do not share knowledge.

Figure 6.1 illustrates that the null relationship and the asocial relationship are actually extremes on continua of two variables. The nature of a relationship can vary from social to asocial and the intensity of a

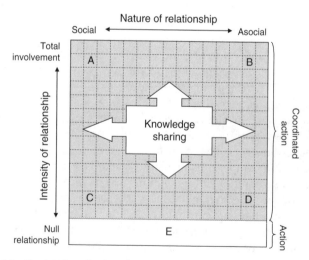

*Figure 6.1*  Knowledge sharing determined by the nature and intensity of a relationship

relationship can vary from a null relationship to total involvement. A third variable, albeit one not depicted in the figure, is the formality or strictness with which people observe the standards of whatever model they are using. As Figure 6.1 indicates, knowledge sharing always implies co-ordinated action within any kind of relationship; sharing knowledge during an intensive workshop among colleagues could be an example of A; a bank clerk sharing the secret code of the bank vault with the robber while being threatened by his gun could be an example of B; C could refer to a situation where someone has a nice brief chat with a stranger and D could refer to a call centre that bothers you with asking stupid questions about a product or service; riding a bike is an example of action that does not involve any relationship nor knowledge sharing. However, note that all these examples could be modelled according to any of the four described relational models.

## Diversity and complexity in social relations

It might seem impossible that only four relational models can explain all complex relationships. However, there are different ways in which diversity based on the four models is established. (After all, there are also just four bases in the genetic code of DNA.) There are three aspects of the construction of social relationships that result in a limitless variety of surface manifestations of a limited set of relatively simple underlying models.

First, the models are in one sense 'empty' principles, which can be realized in behavior only within the context of certain arbitrary cultural rules. *Cultural implementation rules* are rules that stipulate when each model applies and rules that stipulate how to execute each model. Each of the four elementary models can be realized only in some culture-specific manner. There are no culture-free implementations of the models. Each model leaves open a number of parameters that require some determinant setting. Within CS relationships one has to determine what is shared collectively and what is not (for example, goods or thoughts). Within AR relationships the important question is whether people are ranked by age, gender, race, inheritance of or succession to office, or various kinds of achieved status. Questions like 'What counts as equal?' and 'What is appropriate delay before reciprocating?' need to be answered within EM relationships. MP relationships have to determine how prices are set, what counts as an offer of sale or bid to buy and when one can acceptably withdraw from an agreement.

Furthermore, people in different societies commonly use different models and combinations of models in any given domain or context.

Within many Western countries the husband–wife relationship, for example, is primarily based on EM, whereas other cultures consider it as normal that the husband dominates his wife (AR). Relations and operations that are socially significant in one relational structure may not be meaningful in certain others. For example, within a CS mindset the idea of private ownership has no meaning at all, whereas within a MP mindset it is hard to understand that people share goods free of charge.

Second, the four models are ordinarily combined in various ways to yield complex structures, which, though analytically reducible to the four fundamental structures, nevertheless may have emergent properties as a combination. It is quite rare to find a relationship that draws on only one relational model. People commonly use a combination of models, out of which people construct complex social relations. For example, colleagues may share office supplies freely with each other (CS), work on a task at which one is an expert and imperiously directs the other (AR), divide equally the amounts of carpooling rides (EM), and transfer a laptop computer from one to the other for a price determined by its utility or exchange value (MP). Thus, each of the models is operating simultaneously at different levels of a social relationship. Figure 6.2 illustrates how the four basic relational models can be distinguished and how these relations can be combined in hybrid relations.

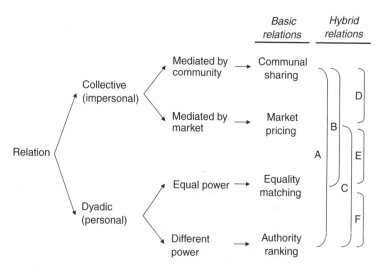

*Figure 6.2*   Distinction between the four basic relational models and their hybrid variations

Third, the recursive application of the same model at successive embedded levels results in a limitless potential for elaboration of any one model. This aspect is further discussed in the section about infocultures.

Finally, the relational models in use are not static, but might change over time. Several theorists have described dynamic sequences of transition in which the dominant form of interaction changes from one of the relational models to another. The relationship between a given pair of people or among the members of a particular group is assumed to transform from MP to EM to CS, or from AR to CS, although sequences may vary. In a society, however, most writers suggest a sequence in the opposite direction that is some subset of the ordering, CS → AR → EM → MP, usually over historical spans of time (for example, transition from primitive tribe to capitalistic society).

## Implications for knowledge sharing

The previous sections have described the four fundamental relational models and how these can establish diverse and complex relationships. Furthermore, it has been asserted that the dynamics of knowledge sharing can be organized according to these relational models. Since the relation models theory intends to describe the elementary 'grammar' of social life in general rather than focussing on the knowledge sharing issue specifically, this section describes how the theory can be specified for knowledge sharing. It is explained how each model conceptualizes knowledge and how each model determines the principles behind knowledge sharing.

Within CS relationships, knowledge is perceived as a common resource, rather than as one's individual property. Knowledge is not personally marked, since it belongs to the whole group. Knowledge is freely shared among people belonging to the same group or dyad, following the idea of 'What's mine is yours'. Whereas the CS relationship described by Fiske primarily refers to an almost pure type of altruism, we suggest a type of communal sharing based on the idea of generalized exchange (Mauss, 1925). The underlying assumption of people sharing knowledge within such a CS relationship is that they expect an unspecified favour from an unspecified group member within an unspecified time span in return. By sharing knowledge within the group or dyad one 'receives' the potential helpfulness of the group in future. The motivation for sharing knowledge is based on intimacy. Knowledge is shared because one thinks that someone else might need it or because someone asks for it. There are no hidden motives for (not) sharing knowledge. The only reason for not sharing knowledge is when one is not capable of sharing or when the desirability for sharing knowledge is unknown.

In order to share knowledge according to CS principles, a bounded group sharing some common substance (such as kinship) is required. It is important to realize that this common substance between people can be based on different *objects* of cohesion and on different *grounds* for cohesion (Lammers, 1964). Although CS is frequently not the dominant structure for sharing knowledge organization-wide (for example object is the university), there might exist some subsets within the organization where knowledge is being shared based on CS (for example object is department within the university). Furthermore, people might share knowledge with others according to CS since they feel connected with them based on shared ideological objectives (ideal cohesion, for example within a political movement), based on shared activities (instrumental cohesion, like between academic staff) or based on solidarity (social cohesion, like fine working environment).

Within AR relationships knowledge is perceived as a means to display rank differences, whether rank is based on, for example, formal power, expertise or age. The higher a person's rank, the better access to better knowledge. A person higher in rank who shares knowledge with someone lower in rank demonstrates his nobility and largesse and expects to get authority or status in return. A subordinate shares knowledge because either he has to or because he wants to ingratiate himself with his superior. In both cases the subordinate can expect a kind of 'pastoral care' or career perspective in return. In this respect knowledge sharing is motivated by power differences. People are less or not willing to share knowledge when it can change their balance of power negatively. 'Negative' knowledge is frequently withhold by window dressing behavior and a knowledge overload may originate from largesse and sweet-talk.

Within EM relationships knowledge is perceived as a means of levelling out knowledge sharing efforts. The principle behind knowledge sharing within an EM relation is based on the exchange of knowledge for similar knowledge. Knowledge is being shared because someone else has shared something similar before or because one expects something similar in return. It is the desire for equality that motivates knowledge sharing in these circumstances. In this respect one can morally oblige a person to share something in return by sharing knowledge oneself. People are less or not willing to share knowledge when nothing similar can be shared in return within a reasonable time span.

Within MP relationships knowledge is perceived as a commodity which has a value and can be traded. Knowledge is being shared because one receives a compensation for it (not being similar knowledge or status). People are motivated to share knowledge by achievement. When the perceived compensation is not high enough, people are less or not willing to share knowledge. In Appendix 1 at the end of this chapter the implications of the four relational models for understanding knowledge sharing are summarized.

Let's illustrate the different knowledge sharing principles for professional knowledge workers. Whereas the university is expected to be a place where knowledge is being shared freely, following the rules of CS, the reality demonstrates that the CS mechanism is hardly present within universities. Of course, scientists are very eager to share their knowledge with other people from the academic community, but only when they are being rewarded for it by prestige (AR) or money (MP). So sharing ideas through scientific publications associated with author names is common practice, just like contributing to a lucrative publication. However, freely sharing knowledge with colleagues in the pre-publication phase (CS) is less likely to occur. In the day-to-day activities of academics, knowledge is commonly shared with colleagues according to EM principles. Only when they acquire valuable knowledge from colleagues, will they share similar knowledge with them (and vice versa). Regularly, academics feel more cohesiveness with the peers who are working on their own research topic than with people from unrelated departments or with the entire university.

A similar line of reasoning exists for ambitious professional consultants. Since these knowledge workers frequently feel more connected with the consulting profession and their own career than with the consulting firm they are temporarily working for, they like to receive intellectual recognition for their own work (AR) more often than a financial reward (MP). After all, they already have achieved a minimum level of income. In contrast to the academics, consultants are frequently not personally rewarded for their intellectual effort. The intellectual outcome is considered to be 'owned' by the whole organization (CS) and therefore the company name is connected to it, rather than the name of the consultant who created it. Some consultancy firms have succeeded in creating an intensive ideal cohesiveness, resulting in CS practices of knowledge sharing.

This section ends with some remarks about the null relation and the asocial relation, since they explain, among other things, why knowledge is not being shared. As has been described before, when there is a null relation between people, knowledge cannot be shared by definition. In these situations it is interesting to find out why there is no longer a relation between the actors involved and if this is problematic. In addition, the degree to which the actors are relating for the sake of the relationship itself (social) or are using each other as means to asocial ends determines if and how knowledge is being shared. In the long run, asocial relationships will discourage or even prevent knowledge sharing.

## Infoculture: recursive application of social relations

To date, the relational models have been described primarily as the mechanisms behind knowledge sharing between individual relationships. One can usually generalize such a relationship towards one dominant model of social relations. The relation between a husband and wife, for example, might be primarily based on EM, even when they also act according to the other models.

The models can also be used to delineate the knowledge sharing mechanisms within organizational settings. After all, organizational actors are embedded within a network of social relations. When the majority of actors within an organizational setting is sharing knowledge according to one particular relational model, the organizational setting can be typified by that dominant model of social relations.

Based on a process of institutionalization (Berger and Luckmann, 1966) not only relationships and organizational settings can be typified by one dominant relational model, but also a country or even a society. Whereas many Western countries are inclined towards MP thinking, for example, many countries from the Middle East are more based on AR.

Let us now focus on the significance of the relational models at the level of organizational settings. Different organizational settings could be characterized according to different dominant relational models. The assumptions underlying a community of practice, for example, are frequently based on CS. In a similar way one might argue that people in a formal work group interrelate according to AR and that project members interrelate according to MP. Partly this can be explained by the time scope of the different organizational settings. The more often people interact, the longer the relationship endures, and the greater the number and diversity of domains in which they interact, the less likely they are to use MP and the more likely they are to relate in a CS mode; EM is in between (Fiske, 1991).

In practice one frequently explains a lack of knowledge sharing by saying that 'there exists a culture that discourage knowledge sharing'. And indeed this 'knowledge-sharing culture' is of crucial importance, but commonly remains rather abstract. In this respect, the four relational models can be seen as different completions of what Ciborra (Ciborra and Patriotta, 1996) refers to as an infoculture and specify this rather abstract, yet interesting theoretical notion.

Although it is possible to use any of the four models to organize any aspect of social relations, some relational models are more obvious to occur in particular situations. For example, work organized along CS lines lacks the long-term productive potential characteristic of division of labour based on differentiated complementarity. Whereas EM is widely used as a means of obtaining supplementary labour at times of peak demand or of tasks that require massed labour, it is never the primary mode of organizing the core group for the entire cycle of production. This is probably because a complete cycle of production can rarely be broken down into tasks that are all the same, and because often there is no great functional advantage in balanced reciprocal exchange of the same task. Market systems governed by prices can be the most efficient mechanism for organizing large-scale production and exchange. In part this is because MP facilitates division of labour and technical specialization, and in part because of its emergent property of conveying information about utilities and costs, permitting the use of this information to guide allocation decisions. On the other hand, many kinds of public goods cannot be produced and allocated by MP alone.

Thus, the four models of human relations are dysfunctional for some purposes in some contexts. Furthermore, they do not work equally well in every domain. Let's take a decision making process as an example. Within CS decision making is based on seeking consensus, within AR relations on authoritative fiat, within EM relations on one person, one vote, and within MP relations on rational cost–benefit analysis. When quick decision making is required, AR is more appropriate than CS, since this last model is cumbersome and time consuming.

## Conflicts: mismatch of relational models

Hitherto, it has been presumed that individuals, groups or organizations sharing knowledge are operating according to the same relational model without problems and that the technologies supporting knowledge sharing are in line with the relational model of their users. However, in practice the distinctness and the congruence of the relational models are not always assured. Three situations can be distinguished where a mismatch of relational models might result in a social conflict: (a) people share knowledge according to the same relational model but disagree about how the model is applied, (b) people share knowledge according to different relational models and (c) the technology or organizational structure supposed to support knowledge sharing is designed according to a different rationale than the relational model of its users. All three situations are now illustrated.

In the first type of situation social conflicts can occur when the people involved have different interpretations of the same relational model in use. Conflicts are the result of applying different cultural implementation rules. An example of such a social conflict in organizational settings is the disturbed relation between an employee from the IT helpdesk and a needy manager from another department. Both individuals might think that their relation is based on AR. The IT-er has a technical expertise that the manager is lacking and the manager has a formal power that supersedes the influence of the IT-er. Thus, the variable on which the hierarchy is based is different. Both are acting and sharing knowledge as if they are the higher in rank, ending in a social conflict. The result is that both evaluate the other's behaviour as inappropriate and both experience a lack of understanding. Similar conflicts might occur between young, recently graduated academics and grown old senior employees, or between a secretary with many years of experience and her new manager.

A second example deals with a different interpretation of how to balance a mutually approved EM relationship. When one person has shared a significant amount of knowledge with someone else and this person only receives insignificant knowledge in return or significant knowledge with an inappropriate delay, a social conflict might occur. This social conflict can be resolved in several ways. The person can continue to share knowledge with the other, so that the relationship might shift from an EM to an AR model. The person acquires a certain expert status implicitly, due to the developed imbalance of knowledge. Or the person can be inclined not to share any knowledge with that person anymore in future. Additional knowledge needs to be shared in order to resolve the conflicts.

The second type of situation results in more serious social conflicts, since the actors involved share knowledge according to different relational models. If one person shares knowledge with someone else, while implicitly adopting a CS model, he would feel offended when the other is asking money for his contribution (MP). When a person starts to behave as an expert to his colleagues (AR), he can expect opposition of them when they are used to share knowledge according to EM.

In the third type of situation conflicts can occur since the technology or organizational structure are designed according to different relational models than their users'. This can be illustrated by considering the development of knowledge repositories in order to share best practices. The rationale behind the design of most current knowledge repositories is based on CS. Knowledge is considered to be a pooled resource that is accessible by everyone and knowledge is considered to be freely shared with others where possible. When the people involved do actually interrelate according to the model of CS, then there is no problem. However, in situations where there exists a difference between the assumed CS rationale behind the technology and the actual relational model in use, problems might occur. For example, when people relate with one another based on AR, they might have difficulties with using a technology that is based on CS. Since information is accessible by everybody including one's superiors, they avoid the knowledge system and share their ideas informally through other media. People do not want to be adjudicated on the basis of some informal premature documents they have put in the system. People acting upon EM have other reasons for (not) contributing to knowledge systems. A frequently expressed argument is that 'people do not want to bring more than they get'. Especially employees who have no intention to remain in an organization for a long time, for example, do not value the importance of retaining experiences for future use by their colleagues, since they won't benefit themselves. People who share knowledge according to MP only contribute to the knowledge repository when they receive an appropriate reward for it. A repository based on CS does not provide such a reward.

Different strategies can be followed to solve these kinds of problems. One can try to change the existing relational model of the user in order to fit the technology to be used, one can try to redesign the existing technology in order to fit the relational model of its user, or a combination of both. The first situation requires a cognitive change of the users which is a time-consuming process, whereas the second situation requires a fundamental reconsideration about the functionalities of the technology. Obviously, in practice it should not be an either or choice, but a combination of both strategies.

Several technical adjustments of the knowledge system can be proposed. The problem within an AR relation might be solved by implementing a double-layer structure in the knowledge system; only the final content is made accessible by everybody, while the rest is only accessible by colleagues of the project team (Ciborra and Patriotta, 1996). In the EM situation, for example, one could redesign the technology in such a way that people can only consult the knowledge system when they also contribute something. In a MP situation people

Textbox 2

---

**Implementing communities**

The last two decennia, a whole range of organizations have reorganized themselves into team-based organizations, since there was widespread agreement that multidisciplinary working was essential in the new competitive environment (Orlikowski, Yates, Okamura and Fujimoto, 1995). While moving from a functionally based company, where experts were located amongst others with similar backgrounds and interests, to one based on project teams, they found out that much cross-fertilization of ideas within disciplines were lost (Blackler, Crump and McDonald, 1999). An increasing number of organizations have tried to solve their problem by creating communities as a way of maintaining connections with peers, continuing the abilities of specialists to work at the forefront of their own fields (Wenger, 1998). Appealing historic examples (Orr, 1990; Wenger and Snyder, 2000) have probably contributed to the desire of many organizations to implement similar communities within or between organizational settings. Although communities benefit from cultivation (Wenger and Snyder, 2000), their fundamentally informal and self-organizing nature makes a simple managerial implementation almost impossible (management paradox). And indeed, in practice many organizations are struggling with facilitating communities and the expected advantages for the knowledge sharing process do not always come off.

---

might be stimulated to contribute to the system by providing financial bonuses. These suggestions for changing the technology should be accompanied by an appropriate change of the relational model (infoculture) of the users.

Just as the rationale of a technology needs to be in line with the relational model of its users, in addition the rationale of the organizational structure needs to fit the relational model of the way people share knowledge. Within organizations with a dominant MP infoculture, it is very hard or even impossible to implement a community of practice based on CS. Thus, reward systems, supporting technologies, organizational hierarchies need to be in line with the relational models in use and vice versa. It is useless to reward people according to MP when they relate to one another based on Authority Ranking (AR).

## Research model

This section presents a conceptual research model for investigating knowledge sharing in practice. The vertical relations in Figure 6.3 describe the argument made in this chapter. It has been argued that the different models of social relations determine the structure behind knowledge sharing processes and that cultural implementation rules are essential for the realization of any relational model in practice. The horizontal relations are implicitly assumed in this chapter, but are important for placing the argument in context. The horizontal relations are now briefly described (for reasons of clarity, not all relations are depicted in Figure 6.3).

In this chapter the focus has been on knowledge sharing within organizational settings. In another paper (Boer, Baalen and Kumar, 2002) we describe how different organizational settings can be described as the context within which knowledge is being shared by using an activity theory approach. However, it is important to realize that knowledge sharing is not an end in itself but a means to an end. The first and most obvious reason for sharing knowledge is that the knowledge is required to execute one's task (activity performance), since the required knowledge is distributed among different people. The need for knowledge sharing depends, among other factors, on the nature of the task (see, for example, information processing theory of Galbraith, 1973).

Besides sharing knowledge in order to execute one's task, a second reason for sharing knowledge is to respond to changes that organizational settings are dealing with continuously (for example, change of task formulation, change of personnel, change of technologies). Such changes might result in knowledge tensions or breakdowns (for example, disagreement about task description, social conflict between people due to acting according to different relational models, incompatibility of technologies). Consequently, it might be necessary to share knowledge in order to solve these kinds of tensions and breakdowns by for example clarifying the problem, suggesting solutions or evaluating alternatives.

As has been addressed in the introduction to this chapter, there are several other factors besides the relational models for explaining why people do or do not share knowledge. However, taking the different relational models into account as principles behind knowledge sharing

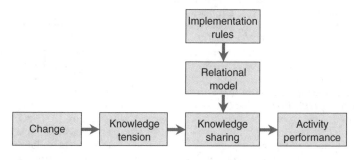

*Figure 6.3* Conceptual model for investigating knowledge sharing

is considered to be crucial, yet the relational aspects of knowledge sharing are frequently underexposed in literature. Of special interest is the link between both types of research, that is how the relational models are influenced by and influence individual, organizational, technical and knowledge factors. For example, when knowledge is specific and uncodified, it is almost impossible to share it according to MP principles. Also the effort to acquire knowledge influences the relational model people will adopt for sharing this knowledge; 'Low profile' knowledge like knowing how to use the coffee machine is likely to take place according to CS, whereas an electronic presentation about a specific subject is more likely to take place according to EM or MP.

This section concludes with some remarks about the way that data can be collected in practice. Table 6.2 describes the major steps one can follow when investigating knowledge sharing in organizational settings. An important issue is how a relational model can be mapped. Fiske argues that there is only one criterion for determining what kind of social relationship (if any) it is that people are engaged in: 'The trick is to figure out what the devil *they* think they are up to.' Thus, the unit of analysis, the locus of the social relationships, is cognitive (in the broad sense). The models are goals, ideals, criteria, rules or guidelines that, under certain circumstances, conceivably may not correspond closely to what any particular observer sees in the manifest action or its outcome. The standard for determining what kind of social relation is operative is not the concrete result of the action either in the short run or the long term;

*Table 6.2* Practical steps for investigating the relational dimension behind knowledge sharing

1. Determine whether there is a social (or an asocial) relation between the actors under investigation. If so, describe how this relationship has developed over time. If not, explain why not and indicate the implications for the organization (position the relation in Figure 6.1);
2. Indicate what (mix of) relational models are actually operative between these actors with respect to different types of knowledge sharing in different phases (select from Figure 6.2);
3. Specify the specific cultural implementation rules of these relational models with respect to knowledge sharing and indicate how these have changed over time (see section 3);
4. Make a detailed description of how knowledge is being shared. Try to find out when people do not share knowledge and why. Give special attention to the three types of conflicts that can occur (see sections 4 and 6);
5. Compare the findings of the actual situation with any other situation, e.g. the dominant infoculture, the proposed or desired situation or the situation after implementing a new supporting technology or organizational structure.

the standard is the conception each person has or what the relationship is (or ought to be). Consequently, different people may reckon that different relationships are in effect. Furthermore, so long as people believe that they are interacting with another person, they may apply the model and operate in a social mode even when no other person is really there.

## Concluding remarks

The message of this chapter is to emphasize the relational and motivational nature of knowledge sharing. Although individual, organizational and technical factors and the nature of knowledge contribute to the understanding of knowledge sharing, much of its dynamics remains unexplained. One important reason for this is that current research about knowledge sharing has been guided largely by one model of social relations, whether this is for example one of altruism or one of rational cost–benefit analysis.

By adopting the four relational models distinguished by the relation models theory of Fiske (communal sharing, authority ranking, equality matching and market pricing) new insights are obtained. It has been described how knowledge is being shared differently within each of the four relational models. Explanations are provided, for example, for why it is so difficult to implement communities of practice within organizational settings based on market pricing, why people do not contribute to knowledge repositories and why it is so difficult to change the infoculture within organizational settings.

The cultural implementation rules, determining when each relational model is applied and how each model is executed, play a central role in the way knowledge is being shared. Some of these implementation rules have been described in this chapter, but much additional research is required to further specify these rules. The research model and the practical guidelines for investigating knowledge sharing presented here are just a start and need further refinement. We would like to invite researchers to join our search for the implications of different models of social relations for understanding knowledge sharing.

It is our conviction that in order to really understand knowledge sharing, one needs to know according to what relational model knowledge is being shared. Consequently, one can better design technologies that support knowledge sharing and design the structure of organizational settings. On the other hand, by knowing the assumptions about the social relations underlying the technical and organizational infrastructure, one can better understand why knowledge is or is not being shared.

## Appendix 1  Knowledge sharing according to different models of social relations

| | Communal sharing | Authority ranking | Equality matching | Market pricing |
|---|---|---|---|---|
| *How is knowledge being perceived?* | As a common resource, rather than as one's individual property. | As a means to display one's superiority; 'Knowledge is power'. | As a means of exchange for other knowledge. | As a commodity which has a value and can be traded. |
| *What are the implications of this perception for the knowledge sharing process?* | Knowledge is freely shared among people belonging to the same group; 'What's mine is yours'. | By sharing knowledge one can demonstrate one's nobility and largesse. The higher a person's rank, the better access to better knowledge. | The knowledge sharing process becomes dependent on similar knowledge sharing processes from the past and/or in the future. | The knowledge sharing process becomes dependent on the value of the knowledge. |
| *Why is knowledge being shared? (push vs pull)* | Because one thinks that someone else might need it; because someone asks for it. Motivated by intimacy. | Because it is requested by someone in a higher rank; because the superior has to share it. Motivated by power. | Because someone else has shared something similar before; because one expects something in return. Motivated by desire for equality. | Because one receives a compensation for it (not something similar). Motivated by achievement. |
| *When might knowledge not be shared even though it is desirable?* | When one is not capable of sharing it or when the desirability is unknown. | When it can change the balance of power negatively. | When nothing similar can be shared in return within a reasonable time span. | When the perceived compensation is not high enough. |

| | | | | |
|---|---|---|---|---|
| *What are the opportunistic motives for (not) sharing knowledge?* | No opportunistic motives. | 'Negative' knowledge is withheld; window dressing. Knowledge overload may originate from largesse and sweet-talk. | By sharing knowledge with someone, one can morally oblige this person to share something in return. | By sharing knowledge below the market value, one might create moral commitment. |
| *How are problems resulting from knowledge sharing being solved?* | By seeking consensus. | By authoritative fiat. | By one person, one vote. | By rational cost-benefit analysis. |
| *By who is knowledge being shared?* | By kinship, minimal groups, national identities (knowledge is not being shared with outsiders). | By people with different hierarchical positions (ranks). | By people at the same horizontal or vertical position in the division of labor. | By the people who receive and provide the compensation. |
| *With what emotion is knowledge being shared?* | It goes without saying, based on idealism. | Mostly not spontaneous but based on sense of duty. | Unproblematic as long as the time span between the return is not too long. | Unproblematic as long as the compensation is appropriate. |
| *What moment is knowledge being shared?* | Unspecified, any time when needed. | Immediately when the superior requests it and otherwise when he has time. | Implicitly specified in (short) future: when there is a (potential) mismatch in sharing. | Direct or at specified moment in time (in contract). |
| *How is knowledge being shared?* | Diverse ways, but in a personal way. | Diverse ways (brief and short). | In a similar way as before or as expected in future. | In a way it is demanded. |
| *Examples of knowledge that is typically being shared* | In principle everything. | Factual knowledge. | Personal background stories. | Functional expertise. |

# References

Adler, P.S. and Kwon, S.-W. (2002) Social capital: prospects for a new concept, *Academy of Management Review*, 27: 17–40.

Anderson, B. and O'Gorman, R. (1983) *Imagined Communities: Reflections on the Origin and Spread of Nationalism*. London: Verso.

Berger, P.L. and Luckmann, T. (1966) *The Social Construction of Reality: a Treatise in the Sociology of Knowledge*. Garden City, NY: Doubleday.

Blackler, F., Crump, N. and McDonald, S. (1999) Managing experts and competing through innovation: an activity theoretical analysis, *Organization*, 6: 5–31.

Blau, P. (1963) *The Dynamics of Bureaucracy*. Chicago: University of Chicago Press.

Blau, P. (1964) *Exchange and Power in Social Life*. New York: Wiley.

Boer, N.I., Baalen, P.J.v., and Kumar, K. (2002) An activity theory approach for studying the situatedness of knowledge sharing, *Hawaii International Conference on System Sciences*. Hawaii: IEEE Computer Society Press.

Boisot, M.H. (1998) *Knowledge Assets: Securing Competitive Advantage in the Information Economy*. Oxford: Oxford University Press.

Brown, J.S. and Duguid, P. (1991) Organizational learning and communities of practice, *Organizational Science*, 2: 40–57.

Buber, M. (1987 [1923]) *I and thou*. New York: Collier-Macmillan.

Ciborra, C.U. and Patriotta, G. (1996) Groupware and teamwork in new product development: the case of a consumer goods multinational. In C.U. Ciborra (ed.), *Groupware and Teamwork*. New York: John Wiley & Sons.

Clark, M.S. and Mills, J. (1979) Interpersonal attraction in exchange and communal relationships. *Journal of Personality and Social Psychology*, 37: 12–24.

Cohen, W. and Levinthal, D. (1990) Absorbtive capacity: a new perspective on learning and innovation, *Administrative Science Quarterly*, 35: 128–52.

Daft, R.L. and Lengel, R.H. (1984) Information richness: a new approach to managerial behavior and organizational design, *Research in Organizational Behavior*, 6: 191–233.

Davenport, T.H. and Prusak, L. (1998) *Working Knowledge: How Organizations Manage What They Know*. Boston: Harvard Business School Press.

Durkheim, E. (1966 [1897]) *Suicide: a Study in Sociology*. New York: Free Press.

Fiske, A.P. (1991) *Structure of Social Life: the Four Elementary Forms of Human Relations*. The Free Press.

Fiske, A.P. (1992) The four elementary forms of sociality: framework for a unified theory of social relations, *Psychological Review*, 99: 689–723.

Galbraith, J.R. (1973) *Designing Complex Organizations*. London: Addison-Wesley.

Giddens, A. (1984) *The Constitution of Society*. University of California Press.

Grant, R.M. (1996) Toward a knowledge-based theory of the firm, *Strategic Management Journal*, 17: 109–22.

Hagstrom, W.O. (1965) *The Scientific Community*. New York: Basic Books.

Hansen, M.T., Nohria, N. and Tierney, T. (1999) What's your strategy for managing knowledge?, *Harvard Business Review*, 106–16.

Huber, G.P. (1991) Organizational learning: the contribution process and the literatures, *Organization Science*, 2: 88–115.

Krech, D. and Crutchfield, R.S. (1965) *Elements of Psychology*. New York: Knopf.

Lammers, C.J. (1964) Uiterlijke samenhang en bindingskracht van de organisatie, *Sociologie van de organisatie*. Leiden: Rijksuniversiteit Leiden.

Lane, P.J. and Lubatkin, M. (1998) Relative absorbtive capacity and interorganizational learning, *Strategic Management Journal*, 19: 461–77.

Latour, B. (1987) *Science in Action*. Cambridge: Harvard University Press.

Leary, T.F. (1957) *Interpersonal Diagnosis of Personality: a Functional Theory and Methodology for Personality Evaluation*. New York: Ronald Cress.

Malinowski, B. (1961 [1922]) *Argonauts of the Western Pacific: an Account of Native Enterprise and Adventure in the Archipelagoes of Melanesian New Guinea*. New York: Dutton.

Mauss, M. (1925) *The Gift: Forms and Functions of Exchange in Archaic Societies*. London: Routledge and Kegan Paul.

Moenaert, R.K., Caeldries, A. and Wauters, E. (2000) Communication flows in international product innovation teams, *Journal of Product Innovation Management*, 17: 360–77.

Orlikowski, W.J., Yates, J., Okamura, K. and Fujimoto, M. (1995) Shaping electronic communication: the metastructuring of technology in the context of use, *Organization Science*, 6: 423–44.

Orr, J.E. (1990) Sharing knowledge, celebrating identity: community memory in a service culture. In D. Middleton and D. Edwards (eds), *Collective Remembering: Memory in Society*. London: Sage.

Piaget, J. (1973 [1932]) *Le jugement moral chez l'enfant*. Paris: Presses Universitaries de France.

Polanyi, K. (1957 [1944]) *The Great Transformation: the Political and Economic Origins of Our Time*. New York: Rinehart.

Raymond, E.S. (2001) *The Cathedral and the Bazaar: Musings on Linux and Open Source by an Accidental Revolutionary*. California: O'Reilly Publications.

Salins, M. (1965) On the sociology of primitive exchange. In M. Banton (ed.), *The Relevance of Models for Social Anthropology*. London: Tavistock.

Szulanski, G. (1996) Exploring international stickiness: impediments to the transfer of best practice within the firm, *Strategic Management Journal*, 17: 27–43.

Tönnies, F. (1988 [1887]) *Community and Society (Gemeinschaft und Gesellschaft)* New Brunswick, NJ: Transaction Books.

Udy, S.H. (1959) *Organization of Work: a Comparative Analysis of Production among Nonindustrial Peoples*. New Haven, CT: Human Relations Area File Press.

Weber, M. (1975 [1916]) The social psychology of the world religions. In H.H. Gerth and C.W. Mills (eds), *From Max Weber: Essays in Sociology*. New York: Oxford University Press.

Wenger, E. (1998) *Communities of Practice: Learning, Meaning and Identity*. Cambridge: Cambridge University Press.

Wenger, E.C. and Snyder, W.M. (2000) Communities of practice: the organizational frontier, *Harvard Business Review*, 78: 139–45.

# 7

# A Knowledge-Sharing Approach to Organizational Change: A Critical Discourse Analysis

*Lesley Treleaven*

> Organisations do not simply work, they are *made* to work.
>
> Tsoukas and Chia (2002: 577)

## Introduction

Knowledge management in organizations has been gaining attention recently for its potential to maximize competitive advantage through deploying organizational knowledge more effectively. However, how knowledge is created, disrupted, shared, lost and re-created *within* the transformative struggles of organizational restructuring processes has, as yet, received less attention. In turn, the impact of knowledge management processes on the restructured organizations remains largely unexamined in empirical studies of organizational change. Such research, however, is crucial to developing organizational learning and capabilities to face uncertain futures in dynamic business environments.

The pragmatic approach taken in most management studies does not conceptualize knowledge management as a social process that is deeply embedded within complex power relations. In fact, knowledge sharing by individuals, within and between groups, and across and beyond organizations, is taken for granted as naturally-occurring and unproblematic. Such conceptualizations have significant effects on studies of knowledge management approached from the fields of both information systems and organizational studies.

First, from an information systems (IS) perspective, when knowledge management is not recognized as a social process situated within the social relations of power, problems related to knowledge sharing are often understood in technological terms. Thus failure to share knowledge is typically attributed to inadequate communication means and a lack of knowledge transfer. As a result, companies often invest in a range of communication technologies (Storey and Barnett, 2000; Schultze and Boland, 2000). However, investments in sophisticated technical 'solutions', such as groupware enabling anonymous participation in organizational change processes, do not necessarily address the complex social conditions within which people participate in their workplaces. Not only do such approaches to knowledge sharing prove of little value to organizations, as numerous studies have demonstrated (see, for instance, Galliers and Newell, 2001; Swan, Newell, Scarborough and Hislop, 1999); indeed, they may add to the 'problem'.[1]

Second, within the broad domain of organizational studies (OS), organizational change processes often meet with what much of the traditional management literature terms as 'resistance' and 'organizational politics'. Addressing the failure of professionals, committed to continuous improvement, to engage in the reflective practice of double-loop learning, Argyris (1990) develops the concept of organizational defensive routines. Arguably, Argyris emphasizes the social processes at work in organizational change. Nevertheless, characteristic of much change management literature, the social relations of power as they function between people required to share knowledge in organizations requires better conceptualization for empirical investigation. For not only do power relations shape the interactions between people, but they also profoundly influence the nature of knowledge and the dynamics of knowledge sharing.

Third, in contrast to both these IS and OS traditions, Foucauldian post-structuralist theory (1980, 1983) attends to the ways in which power and knowledge are both socially constituted and mutually constituting. Thus Foucault's formulation of the power/knowledge nexus can be used to open up questions about the social relations of power in creating and sharing new knowledge required for successful organizational change. Furthermore, knowledge sharing practices may be improved by investigation into how organizational knowledge is excluded, over-looked, disrupted and lost during organizational change processes.

This empirical, interdisciplinary investigation therefore seeks to extend Foucauldian applications of power/knowledge to an emerging domain where knowledge management, organizational change and critical studies in management and organizations intersect. For Foucauldian work has been a growing source of postmodernist exploration within organizational theory (Chia, 2000; Chan and Garrick, 2002; Clegg, 1987; Hassard and Rowlinson, 2002; McKinlay and Starkey, 1998; Knights, 2002; Townley, 1993 and 2002) and been useful in a range of empirical studies of organizations (Brewis, 2001; Brocklehurst, 2001; Fletcher, 1998; Knights and Morgan, 1991; Mahmood, 1994; McKinlay, 2002; Townley, 1993; Xu, 2000) whilst also undergoing considerable critique (Hassard and Kelemen, 2002; Marsden, 1993; Newton, 1998; Rowlinson and Carter, 2002; Wray-Bliss, 2002).

This study therefore adopts a knowledge-based approach to organizational restructuring by investigating, from a Foucauldian perspective, knowledge sharing in one organization undergoing extensive change. Within a context of university restructuring, academics were invited by the University executive to engage in a knowledge sharing process to propose new schools. In the *Guidelines for School Formation Process* (GSFP), the Vice Chancellor (VC) declared:

> It is intended that staff will think laterally and creatively about the opportunities the restructure presents, meet and talk with colleagues on other campuses and design potential Schools which are innovative, flexible, intellectually coherent and capable of developing and adapting to a profoundly transforming educational environment. (GSFP, 2000: 1)

This school formation process called for staff to engage reflectively, to develop and articulate shared understandings with their colleagues about their future school's disciplinary interests, directions and name, and left open the possibility for new, emergent developments of school collations in the process. Why did this opportunity for knowledge sharing fail?

There are six parts to the chapter. The first part discusses Foucauldian theorizations of power and knowledge that form the theoretical framework for the case study. Second, the field site and research methodology are described. Third, the discursive contexts within which the University was situated, and then the competing and contradictory discourses, within which the School of Management was formed, are examined. Next, power/knowledge relations in the formation of the School are analysed. Then the contradictions that disrupted effective knowledge sharing in the study are discussed. Finally, this study highlights how research into knowledge management processes can benefit from applications of Foucauldian poststructuralist theory and discourse analysis.

## Foucauldian theorizations of power and power/knowledge

Better ways of understanding unsuccessful attempts to encourage knowledge sharing may take into account the nexus between power and knowledge. Thus, some useful analytical tools for investigating knowledge sharing in organizations may lie in Foucauldian understandings of power and knowledge (Cooper, 1994; Foucault, 1980 and 1983; McNay, 1992). For with their insistence on the importance of language and practices, Foucauldian poststructuralist theories attempt to come to terms with power as a central problematic in the transformation of social relations that, in turn, discursively shape institutions, such as universities.

Rather than power being conceptualized as a fixed object which some people, institutions or structures possess and which others do not, Foucault proposes that power is both dynamic and relational.

First, instead of trying to identify 'Who has power?' Foucault considers 'How is power exercised?' Accordingly, he explores how power is exercised through the social relations between people. This emphasis on the relational aspect of power between people has received considerable attention in the feminist literature (Gilligan, 1982; Hollway, 1984) for several decades. However, as Townley (1993) observes, general management studies have been slow to incorporate these understandings into studies of organizations where power relations are, nevertheless, underlined.

Second, Foucault (1983) argues that power is exercised indirectly through what we say (language) and what we do (practices) with the effects of power being manifested in people's actions. Power is therefore diffuse and ubiquitous, pervasively flowing through everyday life. Given these characteristics, the analogy between power and electricity is often drawn. For like electricity (power) shining light on the pages of a book we are reading, what we read and what we come to know is an everyday effect of electricity. In this way, power shapes not only what we know (knowledge) but also what we can know, the very objects themselves of our inquiry. It does this since knowledge is formed in and expressed through the language we use. In turn, language itself governs our ways of thinking (meaning, values) and acting (practices):

> The exercise of power itself creates and causes to emerge new objects of knowledge and accumulates new bodies of information... the exercise of power perpetually creates knowledge and, conversely, knowledge constantly induces effects of power ... It is not possible for power to be exercised without knowledge, it is impossible not to engender power. (Foucault, 1980: 52)

To summarize, power is thereby understood as productive of knowledges, meanings and values as well as practices, whilst knowledge is expressed, shared, contested and (re)constructed through language and practices. This power/knowledge nexus is one of Foucault's most widely known formulations.

As we shall see, power was exercised *productively* by the University executive in the creation of guidelines for forming new schools. Power was also exercised *relationally* in the way academics interacted with each other to produce proposals for new schools. Power was also exercised *discursively* throughout the school formation processes by the operation of the *Guidelines* that both opened up and constrained knowledge sharing. Conversely, these proposals (acts of knowledge creation) were assessed by the University executive who then exercised power *coercively* through the actions they took in the approval processes via facilitators. However, arguably, their final decision in favour of one School of Management was powerfully shaped by the executive's lack of collective knowledge to make clear distinctions between the proposals. In this way, power and knowledge are socially constituted and mutually constituting.

## The study

The study presented draws on a decade-long research project on the consultative processes employed in the comprehensive restructurings of one Australian university. Broadly, that research seeks, first, to identify the nature of the participation by the executive, staff and unions in the consultative processes; second, to understand how knowledge was created, communicated and shared during the organizational change processes; and third, to understand the role played by computer-mediated communications (e-mail, intranet and group systems software) in the process of communicating and sharing knowledge during the consultative processes.

### The field site

The research site is located at a 'new' Australian university, referred to here as the University of Eastern Australia (UEA). UEA was created as a federated university in 1989 by the amalgamation of three former Colleges of Advanced Education (CAE). This latest restructuring brings together these three former network members into one 'unified' University, necessitating the formation of four Colleges and 26 schools to replace the former faculties. The UEA's 35,000 students and 2,300 staff are scattered across six campuses situated variously from five to 65 kilometres apart around a large metropolitan centre.

## Research methodology

Comprehensive research data were gathered by three researchers, two of whom were participants in the school formation process. Thus, along with detailed field notes, many documents, e-mail messages, discussions and other materials produced in the University restructuring, were available. Additionally, twenty semi-structured interviews with staff were conducted to identify experiences, attitudes, feelings and insights regarding the school formation process and the extent of knowledge sharing using a range of media including e-mail and intranet. The interviews, lasting between one and two hours, spanned the range of executive, senior and academic staff involved in the restructuring and school formation; they were tape-recorded, transcribed and then checked by participants.

The data analysis was undertaken by initially reviewing these numerous texts and then by subjecting them to critical discourse analysis (Phillips and Hardy, 2002). Critical discourse analysis, as it is employed here drawing on Fairclough (1995), is a means of foregrounding for examination the taken-for-granted factors (historical, social, cultural, educational and political) that shape the language people use. Accordingly, the discourse analysis undertaken here is not only concerned with the content of these empirical materials as texts but also the history and contexts that surround their production, dissemination and reception, thereby constructing different 'realities' (Phillips and Hardy, 2002). This approach, moving in an iterative process between context and text (Fairclough, 1992), is distinguished by Phillips and Ravasi (1998) from social linguistic analysis and critical linguistic analysis, both of which focus more detailed linguistic attention on text. Social linguistic analysis (see, for example, O'Connor, 1995) examines the linguistic mechanisms and strategies that construct emerging discourse while critical linguistic analysis (for example, van Dijk, 1993; Wetherell and Potter, 1992) analyse the microdynamics of power as they construct specific talk and text. The empirical study in this chapter, with its understandings of power drawn from Foucault, is also distinguishable from other critical theory (employed by Lawrence, Phillips and Hardy, 1999) or cognitive orientations (adopted recently by van Dijk, 2003).

Critical discourse analysis was employed as one way of engaging usefully with rich, complex data and its representation of far more complex everyday lives in an organization. Thus the researcher's purpose in making such a discourse analysis was to go 'beyond the text', to foreground the conditions shaping the production of the communications over the 'actual' or 'realist tales' (van Maanen, 1988) that were then placed in the background. A macroanalysis therefore employed Foucauldian concepts and related deconstructive strategies first for critically reading the research data in an iterative process to identify the dominant and alternative discourses. Second, a subsequent analysis, drawing systematically on qualitative research methods (Miles and Huberman, 1994), sought to distinguish in data displays the identified discursive contexts as they operated at different levels of the University to create effects in the formation of the School of Management. A third microanalysis closely examined symptomatic texts for the effects of varying relations of power indicated in language and practices (Fairclough, 1992).

The researchers were positioned actively within the research process itself, renegotiating subjectivities in terms of how they 'read' the material as well as bringing 'insider knowledge' (Adler and Adler, 1987; Clifford and Marcus, 1986) to the empirical study. Such knowledges, though partial of course, are contextualized both historically and in terms of local meanings. Thus it is appropriate to declare the positions of the writer constructing this text as both a feminist collaborative action researcher and as a participant who supported the two schools proposal in its second of three iterations. As such, the way in which the tale has been reconstructed does not claim to represent the only 'truth' of the school formation. Its interest lies not in identifying any correct interpretation, but rather ways in which the dynamics of knowledge sharing may be better understood and enacted.

## Historical contexts and competing discourses

In this second part of the chapter, the discursive contexts within which the School of Management was formed are discussed at three levels (Table 7.1). First, drawing on recent literature, the study is contextualized within the historical discourses shaping the restructuring of Australian universities; second, at the level of the University, two contradictory organizational discourses governing the school formation process are identified in the *Guidelines* and other documents; third, at the level of the School/s of Management, two competing discourses shaping its formation are analysed from symptomatic texts in interviews.

### Historical discourses shaping the restructuring of Australian universities

According to recent studies of the higher education sector in Australia (Currie and Newson, 1998; Dudley, 1998; Marginson and Considine,

*Table 7.1* Historical contexts and competing discourses in UEA School of Management Formation process

| Level of context | Historical context | Competing discourses | Domain of action | Effects |
|---|---|---|---|---|
| **Higher Education in Australia** | Reduced government support | Economic rationalism | Organizational restructure of UEA from federated to unified university | Scarcity of funding, students, staff, resources |
| | | Corporate managerialism | | |
| | Globalization and competitive provision of tertiary education | Entrepreneurialism | | |
| **University of Eastern Australia** | Governance of Federated University unmanageable | Participation in knowledge sharing: University without walls A bottom-up process | Policy and service provision: unification processes | Centralization Managerialism |
| | Budgetary restraint required | Accountability: Evidence-based decision making | Centralized and limited financial delegations | Slow, delayed, decision making |
| | Fiefdoms in federated network members | Parochial network member discourses: practices and positions | UEA School formation process | Insecurity, uncertainty, lack of trust, reduced organizational commitment |
| **School of Management** | Dispersed, isolated groups with different cultures | Operational: big is better | School/s of Management proposal process | Lack of knowledge sharing |
| | | Interdisciplinary: being different | | Overlapping membership of proposed schools |
| | Under resourced, high student numbers | | | |

2000), significant discursive shifts in the last decade towards corporate managerialism, economic rationalism, entrepreneurialism and globalization have necessitated that Australian universities recreate themselves. Concurrently, contradictory shifts in leadership practices and the management of organizational change have emphasized consultative processes and participation of staff in ensuing restructures, enterprise bargaining and accommodations to reduced government funding (Treleaven *et al.*, 1999). Arguably, Australian university staff can no longer engage solely in scholarly pursuits in their discipline; their futures are increasingly shaped by their collective capability to create and share organizational knowledge and learning in an Academy under considerable challenge. Nowhere in Australia is this perhaps more noticeable than in the former CAE sector, where the so-called 'new' universities, formed since 1987, have had to both invent and re-invent themselves to meet increasing local and global competition.

One effect of these changing discourses, summarized in Table 7.1 above, is that the UEA Vice Chancellor, in a bold – and, many would argue, inevitable – move, set out to restructure the competitive UEA federation of network members into a single university. At the outset, two driving forces were named by the executive: budgetary imperatives and the coherence of a unified institution for students, external bodies and the wider community.

### Discourses shaping the University's school formation process

Examination of the University's *Guidelines for School Formation Process* can be seen as a call for knowledge sharing in the formation of new schools. The VC declared the new schools process as:

> an opportunity to create innovative new partnerships, synergies and academic 'friendships' and collaborations across... [UEA]. The new Schools therefore will be a structural manifestation of the 'new'... [UEA]; a University without walls not only externally, but within its own community... In exploring different possibilities we should remember that at the heart of the reorganisation of the University is breaking down old barriers in order to open up academic programs and learning opportunities for students, create a satisfying intellectual and working environment for staff and develop the research and enterprise base of the University. (GSFP, 2000: 1)

The UEA's origins in three CAEs, each with distinctive histories, cultures and practices, contextualize the attempt here by the UEA executive to unsettle historically dominant parochial discourses. The emphasis is placed on schools transcending old network member structures to encompass like groupings across the University, to develop a sound academic rationale and agree on a clearly differentiated name and location within one College.

A set of draft guidelines were circulated, revised and redistributed. Six steps in the process of schools formation were identified. These were collection of all relevant documentary material by the College; calls for and appointment of a facilitation team of senior 'neutral' staff to guide school proposals in each College; submission of school proposals on a proforma to focus discussion of a 'first cut' of possible schools, with several iterations, and posting of all proposals and amendments on a UEA intranet; school proposals finalized by interested staff with the VC having right of veto or taking the decision where proposals competed; appointment of heads of school; and staff location decided with consultation.

Analysis suggests that there are arguably two major discourses, those of participation and accountability, that can be seen as disciplining, in the Foucauldian sense, the school formation process throughout 2000. In the move towards unification, three principles were identified by the Vice Chancellor as important: a university without (external or internal) walls, a bottom-up process, and evidence-based decision making. All three constitute a participatory discourse directed towards knowledge sharing: 'the process for building Schools and Colleges needs to be based on shared assumptions about form, nature and purpose' (GSFP, 2000: 1). Simultaneously, increased governance responsibility, tight budgetary control and restraint, and cost savings generated a discourse of accountability. The account that follows will argue that it was the conflicting practices of these two discourses, and the power relations of those situated differently within them rather than any inherent contradiction between them, that shaped the failure to share knowledge.

### A participatory discourse

In pockets across the University, there was considerable commitment to engage creatively and productively to create new futures in response to newly forming conditions. However, there was no easy agreement or acceptance of the school formation process as being self-evident, as the VC openly acknowledged in the *Guidelines*. Nevertheless, a bottom-up approach was explicitly taken to 'capture, guide and represent clearly the deliberations currently underway in the University on the optimal design of future Schools' (GSFP, 2000: 7).

Potential school proposals for executive deliberation were put forward via facilitators who met weekly (sometimes chaired by the VC) with several executive staff. Whilst the *bottom-up process*[2] was intended to be transparent, interview data show there were many different experiences of its meanings in practice across UEA. For those academics who had participated in earlier restructures employing consultative processes at one network member (Treleaven, Cecez-Kecmanovic and Moodie, 1999), *a bottom-up approach* variously created expectations of co-ordinated autonomy, consultation and collegiate collaboration within specified parameters. For some senior staff, an instrumental belief that *co-operation is more likely* secured through *people's input* underpinned the process:

> If people feel that they're trusted by senior management they're more likely to cooperate and make those decisions than if they think that the decisions are just being made from on high and that they've had no input into the process. (Interview no. 6: 5)

For others, especially academics, the school formation process was perceived as a rather cynical deployment of participation in decisions already taken at senior levels. Another member's history of secession attempts positioned many of its staff, at least initially, as less orientated towards consultation with other former network members.

The deployment of computer-mediated communications (CMC) played a crucial role in the formation of many UEA Schools. CMC facilitated the dissemination of information and the circulation of competing and conflicting viewpoints, as people engaged in what appeared to be a democratization of communication (Cecez-Kecmanovic, Treleaven and Moodie, 2000; Sproull and Kiesler, 1991). Documents, announcements, proposals, discussion papers and other relevant material were distributed via e-mail to all academic and general staff. Discussions about major documents and proposals were also conducted on e-mail and many school proposals posted on the institution's intranet for discussion. Nevertheless, as one senior academic observed, the difference between face-to-face meetings and CMC was pertinent:

> The problem with a bulletin board is the same as email generally – it's impersonal. At least people feel that. [The VC] was very astute in the way that she handled it, in the restructure. She said that – knowing that she couldn't get around all the time, she said, look, send me your comments by email...she was very assiduous at answering every email – eventually...She was also very astute in having public meetings. Large public fora where people were allowed to – they were permitted, they were empowered to – vent. There were some pretty nasty things said at those public meetings...and [the VC and her adviser] just let it wash over them and said: yes, look I can see – either with misinformation they corrected the information or, – I think you misunderstand the meaning of that, what it actually meant was this, or we have actually addressed that and what we've done is y. And then we all said: Yes, we can see the problem um, we haven't thought of that. [The VC] at a number of sessions said quite

openly: haven't thought of that. Thank you for drawing that to my attention, we will do something about it. (Interview no. 1: 27–8)

In recounting his assessment of the VC's *astute* approach to participative processes, there is evidence of an attempt to reach widely across different communication media to deal with individual concerns. This academic leader also indicates his own (and others') learning to position himself in new ways regarding inclusive participation on a wider scale than he has apparently encountered before, moving as he does from *the VC*, to *we*, to *we all*. Further, he also moves from *people were allowed* to *permitted* to *empowered* as he catches himself in conflicting discursive positions of giving permission to expressing concerns through more free and open communication which the VC demonstrated a willingness to accept by acknowledging *we haven't thought of that*. Significantly, his account points to practices consistent with a knowledge sharing approach which the VC was committed to establishing: openness to new information rather than defensiveness, and communicative processes directed towards mutual understanding.

### A discourse of accountability

The broad discursive contexts, discussed above in Subsection 4.1, underline the necessity to make the governance and regulation of the former network members with their variable emergent practices, much more accountable. This impetus was, however, only acknowledged publicly by the Vice Chancellor (Interview no. 18) in retrospect, although it none the less informs the commitment to evidence-based decision making embedded in the *Guidelines*. Associated with this discourse of accountability was a set of prescribed procedures for data gathering, upward communication via facilitators and decision making at different levels. These practices disciplined academic staff throughout the school formation process.

Furthermore, UEA executive and staff participating in the school formation processes were also situated within the wider discourses of Australian higher education, especially those related to scarcity (of funding, students, resources, jobs and futures). The reduction in government funding of UEA, in particular, and the higher education sector generally, was emphasized publicly by the executive in their decisions to rationalize duplication, economize on administrative functions across the former network members and achieve budgetary control within tight constraints. Thus not only was there a local discourse of accountability being generated by the UEA executive, there was also increased bureaucratic centralization of former network members' activities in the attempt to bring them under control and surveillance.

In the interviews and e-mails, it is a matter of considerable angst as to the relative importance of *the budget bottom line [that] became the sort of strategic plan* (Interview no. 9: 4) *in lieu of a strategic organizational process* (Interview no. 19: 5). For the discourse of accountability as it operated across UEA deeply conflicted with the participatory practices of consultation and industrial democracy that called for knowledge sharing.

The discursive effects were to produce a climate of insecurity, uncertainty, fear and lack of trust that mobilized the defensive routines described by Argyris (1990). What this critical discourse analysis is able to demonstrate, however, is that the failure to share knowledge is not the result of defensive individuals refusing to engage productively in the organization's invitation to share knowledge but rather a far more complex situation that implicates relations of power operating discursively throughout the organization and in contexts shaped well beyond, yet nevertheless pervasively, throughout UEA.

## Competing discourses shaping the School/s of Management formation

There is strong evidence, in e-mails and discussions across the University, of acceptance by staff for organizational change. What was contested amongst staff in former schools with some disciplinary relationship to Management was the rationale and membership of the new school/s. This contestation is demonstrated in the linguistic evidence of two oppositional discourses in circulation: *bigger is better* and *but we're different.*

### Bigger is better: an operational perspective

The first proposal that reached an early general consensus, even before the *Guidelines* were published and facilitators were appointed, was that all those associated with the broad discipline of management would form one School of Management. Five meetings at different campuses were held by inviting people via e-mail. Shaping this proposal were assumptions that the large numbers of staff (approximately 70 full-time staff) and students would position such a school favourably to achieve economies in resource allocation:

> I wanted to get a rationalization of what was happening. Because I've seen too many divisions in Management. My way of thinking about Management in [UEA] is that it's under-resourced, understaffed and

has far too great a diversity of programs and courses. That is very much at the expense of the electives that can be put forward. So if we could get a common core, you can run a common core with far fewer staff in a curriculum creation role. (Interview no. 2: 3)

Initially as people met and saw they shared a lot in common, across what was at least seven distinct discipline groups, this 'one school' proposal was uncontested. However, on reflection, some Management academics recognized that there had been no discussion of the substantive issues: of envisioning how the teaching and research might develop in an interdisciplinary sense at school level.

### But we're different: a new interdisciplinary formation

The second proposal was developed in opposition to the early 'one size fits all' proposal. Initially, this second school proposal came out of left field from a small group attempting to differentiate themselves from those offering functional management subjects orientated towards professionally-accrediting bodies. The proposal was seen, ultimately to its disadvantage, in traditional management terms as having its origins in the development of a power base and by other potential colleagues as lacking the inclusivity required to build a wide base of support.

The focus on an innovative approach to understanding management in organizations through the interdisciplinarity of organizational studies and information systems was emphasized as more people contributed to the second proposal. Based on shared understandings and values, this opportunity to bring knowledge sharing into collegiate practice was enhanced by the leadership of a senior academic on their return from sabbatical leave. The difficulty, however, lay not only in making valid distinctions apparent to the facilitators and executive level, but also in engaging those colleagues proposing the one large school:

> [Proponents of the one school proposal] sat back and did nothing which is fairly tactical, of course, because if you don't have the debate then you can't have an argument and nobody can win or lose – so he just said, well I am not arguing with you, we are staying where we are, this is our proposal and that's it. So we were always arguing from behind saying we disagree, we disagree rather than we are one side and they are the other, well, we have two points of view. (Interview no. 5: 6)

The failure to develop mutual understanding as a precondition for knowledge sharing and knowledge creation is significant. More importantly, what will be taken up later is the relation between power as effects on action and, in turn, knowledge sharing.

A third school proposal was presented from a former network member. The facilitators directed that both the second and third proposals be combined and reformulated. In doing so, the academic coherences that had developed around the second proposal were lost and some of those previously keen to support two schools lost interest.

## Analysis of power/knowledge in the School of Management formation process

After many months of delay, achieving an acceptable consensus for school formation by Management academics was deemed unlikely by the UEA executive which took the decision to approve one large school. With overlapping membership on each school proposal, the committee was unable to distinguish between each potential school on the basis of its membership size. Their assumption that evidence-based decision making would be forthcoming was highly problematic:

> whilst I felt that we had the goodwill of a number of the participating parties there, somehow or other the information provided in the final documentation – for whatever reason – was inaccurate. And I think we can all accept that if you've got the absolute facts in front of you, you can start to make sensible decisions. But if it's all still very blurry, then we couldn't make those sensible decisions. (Interview no. 6: 7)

The use of the descriptors *inaccurate* and *absolute* applied to *facts* is indicative of assumptions that do not adequately recognize the relationship between knowledge and power: in this case the power of the proponents of different school proposals to disruptively compete by providing names added to their proposals without the express consent of their colleagues.

One compelling interpretation of the executive's decision to develop one School of Management is that the proposal for one big school was situated more powerfully within a concern for operational matters than in its executive's concern to create innovative school collations. Not only did one school appear to represent cost savings by providing resources for only one school; it also avoided the complexity of needing to distinguish between two schools for operational purposes. Furthermore, the decision to form one School of Management across the whole University potentially represented greater potential for disrupting the social relations of power vested in former network members than in re-forming smaller, campus-based schools.

The school formation process opened up opportunities to establish new alliances and to improve UEA's relative positioning within Australian higher education. However, these moves within the broad field of Management occurred principally without knowledge sharing and thereby did not create new disciplinary groupings within the school formation process.

This failure of knowledge sharing was analysed by examining the research data for tensions, refusals and disruptions in the struggles of different proponents as they positioned themselves in the two competing discourses. The analysis shows, first, how participants' subject positions within classical conceptualizations of power as something that can be gained or lost produced barriers to knowledge creation and sharing. Second, the analysis points to the ways in which different conceptualizations of power are more productive of the conditions for knowledge sharing, though none the less unsuccessful in terms of specific school outcomes. In summary, where power was seen in classical terms, colleagues tried to 'hold on to power' using size as the means to attract resources and 'stay powerful'. Where knowledge sharing was the focus, power was exercised more creatively towards articulating an interdisciplinary direction for a new school. However, in the two school proposal, knowledge sharing was flawed – in fact, its lack of transparency to all potential members became a major weakness, depriving the proposal of sufficient numbers.

One of the facilitators for the School of Management, who had also led his own school successfully through a formation process, implies the constitutive relationship between power and knowledge:

> I was in the privileged position of knowing who to talk to, and what committees to be on to assist [my] School to move into the restructure as best I could...I guess my corporate knowledge of how to work in that environment...meant that I met with and learned who to communicate with – many of the power brokers in the new restructure. (Interview no. 6: 1)

Whilst still perpetuating the notion of power as something you get access to (*knowing who to talk to*) and wielded by *the power brokers in the new restructure*, the facilitator also implies his understanding of power as based relationally between people and exercised through their actions.

The dynamics of power as investigated in this study suggest a distinction needs to be made between resistance to change (*everyone who is fighting a change in their organization*) on the one hand and resistance to the 'status quo' (itself a problematic notion given the dynamics of organizational life) on the other. Cooper's theory of power (1994) as productive proposes that the effects of resistance and transformative struggle may be indistinguishable except for style of engagement:

> The extent to which resistance and other forms of social contestation, such as the drive for transformation, differ is questionable. In a context of permanent instability, saying 'no' to change, i.e. resistance, will not retain the status quo ante but precipitate outcomes that will probably include subsequent struggles. Thus the difference between resistance and transformative struggle may have more to do with the style of engagement with power than with the nature or quality of the outcome. (Cooper, 1994: 453)

The point is not so much the problematic binary, which Cooper does much to disperse anyhow, but rather one of distinction in everyday practice. Resisting change and thus wanting to maintain the status quo, as several of these interviewees indicate, contrasts significantly in intent, and hence the nature of the outcome, with resisting the apparent status quo itself and wanting to transform it. However, investments in the status quo and investments in alternative values differ substantially. 'Organizing out' of opposition was employed by proponents of both school proposals. In contrast, those attempting to engage in knowledge sharing and form a second school, were engaged both in transformative struggle (albeit unsuccessful), and sometimes in a different style of engagement that derived from alternative values in an ideological sense.

> I thought then and I still think that we as a University did not use this opportunity to advance things, to make a quantum leap. Organisational redesign isn't just about shuffling, it's also having a vision … for what it can be in five years time … And it's probably not just by chance that we here developed what we believe is innovative and different from others. So the conditions in which we found ourselves – our dislocation and lack of shared experiences and not knowing each other – allowed us to develop mutual understanding in local groups and share them only when required. Affiliation with a particular proposal developed on disciplinary and geographic bases in most cases. If you imagine a different scenario in which we were

all in one building, I don't think that they [the proposals] would have developed as they did. (Interview no. 13: 3)

Discourse analysis of this version of the school formation suggests an open, inclusive position taken up towards *mutual understanding*; even when this has not occurred, the language used retains the possibility that under different conditions of proximity, shared understandings and trust could have created *a different scenario* with *a quantum leap*. The binary oppositions of *winners and losers* and their accompanying *defensive* positions against loss are noticeably absent in the recognition of missing the opportunity to create a new interdisciplinary school. Thus how participants conceptualize power affects not only the ways in which they engage with others, but also the possibilities of creating new knowledges, in this instance, new academic collations in a new school.

## Disruptive contradictions to knowledge sharing

Extensive examination of the many texts produced in the formation of the School of Management foregrounds five contradictions that disrupted effective knowledge sharing. First, at a conceptual level, there was persistent slippage from knowledge sharing to information dissemination. Second, at a planning level, the function of facilitation was constructed as information processing and upwards transfer of proposals for executive consideration. Third, at the level of practice, the UEA intranet provided for accessible communication across a highly dispersed organization was largely neglected in the School of Management's formation in favour of informal and selective communication. Fourth, the absence of reflexivity privileged defensiveness over open engagement required for generating new knowledge. Finally, in what appears to be the higher order strategic goal of unification across the UEA, organizational knowledge was both disrupted and lost.

### Knowledge sharing as information dissemination

When asked about knowledge sharing, interviewees often slid quickly into talking about data gathering, information processing and information dissemination as though they were synonymous with knowledge sharing. In fact, an argument can be put from discourse analysis of many senior staff's interviews that knowledge sharing was understood as a downward process that they were in control of:

I think that they [the VC and her adviser] have, as we all have, tried to share information, disseminate information as broadly and widely as possible. I think, to some extent, at each level, we probably will achieve it but, to some extent, we haven't. Because there is just so much information locked up inside people's heads and on people's tables, it is just physically impossible to get it all out. (Interview no. 1: 10)

A reading against the grain highlights the power/knowledge relations implicit in this response to a question about knowledge sharing practices. Knowledge sharing is seen here as a technical challenge, and even a *physical* function, of retrieving and distributing what is *locked up inside people's heads and on people's tables*. The *people* are not the academic participants in an open-ended, creative process of school formation but the senior staff with repositories of already-known *information*. This conceptualization, in stark contrast to the *bottom-up approach* that was articulated by the VC in the *Guidelines*, is represented below:

What I found is that everything you write is deconstructed in so many ways, has so many meanings... Words have so much more meaning than they should have and there is no easy way around that except that we are very careful in what we write – always... you have to be very careful in the written word, and in the Chancellery particularly, and in leading this restructure process. The sensitivities are absolutely extreme. We say one word that doesn't seem quite right, then we get pummelled for several days. So some of the real problems in the information sharing is making sure that is received by an audience in a way that it can be used not in a way that can be criticised and it's getting the intended message out. (Interview no. 3: 19)

Here a one-way flow is assumed by the speaker who attempts to control meanings by *being very careful in the written word* without recognizing that effective communication is the creation of shared meanings and mutual understanding, even where there may be no agreement. In fact, in this representation there was an attempt to get fixed meanings *received by an audience in a way that it can be used not in a way that can be criticised*, to get it right... *inside people's heads*.

A persuasive interpretation of these features, together with linguistic evidence in the e-mails for which there is not space here to present, suggests that... *allowing people to have their say* and *a chance to say something* were frequent tags attached to the consultative process, especially in the context of the accessibility and democratizing potential of e-mail. However, these constructions come out of an authoritarian discourse where permission to speak is given. They signal that some of the executive staff charged with the implementation process do not yet comprehend the difference between, on the one hand, creating space to *vent and to ask questions in large meetings* and, on the other hand, ways of encouraging knowledge creation and sharing.

### Facilitation as information processing

The slippage from knowledge sharing to information dissemination was also reproduced in the specified role of the facilitators as negotiators between conflicting and overlapping sets of data and their ensuing proposals:

> ... as a mediator – to try and get all of the information on the table ... and to try and broker exchanges between people who were often angry but for good reason – they were trying to protect their interests – and to bring about a reasonable decision-making process. (Interview no. 6: 2)

In their weekly meeting with the committee charged with oversighting the restructure, facilitators acted as conduits for horizontal co-ordination of information across potential schools and colleges and upward presentation of school proposals for executive consideration.

In this sense, the meaning attached to the term 'facilitator' varied significantly from its use generally, within the UEA and specifically in one of the former network members, as enabling open dialogue. Instead of a set of facilitation processes designed to develop trust, knowledge creation and knowledge sharing, consistent with the espoused 'bottom-up process', a hierarchical structure of information gathering and reporting was imposed via the *Guidelines* as a form of surveillance supporting evidence-based decision making.

### Informal and selective communication

Without a formally-constituted inclusive process, such as a series of facilitated events that included all former school groupings, ad hoc meetings were spread across campuses and called at short notice. The need to develop trust in order to form new school collations was exacerbated by the geographical dispersion:

> ... you can see that the mutual understanding developed between people who were close to each other geographically. People in one network member – they had their own truth, their own views, what it was they wanted ... the same thing happened with us here and others. (Interview no. 13: 3)

Creating a proposal based on mutual understanding required participants to engage in an emergent process with each other across contradictory discourses to fully explore each other's ideas. However, with the emphasis on submitting a proposal for executive consideration, a focus on outcomes militated against adopting processes of open inquiry. Exchanges in the development of proposals were often informal and selective, as one author of a school proposal admitted:

> I didn't use the website very much because it was so tortured getting into it and I am not very patient with technology. I didn't keep following the VC's messages and all that sort of, that kind of stuff – I was too busy – there was too much rubbish – I wiped most of it to be perfectly honest. If it was really important, somebody would tell me. (Interview no. 4: 17)

Despite claims of transparency, none of the Management proposals was publicly posted or discussed on the UEA intranet, where other School proposals were widely accessible and debated. Furthermore, although communication media were available to support information and knowledge sharing, their lack of use within a business faculty throughout the organizational restructure, was notable.

### The absence of reflexivity

Despite the VC's intention to create the opportunity for knowledge sharing between academics to bring forth innovative disciplinary collations in new schools, defensive organizational routines (Argyris, 1990) were enacted at every level according to the interview data. Thus the VC is perceived as being assiduously shielded from 'bad news' by Chancellery staff, senior managers are reported as failing to comprehend or embrace the sea change in attitudes required for knowledge sharing processes, and Management academics reported deep mistrust of the opportunity to be agents in creating their school future.

The importance of reflective practice for breaking out of such defensive routines and developing effective knowledge management processes is thereby underlined. Staff need not only to develop the capacity for reflection on their own actions (reflexivity) but also to make explicit, through such reflection, the rules and principles governing their behaviour (Tsoukas and Vladmirou, 2001). Following Maturana (1980), von Foerster (1984) and Argyris (1992), Tsoukas and Chia (2002: 575) propose that 'reflexivity requires certain conditions to flourish'. This study indicates that sound conceptualization of knowledge management processes and their requisite facilitation of reflective practices are two of these specific conditions for knowledge sharing. Although further investigation is required, this study points explicitly to the link between reflexivity and knowledge sharing, and, in turn, the production of new knowledges.

### The higher importance accorded to strategic cultural change

The capacity for meaningful knowledge sharing and maintenance of organizational knowledge may well be at odds with the intention of disrupting former network member boundaries. As one senior academic considered:

> People suggested to me and I am inclined to agree, that there is a perception that [if you want to] introduce a new system and you don't want to be burdened with everyone saying that's not the way we used to do it, you shuffle everything and everyone into jobs where they don't know what used to happen and you won't have that resistance. (Interview no. 7: 23)

Both within the School and more widely throughout the UEA, everyday exchanges seem to echo elements of this interpretation. In a recent e-mail sent across at least one College, recognition of this loss of organizational knowledge is shared disruptively in a postscript that muses, 'I smile because I don't know what's going on.' The tradeoff in morale and organizational commitment as an effect of losing organizational knowledge merits investigation in this research site. Additionally, organizational capacity to recreate new organizational knowledge without destroying organizational knowledge that is still an asset, requires consideration in other sites throughout UEA.

Yet breaking down barriers of cultural and historical differences could, arguably, have also been achieved by members' commitment to knowledge sharing. Here shared understandings reached through the exploration of differing values and meanings could have accorded just what the unification sought to achieve. Instead, lacking trust in the knowledge sharing processes, control exercised centrally and through a range of discursive mechanisms militated against local, situated interactions and the potential for the university without walls to be established. Accordingly, silos within and around the school were established, seeking to store up the limited resources available and reducing the levels of communication.

## Conclusion

This interdisciplinary field study of knowledge management processes in an organizational restructuring investigated how knowledge functions as a social process within complex social relations of power. Second, using a Foucauldian discourse analysis, the study examined how knowledge sharing was disrupted by competing and contradictory discourses and thereby indicated better ways of encouraging and supporting knowledge sharing in organizations. Third, the chapter demonstrated how applying Foucauldian poststructuralist concepts opened up useful questions for knowledge management processes directed towards developing new capabilities within organizations.

First, the analysis of the discursive construction of the school formation process shows that opportunities for knowledge sharing were both created and disrupted in the contradictions and instabilities of the organization and its social relations of power. The *Guidelines* presented the opportunity for a creative process of school formation that would be largely self-determining and emergent (Tsoukas and Chia, 2002). Yet, at the level of the University, there were multiple, competing and contradictory discourses operating. At the level of the School, the tensions, refusals and disruptions in the struggles of different proponents to position themselves in these discourses produced contradictory assumptions, beliefs and values of the one/two school proponents which remained in the background, rarely articulated and unreflectively examined. Knowledge sharing required engaging with these contradictions and different meanings reflectively so as to create new schools.

Second, although this study identifies how knowledge sharing was disrupted and failed, these conditions may also be read as indicative for encouraging and supporting more successful knowledge sharing in organizations. Such a move involves reconceptualizing knowledge management processes as well as changing practices.

Accordingly, organizations wanting to deploy knowledge creation and knowledge sharing processes will need to develop the capabilities to understand, design and facilitate them as human social processes recognizing that such processes are not naturally occurring. For, as Tsoukas and Chia (2002: 579) elegantly write: 'the introduction of a new discursive template is only the beginning of the journey of change, or to be more precise, it is a punctuation of the flow in organisational life'. Organizations will need to do much more than just provide communication technologies and digitalized information; they need to investigate new ways to assist all participants at varying levels throughout an organization to engage reflectively across contradictory discourses to explore in greater depth different beliefs, values and assumptions. As such they will need a willingness to disturb the social relations of power that inhibit, control and ignore knowledge sharing and co-creation processes.

Finally, in seeking to advance the understanding and practice of knowledge management processes in the complex, messy and dynamic environments of ubiquitous organizational restructuring, applications of Foucauldian concepts may open up new perspectives. In particular, questions that challenge taken-for-granted notions of power and the discursive effects of organizational change practices shaped within them, can lead to better understandings of power/knowledge within the emergent field of knowledge management and its contributions towards developing new capabilities within organizations.

## Acknowledgements

This chapter has been substantially developed since it was first presented at OKLC in Athens, April 2002. The research was conducted as part of the Australian Research Council (ARC) SPRIT Grant No. C00002546: 'Knowledge Management Enabling Environment–A New Concept, Technology and Methodology'. I gratefully acknowledge Cate Jerram for undertaking and transcribing the interviews that form much of the data for the analyses. I thank Dubravka Cecez-Kecmanovic for her insights into the restructuring and UEA staff for agreeing to reflect on the school formation process and to make their interviews available. I also thank Haridimos Tsoukas, as editor, for his valuable feedback on the earlier version.

## Notes

1. A word is placed in inverted commas, to indicate that its meaning cannot be taken for granted and is hence under 'revision'.
2. For ease of reading, words are placed in italics when they form part of the research data as written documents or spoken texts in interviews.

## References

Adler, P.A. and Adler, P. (1987) *Membership Roles in Field Research*, vol. 6. Sage University Paper Series on Qualitative Research Methods. Newbury Park, CA: Sage Publications.

Argyris, C. (1990) *Overcoming Organizational Defenses: Facilitating Organizational Learning*. Boston, MA: Allyn and Bacon.

Argyris, C. (1992) *On Organizational Learning*. Oxford: Blackwell.

Brewis, J. (2001) Foucault, politics and organizations: (Re) Constructing sexual harassment, *Gender, Work and Organization*, 8(1): 37–61.

Brocklehurst, M. (2001) Power, identity and new technology homework: implications for 'new forms' of organizing, *Organization Studies*, 22(3): 445–66.

Cecez-Kecmanovic, D., Treleaven, L., and Moodie, D. (2000) *CMC and the Question of Democratisation: a University Field Study*. Paper presented at the 33rd Annual Hawaii International Conference on System Sciences (HICSS-33), Maui, Hawaii, 3–8 January. Retrieved October 25, 2002, from http://computer.org/proceedings/hicss/0493/04931/04931006.pdf.

Chan, A. and Garrick, J. (2002) Organization theory in turbulent times: the traces of Foucault's ethics, *Organization*, 9(4): 683–702.

Chia, R. (2000) Discourse analysis as organizational analysis, *Organization*, 7: 513–18.

Clegg, S.R. (1987) The language of power and the power of language, *Organization Studies*, 8: 61–70.

Clifford, J. and Marcus, G. E. (eds) (1986) *Writing Culture: the Poetics and Politics of Ethnography*. Berkeley: University of California Press.

Cooper, D. (1994) Productive, relational, everywhere? Conceptualising power and resistance within Foucaulidan feminism, *Sociology*, 28(2): 435–54.

Currie, J. and Newson, J. (eds) (1998) *Universities and Globalisation: Critical Perspectives*. Newbury Park, CA: Sage Publications.

Dudley, J. (1998) Globalisation and education policy in Australia. In J. Currie & J. Newson (eds), *Universities and Globalisation: Critical Perspectives*. Newbury Park, CA: Sage Publications.

Fairclough, N. (1992) *Discourse and Social Change*. Cambridge: Polity Press.

Fairclough, N. (1995) *Critical Discourse Analysis: the Critical Study of Language*. London: Longman.

Fletcher, J.K. (1998) A feminist reconstruction of work, *Journal of Management Inquiry*, 7(2): 163–86.

Foucault, M. (1980) Prison talk (C. Gordon, J. Marshall, J. Mepham and K. Soper, trans.) In C. Gordon (ed.), *Power/Knowledge: Selected Interviews and other Writings 1972–1977 by Michel Foucault*. Hemel Hempstead: Harvester Wheatsheaf.

Foucault, M. (1983) The subject and power. In H. Dreyfus and P. Rabinow (eds), *Michel Foucault: Beyond Structuralism and Hermeneutics*. Chicago: The University of Chicago Press.

Galliers, R. and Newell, S. (2001) *Back to the future: from knowledge management to data management*. Paper presented at the European Conference On Information Systems ECIS 2001, Bled, Slovenia.

Gilligan, C. (1982) *In a Different Voice: Psychological Theory and Women's Development*. Cambridge, MA: Harvard University Press.

Hassard, J. and Kelemen, M. (2002) Production and consumption in organizational knowledge: the case of the 'paradigms debate', *Organization*, 9(2): 331–55.

Hassard, J.S. and Rowlinson, M. (2002) Researching Foucault's research: organization and control in Joseph Lancaster's monitorial schools, *Organization*, 9(4): 615–40.

Hollway, W. (1984) Gender difference and the production of subjectivity. In J. Henriques *et al.* (eds), *Changing the Subject: Psychology, Social Regulation and Subjectivity*. London: Methuen.

Knights, D. (2002) Writing organizational analysis into Foucault, *Organization*, 9(4): 575–94.

Knights, D. and Morgan, G. (1991) Corporate strategy, organization, and subjectivity: a critique. *Organization Studies*, 12(2): 251–73.

Lawrence, T., Phillips, N. and Hardy, C. (1999) Watching whale-watching: a relational theory of organizational collaboration, *Journal of Applied Behavioural Science*, 35: 479–502.

Mahmoud, E. (1994) Organizational change and accounting: understanding the budgeting system in its organizational context, *Organization Studies*, 15(2): 213.

Marginson, S. and Considine, M. (2000) *The Enterprise University: Power, Governance and Reinvention in Australia*. Cambridge: Cambridge University Press.

Marsden, R. (1993) The politics of organizational analysis, *Organization Studies*, 14(1): 93.

Maturana, H. (1980) Biology of cognition. In H. Maturana and F. Varela (eds), *Autopoesis and Cognition*. Dordrecht: Reidel.

McKinlay, A. and Starley, K. (eds) (1998) *Foucault, Management and Organization Theory*. Thousand Oaks, CA: Sage Publications.

McKinlay, A. (2002) Dead selves: the birth of the modern career, *Organization*, 9(4): 595–614.

McNay, L. (1992) *Foucault and Feminism: Power, Gender and the Self*. Cambridge: Polity Press.

Miles, M.B. and Huberman, A.M. (1994) *Qualitative Data Analysis: an Expanded Sourcebook*. Thousand Oaks, CA: SaGE.

Newton, T.J. (1998) Theorizing subjectivity in organizations: the failure of Foucauldian studies?, *Organization Studies*, 19(3): 415–47.

O'Connor, E.S. (1995) Paradoxes of participation: textual analysis and organizational change, *Organization Studies*, 16: 769–803.

Phillips, H. and Hardy, C. (2002) *Discourse Analysis: Investigating Processes of Social Construction*. Thousand Oaks, CA: Sage Publications.

Phillips, N. and Ravasi, D. (1998) *Analysing social construction in organizations: Discourse analysis as a research method in organization and management studies*. Paper presented at the Third International Conference on Organizational Discourse: Pretexts, subtexts and Contexts, London, July.

Rowlinson, M. and Carter, C. (2002) Foucault and history in organization studies, *Organization*, 9(4): 527–48.

Schultze, U. and Boland, R. (2000) Knowledge management technology and the reproduction of work practices, *Journal of Strategic Information Systems*, 9: 193–212.

Sproull, L. and Kiesler, S. (eds) (1991) *Connections: New Ways of Working in the Network*. Cambridge, MA: MIT Press.

Storey, J. and Barnett, E. (2000) Knowledge management initiatives: learning from failure, *Journal of Knowledge Management*, 4: 145–56.

Swan, J.S., Newell, S., Scarbrough, H., and Hislop, D. (1999) Knowledge management and innovation: networks and networking, *Journal of Knowledge Management*, 3(4): 262–75.

Townley, B. (1993) Foucault, power/knowledge, and its relevance for human resource management, *Academy of Management Review*, 18(3): 518–46.

Townley, B. (2002) Managing with modernity, *Organization*, 9(4): 549–74.

Treleaven, L., Cecez-Kecmanovic, D. and Moodie, D. (1999) Generating a Consultative Discourse: a decade of communication change, *The Australian Journal of Communication*, 26(3): 67–82.

Tsoukas, H. and Chia, R. (2002) On organizational becoming: rethinking organisational change, *Organization Science*, 13(5): 567–82.

Tsoukas, H. and Vladimirou, N. (2001) What is organizational knowledge?, *Journal of Management Studies*, 38(7): 973–93.

Van Dijk, T.A. (1993) Principles of critical discourse analysis. *Discourse and Society*, 8: 5–6.

Van Dijk, T.A. (2003) The discourse–knowledge interface. In G. Weiss and R. Wodak (eds), *Critical Discourse Analysis: Theory and Interdisciplinarity*. Palgrave-Macmillan, Houndsmill, UK: 85–109.

Van Maanen, J. (1988) *Tales of the Field: On Writing Ethnography*. Chicago: University of Chicago Press.

Von Foester, H. (1984) On constructing a reality. In P. Watzlawick (ed.), *The Invented Reality*. New York: W.W. Norton.

Wetherell, M. and Potter, J. (1992) *Mapping the Language of Racism: Discourse and the Legitimation of Exploitation*. New York: Harvester.

Wray-Bliss, E. (2002) Abstract ethics, embodied ethics: the strange marriage of Foucault and positivism in labour process theory, *Organization*, 9(1): 5–40.

Xu, Q. (2000) On the way to knowledge: making a discourse at quality, *Organization*, 7(3): 427–54.

# 8

## 'Knowing' as an Activity: Implications for the Film Industry and Semi-Permanent Work Groups

*Maria Daskalaki and Helen Blair*

### Introduction

The central concern of this chapter is to provide a theoretical explanation of the nature of knowing in an industry organized around project-based work, the film industry. In particular, it explains how knowledge of the work process, culture and rules of film production are gained and stored by both individuals and semi-permanent work groups (SPWGs, Blair, 2000) and then contributed for a short time to organizations. This exploration is particularly interesting as the film industry presents a context in which production organizations are temporary entities and there are no permanent organizational structures through which knowledge can be communicated and maintained.

Previous research in the areas of new product development (Boutellier *et al.*, 1998), virtual teams (Strauss and Olivera, 2000) and global teams (Harvey and Novicevic, 1999, 2002) has demonstrated that teams which are geographically dispersed potentially provide a flexible response and a diverse platform of expertise and talent that contributes innovative ideas and improved project quality to rapidly changing markets. However, cross-functional and cross-national teamwork, as contrasting evidence suggests, may be impeded by miscommunication, logistical and technological constraints and a lack of trusting relationships and 'mutual knowledge' (Sole and Edmondson, 2002).

Moreover, much management theory, and theories of knowledge in that sphere, assumes the notion of organizational permanence (or at least its desirability). By contrast, in project-based organizations resources are assembled (financial, human and technical) on a one-off basis, with the explicit intention that they will be dispersed on completion of the task (DeFillippi and Arthur, 1998; Jones, 1996). Yet, as a consequence of temporary organization, the importance of organizational learning is much reduced and notions of knowledge resources providing long-term competitive advantage for a particular unit of capital are largely redundant (Corrado *et al.*, 2001).

This chapter is going to explore collaborative work and team learning processes within a project-based work context through the presentation and analysis of a case study. This case study, in the main, describes the interrelationships that develop between the members of a film crew and deconstructs their activities as members of a project-based industry. In particular, we are going to present and discuss the processes that govern knowledge sharing and maintenance within and between projects in the film industry and analyse the 'learning interactions' observed within project teams.

As filmmaking is a complex, ambiguous and uncertain process, the knowledge of film freelancers becomes key to the creation of a film (Blair, 2001a). As a consequence, the individual freelancers who comprise each project through their membership of semi-permanent work groups become the 'storage units' for the industry-wide norms, culture and rules. Nevertheless, the potential for knowledge to be 'lost' is considerable. In this chapter we will suggest that as membership of SPWGs remains fairly consistent over a series of projects, a group memory develops, consisting of both individual and collective experiences. In addition, the longitudinal existence of SPWGs from project to project assists in the dissemination, maintenance and re-negotiation of various forms of industry knowledge. Although the combination of individuals and groups may vary on each film project, the 'core' in some cases, remains the same. As a result, knowledge is both socially distributed within the SPWGs and spatially distributed throughout the industry.

In particular, teams are, in the instance of 'producing knowledge', coming together to share and reproduce what they have assimilated and accumulated during their previous common experiences as well as temporary separations. In the process of their collaboration, they are not only sharing and reproducing but they also create new knowledge embedded and situated in the socio-technical 'spaces' in which they coexist. A film production, we suggest, in this case, becomes a learning episode for the members of the teams as well as an opportunity for them to enhance their ability as collaborators in future projects.

Therefore, this chapter considers the role of SPWGs in the maintenance of industry knowledge and their contribution to learning within project organizations. We will treat learning as a social activity, adopting a form of Activity Theory (Engeström, 1987) as the basis for our exploration. Rather than draw a sharp distinction between individual and organizational learning, which is in many ways redundant in the temporary organization contexts, we will consider the set of social relations – which comprises film production – as an activity system. Within that system, the social relations that develop within SPWGs become the platform upon which technical and social knowledge is negotiated, shaped and reshaped.

Activity Theory (AT) according to Blackler (1995) has its origins in the Marxian approach of Vygotsky (1978) according to which social experiences shape consciousness (instead of human consciousness determining social being). More recent approaches emphasize the collective nature of knowing, concentrating on the processes through which people develop shared conceptions of their activities (Brown *et al.*, 1989; Lave and Wenger, 1991). They also stress the relationships that exist between collective interpretations of activities and the socio-cognitive and material resources through which these interpretations are enacted (Hutchins, 1983; Engeström, 1987, 1993). According to these approaches, learning is a non-individualistic process and an active, community-based social practice that involves participation, activity and negotiation of meaning (Lave and Wenger, 1991). AT, therefore,

> [in] contrast to other traditions in psychology, such as behaviorism, … conceives learning and mental development as a process mediated by social relations; in this, dialogue comes to be seen not only as a means of transmitting information or an overlay on cognition, but a constitutive dimension of the activity systems that construct and display thinking. Work on inquiry and activity systems, and related work, has pointed to the idea of shared thinking, or distributed intelligence, as a basic metaphor for how knowledge is formed … Learning aims are seen in terms of group dynamics and meaning-making, and not only as individual achievements among the participants. Once again, dialogue plays a central role because it is a medium through which participants are able to share their conceptions, verify or test their understandings, and identify areas of common knowledge or of difference. (Burbules and Bruce, 2001)

The film industry, we suggest, is an exemplar for other project-based sectors that can also be analysed by AT. Contemporary systems of work are 'becoming more complex and interdependent, objects of activity more abstract and emergent, and communities [or "spaces"] of activity more transient' (Blackler *et al.*, 2000: 294). Within these communities, learning cannot be divided into individual and organizational since it takes place in a participative, social context, where individuals act and communicate their own personal 'meanings'. That is, learning is the result of social interaction and a 'praxis' – derived from the Greek word 'pratto', meaning to engage in an activity within a context – during which individuals become involved in a dynamic interdependent exchange of information and experiences.[1] 'Activity spaces', in this context, are considered to be complex patterns of practice that develop over time as culturally situated and socially distributed phenomenon (Blackler *et al.*, 2000). The concept of activity, as rightly stated by Blackler (1993), is compatible with the notion of 'frame' (Goffman, 1974), 'social worlds' (Lévi-Strauss, 1978) or 'habitus' (Bourdieu, 1977), with activity theory (AT) focussing more on the interpersonal relations and the network connections present within overlapping systems that mediate processes and interactions within the group.

Additionally, initial research on activity systems and knowledge focussed on organizations that are 'permanent' and 'integrated' systems with a geographical and social space clearly defined and historically construed. This chapter suggests testing this theoretical position in the absence of organizational boundaries formalized social activities and institutional codes to support and 'contain' a databank of knowledge. We support that knowledge in project-based teams[2] is geographically and temporally 'distributed' between SPWGs who achieve a task the quality of which is highly dependent on the interdependence of their activities. Therefore, 'strategic advantage' or 'organizational capabilities' of the film project as a whole could be considered as socially and topographically dispersed in a space (or network) that differs from the traditional organizational spaces. Its semi-permanent nature and its spatial and temporal configuration become determining factors of the members' activities, knowledge structures and systems as well as their subjectivities and interrelationships.

The ties and inter-subjectivities that such systems entail result in organizational spaces which are continuously recreated every time teams come together. Similarly, when these teams are dismantled, their knowledge is re-distributed in the social-communicative environment in which they operate (the industry networks). In addition, the interdependence of these teams does create a new form of spatiality by utilizing looser recurrent groupings to ensure relational continuity. This new space created is held together through the invisible connections that exist for each team member and their network. Meaning therefore within these networks is 'mutually constituted in relations between activity systems and persons acting and has a relational character' (Lave, 1993). Thus, sensemaking and learning are two processes that require dialogue and open communication channels between potential or present team members.

In turn, this demands individuals to come together and collectively create new meaning and new routines or negotiate and re-establish old ones. This is what Dixon (1994) called 'public map making' according to which tacit collective meaning structures – a kind of defensive routines that have become tacit and part of the previous project's collective meaning structures – should be placed back 'into the accessible meaning of the individuals, where [they] can be challenged, tested and altered' (Dixon, 1994). This, we suggest, will allow the reconstitution of the team around a different project (another production) that may require alternative cognitive structures and will allow the creation of new knowledge and capabilities to emerge for the team in recurrent collaborative activity.

However, in order to achieve that, members of the team ought to critically examine their knowledge structures and be willing to share their previously acquired experience with the team members, that is view filmmaking as a shared experience. This is a situation that could also potentially evoke contradictions, uncertainty and conflict between collaborators unless their activity system integrates 'the subject, the object and the instrument (material tools as well as sign and symbols) into a unified whole' (Engeström, 1993). According to Engeström, activity systems are built based on the relations between agents (like actors, producers, directors etc.), the community of which they are members (industry members and their interrelated activities) and the conception people have about their activities. These relations necessarily also involve the mediated role of technologies or techno-actors or 'actants' (Latour, 1987) (cameras, photography, other equipment etc.), language (industry jargon) and implicit and explicit social rules, systems and division of labour prevalent in their 'communities of practice' (Lave and Wenger, 1991).

In the next section, we address semi-permanent work groups and their activities as 'socially distributed' entities and explain their role in the filmmaking activity. To illustrate the role of SPWGs in project-based learning, we then provide some concrete examples of their function in a particular film production. Knowledge is then articulated as an emergent and distributed social activity and that understanding is applied to SPWGs within the activity system. Implications for further research are then discussed, prior to drawing our conclusions.

## Semi-permanent work groups and film-making

This section describes some of the characteristics of the SPWGs. The semi-permanent work group defines an informal work unit prevalent in the film industry which comprises a relatively stable membership that moves as a collective unit from project to project (Blair, 2001a). This type of unit exists in industries such as film, television, architecture and construction, where there is a high level of uncertainty and organizations are organized on a temporary basis (DeFillippi and Arthur, 1998). There is a growing literature concerning project and temporary organization as these forms of co-ordination have become more prevalent (Ayas, 1996). Goodman and Goodman consider a temporary system as a 'set of diversely skilled people working together on a complex task over a limited period of time' (Goodman and Goodman, 1972: 494).

Further, much management and economic theory, as well as theories of knowledge in the business context, assume the notion of organizational permanence (or at least its desirability). These approaches assume a very rigid conceptualization of the term 'knowledge', attaching a far greater importance to the impact of geographical boundaries and permanent structures on the process of learning. Yet, structures, roles, rules and norms are required to exist to facilitate the recreation of each discrete project organisation (Jones, 1996). Here, we suggest that these exist at an interpersonal rather than organizational level.

In this uncertain and fluid type of environment one important means of passing on relevant knowledge is through more stable interpersonal relationships, and often these form within the context of a work group. A semi-permanent work group comprises a number of individuals (usually those required to form a 'department' or team) who work together on an almost permanent basis. The group will move from job to job in its entirety with the members remaining the same (Blair, 2001a). Therefore, ongoing contacts exist between each member of the group but also significantly between the head of department (who sources and then supplies employment opportunities) and group members. Although these groups may remain stable for a number of years, their configuration is not career-long as individuals may leave (for career progression purposes, for example) or may be expelled (if, for example, performance is not satisfactory).

Unsuccessful working relationships may affect both the work process and the product and therefore managers tend to avoid the risk of bringing in a group of 'strangers' to work together. Failing work relationships may also affect the reputations of the individuals involved and the head of department associated with those people, and so they tend also to be avoided by the members of the teams. Working with people they worked before should facilitate a more effective, less stressful working relationship. In this instance, networking, being a social mechanism for exchanging resources (in the main, information) becomes very important when building these working relationships (Blair and Daskalaki, 2002). Exchange of information, in turn, facilitates the repeated assemblage of established SPWGs and the continuity of the same work groups. Furthermore, the prevalence of SPWGs demonstrates the tendency of filmmakers to move jobs in-groups, with people they had worked with previously (Blair, Grey and Randle, 2001), who most probably constitute their network of contacts. In addition, SPWGs appear to be an effective 'solution' for (a) an industry dominated by 'flexible'[3] employment forms and (b) a 'product' that 'promises' high job mobility but at the same time, demands social interdependence.

This chapter proposes that the freelance-dominated labour market is characterized by uncertainty and often turbulent, cyclical environmental conditions. During periods of intense work, however, strong links are built with colleagues and if these are maintained, those individuals will be able to pass information to future 'employers'[4] related to their contact's (link's) personality as well as skills and abilities. Thus, the maintenance of network links or connections and the social and professional support provided through them, become the industry's means to deal with the insecurity of temporary work and uncertainty of freelance employment. Indeed, as research by the authors suggests, the film industry provides a particularly extreme case of networking, demonstrating the importance of informal means of learning of and getting, jobs (Blair and Daskalaki, 2002). Therefore, the assembly of established work groups can be viewed as a mechanism to reduce the uncertainty of getting work on the part of the freelancers and of potentially unsuccessful working relationships on the part of both the head of department and group members (Pfeffer *et al.*, 1976).

### SPWGs: socially distributed activities and intentional communities

This part of the chapter focusses on the cognitive functioning of SPWG participants and the way they process their cognitive scripts and routines within diverse activity contexts. We suggest that freelancers in the film industry participate in a collaborative environment where the exchange and sharing of knowledge and meaning are not only encouraged but also considered crucial for both the initiation and completion of projects. It is suggested that within these contexts, members experience high levels of uncertainty, ambiguity and mistrust (DeFillippi and Arthur, 1998; Blair, 2001b). Therefore, the formation of enduring teams that conduct an activity in a temporary organization (for example designing, creating and producing, the hair and make-up effects) is an attempt to reduce uncertainty and relationship ambiguity based on a culture of high trust. These cultures can be viewed as 'systems of enduring socially agreed-on meanings that guide behavior' (Berger and Luckmann, 1966) the study of which can offer a better understanding of how SPWGs 'behave' (use accumulated experiences) and 'learn'.

Finley and Mitroff (1986) refer to schemata and scripts as 'consensual' tools, shared by project members. Schemata are considered to be cognitive structures through which information is analysed and shared between and among groups. Moreover, scripts can become carriers of socially constructed meaning or 'relatively predetermined and stereotyped sequences of action which come into play by particular and well-recognized cues or circumstances which we acquire knowledge through the process of socialisation' (Mangham, 1978). Following this, project cognitive structures are expected to be 'socially shared' and project members 'co-implicated' to each others' actions (Star, 1992). Thus their consensual cognitive schemata are exchanged and reshaped by their interaction in practice.

Therefore, knowledge is positioned in neither individual nor in a social domain but is thought of as shared cognitive structures and relationally developed meanings that is 'situated' (within teams) and 'distributed' (within networks) not in a clearly defined organizational space but in a spatially disperse 'activity system'. This has clear application in the film industry context and other project-based organizations where employment arrangements are not permanent[5] and teams combine knowledge resources on individual projects and may subsequently pass knowledge to network contacts or work with different teams on future projects.

However, in contrast to Wenger's (1998) 'communities of practice' (COP) that are framed around shared culture and practice, film SPWGs' joint activity is

> accomplished by the assembling of sets of individuals derived from overlapping constellations of personal networks. These individuals have to create sufficient shared understanding to get work done, but such understanding must be collectively constructed rather than existing historically in an ongoing community. (Nardi *et al.*, 2002: 224)

Here, Nardi *et al.* (2002) suggest that personal networks are constructed and maintained by individuals or sets of individuals who intentionally get together in order to constitute groups that are more heterogeneous than those implied by COP approaches. Similarly, film production consists of personal, intentional networks in the form of SPWGs groups (which form individual 'departments' such as camera, sound, art etc.), the practices of which enable the production of a complex and unique product. In some instances, these groups are situated in geographically dispersed places (virtual teams) and they collaborate within an emergent electronic 'space'.

As our findings suggest, the high degree of interdependency existing between the activities of film production – combined in a single, final product (Blair, 2001b) – creates high levels of interdependency between teams or groups. Within this transient context, the existence of SPWGs provide a site for both the retention and distribution of the industry culture, knowledge and routines that are reproduced each time a film project is enacted. This is a complex activity that for the past 40 years has been conducted in temporary organizations, with organizational structures and resources being constructed and assembled on a recurrent but temporal basis (DeFillippi and Arthur, 1998). The following section investigates this activity further, providing evidence from the case study.

## Semi-permanent work groups: case study of a film production

Knowing[6] refers to an emergent and distributed social practice. Further, systems (or distributed organizational units) are analysed as 'activity networks' (Blackler *et al.*, 2000), that is, as overlapping communities of activity the members of which 'recognise shared work priorities, work with a common cognitive and technological infrastructure, and support each other's activity' (Blackler *et al.*, 2000: 282) towards an emergent object. This object, the product of collective expertise and co-operative interrelations, is the film. Thus, viewing, knowing and learning as activities (see Blackler, 1995) could facilitate our examination of whether and how SPWGs in the film industry retain and create long-lasting organizational routines, build trust and develop organizational capabilities. The chapter examines film production and the individuals involved with it as a constellation of 'knowledge-based systems' (Tsoukas, 1996).

The data, on which this chapter is based, originate from a case study of a film production identified by the pseudonym TeenComedy.[7] It is designed to illustrate the stability of the SPWGs over time and their composition and point to the shared development and understanding of the groups' practices. Three of the 'departments'[8] on this film can be described as semi-permanent work groups: camera, sound and assistant directors' teams. The camera team is the most complex example of semi-permanent groups evidenced on the case film. As can be seen in Figure 8.1, the work group is comprised of the director of photography (DOP – head of department), focus puller, grip, gaffer and clapper/ loader. Prior to joining the present group configuration the focus puller and clapper/loader had an established work relationship. When the focus puller joined the above group, he brought the clapper/loader with him. Similarly, the grip had worked with both the focus puller and clapper/loader prior to joining this group.

Figure 8.1 also illustrates the longevity of the relationships between different members of the group and so it can be seen that the focus puller, and clapper/loader have completed between eight and ten jobs with the DOP, with the grip having worked with him over some three years. That principle can also be seen to apply with the gaffer who engages in repeated working relationships with the same electricians. This group therefore moves from film to film with that combination of personnel. Since the case film, this semi-permanent work group have completed at least one other project together.

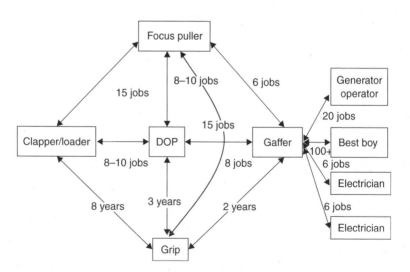

*Figure 8.1*  Pattern of working relationships in the camera/electrical department

Through these ongoing relationships collective understandings and knowledge are built and reshaped. Knowledge concerning the rules and roles of the industry and the relationships between teams, is passed on to the more junior members of the group through interactive social processes, such as storytelling, instruction and illustration.

The team of assistant directors (ADs) comprises the head of department (the first AD) and two assistants (second and third ADs). Of the two assistants, the second had completed three jobs with the head and two with the third assistant (Figure 8.2). Having joined the group after the second, the third had also undertaken two jobs with the third assistant. Since the case film that unit have gone on to complete another job together.

In the sound team (Figure 8.3), having been the sound mixer's trainee, the boom operator has worked for him for the past nine years. This established relationship therefore came into being through the traineeship and then an opportunity at the next level (boom operator) became available which the present operator secured. From that time the boom swinger has worked on an ongoing basis with the mixer.

These interrelationships give some indication of the established, long-term nature of the groups. Their 'permanent' status can also be evidenced in the manner in which members of the group view their relationship to the group and to their head of department in particular (as

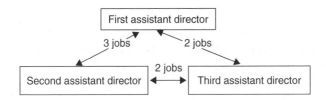

*Figure 8.2*  Pattern of working relationships in the assistant director department

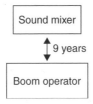

*Figure 8.3*  Pattern of working relationships in the sound team

the key employment supplier). One member of the crew noted, regarding not having found work since involvement in the case film, that:

> it hasn't bothered me finishing [the case film] ... we had nothing definite. I mean I tend to work with [the head of department] more or less permanently these days. Stephen

Significantly, this interviewee uses the word 'we', inferring identification with a pre-existing group of people and their collective. Or, as another interviewee points out:

> It's watching their backs and making sure that they've got everything they need and everything we need cos if [the HoDs] team make him look good then he'll get more jobs and that means we'll work, we'll get more work. So its all about looking after each other. Susan

'Stephen' also states that that head of department is more or less his 'permanent employer'. Going on, he says:

> we work, within our group people work together quite [a lot] ... that might be seen as a little more unusual. People tend to work with people they know as much as they can. Whether we're usual in so much as having worked with [the head of department] for quite a few films I don't know.

Again this infers a notion of permanency which, although the interviewee indicates some reservations as to their typicality, is taken up by other case film crew members:

> As I work with [the head of department] a lot ... he gets the job and (pause) and, and he tells production he wants me to do it. John

and

> I'm in with this team and we don't stop working and it is very secure at the moment. Susan

There are two related reasons for the 'departmental nature' of SPWGs. The first reason is functional, in as much as film production brings together a range of discrete technical and creative skills which lead to 'departments' or teams being comprised of distinct skill groups. The camera and sound teams perform tasks that require different skills, for example. As each team is quite distinct in skill demarcation, the formation of semi-permanent work groups offers considerable benefits to task performance and role fulfillment. The second reason for configuring groups around 'departments' is operational and relates to the recruitment and selection process. Because heads of department are responsible for recruiting and selecting staff for their teams only, any ongoing relationships between the head of department and his or her staff will take place within that group boundary. As a result of these two factors, semi-permanent work groups are based around 'departmental' boundaries.

Additionally, employment security and other benefits raise issues of expectancy (that the head of department will, as a group leader, do a job and that the group members will respond positively when asked) and dependency. This chapter suggests that within the wider film activity system SPWGs are important sets of social relations within which knowledge is both held and shared. Industry norms, culture and rules are modified and re-enacted within the groups, as are the relations between teams, as a result of socialization[9] within a given SPWG. Furthermore, the ways of working and behaving of that particular SPWG are also shaped, reshaped and shared within the group context.

Nevertheless, these participative environments inherently entail situations of uncertainty, ambiguity and conflict. According to Engeström (1993), these tensions and conflicts between activity systems are the result of the division of labour in capitalist society and commodification of activity. In the situation of the film industry this is intensified by the uncertainty regarding the success of the product. Although most of the members of a film crew may have fixed payment contracts, the success of the film (object) as well as the effectiveness of the collaboration (social and interactive aspects of the relationship) will determine the involvement of filmmakers with future projects and, in effect, career progression and survival:

> We did very well as a team. If you find one then you stick together and then you have greater potential for success in later projects. You know your boundaries, you don't step on the field of the other and you accept what the other person is doing. It becomes a family ... it is a very intimate process ... you have the same vision and creativity is intimacy. (Interviewee A)

According to Blair (2001c), 'pre-existing connections and linkages are explicitly drawn upon in a project context to minimize the uncertainty and risk of one-off transactions in key resource areas'. It appears there-fore that unity of teams in both a horizontal and vertical manner could facilitate decision making and communication. Furthermore, following AT, this becomes possible through collaborative accounts of knowing that discourage the separation of the individual from the collective and the social from the technical.

### Activity- and project-based learning in film

The case production involved a crew of some sixty (a relatively small number), yet the number of layers between junior and senior members is considerable. For example, between the clapper/loader (a junior member of the camera 'department') and the director there are four layers (Figure 8.4).

In the instance of the camera 'department', for example, each grade completes tasks directly for the next grade. A similar system was observed in all teams, where tasks undertaken at a 'lower' level directly enabled those further up the hierarchy to complete their tasks. In the costume team, the costume assistant would wash and ready clothes for the next days shooting so that the dresser/wardrobe supervisor could dress the actors/esses the following day.

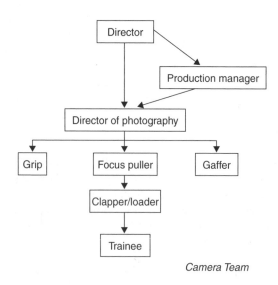

*Camera Team*

*Figure 8.4*　Formal structure of the camera 'department'

Yet the interrelated nature of various agents' actions and their co-dependency and, at the same time, the blurred boundaries and potentially conflicting individual and group interests give rise to tensions and potential conflict within and between teams. This tension – which emerges due to the division of labour observed in the process of filmmaking (Blair, 2001c) – could be considered to be the outcome of the co-presence of various activity sub-systems organized around (sometimes) competing actions and differing interests. For example, potential tensions may arise if the make-up artists express concerns over an actor's appearance in a particular scene while the producer is concerned with meeting the deadline initially agreed with the distribution and marketing teams.

However, this tension will be minimized or avoided through 'attachment to work groups and networks of contacts ... [which becomes] the primary conduit for training and learning opportunities' (Blair, 2001c). The constitution and re-constitution of the team relies heavily upon informed, conscious decisions regarding 'who' will be joining the network of contacts of members within the industry as well as the production teams for individual projects:

> you want to work with somebody you have to know that they understand what you mean from the outset – this is the level in which we are operating so trust and shared understanding are enormously important. Because you are creating something from nothing, a lot of problems may come from the two parties, or three parties or ... whatever, providing service to each other ... You prefer to work with people you know, mainly because you have worked with in the past and you share a common language. (Interviewee B)

Thus, we suggest that tensions between groups can be exacerbated as groups close in on themselves and look inwards during inter-group conflict. As already suggested, for the majority of the time these groups are, the outcome of the *deliberate* activation of various relationships that have been cultivated over long periods. As a result, remembering and communicating allows flexible and desirable configurations of members within the groups (Nardi *et al.*, 2002). These configurations facilitate conflict resolution and learning during film making activities.

Activity Theory and its focus on mediated interactions between individuals or groups and their interpretative contexts provides a very useful tool for studying filmmaking as a social practice. For example, consider two systems that have to share information in order to complete a task. Yet this information or knowledge is distributed or situated across different task performers (Hutchins, 1983). Competent performance and completion will require integration of tasks, skills and knowledge achieved by 'structuring mechanisms' such as roles, division of labour (Leont'ev, 1978, 1981) and rules tacitly shared by all participants (Engeström, 1993; Figure 8.5).

In detail, by focussing on the interpersonal distribution of knowledge within the film industry, we assessed the importance of the 'distributed' qualities of learning and the relational character of professional identities within SPWGs and their activities. Moreover, the film (the outcome of this 'relationality') was not treated as the 'goal' of film production. A goal, in AT, is a conscious, short-lived action. Instead, following the model of the basic structure of human activity system, we define film as the *outcome* of collaborative activity systems that encompasses embodied knowledge and mediated presence. The other elements of an activity system are translated as components of a film production below (Table 8.1).

Furthermore, learning is the outcome of collective problem solving accumulated during the repeated interactions of the team members in

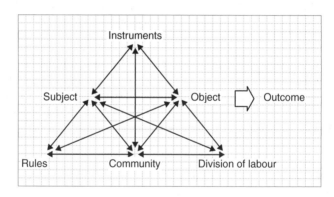

*Figure 8.5* The structure of a human activity system (Engeström, 1987: 78)

Table 8.1 The components of an activity system: the film industry

| Subject | SPWG |
| --- | --- |
| Object | The intended audience |
| Outcome | The film |
| Rules | Norms, values, regulations, generic constraints, relationships, guide for interactions |
| Instruments | Technology, equipment, lists, materials, plans |
| Division of Labour | Tasks of SPWGs/teams, decision-making power |
| Community | The totality of the film crew |

previous collaborations. As a result, interaction in a SPWG leaves behind a 'transformed network' as a result of the activity, suggesting that 'the historical experiences of workers in intentional networks qualitatively change the way they behave towards one another in their networks in future interactions' (Nardi *et al.*, 2002: 228).

Networking activities are absolutely crucial for filmmakers' survival as active members of the industry. Further, these activities, in the main, involve strategic information exchange and knowledge sharing of prospective collaborators (Blair and Daskalaki, 2002). As one of the interviewees stated:

> Networking, as I understand it, is a means of sharing and gathering information that is useful to one for creative and personal development… it is about having an exchange. (Interviewee C)

Thus, knowing (as embedded in participants-in-interaction) and 'temporarily strong relational ties'[10] (outcome of co-ordination, negotiation, intentional collaboration and trust) may counter the instability and uncertainty of the film production process. By participants-in-interaction, we define an alternative spatial context within which teams collectively accumulate experiences and knowledge; knowing therefore in these environments becomes a dynamic activity reshaped within different activity contexts, in this case of different film productions. Thus, the spatiality of the activity gains secondary importance in contrast to its interrelational aspect which becomes the primary 'field' of knowing for each interacting resource group. By 'interrelational', here, we refer to the dynamics of recurrent interactions that develop between specific individuals (for example director–editor, director–cinematographer, director–production designer or director–composer; see Corrado *et al.*, 2001) during semi-permanent collaborative activities.

In 2000, Engeström expanded his activity systems theory, which emerged from his studies of the Finnish health care system, and devised the term 'knotworking' in an attempt to describe a new form of work organization. He suggested that the notion of 'knot' describes a

> rapidly pulsating, distributed and partially improvised orchestration of collaborative performance between otherwise loosely connected actors and activity systems. A movement of tying, untying together seemingly separate threads of activity characterizes knotworking. (Engeström, 2000: 971)

However, Engeström's (2000) 'knotworking' has neither a clear deadline nor a stable centre of activities. SPWGs in the film industry allow for co-configuration work to take place due to the repeated interactions that co-implicate the same or interrelated networks of individuals, teams or institutions. In this chapter, instead of taking as our level of analysis the task or the product (outcome of the activity), like Engeström, we focussed on the actors (subjects) and the processes of knowing within the community (see Table 8.1). As a result, we proposed that SPWGs in the film industry constitute dispersed 'networking systems', the activities of which re-enact intentional communities and re-constitute the outcome of their collaboration.

## Implications for future research

In contrast to much of the popular, prescriptive literature surrounding the management of creative labour, the co-ordination of film production is highly hierarchical (Blair, 2001c). By reflecting on this issue at this point, we would like to address the connection between power, structures and knowledge and suggest a theme for future research: how hierarchical structures and power relationships may affect project-based learning and knowing of SPWGs. Though unpacking these themes has not been the main purpose of the chapter, previous research (Blair, 2001c) has touched upon related issues.

The hierarchical organizing of film production is reinforced by a large number of commonly held assumptions and rules which are instilled in junior members of staff as they work their way through the grades and are based upon skill levels, length of attachment to a group and task allocation. Thus, it appears that a clear hierarchy in co-ordinating and controlling the vertical division of labour is observed in the organization of work in the film industry. The departmental hierarchies evidenced in the case production involved strict task demarcation and clearly defined reporting relationships between different levels of the organization. Each lower grade is supervised by the one immediately above, with the clapper loader describing his job as follows:

> Well basically it's assisting the focus puller. Obviously the camera-man, but you're mainly assisting the focus puller. You come in and you mark the clapper boards up with the correct date, make sure the film is loaded in the magazines, which means the film would be in rolls in a can. You put the film from the cans into the magazines and

the magazines are the items which go on the camera, its like a big metal case with film that goes on the camera. So you would check that you've got the right stock, film stock... basically go on the floor and start off and you listen to what, the cameraman wants – a change of filters you would sort of automatically go to, or change lenses, you would go to the box to get'em [*sic*] for the focus puller. Once you get the lens to them, where the camera is, you'd pass it over to the focus puller. He would then put it on the camera. You'll take the lens that was on the camera back to the lens box, put it in. You make sure that the lens is clean before you give it to the focus puller and if it's not clean either you would clean it yourself or you would say to the focus puller 'Oh there's a smudge on the front or the back'. And that's the same with filters; you would do that with filters. Allan

It is also illustrated through the view of one camera team member, concerning his career progression:

the next progression obviously is going to stay focus pulling for quite a number of years but then hopefully move up to camera operator and maybe one day in the distant future cameraman. But you know... I take one step at a time.

However, as this chapter proposed film is the outcome of the interrelational qualities of different knowledge systems, activities and professional identities; thus, film production is a form of social interaction, a mode of action and a systemic activity. As a result, we would not expect the hierarchical organization of film production to hinder learning and collaboration in the film industry. In other words, one would expect the power relationships that may develop during film production interactions to follow the Foucauldian route of constitutive qualities rather than the general schema of 'domination-repression' (Smart, 1985).

Therefore, potential points of tension, we would expect, will provide a platform for seemingly powerless individuals or groups within the hierarchy to negotiate, shape and enact technical and social knowing. It is within this context where conflict and tension – inherent elements of activity systems – fail to hinder learning and completion of the project of the SPWGs during film production. This, we propose, yields for re-evaluation of the notions of subjectivity, action and hierarchy of relations when these are studied in relation to project teams and particularly, semi-permanent work teams. Further research could investigate the issue in greater depth by building upon this case study's preliminary findings and theoretical contributions.

## Conclusion

Over the past two decades, delayering, cross-functional teams, flexible work patterns, portfolio work and other managerial 'innovations' have led companies towards the development of 'boundaryless' organizational structures. Collaborative work and group learning within these particular organizational forms have become crucial not only for the achievement of organizational success and innovation, but also for survival and the development of organizational capabilities. The case study used as an example in this chapter demonstrated knowledge sharing and collaborative learning between the members of teams who temporarily form a group in order to engage in an activity – namely, to create a film. Filmmaking was treated as paradigmatic of the relationships that develop within other cross-functional teams within 'permanent' and 'semi-permanent' organizations.

We suggested that the knowledge produced within a team context is transferred to the next project by the members of the team. Thus, the ongoing work groups (called Semi-Permanent Work Groups (SPWGs) here) are the main 'site' for the transmission and maintenance of work and social norms as well as technical know-how. The chapter, adopting a version of Activity Theory, provided an alternative formulation as to how individuals and teams learn and how SPWGs survive and evolve. Semi-permanent work groups and project-based work lacks the traditional organizational structures and processes to integrate capabilities, knowledge and talent. We drew attention towards networks of contacts that assist members of the film industry to maintain relationships, participate in collective learning and, eventually, get jobs. We proposed that networks, in this situation, act as the 'invisible boundaries' of every potential film project.

Activity Theory provided useful insights into how knowledge is maintained these industry 'boundaries' and how each project becomes an opportunity for stronger links within the teams, leading the teams towards more effective collaborations in the future. Activity systems guide the interrelationships between SPWGs and their members as well as enabling the recomposition or deliberate reactivation of the 'core' of a film crew from one project to the next. Thus, it is the recurrent interactions that develop between specific individuals or activity sub-systems over time that substitute for the traditional 'pool' of resources found in 'permanent' organizations. The chapter also supported the idea that film production entails periods of tension and conflict that won't hinder but instead, facilitate the negotiation of meaning and the cycle of knowing within and between various activity contexts. This is due to the fact that film production groups do not simply work together but their work activities are achieved via the *intentional* maintenance of their personal networks and *re-enactment* of their collaborative relationships. We considered this as a starting point for future research in the area.

Finally, this chapter introduced a theoretical framework that will facilitate and expand the analysis of the activities of SPWGs in the creative industries. In terms of the nature of learning, we suggested that it is a social activity. Given that in the film and many other creative industries, organizations are not permanent, it is important to ask how individual members gain and store knowledge in that transient environment. In contrast to DeFillippi and Arthur's (1998) suggestion that organizational memory disappears once project tasks are accomplished, we suggested that knowledge (or knowing) is embedded in the interrelationships and the links that develop and/or are re-enacted during film production interactions. Consequently, the chapter proposed that the concept of organizational memory has to be revisited taking into consideration project-based work organizations and the relationships and processes they entail.

## Acknowledgements

We are indebted to Stephen Gourlay (Kingston Business School) for the valuable comments on an earlier draft. Special thanks to the organizers (and editors of this book) and participants of the 3rd European Conference on Knowledge, Learning and Organizational Capabilities (2002) for their helpful feedback on earlier versions of this chapter.

## Notes

1. This is in accordance with Brown and Duguid's (2001) 'practice perspective' on knowledge and knowledge-acquisition-and-use. See also Chaklin and Lave (1996).
2. The use of the term 'teams' in this chapter does not follow the traditional definition of the term 'organizational teams'. Instead, the term can be read as

'loosely connected actors and activity systems' or 'combinations of people, tasks and tools [ that] are unique and of relatively short duration' (Engeström *et al.*, 1999).

3. This mainly represents freelance working patterns and/or project-based employment.
4. In the film industry, the concept of 'employer' is different from the one used in other sectors.
5. 'Permanent' here refers to the length of the relationship and denotes a 'job for life' employment pattern, that most of the time may not be the case in practice.
6. 'Knowing' rather than knowledge is used here to signify the dynamic and processual qualities of what is widely addressed as 'knowledge'.
7. The 'case film' here refers to a case study by one of the authors; it has been documented elsewhere as 'Teen Comedy'.
8. As with the concept of 'employer', 'department' here does not have the traditional meaning when used in the film industry. It is an alternative term for SPWGs or teams and thus used interchangeably.
9. Or in the terms of Lave and Wenger (1991: 29) term, 'legitimate peripheral participation': 'process by which newcomers become part of a community of practice [... or ...] full participants in a sociocultural practice'.
10. Ongoing research by the authors confirms Nardi *et al.*'s (2002) suggestion that 'strength and weakness of ties are not so much stable properties of an intentional network as they are variable manifestations of ongoing processes of network activation as they occur through actions of remembering and communicating' (Nardi *et al.*, 2002: 231). This invites re-conceptualisation of Granovetter's (1973) notion of ties.

## References

Ayas, K. (1996) Professional Project management: a shift towards learning and a knowledge creating structure, *International Journal of Project Management*, 14(3): 131–6.

Berger, P. and Luckmann, T. (1966) *The Social Construction of Reality: a Treatise in the Sociology of Knowledge*. Harmondsworth: Penguin Books.

Blackler, F. (1993) Knowledge and the theory of organisations: organisations as activity systems and the reframing of management, *Journal of Management Studies*, 30: 865–84.

Blackler, F. (1995) Knowledge, knowledge work and organisations: an overview and interpretation, *Organization Studies*, 16: 1021–46.

Blackler, F., Crump, N. and McDonald, S. (2000) Organizing processes in complex network activities, *Organization*, 7(2): 277–300.

Blair, H. (2000) Working in film: employment in a project-based sector, *Personnel Review*, 30(2): 170–85.

Blair, H. (2001a) The labour process and labour market in the British film industry, *Work, Employment and Society*, 15(1): 1–21.

Blair, H. (2001b) Responsible autonomy in conditions of uncertainty: the case of film production, 19th International Labour Process Conference, Royal Holloway (University of London). 26–28 March.

Blair, H. (2001c) Beyond the film? The social and spacial dynamics of project-organisation, International Workshop, 26–29 April 2001, University of Bonn.

Blair, H. Grey, S. and Randle, K. (2001) Working in film: employment in a project based industry, *Personnel Review*, 30(2): 170–85.

Blair, H. and Daskalaki, M. (2002) Women's experiences of interpersonal networks in the UK film and television sectors. *Report of Findings*. UK: Economic and Social Research Council.

Bourdieu, P. (1977) *Outline of a Theory of Practice*, translated by R. Nice. Cambridge: Cambridge University Press. (First published in French, 1973.)

Boutellier, R.O., Gassmann, O., Macho, H. and Roux, M. (1998) Management of dispersed product development teams: the role of information technologies, *R&D Management*, 28(1): 13–26.

Brown, J.S., Collins, A. and Duguid, S. (1989) Situated cognition and the culture of learning, *Educational Researcher*, 18(1): 32–42.

Brown, J.S. and Duguid, P. (2001) Knowledge and Organisation: a Social-Practice Perspective, *Organization Science*, 12(2): 198–213.

Burbules, N.C. and Bruce, C.B. (2001) Theory and research on teaching as dialogue. In V. Richardson (ed.), *Handbook of Research on Teaching*, 4th edition. US: American Educational Research Association.

Chaklin, S. and Lave, J. (1996) *Understanding Practice: Perspectives on Activity and Context*. Cambridge: Cambridge University Press.

Corrado, R., Ferriani, S. and Boschetti, C. (2001) Managing knowledge and resources in highly creative contexts: new insights from the US movie industry, paper presented in the British Academy of Management Conference, Cardiff.

Daskalaki, M. (2000) Induction programmes in the age of 'corporate culture': the 'sophisticated subject', *Business and Professional Ethics Journal*, 19(3/4): 199–231.

DeFillippi, R.J. and Arthur, M.B. (1998) Paradox in project-based enterprise: the case of film making, *California Management Review*, 40(2) (Winter): 125–39.

Dixon, N. (1994) *The Organizational Learning Cycle: How we can learn collectively*. London and New York: McGraw-Hill.

Engeström, Y. (1987) *Learning by Expanding: an Activity Theoretical Approach to Developmental Research*. Helsinki: Orienta-Konsultit.

Engeström, Y. (1991) Developmental Work Research: Reconstructing Expertise through Expansive Learning. In M. Nurminen and G. Weir (eds), *Human Jobs and Computer Interfaces*. Amsterdam: North Holland.

Engeström, Y. (1993) Work as a Testbed of Activity Theory. In S. Chaiklin and J. Lave (eds), *Understanding Practice: Perspectives on Activity and Context*. Cambridge: Cambridge University Press.

Engeström, Y. (2000) Activity theory as a framework for analysing and redesigning work, *Ergonomics*, July, 7: 960–77.

Engeström, Y., Engeström, R. and Vahaaho, T. (1999) When the centre doesn't hold: the importance of knotworking. In S. Chaiklin, Hedegaard, and U. Jensen (eds), *Activity Theory and Social Practice: Cultural-Historical approaches*. Aarhus, Denmark: Aarhus University Press.

Finley, M. and Mitroff, I. (1986) Strategic Plan Failures. In P.H. Sims, A.D. Gioia and Associates (eds), *The Thinking Organisation*. San Francisco: Jossey-Bass.

Foucault, M. (1980) *Power/Knowledge: Selected Interviews and Other Writings 1972–1977*. Hemel Hempstead: Harvester Wheatsheaf.

Fox, S. (2000) Communities of practice, Foucault and actor–network theory, *Journal of Management Studies*, September, 37(6): 853–68.

Goffman, I. (1974) *Frame Analysis: an Essay on the Organization of Experience*. New York: Harper & Row.

Goodman, L.P. and Goodman, R.A. (1972) Theatre as a temporary system, *California Management Review*, 15(2): 103–8.

Granovetter, M. (1973) The strength of weak ties, *American Journal of Sociology*, 78(6): 1360–80.

Harvey, M. and Novicevic, M. (1999) The trials and tribulations of addressing organizational ignorance. *European Management Journal*. 17(4): 431–43.

Harvey, M. and Novicevic, M. (2002) The coordination of strategic initiatives within global organizations: The role of global teams, *International Journal of Human Resource Management*, 13(4): 660–76.

Hutchins, E. (1983) Understanding Micronesian Navigation. In D. Gentner and A.S. Stevens (eds), *Mental Models*. Hillsdale, NJ: Lawrence Erlbaum Associates.

Jones, C. (1996) Careers project-networks: the case of film industry. In M.B. Arthur and D.M. Russeau (eds), *The Boundaryless Career*. New York: Oxford University Press, N.Y.

Latour, B. (1987) *Science in Action*. Cambridge, MA: Harvard University Press.

Lave, J. (1993) The practice of learning. In S. Chaklin and J. Lave (eds), *Understanding Practice: Perspectives on Activity and Context*. Cambridge: Cambridge University Press.

Lave, J. and Wenger, E. (1991) *Situated Learning: Legitimate Peripheral Participation*. Cambridge: Cambridge University Press.

Leont'ev, A.N. (1978) *Activity, Consciousness, Personality*. Englewood Cliffs, NJ: Prentice Hall.

Leont'ev, A.N. (1981) The problem of activity in psychology. In J. Wertsch (ed.), *The Concept of Activity in Soviet Psychology*. Armonk, New York: M.E. Sharpe.

Levi-Strauss, C. (1978) A Social World Perspective, *Studies in Symbolic Interaction*, 1: 119–28.

Mallon, M. (1998) From Public Sector Employees to Portfolio Workers: Pioneers of New Careers? In C. Mabey, D. Skinner and T. Clark (eds.), *Experiencing Human Resource Management*, London: Sage.

Mangham, I.L. (1978) *Interactions and Interventions in Organisations*. Chichester: Wiley.

Mills, S. (1997) *Discourse*. London: Routledge.

Nardi, B., Whittaker, S. and Schwarz, H. (2002) NetWORKers and their Activity in Intentional Networks, *Computer-Supported Cooperative Work, Special Issue*, January, 11(1–2): 205–242.

Pfeffer, J., Salancik, G. and Leblebici, H. (1976) The Effect of Uncertainty on the Use of Social Influence in Organizational Decision Making, *Administrative Science Quarterly*, 21: 227–45.

Sawicki, J. (1998) Feminism, Foucault and Subjects of Power and Freedom. In J. Moss (ed.), *The Later Foucault*. London: Sage.

Smart, B. (1985) *Michel Foucault*. London: Routledge.

Sole, D.L. and Edmondson, A.C. (2002) Bridging Knowledge Gaps: Learning in Geographically Dispersed, Cross-functional Development Teams. In N. Bontis and C.W. Choo (eds), *Strategic Management of Intellectual Capital and Organizational Knowledge*. Oxford: Oxford University Press.

Star, S. (1992) The Trojan Door: Organisations, Work and the 'Open Black Box', *Systems Practice*, 5: 395–410.

Straus, S.G. and Olivera, F. (2000) Knowledge Acquisition in Virtual Teams, *Researchand Managing Groups and Teams*, 3: 257–82.

Tsoukas, H. (1996) The firm as a distributed knowledge system: a constructionist approach, *Strategic Management Journal*, 17: 11–25.

Vygotsky, L.S. (1978) *Mind in Society*. Cambridge, MA: Harvard University Press.

Wenger, E. (1998) *Communities of Practice*. Cambridge: Cambridge University Press.

# Part III

# Organizational Knowledge and Dynamic Capabilities

# 9
# Knowledge Creation and Organizational Capabilities of Innovating and Imitating Firms

*Arie Y. Lewin and Silvia Massini*

## Introduction

Knowledge, innovation and technological progress have been central themes of research in macro- and microeconomics, innovation processes and strategy. Schumpeter's (1942) seminal book *Capitalism, Socialism and Democracy* is often credited with originating and stimulating interest, theoretical development and research on processes of creative destruction, involving new products, processes, markets, resources and organizations, and the role of the entrepreneur.

Empirical studies on the role of technological progress in economic growth models probably originated with the work of Solow (1956, 1957). These studies have progressed at different levels of analyses: country, industry or sector, and technology. At a macro level, another dimension involves the role of National Systems of Innovation (Freeman, 1987; Lundvall, 1992; Nelson, 1993). Sectoral studies have explored specific patterns of innovation (Pavitt, 1984), technological trajectories (Malerba and Orsenigo, 1996, 2000) as well as the structure and functioning of technological systems (Carlsson, 1995; Edquist, 1997).

With the exception of case studies (for example, Henderson, 1994; Tushman and Anderson, 1997; Clark and Fujimoto, 1991; Burgelman, 2002), this body of research focusses either on a population of firms (industry, sector) or on a technology or on the characteristics of the evolution of science and technology (such as patterns of patents dynamics). Although it is widely recognized that the firm and its unique capabilities is the major source of heterogeneities in the population

(Lewin *et al.*, forthcoming 2003b), few studies have empirically supported a causal link between firm innovation capabilities and competitive advantage (or superior performance).

The major focus of this chapter is on *innovating* and *imitating* firms and their capabilities for knowledge creation within neo-evolutionary economics frameworks (Nelson and Winter, 1982; Dosi, 1982, 1988). We conjecture that *innovating* firms have internalized configurations of organizational know-how, dynamic capabilities or regimes of routines for facilitating and managing innovation and knowledge creation processes that are superior to those of *imitating* firms. Paralleling arguments of the resource-based view of the firm, we consider such organizational knowledge and capabilities to be unique, inimitable and immobile resources partly because these capabilities have been developed within an organization over time, and therefore are neither purchasable in the market nor imitable in the short term. Teece and Pisano (1994) and Teece *et al.* (1997) suggest that dynamic capabilities – the mechanisms through which firms develop and internalize new capabilities in changing environments – form a primary source of competitive advantage. Thus, we proceed on the assumption that *innovating* firms have developed, retained and replicated innovation and knowledge creation routines that are dependent on learning processes and routines specific to the organization that are difficult to imitate and that are the source of strategic advantage. This is also consistent with the perspective that knowledge creation and integration are perhaps the most important strategic assets of the firm (Dierickx and Cool, 1989; Leonard-Barton, 1992; Conner and Prahalad, 1996; Grant, 1996).

However, certain key concepts such as resources or capabilities have proved difficult to observe or measure directly (Godfrey and Hill, 1995; Reed and DeFillippi, 1990; Robins and Wiersema, 1995). As a result, empirical studies have relied on proxy and more distant measures for firm capabilities such as R&D intensity, advertising intensity, and capital intensity as substitutes for directly estimating single or configurations of capabilities. This is also the case with empirical studies in evolutionary economics, where much of the support for the theory is built on simulation studies and illustrative case research. It is altogether clear that the need persists for investigating and understanding the knowledge content of organizational routines, their operationalization, and their dynamics and that the link, if any, between regimes (configurations) of routines and capabilities involving innovation and performance of *innovating* and *imitating* firms remains to be established empirically.

Specifically in this chapter we argue that *innovating* firms (for example, first movers, fast followers or early adopters) differ from *imitating* firms (for example, late adopters, laggards) in the configuration of routines and dynamic capabilities for managing the level of adaptive tension (McKelvey, forthcoming 2003) (for example, meta rules for anchoring adaptation trajectories to different comparison groups), and for managing variation, selection and retention processes, such as exploration and exploitation (March, 1991; Lewin and Volberda, forthcoming, 2003), learning-by-doing, learning-by-using and learning-to-learn (Rosenberg, 1982). *Innovating* firms are also more likely to develop their own unique technical or product or business methods capabilities and applications and are more likely to be actively engaged in the evolution of population-wide practices that ultimately define the new dominant design (Abernathy and Utterback, 1975; Utterback and Abernathy, 1978). Ceteris paribus, these firms are also better positioned to exploit opportunity for rents during the early stages of emergence, evolution and maturation of new dominant logics and designs.

In the sections that follow we briefly review knowledge, technological progress and innovation in economics and the influence of national innovation systems. The chapter discusses routines that are source of firms' heterogeneity. The major contribution of the chapter is a model of organizational capabilities that distinguishes between *innovating* and *imitating* firms.

## Knowledge, technological progress and innovation

Knowledge is clearly a central concept in many social science theories. It is viewed as a crucial component of national economic development and growth and is considered to be the key source of firm capabilities to adapt and create new wealth. Moreover, there is a deep level of belief in society in the central role of knowledge. This is reflected in national policies designed to stimulate technological innovation, in firm strategies for investing in knowledge management systems, in firms striving to transform themselves into learning organizations, in training workers to become knowledge workers and in strategies for protecting and leveraging propriety knowledge. Although a full review and discussion of these theories is beyond the scope of this chapter, it is clear that knowledge is a concept of great significance to theories of the firm, industry-competitive dynamics, political economy, developmental economy, international trade theory and innovation research.

Robert Solow (1957) is often recognized as the first macroeconomist to focus attention on the role of technological change (technological knowledge) in explaining economic growth. He provided estimations of aggregate production functions modeling gross output per man-hour as a function of capital per man-hour. Solow observed that for the period 1909–49 12.5 per cent of the gross output growth was attributable to the increased use of capital and the remaining 87.5 per cent was due to technical change. For Solow 'technical change' means '*any kind of shift* in the production function: thus slowdowns, speedups, improvements in the education of the labor force and all sorts of things will appear as "technical change"' (p. 312, italics in the original). Therefore, if growth models explicitly included variables for innovation and technological change, it would be possible to identify and measure their specific contribution to economic growth. Jorgenson and Griliches (1967) estimated the average annual rate of growth in total output over the period 1945–65 to be 3.49 per cent and the average annual rate of growth in total inputs and total factor productivity to be 1.83 per cent and 1.60 per cent respectively. Thus, the rate of growth in total inputs explains 52.4 per cent in total output. The remainder is explained by changes in total factor productivity which also includes technological progress embedded in new capital investments, research and development activities, human capital effectiveness and organizational knowledge. Although technological innovations and other factors such as improved managerial and organizational knowledge are now accepted as important variables for explaining economic growth, they have proved to be difficult to quantify analytically.

Since Solow's seminal insights, much theoretical and empirical research has extended the work on aggregate production functions and related total factor productivity functions. For example, the New Growth Theory (Romer, 1986, 1990) represents an attempt to incorporate human capital as an endogenous growth variable. Building on empirical evidence on the importance of investments in research and training to develop skilled labour, these models introduce employment of skilled human capital and investments in research, with increasing marginal productivity, to formulate a dynamic production function. The models assume that the stock of technological knowledge is embodied in people with a finite life, and that human capital must be renewed continuously. The models also assume learning-by-doing processes and cumulative learning (Lucas, 1988). These models claim to incorporate technological progress endogenously. In reality, however, their models do not capture actual processes for generating, developing and improving technological knowledge and learning, beyond introducing new human capital and continue to rely on the average representative firm as the basis for their aggregate studies.

Applied economists have specified models that decompose knowledge elements of Solow 'residual'. By introducing additional independent variables in the production function that can represent technological change, such as R&D expenditures and patents, Zvi Griliches (1986, 1991) and his collaborators have provided important empirical evidence of the role of innovative activities on macro and micro growth. At the macro level improvements in science and technology, proxied by national efforts in R&D expenditures or number of patents, have been shown to be equally important as capital accumulation and skilled labour in explaining the upward shift in the aggregate production. At the micro level it emerges that discretionary investments in, for example, research and development (for example, Griliches and Mairesse, 1981) and changes in work practices (for example, Ichniowski *et al.*, 1997) are significant factors in accounting for changes in firm growth and productivity.

Griliches (1991, 1995) showed that, in addition to the firm's own R&D efforts, it is also important to consider the cumulative R&D undertaken by other firms operating in horizontally and vertically contiguous sectors in explaining firm growth. The pool of collective knowledge in an economy or industry increases the effectiveness of individual efforts in creating and developing new knowledge. At the same time, firms that intend to benefit from knowledge developed elsewhere cannot expect to do so passively, but need to invest in developing their own knowledge and competencies to be ready and able to recognize, evaluate and appropriate valuable external knowledge and use it effectively (Cohen and Levinthal, 1989, 1990; see also the recent review by Zahra and George, 2002). Moreover, in order to benefit from knowledge spillovers across organizational boundaries and other externalities, firms need to have or to develop similar, complementary knowledge capabilities and be in proximate technological (Jaffe, 1986, 1988) and geographical (Howells, 1990; Feldman, 1993; Jaffe *et al.*, 1993) locations.

Debates within the field of industrial organization economics also serve to highlight the importance of firm-specific path dependence, strategic choices and capabilities in explaining industry conduct and performance. The existence of diversity and variation among firms within an industry is due to 'differing histories of strategic choice and performance' (Rumelt, 1984: 558) or to different managerial decision making. Empirical studies testing the relative importance of industry and firm effects in predicting performance have found that industry effects only explained about 17 to 20 per cent of the variance in financial performance (Schmalensee, 1985; Wernerfelt and Montgomery, 1988; Rumelt, 1991). However, Rumelt (1991), distinguishing between stable and yearly fluctuating performance effects, found that stable industry effects only explained 8 per cent of the variance in business performance and business-specific effects explained 46 per cent of the variance in performance. Wernerfelt and Montgomery (1988), using Tobin's q as performance variable, found strong firm-specific effects that were roughly 13–21 per cent larger than the industry effects. Consistent with Wernerfelt and Montgomery (1988), Hansen and Wernerfelt (1989) found that organizational factors were about twice as important as industry effects. Cubbin and Geroski (1987) found strong heterogeneity within most industries, as well as a lack of common industry-wide response to change among almost half of the firms studied. More recently, Mauri and Michaels (1998) and Brush *et al.* (1999) found that firm effects outweighed industry effects in affecting firm performance. However, it is altogether clear that roles of organizational knowledge and capabilities in explaining performance at the level of organization-specific routines and dynamic capabilities have not advanced beyond better estimates of the knowledge components in the random error.

Schumpeter (1942: 83) pointed out that 'the fundamental impulse that sets and keeps the capitalist engine in motion comes from the new consumers' goods, the new methods of production or transportation, the new markets, the new forms of industrial organization that capitalist enterprise creates'. Yet most innovation studies tend to concentrate on product or process innovations. By observing adaptation, change and progress in economic society at the time, the Austrian economist directed attention to the incessant destruction of the old economic structure and the incessant creation of a new one. He also explored differences between role of larger modern corporations and smaller entrepreneurial enterprises in developing innovations. Larger firms have resources for creating formal R&D laboratories, exploiting economies of scale in the R&D function itself, better access to external finances, and benefit from complementarities between R&D, manufacturing and non manufacturing activities. By deploying resources to explore new technological opportunities large firms can originate new products and processes and thereby strengthen their market power further. However, Schumpeter also noticed a high degree of bureaucratization in research and innovation activities that impedes development of capitalism and opens opportunities for smaller firms with greater flexibility for innovation and new ventures in the economy. Schumpeterian ideas unleashed an enormous empirical literature investigating effects of firm size and market concentration on innovation and direction of causality (Cohen and Levin, 1989; Cohen, 1995). These studies conclude that there is a positive monotonic relationship between firm size and R&D, but that innovative output appears to be less than proportional to size, and therefore R&D productivity declines with size. However, the relationship between market concentration and innovation is not very strong and seems to reflect more fundamental characteristics of industries, such as opportunity and appropriability conditions (Cohen, 1995).

A number of historical case studies have also investigated evolution, development and management of technologies (Van de Ven *et al.*, 1989; Henderson and Clark, 1990; Jelinek and Schoonhoven, 1990; Morone, 1993). These studies have a process focus and explore dynamics of resolving unanticipated technical problems in different areas that emerge when a new technology is being developed. In the process of solving a problem in one area scientists and engineers are likely to find new problems in related technological areas. The process of developing and shaping new technologies is not linear or intendedly rational. It involves many dead ends, new beginnings and a series of bottlenecks that are overcome through combination and recombination of existing known solutions and, on occasion, discovery of entirely novel technological advances (Van de Ven *et al.*, 1989). It appears that technologies tend to develop within technological paradigms (Dosi, 1982) that offer technology specific opportunities and along trajectories (Nelson and Winter, 1977) that to some extent are decoupled from market influences.

Mechanisms of development and diffusion of new and competing technologies have also been explored within various simulation models. Arthur (1989) developed a probabilistic model, demonstrating that when two new technologies appear in the market it is not always the case that the superior technology emerges as the dominant design. Dynamic increasing returns to adoption may shift the adoption preference to the more highly adopted technology, because related services are likely to emerge sooner, because of network and externality effects and establishment of technical standards. Classical examples include the QWERTY keyboard (David, 1985) and VHS/Betamax case (Cusumano *et al.*, 1997).

Another characteristic of technological development and evolution involves the localized nature of innovation research and development. In general, firms tend to explore new opportunities and technical advances by searching and learning in areas closely related to or adjoining their existing applications and practices (Cyert and March, 1963; Nelson and Winter, 1982). Existing applications and knowledge may be sub-optimal or inadequate, but for reasons of bounded rationality, satisficing decision making and technological and organizational lock-in the firm may be unable or unwilling to search for or adopt new technological solutions or make changes to the hierarchy of routines. Kogut and Zander (1992) have argued that *innovating* firms need to develop combinative capabilities as exploration mechanisms for facilitating dynamic transformation of current knowledge and acquisition of new knowledge and for generating new application from existing knowledge. More generally, the dynamic capability of firms determines their ability to respond to competition in a rapidly changing environment by effectively adapting, integrating, co-ordinating and reconfiguring internal and external organizational skills, resources and functional competencies (Teece *et al.*, 1997). The organizational capacity for dynamically combining and recombining knowledge is a distinguishing characteristic of *innovating* and *imitating* firms because the capabilities of a firm cannot be separated from its current organization.

Absorptive capacity (Cohen and Levinthal, 1989, 1990; Zahra and George, 2002) for assimilating new knowledge has clearly emerged as another organization capability that distinguishes between *innovating* and *imitating* firms. Cohen and Levinthal (1989, 1990) argued that the acquisition, transformation and internalization of external knowledge, requires firms to have an internal knowledge configuration (for example stock, organization structure, practices, etc.) that enables screening, identification and absorption of potentially useful new external information and knowledge. Firm-specific investments in R&D generate new knowledge and innovations, facilitate learning and develop absorptive capacity, that become the basis for evaluating and exploiting external knowledge.

Organizational absorptive capacity, however, does not only involve organizational routines for acquiring and assimilating new knowledge and information. It also requires organizational routines and capabilities for integrating and exploiting this new knowledge. It implies development and internalization of effective routines for transferring knowledge across and within subunits; exchanging and sharing knowledge with competitors, partners, suppliers and customers; appropriating knowledge from spillovers; and safeguarding crucial internal knowledge from imitation. Furthermore, absorptive capacity also depends upon prior knowledge and facilitates cumulative learning of new related knowledge, efficient and effective co-ordination or integration of activities internal to the firm, as well as external co-ordination of activities and technologies, via strategic alliances, outsourcing, technological collaborations, formal or informal networks between industries, and between industry and university laboratories. Clearly, organization structures are critical for facilitating and assimilating knowledge creation. However, while important research identifies absorptive capacity as a lynchpin capability of *innovating* firms, the actual bundles of routines and capabilities that distinguish *innovating* from *imitating* firms remains to be studied at the level of organizational routines.

The discussion so far has treated innovation research as applying universally, independent of the influence of nation-state institutional configurations (Lewin and Kim, forthcoming 2003). However, technological opportunities, appropriability regimes and mechanisms, spillover effects tend to vary across industry (Pavitt, 1984) and countries (Malerba and Orsenigo, 1996). Therefore, the dynamics of innovation should vary across countries, sectors and firms. It is the configuration of organizations, institutions, formal structures with explicit goals and purposes, and the sets of habits, routines, rules, norms and legal statutes, that regulate the relations and interactions between actors (people, organizations, etc.) and constitute National Innovation Systems (Lundvall, 1992; Nelson, 1993). Technological innovations and knowledge develop faster or at lower costs through collaborations and interactions between scientists and engineers affiliated with different firms and laboratories. It is the network configuration of institutions in public and private sectors (firms, banks, universities, governments, and so on), and the structure of incentive for promoting and protecting new intellectual property that shape National Systems of Innovation (Freeman, 1987; Lundvall, 1992; Nelson, 1993) and influence rate and direction of technological learning in a country (Patel and Pavitt, 1992).

From the above analysis, it is clear that National Innovation Systems influence the processes of interactions, initiation and diffusion of new technologies, scale of R&D and other technical activities, as well as organization and allocation of resources at the national, industry and enterprise level. Therefore, we expect that firm-specific innovation regimes will differ across countries within same sectors. However, it is beyond the scope of this chapter to develop these differences in depth (see Massini *et al.*, 2002; Whitley, 2002; Lewin and Kim, forthcoming 2003).

## Firm heterogeneity and competitive advantage: unpacking the black box

Collectively, firm-level theories serve to elaborate population heterogeneity due to differences within firms. The resource-based view (Penrose, 1959; Wernerfelt, 1984; Barney, 1991), the behavioural theory of the firm (Cyert and March, 1963), strategic choice (Child, 1972; Miles and Snow, 1978), punctuated equilibrium (Tushman and Romanelli, 1985; Gersick, 1991), and transaction cost theory (Coase, 1937; Williamson, 1975, 1985) all focus on differences in adaptation at the level of the firm. Evolutionary economics (Nelson and Winter, 1982) is an economic theory of technological change. It focuses on technological development and adaptation as embedded in organizational capability to develop and improve practiced routines. These processes involve information processing, decision making, search and selection as well as imitation of best practices from the environment. Neo-evolutionary models, as a class, have the advantage of considering organization change as emergent outcomes deriving from interaction of firm level processes (including managerial intentionality) and environmental selection.

Evolutionary economics builds on the behavioural theory of the firm (Cyert and March, 1963). It extends principles of bounded rationality, satisficing, aspiration level adaptation (March and Simon, 1958), local rationality, adaptation level decision rules, feedback-react decision procedures, problemistic search, and organizational learning, to describe how firms change and adapt their technologies, both internally and as an outcome of interaction with the environment. Evolutionary economics stresses the existence of differences in technology, productivity and profitability among firms, and provides an explanatory foundation for sources of such heterogeneity. Nelson and Winter (1974, 1982) developed simulation models of interaction of heterogeneous firms over time and reproduced estimations of aggregate production function and economic growth as in Solow (1957). Evolutionary economics advances a theory of economic growth in which technological change is simultaneously endogenous and exogenous, and where innovation processes and research activities are explicitly described. The theory clearly assumes that, regardless of industry, exceptional performance derives from superior internal hierarchies of routines. The theory implies that in highly competitive environments successful firms experience superior survival and growth rates because their superior capabilities enable them to consistently sustain innovation, new knowledge creation, recombining of existing capabilities and reinventing and updating their underlying routines. The less successful firms are assumed to be selected out at increasing rates because they lack comparably developed innovation and new knowledge creation routines (Nelson and Winter, 1982).

Evolutionary economics stresses differences in technology, productivity and profitability among firms, and provides an explanatory foundation for sources of such heterogeneity. It models the firm as a hierarchy of practiced routines that change over time in response to problems, organization learning and innovation. Routines consist of rules, heuristics and norms that are expressed at different levels of organizational activities. They range from simple rules, involving problem search, local search, to higher-level routines that regulate innovation and change, as well as interaction with the environment. Evolutionary economics assumes that new technologies, processes or business methods have to be internalized into the hierarchy of existing routines and capabilities through firm-specific variation, selection and replication processes. It specifically recognizes dynamic interaction of internal and external variation, selection and replication processes in knowledge creation and change over time. The expected outcomes are new superior routines and capabilities, and creation of new knowledge.

The execution of routines does not assume or require understanding of the knowledge base underlying the routine, which ranges from codified to tacit (Polanyi, 1967). Codified knowledge is embodied in decision rules, and practiced routines may embody tacit idiosyncratic knowledge. The knowledge basis of decision rules is modified through problemistic search, trial and error, random improvisation, and directed search. Capabilities are viewed as bundles of routines, and the theory posits that capabilities and routines change and adapt via internal search, selection, and replication processes; it also posits imitation processes based on interaction between internal and external environments. In a broader sense, the theory provides a basis for modelling intra-firm variation, selection and retention (VSR) processes and the emergent outcome of external selection environment.

## Distinguishing *innovating* from *imitating* firms

The performance implications of evolutionary economics are of specific interest to this chapter. The theory clearly assumes that, regardless of industry, exceptional performance derives from superior internal hierarchies of routines. Moreover, configurations of routines and capabilities are context-specific and also reflect differences in national institutional configurations. Thus, for example, capabilities for absorbing new knowledge can be expected to consist of more elaborated bundles of routines in R&D intensive than in low R&D intensive industries and vary by country (Massini *et al.*, 2002).

Econometric estimations of knowledge production function have provided strong inferential support for contribution of knowledge

(R&D, patents and training) to macroeconomic growth models and firm productivity (Griliches, 1995; Jorgenson and Fraumeni, 1992) and performance (market value) (Bosworth and Rogers, 2001; Hall *et al.*, 2001). Case studies on firm capabilities and adaptation have primarily served to greatly explicate sources and cause of structural inertia and why firms are not able to adapt (for example, Leonard-Barton, 1992). Simulation studies have been important sources of new theoretical insights regarding, for example, relationship between exploration and exploitation in organizational learning (March, 1991), ineffectiveness of strategies based on imitating complex capabilities of competitors (Rivkin, 2000), and random sources of learning and adaptation (Cohen *et al.*, 1972).

The inescapable conclusion is that few studies have empirically supported a causal link between knowledge and competitive advantage or superior performance, or investigated the relationship between competitive advantage and firm capabilities and routines. In spite of much inferential and circumstantial evidence on the importance and value of knowledge, there is no direct empirical support linking superior knowledge and knowing capabilities to exceptional performance or competitive advantage (McEvily and Chakravarty, 2002). Ceteris paribus, successful firms are assumed to experience superior survival and growth. Less successful firms are assumed to be selected out at increasing rates because they lack comparably developed innovation and new knowledge creation routines. Clearly the need persists to investigate and understand the knowledge content of organizational routines and their operationalization, and the link between superior routines and capabilities to performance of successful firms.

The most plausible explanation for the conclusion of McEvily and Chakravarty (2002) is the very small representation of *innovating* firms in the population being studied. Indeed, various theories distinguish between firms that initiate change, such as early entrants, early adopters and fast followers, and those that adopt change once it is matured, codified and fully understood. Institutional theory describes how original diversity and variation among organizations (initial stage of innovation and change) is replaced by a process of institutionalization and homogenization (DiMaggio and Powell, 1991). The diffusion of institution isomorphism is posited to occur through three mechanisms – coercive, mimetic and normative. Coercive isomorphism primarily results from political pressure for legitimacy, exerted by external institutional environment or by large organizations that control significant resources or market shares. In the face of technological or strategic uncertainties initiated by new entrants (technological innovators) organizations are posited to mimic practices and strategies of organizations perceived as successful implementers. Thus mimetic isomorphic pressure leads organizations to imitate others by modelling themselves after successful competitors. In the case of new technologies, mimetic organizations adopt technologies of early adopters because of desire to increase organization legitimacy. Normative isomorphic pressures arise from the need to conform to professional standards, such as formal education and industry standards such as manufacturing standards. Thus once an innovation begins to mature in the form of standards, normative isomorphic pressure explains the spread of the standard throughout the population.

Population ecology generally perceives organizations as being unable to adapt (Hannan and Freeman, 1984). Over time, environmental change driven by a few new entrants results in a mis-alignment between incumbent organization forms and new entrants. The inability of incumbents to change creates opportunities for new entrants to establish new organization forms with a better fit to the environment, thereby introducing variation that triggers increasing selection rates. Once viability of new organization forms becomes visible, density of organization founding and disbanding increases. Density-dependent population dynamics explain why intra-population processes of founding and disbanding follow a concave pattern of growth and decline. Initial growth in population density (number of organizations with new forms) increases the legitimacy of the new population. Legitimacy gained from greater population density leads to an increase in founding rates and a decrease in failure rates in new organization forms.

Similar findings are observed in diffusion of innovation literature and widely observed S-shaped profile of the diffusion of an innovation. The emerging empirical regularity supports a phenomenon of a few actors or firms involved in the early stages of initiating and shaping an innovation, with most firms adopting innovation past a certain level of codification and standardization (Bass, 1980; Rogers, 1983; Mahajan *et al.*, 1990). The development process of a new technology and its diffusion can be quite long, because of technological uncertainties characterizing the initial phase of new product development. It has been observed that the time before a technology takes off (ahead of S-shaped diffusion profile becoming convex) can be quite extensive (Stoneman, 1983). Moreover, during the period when technological experimentation is taking place, industries experience a high degree of turbulence due to high number of new entries and deaths (Abernathy and Utterback, 1975; Utterback and Abernathy, 1978; Klepper, 1997).

The theoretical literature on parametric and non-parametric estimation of Pareto performance frontiers (Lewin and Lovell, 1990, 1995) also demonstrates that only a few firms define the frontier. Most firms in an industry operate below the performance frontier. One model shows where the life chances of firms increase with proximity to Pareto performance frontiers. In other words, successful firms (those defining the performance frontier over time) experience lower selection rates than firms below the frontier and selection rates increase with distance from the frontier. Firms defining the Pareto performance frontiers (including those that leapfrog onto the frontier) possess superior organizational capabilities and hierarchies of routines that distinguish them from other firms in the population.

We have argued that *innovating* firms or firms that define the Pareto performance frontier in an industry represent a small outlier group of their respective populations. Consistent with Cohen and Klepper (1992) we believe that the population of firms within and across sectors consists of a bimodal distribution, where the frequency of *innovating* firms is much smaller than the frequency of *imitating* firms. Therefore, it is plausible to conjecture that adaptation strategies, adaptation trajectories and configurations of organizational routines and capabilities of *innovating* firms should be significantly different from the rest of the population. Of specific interest to this chapter are differences in configuration of routines and capabilities of *innovating* and *imitating* firms applied to new knowledge creation, absorption and adaptation. In our view, the few *innovating* firms (first mover, fast followers, early adopter) who participate in developing, shaping and adoption of new innovations (technologies, processes or business methods), internalize more elaborate organizational routines and adaptation capabilities for driving change, such as experimentation, trial and error and learning-by-doing than *imitating* firms (late adopters, laggards) who are less likely to exhibit such organizational regimes and will tend to introduce changes only once they become commonly accepted in the population, codified and easier to implement (Kieser, 1997; Abrahamson and Fairchild, 1999).

Early adopters of technological innovations are more likely to act like lead users (von Hippel, 1986). They conceive and contribute new applications for these technologies not initially thought of by their developers, because they internalize routines that facilitate exchanging and sharing information affecting various aspects of new technologies. Firms that aspire to become early innovators, but do not have the supporting organizational capabilities, are more likely to fail in the dynamics of shaping the new dominant design, and therefore will fail to appropriate any rents. Late adopters who possess the supporting organizational routines are more likely to succeed in adopting new dominant design at the state of the art, but will only appropriate some of the rents, because of their very lateness. Firms who adopt new dominant design because of normative or mimetic isomorphic pressure, or because decisions for change are triggered by a crisis (late adopters), are more likely to adopt codified dominant design (without tacit or more idiosyncratic extensions) and are least likely to appropriate rents.

Two cases serve to illustrate our argument. Wal-Mart and Kmart evolved along opposite paths in application of IT to mass merchandising. From the early days of point of sales terminals (POS), through scanner technologies, electronic data interchange (EDI) technologies and satellite networks, Wal-Mart was an early participant in developing supply chain management capabilities. Although supply chain IT solutions are now widely available, it was Wal-Mart and a few other mass retailers and manufacturers, such as P&G, who collectively developed the applications that gave them significant cost advantages early on. For example, P&G and Wal-Mart pioneered the capabilities of supplier self-replenishing of inventory based on sophisticated routines using store scanner data. Wal-Mart has also developed routines for suppliers to self-stock shelves in its stores. The rest of the story is well documented (Hunter, 1999). Kmart had the same opportunities as Wal-Mart to be an early participant in developing IT capabilities that reinvented supply chain management in the mass merchandiser sector, but it did not do so. In one sense, this is surprising since Kmart pioneered the mass merchandising discount concept (Hunter, 1999). Regardless, in the context of evolutionary economics theory, we would conjecture that Kmart did not internalize a set of strategies and organization routines intended to reinvent and update its business model over and over again.

The Dell company represents another example in an entirely different industry. In a similar manner to Wal-Mart, Dell invented an IT-based business model that combines mass customization build-to-order (on basis of online booking of orders) capabilities with supply chain management that is superior to traditional retail distribution model employed by its competitors. Again, as with Wal-Mart, Dell did not invent these capabilities instantaneously. They emerged after several years of trial and error and learning-by-doing. Competitors such as HP, Compaq and IBM, by not themselves participating in early phases of development and adoption of these applications, and because they were, perhaps, unable to devise strategies that would allow them to simultaneously manage two distribution channels (traditional retail and online), essentially fell behind Dell and conceded significant cost advantages to Dell. Most recently, during the downturn in the PC sector this advantage allowed Dell to grow market share by unleashing price competition in the industry. Moreover, Dell is now adapting its business model for competition in adjacent sectors such as inkjet printers, servers, storage devices and routers. If Dell were to be successful in its expansion into these adjacent lines of business, it would support the argument that Dell has internalized strategies and organizational regimes appropriate for reinventing and adapting themselves over time.

Evolutionary theory discusses mainly external VSR routines and the resulting dynamics at the population level have been widely studied empirically (see, for example, Dosi *et al.*, 2000). However, internal VSR routines as represented by organizational routines, and how they interact with external VSR processes, are less studied. We argue that although internal VSR routines tend to be technology and organization specific, early adopters will exhibit similarity in meta-routines, organization culture and management philosophy, regardless of technology or business method being developed. Such firms are likely to share common organization characteristics, mainly those related to their capability to internalize external knowledge and to enable them to be more receptive and adaptive to adopt new, ill understood, and risky technologies. Our view, therefore, goes beyond the explanation of first mover advantage. As the Wal-Mart and Kmart comparison suggests, and as the empirical literature on first mover advantages has shown (for example, Silverberg *et al.*, 1988), first mover strategies do not necessarily lead to first mover advantage. For this advantage to materialize, the firm must also be able to employ structures, processes and hierarchies of routines that collectively support emergence, improvisation, trial and error, experimentation, learning-by-doing, recombination of existing capabilities, externalization and sharing, appropriation of spillover knowledge and internalization (retention and replication) of the new routines. This is consistent with the statement 'The strategy was right but the execution failed' often espoused by senior managers. Such routines and capabilities make up the knowledge spiral (Nonaka and Takeuchi, 1995) and distinguish absorptive capacity for assimilating internal and external new knowledge between firms.

## Towards a model of organizational capabilities of *innovating* and *imitating* firms

In this section we outline the basic elements of a model of organizational routines and capabilities that distinguishes between *innovating* and *imitating* firms at two levels of analysis. First, we consider the meta-routine that defines level of adaptive tension. This meta-routine is the gene (Nelson and Winter, 1982), or meme (Aldrich, 1999) or genotype (Anderson, 1999), that regulates change (rate and magnitude). Second, we consider configurations of routines that define *innovating* and *imitating* absorptive capacity capabilities.

## Level of adaptive tension

Following Cyert and March (1963), we assume that organizational goals for change (incremental improvements, cost reduction, innovation, etc.) are a function of (1) goal in previous period, (2) organizational past experience with respect to change for a specific dimension, and (3) information about experience and/or performance of a reference group for this change dimension.

A linear representation of the functional form for establishing level of adaptive tension (*LOT*) at time *t*, for change dimension *i*, is shown in the equation below:

$$LOT_{t,i} = a_1 LOT_{t-1,i} + a_2 E_{t,i} + a_3 R_{t-1,i} \qquad i = 1,..., N$$

Where *LOT* is the level of adaptive tension; *E* is cumulative past experience $E_t = \Sigma_{j=1,...,J} \omega_{t-j} E_{t-j}$, where weights $\omega_{t-j}$ decrease with age; and *R* is a summary measure of reference, or comparison, group experiences. The sum of the weights $a_1 + a_2 + a_3$ is equal to 1. The index *i* represents different dimensions of change for a particular firm, such as cost reduction, new product introduction, and time to market. In the discussion that follows we simplify the equation by not considering the effect of *LOT* in previous period, $LOT_{t-1}$, and focus mainly on role of past experience and reference group. Thus,

$$LOT_{t,i} = \alpha E_{t,i} + \beta R_{t-1,i}$$

where $\alpha + \beta = 1$. This function represents several important attributes of organizational adaptation. The weights $\alpha$ and $\beta$ represent relative weights that an organization assigns to its own experience in revising its aspiration for $LOT_t$ and its sensitivity to the performance of competitors. It should become evident that one source of heterogeneity of firms in a population is expressed by firm-specific preferences for $\alpha$ and $\beta$. In addition, $\alpha$ and $\beta$ change with experience. As firms experience success with a technology or process the weight assigned to own past experience $\alpha$ will increase, and the sensitivity to the performance of competitors $\beta$ will decline. The extreme case of firms unable to adopt and adapt to competency destroying technological change (Anderson and Tushman, 1990; Christensen, 1997) could be represented in this equation with $\alpha = 1$ and $\beta = 0$.

A second source of firm heterogeneity is associated with the selection of reference or comparison group. Research on level of aspiration (Lewin *et al.*, 1944) and social comparison theory (Festinger, 1954) suggest that most individuals and organizations have a preference for selecting a reference group that reflects average performance of peers as distinct from individuals or groups defining performance frontier. In other words, individuals and organizations tend to select reference groups close to themselves or to firms that they dominate. In addition to psychological explanations, the asymmetric reward structure of organizations (Schiff and Lewin, 1970) motivates managers to bargain for performance goals that are within their level of aspiration range (defined as probability of success $> 0.5$) composed of unit-specific historical experience and average performance of industry peer group. Although the business process engineering movement introduced the idea of benchmarking to best in class, most firms employ the language of *best in class*, but in reality compare to an *average* benchmark (Hammer, 1996). If all firms held their managers accountable to achieve performance goals that match or exceed the best in class (firms defining the Pareto performance frontier), few managers would be awarded their performance bonuses. Not surprisingly, most firms devise adaptation strategies that anchor bonus payouts to improvements over the previous period and to a lesser extent to expectation of matching or slightly exceeding average performance of competitors. *Innovating* firms, we conjecture, select their reference group from among other *innovating* firms or from those defining the Pareto performance frontier. However, they eschew the matching adaptation strategies of *imitating* firms. *Innovating* firms use their reference group information as an anchor for differentiating themselves from other *innovating* firms by, for example, employing strategies of hyper-competition (D'Aveni, 1994, 1999; Illinitch *et al.*, 1998), escalation of competition, leapfrogging, etc. As a result *innovating* firms introduce and increase variety.

Massini *et al.* (2003), in a study of adoption of new organization routines assumed to increase firm structural and procedural flexibility, have explored the role of comparison groups in determining the pattern of adoption. Regardless of cross-national differences, the small number of leading edge adopters (*innovating* firms) was more likely to use the top quartile population as their benchmark. The majority of the firms in the population adopted incremental changes or made no change (*imitating* firms). These firms were more likely to use the average of their respective subpopulation as their benchmark and their adaptation pattern is more consistent with matching or slightly exceeding subpopulation average. *Innovating* firms appear to anchor their adaptation pattern to the average of top quartile; however, the variance in the adaptation pattern was significantly higher than for *imitating* firms supporting arguments of differentiation strategies for the *innovating* firms.

In summary, we argue that most firms anchor their level of adaptive tension to their past experience and to average experience of their competitors. Therefore, firms are more likely to consider adopting a technological innovation once the adoption trend is visible, when emerging underlying standards have been formalized and adopted by industry setting bodies, or technology is sufficiently codified, so that adoption represents significant lower levels of uncertainty. In other words, behaviour of late adopters is consistent with normative and mimetic isomorphism. *Innovating* firms, we conjecture, are more likely to select other *innovating* firms as their reference group. More generally, we expect firms that are near or on the Pareto performance frontiers to use the comparison to a subset of other firms that define the frontier as an anchor and as the basis for differentiating themselves from other *innovating* firms. The level of adaptive tension of *innovating* firms, therefore, is more likely to be anchored to that of other *innovating* firms. But the firm-specific technological development will reflect its own unique contributions to shaping the emerging technology and at the same time mirror the leading edge technological trajectory. Thus, firms whose LOT meme anchors change to performance frontier are more likely to be first movers, fast followers or early adopters, and should have higher odds of capturing abnormal rents. Firms whose LOT meme anchors change to average of peers can at best expect to capture average rents or less. In other words *innovating* firms are more likely to establish their innovation aspirations by comparisons with other firms that define the technological frontier, whereas *imitating* firms are more likely to establish their innovation aspirations at the level of the population average.

## Absorptive capacity capabilities

Although absorptive capacity is a central construct for explaining innovation and knowledge creation, the configuration of routines that make up absorptive capacity capabilities have not been empirically researched and explicated. In our view, regardless of sectors, firms with superior innovation and knowledge creation performance have more sophisticated, more highly developed and elaborated knowledge creation routines, and learning regimes. The configurations of routines and capabilities are context-specific and, therefore, the absorptive capacity capabilities of *innovating* firms consist of more elaborated bundles of routines than of *imitating* firms. For example, Simon (1962) describes combinative capabilities as the routines for decomposing internal, existing and old knowledge and recombining it. *Innovating* firms are more likely to have configured routines for this process than *imitating* firms. Similarly, *innovating* firms are more likely to develop reflection routines that govern updating of routines and increase retention of superior, successful routines (Zollo and Winter, 2002).

Nonaka and Takeuchi (1995) described four phases of evolution of tacit and explicit knowledge and new knowledge creation: socialization (tacit to tacit), externalization (tacit to explicit), combination (explicit to explicit), and internalization (explicit to tacit). They describe the characteristics of representative Japanese firms and do not distinguish between highly effective and less effective knowledge creation firms. We argue that *innovating* firms are more likely to develop routines for each of these phases. More generally, *innovating* firms are likely to internalize and elaborate routines and capabilities for facilitating variation (improvisation, balancing exploration and exploitation, enabling emergence); combinative capabilities and internal selection regimes (decomposing and recombining); reflection and updating routines; and selecting, assimilating and integrating superior routines and capabilities. In addition, *innovating* firms are more likely to develop routines for exchanging and sharing information with partners, suppliers, customers and competitors; participating in shaping technological standards and industry practices; transferring knowledge across and within subunits; appropriating spillovers; and safeguarding crucial internal knowledge.

*Innovating* firms vary in terms of internal and external absorptive capacity. For example, internal absorptive capacity relates to such routines as combinative capabilities, internal selection regimes, assimilating and integrating new knowledge generated internally. External absorptive capacity relates to routines for exchanging and sharing information with partners, suppliers, customers and competitors, shaping standards, and appropriating spillovers. External absorptive capacity is not a necessary condition for effective internal absorptive capacity; however, effective external absorptive capacity does require complementary internal absorptive capabilities. Firms with effective external absorptive capacity routines (or capacity to absorb external knowledge) are more likely to select their comparison group from firms defining the technological frontier. Furthermore, the effectiveness of absorptive capacity routines of *innovating* firms will depend on internalization of complementarities mechanisms (Milgrom and Roberts, 1990, 1995; Ichniowski *et al.*, 1998; Massini and Pettigrew, 2003), which regulate the overall effectiveness of configuring, implementing and adapting absorptive capacity routines and capabilities.

## Discussion

In this chapter we have argued that a critical gap in the literature describing sources of firm heterogeneity relates to an absence of empirical research that unpacks the routine bases of variation, selection and retention processes. In particular, we explored the differences in innovation, knowledge creation and absorptive capacity capabilities of *innovating* and *imitating* firms. Prior empirical research has not found direct empirical support linking superior knowledge and knowing capabilities to superior performance (McEvily and Chakravarty, 2002), probably because of the very low frequency of *innovating* firms in the population being studied. The theoretical model developed in this chapter describes micro-adaptation processes that explain population level normative and mimetic isomorphic phenomena.

*Innovating* firms differ from *imitating* firms for two fundamental reasons. The first relates to the meta-routine (or meme) that regulates change. We refer to this meta routine as level of adaptive tension. In addition, the configuration of absorptive capacity capabilities differs between *innovating* and *imitating* firms. The level of adaptive tension combines firm-cumulative past experience and a summary measure of the performance of comparison groups. The difference between the LOT of *innovating* and *imitating* firms derives from the selection of the comparison groups and the sensitivity to the performance of this group. *Innovating* firms, we argue, are more likely to select their comparison group from the population of firms that define the technological frontier. *Imitating* firms are more likely to select their comparison group from firms representing the average of the population or firms they dominate. In addition, *innovating* firms are more sensitive to the performance of their comparison group ($\beta$ innovating $> \beta$ imitating) because that information anchors their differentiating strategies from other firms defining the technological frontier. The distribution of the weights assigned to own experience and the performance of comparison groups and the selection of comparison groups is a new source of firm heterogeneity that has not been heretofore explored in the literature.

In summary, the level of adaptive tension of *innovating* firms is more likely to be anchored to that of other *innovating* firms and firm-specific technological development is more likely to mirror the leading edge technological trajectory of the industry. Firms whose LOT meme anchors change to performance frontier are more likely to be first movers, fast followers or early adopters, and should have higher odds of capturing abnormal rents. Analogously, firms whose LOT anchors change to average of peers can at best expect to capture average rents or less. In other words, *innovating* firms are more likely to establish their innovation aspirations by comparisons with other firms that define the technological frontier, whereas *imitating* firms are more likely to establish their innovation aspirations at the level of the population average, or firms in the same position in the distribution.

We have also explored the differences in the configuration of routines that make up the absorptive capacity capabilities of *innovating* and *imitating* firms. In particular, we argue that the absorptive capacity of *imitating* firms is limited to adopting codified and mature knowledge, whereas *innovating* firms develop internal and external absorptive capacity for innovation and creation of new knowledge.

The model has several implications for further theoretical development. For example, do firms with low internal capabilities for innovation and knowledge creation favour external sourcing strategy (for example, learning alliances) as a means to gain access to complementary knowledge and expertise? All else being equal, do firms in R&D-intensive sectors have more elaborated innovation and absorptive capacity capabilities than firms in low-tech sectors? Similarly, are firms in industries that experience rapid change and technological progress more likely to have developed external absorptive capabilities? The absorptive capacity of *innovating* firms is differentiated along the configuration for internal absorptive capacity, external absorptive capacity, and the complementarity mechanisms that regulate the overall effectiveness of configuring, implementing and adapting absorptive capacity routines and capabilities. Do these complementarity mechanisms introduce a level of complexity that differentiates among *innovating* firms and directly affects the challenge of imitation?

In conclusion, this chapter advances a new theoretical framework for research on firm-level innovation and knowledge creation capabilities consistent with the view that only a few firms initiate technological change that diffuses throughout the population of firms. It is altogether clear that the need persists for investigating and understanding the knowledge content of organizational routines, their operationalization, and their dynamics and that the link, if any, between regimes (configurations) of routines and capabilities involving innovation and performance of *innovating* and *imitating* firms remains to be established empirically.

## Acknowledgements

The first draft of this chapter was presented at the Third European Conference on Organizational Knowledge, Learning and Capabilities, Athens, April 2002. It has subsequently benefited from presentations at faculty seminars at Said School of Business, Copenhagen Business School and the 2003 Organization Science Winter Conference, Steamboat Spring Colorado.

## References

Abernathy, W.J. and Utterback, J.M. (1975) Patterns of Industrial Innovation, *Technology Review*, 80: 41–7.

Abrahamson, E. and Fairchild, G. (1999) Management fashion: lifecycles, triggers, and collective learning processes, *Administrative Science Quarterly*, 44: 708–40.

Aldrich, H.E. (1999) *Organizations Evolving*. Thousand Oaks, CA: Sage.

Anderson, P. (1999) Complexity theory and organization science, *Organization Science*, 10: 216–32.

Anderson, P. and Tushman, M.L. (1990) Technological discontinuities and dominant design: a cyclical model of technological change, *Administrative Science Quarterly*, 35(4): 604–33.

Arthur, B. (1989) Competing technologies, increasing returns and lock-in by historical events, *Economic Journal*, 99: 116–31.

Bain, J.S. (1968) *Industrial Organization*. New York: Wiley.

Bass, F.M. (1980) The relationship between diffusion rates, experience curves, and demand elasticities for consumer durables technical innovation, *Journal of Business*, 53(3): 51–67.

Barney, J.B. (1991) Firm resources and sustained competitive advantage, *Journal of Management*, 17(1): 99–120.

Bosworth, D. and Rogers, M. (2001) Market value, R&D and intellectual property: an empirical analysis of large Australian firms, *The Economic Record*, 77(239): 323–37.

Brush, T.H., Bromiley, P. and Hendrickx, M. (1999) The relative influence of industry and corporation on business segment performance: an alternative estimate, *Strategic Management Journal*, 20: 519–47.

Burgelman, R.A. (2002) Strategy as vector and the inertia of coevolutionary lock-in, *Administrative Science Quarterly*, 47: 325–57.

Calori, R., Lubatkin, M., Very, P. and Veiga, J.F. (1997) Modelling the origins of nationally bound administrative heritages: a historical institutional analysis of French and British firms, *Organization Science*, 8(6): 681–96.

Carlsson, B. (1995) *Technological Systems and Economic Performance: the Case of Factory Automation*. Dordrecht: Kluwer Academic Publishers.

Child, J. (1972) Organization structure, environment and performance: the role of strategic choice, *Sociology*, 6(1): 1–22.

Christensen, C.M. (1997) *The Innovator's Dilemma. When New Technologies Cause Great Firms to Fail.* Boston, MA: Harvard Business School Press.

Clark, K.B. and Fujimoto, T. (1991) *Product Development Performance: Strategy, Organization, and Management in the World Auto Industry.* Boston, MA: Harvard University Press.

Coase, R.H. (1937) The nature of the firm, *Economica*, 4: 386–405.

Cohen, M.D., March, J.G. and Olsen, J.P. (1972) A garbage can model of organizational choice, *Administrative Science Quarterly*, 17(1): 1–25.

Cohen, W.M. (1995) Empirical studies of innovative activities. In P. Stoneman (ed.), *Handbook of the Economics of Innovation and Technological Change.* Oxford: Blackwell.

Cohen, W.M. and Klepper, S. (1992) The anatomy of industry R&D intensity distributions, *American Economic Review*, 82(4): 773–99.

Cohen, W.M. and Levin, R.C. (1989) Empirical studies of innovation and market structure. In R. Schmalensee and R. Willig (eds), *Handbook of Industrial Organization.* Amsterdam: North Holland.

Cohen, W.M. and Levinthal, D.A. (1989) Innovation and learning: the two faces of R&D, *Economic Journal*, 99: 569–96.

Cohen, W.M. and Levinthal, D.A. (1990) Absorptive capacity: a new perspective on learning and innovation, *Administrative Science Quarterly*, 35: 128–52.

Conner, K.R. and Prahalad, C.K. (1996) A resource-based theory of the firm: knowledge versus opportunism, *Organization Science*, 7(5): 477–501.

Cubbin, J. and Geroski, P. (1987) The convergence of profits in the long run: inter-firm and inter-industry comparisons, *Journal of Industrial Economics*, 35(4): 427–42.

Cusumano, M., Mylonadis, Y. and Rosenbloom, R. (1997) Strategic manoeuvring and mass-market dynamics: the triumph of VHS over Beta. Chapter 6 in M.L. Tushman and P. Anderson, *Managing Strategic Innovation and Change. A Collection of Readings.* Oxford: Oxford University Press. Reprinted from *Business History Review*, 1992.

Cyert, R.M. and March, J.G. (1963) *A Behavioral Theory of the Firm.* Englewood Cliffs, NJ: Prentice Hall.

D'Aveni, R. (1994) *Hypercompetition: Managing the Dynamics of Strategic Maneuvering.* Simon & Schuster. New York: The Free Press Division.

D'Aveni, R. (1999) Strategic supremacy through disruption and dominance, *Sloan Management Review*, 40: 3.

David, P.A. (1985) Clio and the economics of QWERTY, *American Economic Review Proceedings*, 75: 332–7.

Dierickx, I. and Cool, K. (1989) Asset stock accumulation and sustainability of competitive advantage, *Management Science*, 35: 1504–11.

DiMaggio, P.J. and Powell, W.W. (1991) Introduction. In P.J. DiMaggio and W.W. Powell (eds), *The New Institutionalism in Organizational Analysis.* Chicago: University of Chicago Press.

Dosi, G. (1982) Technological paradigms and technological trajectories: a suggested interpretation of the determinants and direction of technical change, *Research Policy*, 11: 147–62.

Dosi, G. (1988) Sources, procedures, and microeconomic effects of innovation, *Journal of Economic Literature*, 26(3): 1120–71.

Dosi, G., Nelson, R.R. and Winter, S.G. (eds) (2000) *The Nature and Dynamics of Organizational Capabilities*. Oxford: Oxford University Press.

Edquist, C. (ed.) (1997) *Systems of Innovation: Technologies, Institutions and Organizations*. London: Pinter.

Feldman, M.P. (1993) An examination of the geography of innovation, *Industrial and Corporate Change*, 2: 451–70.

Festinger, L. (1954) A theory of social comparison processes, *Human Relations*, 7: 117–40.

Freeman, C. (1987) *Technology Policy and Economic Performance: Lessons from Japan*. London: Pinter.

Gersick, C.J.G. (1991) Revolutionary change theories: a multilevel exploration of the punctuated equilibrium paradigm, *Academy of Management Review*, 10(3): 421–34.

Godfrey, P.C. and Hill, C.W. (1995) The problem of unobservables in strategic management research, *Strategic Management Journal*, 16: 519–33.

Grant, R.M. (1996) Prospering in dynamically-competitive environments: organizational capability as knowledge integration, *Organization Science*, 7(4): 375–87.

Griliches, Z. (1986) Productivity R&D and basic research at the firm level in the 1970s, *American Economic Review*, 76: 141–54.

Griliches, Z. (1991) The search of R&D spillovers, *The Scandinavian Journal of Economics*, 94: 29–47.

Griliches, Z. (1995) R&D and productivity: econometric results and measurement issues. In P. Stoneman (ed.), *The Handbook of Innovation and Technological Change*. Oxford: Blackwell.

Griliches, Z. and Mairesse, J. (1981) Productivity and R&D at the firm level, NBER Working Paper no. 826.

Hall, B.H., Jaffe, A. and Trajtenberg, M. (2001) Market value and patent citations: A first look, IBER, Economics Department Working Papers, Paper E01-304, University of California, Berkeley.

Hammer, Michael (1996) *Beyond Reengineering*. New York: HarperCollins.

Hannan, M.T. and Freeman, J.H. (1984) Structural inertia and organizational change, *American Sociological Review*, 49: 149–64.

Hansen, G.S. and Wernerfelt, B. (1989) Determinants of firm performance: the relative importance of economic and organizational factors, *Strategic Management Journal*, 10: 399–411.

Henderson, R. (1994) The evolution of integrative capability: innovation in cardiovascular drug discovery, *Industrial and Corporate Change*, 3(3): 607–30.

Henderson, R.M. and Clark, K.B. (1990) Architectural innovation: the reconfiguration of existing product technologies and the failure of established firms, *Administrative Science Quarterly*, 35: 9–30.

Howells, J. (1990) The location and organisation of research and development: new horizons, *Research Policy*, 19: 133–46.

Hunter, S.D. (1999) *Information Technology and Organization Structure*, Fuqua School of Business, Duke University, NC.

Ichnioswski, C., Shaw, K. and Prennushi, G. (1997) The effects of human resources management practices on productivity: a study of steel finishing lines, *American Economic Review*, 87(3): 291–313.

Illinitch, A.Y., Lewin, A.Y. and D'Aveni, R. (1998) Introduction. In A.Y. Illinitch, A.Y. Lewin and R. D'Aveni (eds), *Managing in Times of Disorder: Hypercompetitve Organizational Responses*. Thousands Oaks, CA: Sage.

Jaffe, A.B. (1986) Technological opportunity and spillovers of R&D, *American Economic Review*, 76: 984–1001.

Jaffe, A.B. (1988) Demand and supply influences on R&D intensity and productivity growth, *The Review of Economic and Statistics*, 72: 431–37.

Jaffe, A.B., Henderson, R. and Trajtenberg, M. (1993) Geographic localization of knowledge spillovers as evidenced by patent citations, *The Quarterly Journal of Economics*, 108: 576–98.

Jelinek, M. and Schoonhoven, C.B. (1990) *The Innovation Marathon: Lessons from High Technology Firms*. Oxford: Basil Blackwell.

Jorgenson, D.W. and Griliches, Z. (1967) The explanation of productivity change, *The Review of Economic Studies*, 34(3): 249–83.

Jorgenson, D.W. and Fraumeni, B.M. (1992) Investment in education and US economic growth, *Scandinavian Journal of Economics*, 94, Supplement: 51–94.

Kieser, A. (1997) Myth and rhetoric in management fashion, *Organization*, 4: 49–74.

Klepper, S. (1997) Industry life cycle, *Industrial and Corporate Change*, 6(1): 145–81.

Kogut, B. and Zander, U. (1992) Knowledge of the firm, combinative capabilities, and the replication of technology, *Organization Science*, 3(3): 383–97.

Leonard-Barton, D. (1992) Core capabilities and core rigidities: a paradox in managing new product development, *Strategic Management Journal*, 13: 111–25.

Lewin, A.Y., Greve, H., Sakano, T., Seiford, L. and Zhou, J. (2003) Mixing up: Organizational efficiency, selection and adaptation in the cement industry, working paper.

Lewin, A.Y. and Kim, J. (forthcoming 2003) The nation-state and culture as influences on organizational change and innovation. In M.S. Poole (ed.), *Handbook of Organizational Change and Development*. Oxford: Oxford University Press.

Lewin, A.Y. and Lovell, C.A.K. (eds) (1990) Frontier analysis. Parametric and non-parametric approaches, *Journal of Econometrics, Special Issue*, 46, 1 and 2.

Lewin, A.Y. and Lovell, C.A.K. (eds) (1995) Productivity analysis. Parametric and non-parametric applications, *European Journal of Operational Research, Special Issue*, 80: 3.

Lewin, A.Y. and Volberda, H.W. (eds) (forthcoming 2003) *The Coevolution Advantage: Mobilizing The Self-Renewing Organization*. Armonk, NY: M.E. Sharpe.

Lewin, A.Y., Weigelt, C.B. and Emery, J.B. (forthcoming 2003b) Adaptation and selection in strategy and change: perspectives on strategic change in Organizations. In M.S. Poole (ed.), *Handbook of Organizational Change and Development*. Oxford: Oxford University Press.

Lewin, K., Dembo, T., Festinger, L. and Sears, P. (1944) Level of aspiration. In J.M. Hunt (ed.), *Personality and the Behavior Disorder*, vol. 1. New York: Ronald.

Lucas, R.E. Jr (1988) On the mechanics of economic development, *Journal of Monetary Economics*, 22: 3–42.

Lundvall, B.-A. (1992) *National Systems of Innovation*. London: Pinter.

Mahajan, V., Muller, E. and Bass, F. (1990) New product diffusion models in marketing: a review and direction for research, *Journal of Marketing*, 54: 1–26.

Malerba, F. and Orsenigo, L. (1996) The dynamics and evolution of industries, *Industrial and Corporate Change*, 5(1): 51–87.

Malerba, F. and Orsenigo, L. (2000) Knowledge, innovative activities and industrial evolution, *Industrial and Corporate Change*, 9(2): 289–314.

March, J.G. (1991) Exploration and exploitation in organizational learning, *Organisation Science*, 2(1): 71–87.

March, J.G. and Simon, H.A. (1958) *Organizations*. New York: Wiley.

Massini, S., Lewin, A.Y. and Greve, H.R. (2003) Comparisons groups and the adaptation patterns of organizational routines, presented at the IoIR-ASEAT conference 'Knowledge and economic and social change: New challenges to innovation studies', Manchester, 7–9 April.

Massini, S., Lewin, A., Numagami, T. and Pettigrew, A.M. (2002) The evolution of organisational routines among large western and Japanese firms, *Research Policy*, 31: 1333–48.

Massini, S. and Pettigrew, A.M. (2003) Complementarities in Organizational Innovation and Performance: Empirical Evidence from the INNFORM survey. In A.M. Pettigrew, R. Whittington, L. Melin, C. Sanchez-Runde, F. van den Bosch, W. Ruigrok and T. Numagami (eds), *Innovative Forms of Organizing. International Perspectives*. London: Sage.

Mauri, A.J. and Michaels, M.P. (1998) Firm and industry effects within strategic management: An empirical examination, *Economics and Organization*, 7: 1–25.

McEvily, S. and Chakravarty, B. (2002) The persistence of knowledge-based advantage: an empirical test for product performance and technological knowledge, *Strategic Management Journal*, 23: 285–305.

McKelvey, B. (forthcoming 2003) Dynamics of new science macroleadership: strategy, microevolution, distributed intelligence, complexity. In A.Y. Lewin and H.W. Volberda (eds), *The Coevolution Advantage: Mobilizing The Self-Renewing Organization*. Armonk, NY: M.E. Sharpe.

Miles, R.E. and Snow, C.C. (1992) Causes of failure in network organizations, *California Management Review* (Summer): 53–72.

Milgrom, P. and Roberts, J. (1990) The economics of modern manufacturing: technology, strategy, and organization, *The American Economic Review*, 80(3): 511–28.

Milgrom, P. and Roberts, J. (1995) Complementarities and fit. Strategy, structure, and organizational change in manufacturing, *Journal of Accounting and Economics*, 19: 179–208.

Morone, J.G. (1993) *Winning in High-Tech Markets: the Role of General Management: How Motorola, Corning, and General Electric Have Built Global Leadership Through Tech.* Boston, MA: Harvard Business School Press.

Nelson, R.R. (ed.) (1993) *National Innovation Systems: a Comparative Analysis*. Oxford: Oxford University Press.

Nelson, R.R. and Winter, S.G. (1974) Neoclassical vs. evolutionary theories of economic growth: critique and prospectus, *Economic Journal*, 84: 886–905.

Nelson, R.R. and Winter, S.G. (1977) In search of a useful theory of innovation, *Research Policy*, 6: 36–76.

Nelson, R.R. and Winter, S.G. (1982) *An Evolutionary Theory of Economic Change*. Cambridge, MA: The Belknap Press, Harvard University Press.

Nonaka, I. and Takeuchi, H. (1995) *The Knowledge-Creating Company: How Japanese Companies Create the Dynamics of Innovation*. Oxford: Oxford University Press.

Patel, P. and Pavitt, K. (1992) Large firms in the production of the world's technology: an important case of non-globalisation. In O. Granstrand, L. Håkanson and S. Sjölander (eds), *Technology Management and International Business: Internationalisation of R&D and Technology*. Chichester: John Wiley and Sons Ltd.

Pavitt, K. (1984) Patterns of technical change: towards a taxonomy and theory, *Research Policy*, 13(6): 343–73.

Penrose, E. (1959) *The Theory of the Growth of the Firm*. Oxford: Basil Blackwell.

Polanyi, M. (1967) *The Tacit Dimension*. Garden City, NY: Doubleday Anchor.

Reed, R. and DeFillippi, R.J. (1990) Casual ambiguity, barriers to imitation, and sustainable competitive advantage, *Academy of Management Review*, 15: 88–102.

Rivkin, J. (2000) Imitation of complex strategies, *Management Science*, 46(6): 824–44.

Robins, J. and Wiersema, M.F. (1995) A resource-based approach to the multibusiness firm: Empirical analysis of portfolio interrelationships and corporate financial performance, *Strategic Management Journal*, 16: 277–99.

Rogers, E.M. (1983) *Diffusion of Innovations*. New York: Free Press.

Romer, P.M. (1986) Increasing returns and long-run growth, *Journal of Political Economy*, 94: 1002–37.

Romer, P.M. (1990) Endogenous technological change, *Journal of Political Economy*, 98: 71–102.

Rosenberg, N. (1982) *Inside the Black Box: Technology and Economics*. Cambridge: Cambridge University Press.

Rumelt, R.P. (1984) Towards a strategic theory of the firm. In R.B. Lamb (ed.), *Competitive Strategic Management*, Englewood Cliffs, NJ: Prentice-Hall.

Rumelt, R.P. (1991) How much does industry matter?, *Strategic Management Journal*, 12: 167–85.

Schmalensee, R. (1985) Do markets differ much?, *American Economic Review*, 75(3): 341–51.

Schiff, M. and Lewin, A.Y. (1970) The impact of people on budget, *The Accounting Review*, XLV(2): 259–68.

Schumpeter, J. (1942) *Capitalism, Socialism and Democracy*. New York: Harper.

Silverberg, G., Dosi, G. and Orsenigo, L. (1988) Innovation, diversity and diffusion: a self-organization model, *Economic Journal*, 98: 1032–54.

Simon, H.A. (1962) The architecture of complexity, *Proceedings of the American Philosophical Society*, 106: 467–82.

Solow, R. (1956) A contribution to the theory of economic growth, *Quarterly Journal of Economics*, 70: 65–94.

Solow, R. (1957) Technical change and the aggregate production function, *Review of Economics and Statistics*, 39: 312–20.

Stoneman, P. (1983) *The Economics of Technological Change*. Oxford: Oxford University Press.

Teece, D. and Pisano, G. (1994) The dynamic capabilities of firms: an introduction, *Industrial and Corporate Change*, 3(3): 537–56.

Teece, D., Pisano, G. and Shuen, A. (1997) Dynamic capabilities and strategic management, *Strategic Management Journal*, 18: 509–533.

Tushman, M.L. and Anderson, P. (eds) (1997) *Managing Strategic Innovation and Change: a Collection of Readings*. Oxford: Oxford University Press.

Tushman, M.L. and Romanelli, E. (1985) Organization evolution: a metamorphosis model of convergence and reorientation. In L. Cummings and B. Staw (eds), *Research in Organizational Behavior*, vol. 7. Greenwich: JAI Press.

Utterback, J.M. and Abernathy, W.J. (1978) A dynamic model of process and product innovation, *Omega*, 3: 639–56.

Van de Ven, A.H., Angle, H.L. and Poole, M.S. (1989) *Research on the Management of Innovation*. New York: Harper and Row.

Von Hippel, E. (1986) Lead users: a source of novel product concepts, *Management Science*, 32(7): 781–805.

Wernerfelt, B. (1984) A resource-based view of the firm, *Strategic Management Journal*, 5(2): 171–80.

Wernerfelt, B. and Montgomery, C.A. (1988) Tobin's q and the importance of focus on firm performance, *American Economic Review*, 78: 246–51.

Whitley, R. (2002) Developing innovating competencies: the role of institutional frameworks, *Industrial and Corporate Change*, 11(3): 497–528.

Williamson, O.E. (1975) *Markets and Hierarchies: Analysis and Antitrust Implications*. New York: Free Press.

Williamson, O.E. (1985) *The Economic Institutions of Capitalism: Firms, Markets and History*. Cambridge: Cambridge University Press.

Zahra, S.A. and George, G. (2002) Absorptive capacity: a review, reconceptualization, and extension, *Academy of Management Review*, 27: 185–203.

Zollo, M. and Winter, S.G. (2002) Deliberate learning and the evolution of dynamic capabilities, *Organization Science*, 13(3): 339–51.

# 10
## Edith Penrose's Organizational Theory of the Firm: Contract, Conflict, Knowledge and Management*
*Christos Pitelis*

### Introduction

In 1959 Edith Penrose published *The Theory of the Growth of the Firm* (TGF). This book marked the first attempt by an economist to examine the internal workings of firms, in order to explain endogenous knowledge creation, innovation and firm growth. Penrose saw the external environment as an 'image' in the minds of management, and suggested a dynamic interaction between the internal and external environments, which defined what she called firms' 'productive opportunity'. She placed particular importance on human resources – in particular management – and saw managerial constraints as limiting the rate of growth of firms, albeit not their size per se.

In Penrose's approach, managers are prime actors, whose 'preferences' are partly endogenous. They are shaped by the macro-environment (capitalism) and by the internal structure and dynamics of firms, their perception of this external (and internal) 'reality', and their own motivation, which includes profits, but also power and the love of the game. The focus on firms as real life organizations, on human resources, on intra-firm learning, on endogenous knowledge, innovation and growth, and on the interaction of exogenous and endogenous, to include non-economic factors in determining managerial motivations and firms' growth, places Penrose's analysis in a unique category. We claim here

* I am grateful to numerous colleagues for comments and discussion pertaining to the issues covered in this paper, notably Perran Penrose, Anastasia Pseiridis, Haridimos Tsoukas and an anonymous referee. Errors are mine.

that in fact hers was the first organizational theory of the firm, going beyond the 'Organizational Economics' approaches of the transaction-costs type and providing a natural link between 'Organizational Economics' and 'Organizational Studies' more generally.

The aim of this chapter is to place Penrose's ideas within the context of the debate concerning the organizational nature and functions of the business firm, to examine its extant and potential contribution to this debate, but also to explore some apparent limitations of the study and look at ways in which these can be addressed.

In section 2 of this chapter we expound the Penrosean ideas and place these within the context of current debates concerning the nature and the role of the firm in capitalist economies. Section 3 focusses on the role of contract and conflict within organizational theories of the firm. Section 4 argues that 'conflict' and 'contract' are both compatible with, and can serve, the Penrosean perspective. Finally, section 5 offers some concluding remarks.

## Edith Penrose's theory and approach

In Penrose's words, firms are 'flesh-and-blood' real life *organizations*, rather than points on a cost curve. They consist of human and non-human resources, under administrative authoritative co-ordination and communication. Human, and especially managerial, resources are the most important. Resources provide multiple potential *services*. Firms use their resources to perform *activities* that result in products for sale in the *market* for a *profit*. Firms differ from markets, their *boundaries* defined by the reach of authoritative co-ordination and communication. For reasons related to resource indivisibilities and the 'balance of processes', firms always have *'excess' resources*. The very performance of activities within firms creates new knowledge through specialization, division of labour, resource combination, teamwork and learning.[1] This reduces the time required for the implementation of current activities, thereby generating further 'excess resources', namely human and non-human resources, which are not fully utilized at any given point in time.

The cohesive shell of the organization is of essence in facilitating learning. As excess resources can provide services at zero marginal cost, in that they have already been hired to provide services for a specified amount of time, they motivate managers-entrepreneurs to apply them to new activities, engendering *endogenous innovation and growth*. The profitable marketization of new innovations requires entrepreneurial thinking, which involves the identification and creation of markets.

The external environment, markets and demand, are perceptions, 'images' in the entrepreneur's mind. Supply and demand are inextricably linked, as planned supply responds to perceived demand. There is a dynamic interaction between the perceived internal and external environments, which defines a firm's *productive opportunity*. The direction of expansion is motivated and shaped by the productive opportunity. There are limits to the growth of the firm, but not to its size. The conception and implementation of expansion requires managers whose firm-specific knowledge is a prerequisite for the successful planning and implementation of expansion, who, therefore, are not available in the open market. This *limits the rate of growth* and explains the pre-eminence Penrose attributes to management.

Penrose applied her insights to mergers, vertical integration, industry concentration, small firms and industry organization more generally, as well as to business strategy and government competition policy (see Pitelis (2002) for an extensive discussion). Her views have served as a basis for Richardson's (1972) seminal attempt to explain inter-firm co-operation. For Richardson, market, integration (firm) and co-operation are three different modes of organizing production. In terms of productive efficiency, similar (in terms of underlying capabilities) and complementary activities are best undertaken within firms. By contrast, dis-similar, but complementary activities are best organized through inter-firm co-operation. Dis-similar and non-complementary activities are best performed through markets. Through Richardson's contribution, Penrose's ideas have also anticipated the large and rapidly growing literature on inter-firm co-operation, networks, clusters, alliances and the like. This literature is closely related to issues of trust, social capital, shared visions and culture, and 'the ethical dimension' (Etzioni, 1988), often seen as means of reducing transaction costs and/or increasing productivity and (through) innovation (see Martin and Sunlay, 2003). These issues are also central to more recent approaches that view non-market elements as crucial for the efficiency of the market system (Pitelis, 1991; Nahapiet and Ghoshal, 1998; Gulati *et al.*, 2000), pointing to the versatility and the embracing nature of Penrose's contribution.

What is it in this contribution that has made it so attractive and influential? We believe that the main reasons are both the argument and the method-epistemology. The argument, first, is not just about the theory of the growth of the firm; it is an argument about the theory of growth of knowledge. For anything and everything new to even be conceived or perceived, let alone implemented, one needs some prior knowledge, including the very capacity to obtain knowledge – that is, to learn.

There are a variety of institutions that can assist in this process: families, schools, norms, customs and traditions, human interaction in society at large. Hayek's (1945) view was that this knowledge is dispersed and that there is, at least in the capitalist economies, an institution par excellence, the market, that facilitates its creation and transmission and thus the co-ordination of individual plans and in the society at large. This is a fundamental insight. Important in our view is that Hayek (1945) himself underplayed the importance of institutions – even the market, in *creating new knowledge*. Markets can be fundamental to the process of creating new knowledge. Even learning about other people's plans may help to modify someone's plans; this is as much about transmitting and distributing existing knowledge as it is about generating new knowledge. Yet the important point is that for Penrose it is *firms* which help to create knowledge, indeed firms are better in doing so than markets. If so, Penrose both critiques Hayek, since firms involve planning, and complements him, since private firms and markets together – the market system – both create new and transmit (dispersed) knowledge. This has crucial implications for the efficiency of the system as a whole.

However, Penrose's contribution goes much deeper than this. If knowledge in general, or even a type of knowledge most suitable for production-related activities, is generated better within firms and/or through inter-firm co-operation, than outside firms, and to the extent that this knowledge is of relevance or use to society as a whole, everything and anything we conceive of or perceive and the lens through which we do so, is predicated upon the existence and functioning of firms. Our very perceptions are a function of firms' functioning, in the deep sense of them providing us with a lens through which we perceive the wider environment and even life as a whole. It is in this sense that Penrose's contribution is beyond the normally conceived bounds (even in her analysis).

The second major reason for the attractiveness of the Penrosian perspective is her epistemology. This involves a dynamic interplay between induction and deduction, structure and agency, in the context of a history-informed path-dependent evolutionary dynamic, shaped by actors' conscious, yet path-dependent and structure-moulded actions, in the context of a purposive organization, the firm. Penrose rejected explicitly biological analogies in the theory of the firm for failing to account for human agency. Her approach anticipates more recent arguments, for example Giddens' (1984) 'duality of structure' and adds a cognitive turn in the form of the concepts such as 'image' and 'productive opportunity' (see Turvani, 2002 for a discussion of Penrose and cognitive science). These socio-psychological aspects of Penrose's work take her beyond economic-based perspectives and bring her closer to sociological theories of the firm.

It is beyond the scope of this chapter to pursue the full ramifications of the above (more is to be found in Pitelis, 2002). Here we focus on assessing Penrose's contribution to economics in general and organizational economics in particular, aiming to draw out the distinctiveness of the Penrosian perspective on the firm.

One can effectively divide economics in two major camps; one focussing on efficient allocation of resources, often assumed to be scarce, the other focussing on resource and wealth creation. Most classical economists, notably Adam Smith and Karl Marx, but also more recent contributors, such as Joseph Schumpeter (1942), have paid attention to the issue of resource and wealth creation. To varying degrees, these economists also dealt with the related issue of resource allocation. Adam Smith, for example, arguably owes his place as the father-figure of modern (neoclassical) economics to his analysis of the allocative and co-ordination role of the 'invisible hand', the market. Yet he believed in the labour theory of value, and attributed wealth creation to labour productivity engendered within firms. Smith wrote about markets and about firms, like his famous pin factory, the point from where *The Wealth of Nations* starts. In the pin factory, labour productivity is achieved through specialization, the division of labour and teamwork, which leads, among other things, to new inventions by those closer to the production process, that is the labourers. The sources of labour productivity, inventions and the wealth of nations are thus to be found within firms. These are only limited by the size of the market. In Allyn Young's (1928) powerful insight, the size of the market itself is determined by specialization and the division of labour; the latter leads to both more elaborate subdivision of labour and extends the size of the market. In a sense, it is specialization and the division of labour that determines specialization and the division of labour, thus productivity and the wealth of nations!

Penrose holds a prominent place in this debate. As Loasby (1999) suggests, Penrose has been able to 'reinvent' this classical tradition, which at the time of her writing was all but extinct. At this time, the battle on the nature and scope of economics had already been won by the efficient allocation of the (scarce) resource perspectives of Jevons, Walras and their followers – what we now call the 'neoclassical perspective'. According to these economists, the scope of economics as a science should appropriately be the analysis of efficient allocation of (scarce) resources. 'Reinventing' the classical perspective was no small feat. Yet I believe Penrose went well beyond reinventing the classical tradition.

Penrose's endogenous knowledge perspective goes beyond Allyn Young in explaining why and how the size of the market is itself determined by specialization and the division of labour (as well as vice versa). It provides the requisite perspective and knowledge to approach the synthesis between dynamic innovation, knowledge and productivity growth perspective and (dynamic) co-ordination through the knowledge provided by firms' own operations and the perceived equivalence (in part achieved through firms' own conscious efforts) of supplies and demands. It helps to bring together resource creation and efficient allocation in a fundamental way; given that it is the internally generated knowledge that supplies firms with the tools to achieve efficient resource allocation, rather that assume they know how to do so.

In this sense, Penrose's contribution is seminal. Knowledge is internally generated, is an input to what they know, what they do, how they do it, every other issue we referred to and more. Her approach is more than a re-invention, however important this re-invention is. Smith, Marx, Young and Schumpeter have not dealt with endogenous innovation and knowledge-growth creation. This is also true of other eminent contributors that dealt with related issues, such as Ronald Coase, Alfred Chandler, Nicholas Kaldor, Michal Kalecki, Stephen Hymer, Gunnar Myrdal, and Douglass North. This is crucial. In a world where 'there is nothing new under the sun', to come up with such a unique insight is as good as it can get, especially when this is one that also helps to explain the very process of perceiving whether, why, and how 'new' is new. An important aspect of this insight, for example, is the endogenous incentive to make profitable use of 'excess resources'. This is far more subtle and powerful than the exogenous profit maximization motive. While the two are related – the latter in part motivating the former – making productive and profitable use of employed resources is a challenge, because it can help to upgrade the resource, because of the personal opportunity cost of (in)ability to delegate, and for numerous socio-psychological reasons not accounted for by an exogenously imposed profit motive (Penrose herself favoured such a broader explanation for the motive of firms, one that includes power, and sociological factors, to include the love of the game). Significantly the very process of thinking what to do about the resources one employs, is itself innovation therefore (new) knowledge.

## Contract and conflict in organizational economics

In his classic 1937 article Coase first pleaded for clearer definitions and then proceeded to define the firm as a multi-person hierarchy, its nature lying in the 'employment contract' between employers and employees. In this sense, Coase focussed on the capitalist firm, as opposed to both non-capitalist firms, and non-firm-like forms of early capitalist production, such as the 'putting-out' system. He went on to explain the 'employment contract' in terms of transaction-costs-related market failures. He regarded savings in transaction costs by firms as the reason why labourers 'agreed' to work under the authority (or direction) of the capitalist-entrepreneur.

Later, Coase (1993a) regretted his emphasis on the 'employment relationship'. He claimed that this had limited the focus onto the issue of the 'nature' of the firm, while one should also look at the issue of the 'essence' of firms – that is, what is involved in 'running a business'. This involves not just an employment contract between capital and labour, but also using other resources and one's own time and abilities to produce. Penrose clearly dealt with the 'essence', having taken the 'nature' for granted. She also looked at the capitalist firm, which is once again a multiple-person hierarchy, under administrative co-ordination by human resources of both human and non-human resources, for production of a product for sale in the market. In this sense, there is, in her definition, more than there is in Coase – although it does, of course, omit the 'employment relation'.

In the Penrosean perspective, the 'employment relation' can be explained in terms of efficiency gains, affected through productivity enhancements, through endogenous innovation and knowledge growth (see Pitelis and Wahl, 1998). To the extent that dynamic (by definition given Penrose's framework) transaction costs can also be of relevance here, it will be the overall dynamic transaction costs reductions cum knowledge-induced productivity benefits that could explain the capitalist firm. Importantly, the very perception of when and how to reduce transaction costs can be afforded through intra-firm knowledge generation (see, among others, Fransman, 1994; Pitelis and Pseiridis, 1999). To assume that firms know this beforehand is unrealistic (and in contrast to Williamson's (1975) own insistence on 'bounded rationality'). How can one be boundedly rational and still get it always right in integrating, and only if in so doing one reduces market transaction costs by more than one increases intra-firm transaction (managerial, administration) costs? Somehow it feels that this is ultra-rationality of the highest 'order![2]

The Penrosean 'insight' leads us further afield. The nature of knowledge – tacit and hard to transmit across markets – deals a blow on the Coasean explanation of the 'nature' of firms. To explain firms from a situation of no firms at all, one requires an entrepreneurial idea aimed to be put in practice. Selling this idea in the open market may be difficult. First, being tacit, the idea may be hard to transmit. Second, if in addition this idea has public goods characteristics, explaining it to anyone can lead to it being expropriated. Among others, this can lead to a competitor (if the original conceiver even manages to go ahead with using it). So we have a two-pronged type of market failure, which, however, is not directly linked to transaction costs. Transaction costs can enter the story only if one suggests that, in their absence, one could conceive of contractual means of addressing the problems. To claim, however, that transaction costs are the main reason, as opposed to the tacitness and public goods aspects of entrepreneurial ideas, is not evident at all. The control afforded to entrepreneurs on their ideas, in the cohesive shell of the firms and the difficulties of transmitting tacit knowledge, can be an adequate initial reason for not selling the idea in the open market. Note that this point is prior to, and complements, the idea that firms may have productivity benefits vis-à-vis markets, which can also be an adequate non-transaction-costs-related explanation of the 'nature' of firms.

The Penrosean input to the 'nature' story (knowledge-related advantages from intra-firm activities) is a (production) efficiency-based complement to the Coasean insight. However, this still fails to explain why labour 'accepted' to work for capital. Efficiency benefits per se are not sufficient to explain why one should accept to work under the authority of another person voluntarily, whether the relationship is contractual or predatory.

Among those who originally dealt with these issues, notably Karl Marx, Knight (1921), and Ronald Coase, the issue was why independent producers accepted to work under dependent employment for an employer-capitalist. As is well known, Marx stressed capitalist coercion that created the proletariat through the barrel of a gun, with the helpful hand of the Crown – through, for example, the farm enclosures. Excellent accounts are in Hymer (1979) and in Heilbroner (1991). For Knight (1921), the reason is different attitudes towards risk. The risk takers insure the timid and risk-averse by providing them with a relatively secure income-wage rate; it is, in effect, a division of tasks. North (1981, 1991), for example, has sided with Marx and Hymer in adopting the predatory (not contractual – co-operative) perspective. It appears to us that Marx, Knight, Coase and Penrose are all correct! In deciding whether and why to be an employee, coercion (thus restricted choice), potential benefits (from transaction costs and/or production efficiencies) and attitudes towards risk are relevant and useful. One factor is differential ability-knowledge by one party in exploiting the benefits from specialization, division of labour and teamwork (see Marglin, 1974).

There is little of the above in organizational economics. Instead, given the 'employment relation' and potentially conflicting interests, there become important for economists what today we call 'agency', moral hazard, 'monitoring' and the like. The literature on these issues is huge, notable contributions being those of Alchian and Demsetz (1972) and Jensen and Meckling (1976). In brief, the issue here is that whenever a 'principal–agent' relationship exists, like, for example, employer–employee, or shareholder–manager, and when the interests of the two parties are not *ex ante* fully aligned, agents may have discretion to pursue their own interests. When this is the case, it becomes important for principals to devise means for aligning the incentives of employees to their own. For Alchian and Demsetz, the question is applied to the very issue of obtaining the productivity benefits of the employment relationship and it is used for a conceptual justification of the need for private ownership and control of firms. Specifically, it is observed that in any team effort, shirking is likely to occur due to difficulties in measuring individual outputs. To ensure that productivity is not thus prejudiced, it becomes necessary to monitor teamworkers. However, the monitor needs, in turn, to be monitored. To avoid an infinite regress situation, it is best if the monitor is self-monitored, by becoming a residual claimant of any surplus left after expenses to the other members of the team, etc., are paid.

The contribution of Alchian and Demsetz is of significance in this regard. It addresses one of the most important issues in political economy, that of extracting labour from labour power, or more generally that of transforming work potential to work. It is part and parcel of a broader category of issues that relate to potentially differing objectives, interests, etc. of groups of people. The archetypal form is that of the Marxian notion of class struggle. In the context of the factory system, this takes the form of the capitalist employer being able to increase the rate of surplus value by intensifying work and/or by introducing labour-saving technical progress (see Marglin, 1974). However, one does not have to take a classical or Marxist view to recognize conflicting interests in firms. Besides Alchian and Demsetz, and Jensen and Meckling, managerial and behavioural theories of the firm are based on similar concerns. Managerial theories rely on different utility functions by managers, plus control on their part, and (thus) the ability to pursue non-profit (including growth) objectives (see Marris, 1996). The behavioural theory goes further, in suggesting the pervasiveness of conflicting objectives by different groups within firms, which, alongside bounded rationality, questions the very sacred cow, the profit motive. In view of conflicting intra-firm interests, and bounded rationality, 'satisficing' is more likely to be the firms' motive (Cyert and March, 1963).

While economics-based solutions to intra-firm conflict are the focus of this chapter, they are neither the only game in town, nor the most important one. Other, organizational, sociological and psychological factors – including leadership, morality, culture, legitimacy and shared vision – can be relevant and important. We return to this issue below.

## Beyond conflict and contract: Penrose, knowledge and management

Unlike other economics-based theories of the firm, there is no conflict of any kind within the production process as described in Penrose. This is almost paradoxical, given in particular Penrose's implication for managerialist literature (see, for example, Slater, 1980). Her story has precious little to do with utility-maximizing managers, favouring growth. Nevertheless, one might have expected that the issue of potentially divergent objectives might have been given a fraction more prominence. While nobody can deal with all issues, and for her own purposes, Penrose might have needed to eschew from intra-firm conflicts (which could well be a separate book), I believe her analysis could be usefully enhanced by allowing intra-firm conflict to enter it.

Penrose's approach was to look at the outside environment by first looking at what she called the 'nature' of the firm (not just Coase's 'employment contract' but the very internal workings of the organization she called a firm). She went on to posit a dynamic interaction between the internal and external environments. The latter includes other firms, and Penrose went on to discuss the importance of oligopolistic interaction and inter-firm competition. In this sense, it is clearly in line with her own focus to also consider intra-firm competition. As already discussed, this can take many forms and apply to many groups. Clearly, however, the conflict par excellence is that between employer and employee, as discussed by Marx, Alchian and Demsetz, and others. Recognizing this can help Penrose's analysis in various ways. First, it provides us with an extra reason for thinking by entrepreneurs-management of how to address this issue – this of course is innovation-knowledge generation. Second, it helps explain-predict, at least partly, the direction and results of such thinking. An example is the proposition of labour-saving technological progress proposed by Marxian theory and its related prediction of a declining profit rate. Last, but not least, conflict can lead to creative tension, and thus be a source of new information and knowledge and productivity advantages (Pitelis, 2002).

On the negative side, the recognition of intra-firm conflict questions efficiency-only-based explanations of organizational change, including that of Penrose. As argued by others, for example Marglin (1974), conflict can lead to a choice of technology that favours sectional interests, not necessarily societal ones – such as, labour-saving technology and (as) labour control devices – leading to a declining rate of profit, and other labour control devices. Such choices by management can help to intensify conflict. This renders crucial the role of non-economic factors that help to establish shared morals and vision through, for example, leadership, ideology, legitimization, shared vision, culture and enablement (see Boddewyn, 2002 for a recent critical account).

There is little of that in Penrose. Instead, interest alignment appears to be in part *ex ante* present, but also affected *ex post* through managerial leadership and its ability to implant its vision to other groups within the organization. Whilst this may well be possible it is neither self-evident nor cost-free. In this context, the failure of Penrose to also discuss in detail issues such as leadership, ideology, legitimization and the effecting of shared values, beliefs and common moralities in organizations is certainly a limitation. As in the case of intra-firm conflict, a more careful examination and discussion of such issues could strengthen the Penrosean story. As it stands, Penrose falls within the camp of organizational economics, plus knowledge minus intra-firm conflict and 'agency'. That it lacks detailed discussions or 'softer' management-related issues is a limitation – one that can be justified in terms of specialization and division of labour. However, unlike other 'organization economics-based' theories of the firm which lack 'insides', the Penrosean story readily lends itself to the discussion of such issues (by virtue of its very focus on human resources, management and knowledge) and can serve as a glue that binds together organization economics and organization studies.

While Penrose's approach is analytic and not prescriptive, there exists an interesting implication in it concerning managerial practice. Perhaps it is exactly the assumption that provides the solution? Could it be that it is through the relentless pursuit of innovation and productivity that, up to a point, conflict can be by-passed and shared-visions, values and moralities emerge? At least to the present author, this looks plausible. This positive-sum approach to problem-conflict solution brings Penrose's theory close to non-economic theories, such as the stakeholder and institutional approaches. It points to enabling employees (as opposed to control-based "incentives") as a managerial strategy for long-term performance (Perrow, 1986; Granovetter, 1985; Powell and DiMaggio, 1991; Clarkson, 1998; Boddewyn, 2002), and even serves as a means of going beyond the 'constraint-plus enabling' perspective to a dialectic synthesis of the two. If so, conflict and contract are shaped, and both in turn shape, the relentless pursuit of productivity and innovation, which is itself driven by objective factors (excess resources through knowledge generation) and subjective factors- agency (the pursuit of maximum feasible profit, power, recognition and the love of the game), by firms' management. Interestingly, the very process of generating intra-firm knowledge helps management enhance its problem-solving capabilities. Managerial knowledge can serve as a means of going beyond 'contract' and conflict.

Penrose's argument and epistemology is also consistent with ideas from psychology. Drawing, for example, on Freud (1967), one can attribute productivity advantages of organizations to psychological and sociological aspects of human behaviour, such as a need for leadership, recognition by one's peers and the existence of competitors. Crafting such further sociological and psychological insight into the Penrosean story helps strengthen her productivity-based arguments and can serve as a basis for a social-science-based theory of the firm. This, however, is beyond the scope of this chapter.

By focussing on the relentless internal and external pressures for innovation and productivity and the problem-solving ability of management, Penrose's theory is more in line with stakeholder, institutional and cultural perspectives of the firm, and provides an economic, action-based means of linking confict and contract, constraint and enablement.

## Concluding remarks

Edith Penrose's contribution to the organizational theory of the firm is seminal. Hers is the first economics-based examination of the internal dynamics of the firm. It recognizes the importance of human resources, of management, of organizational learning, of the interaction between external and internal environments, of the importance of non-economic factors such as the 'image' and 'productive opportunity' in shaping and moulding preferences, objectives, functions and outcomes. While it is limited in that it eschews from dealing explicitly with 'conflict' and 'contract' within firms, the Penrosean approach is amenable to and can benefit from the introduction of such issues as well as further socio-psychological insights. It can serve as an anchor point for building a social-science-based organizational theory of the firm and provides a clue as to how the relentless pursuit of innovation and productivity can serve as a means of dialectically synthesizing 'contract' and 'conflict and strategy'.

## Notes

1. This includes learning by doing; to work with others; to re-combine resources; learning what, how and why; learning to learn; hopefully learning to unlearn; learning oneself; and more generally as ancient Greek philosopher and legislator Solon put it 'getting on always learning'.
2. Coase (1993b) himself considers bounded rationality (or any concept of rationality at all) to be little more than nonsense! We submit that the Penrosean insight helps address Williamson's 'inconsistency' and Coase's own dislike of the rationality concept. In Penrose 'rationality', too, is endogenously generated through perennial learning.

## References

Alchian, A. and Demsetz, H. (1972) Production, information costs, and economic organization, *American Economic Review*, 62: 777–95.

Boddewyn J.J. (2002) The meanings and implications of 'nonmarket', mimeo, Baruch College (CUNY).

Clarkson, M.B.E. (1998) Introduction. In M.B.E. Clarkson (ed.), *The Corporation and Its Stakeholders: Classic and Contemporary Readings*. Toronto: University of Toronto Press.

Coase, R.H. (1937) The nature of the firm, *Economica*, 4: 386–405.

Coase, R.H. (1993a) 1991 Nobel Lecture: the institutional structure of production. In O.E. Williamson and S.G. Winter (eds), *The Nature of the Firm*. Oxford: Oxford University Press.

Coase, R.H. (1993b) Coase on Posner on Coase, *Journal of Institutional and Theoretical Economics*, 149(1): 90–8.

Cyert, R.M. and March, J.G. (1963) *A Behavioural Theory of the Firm*. Englewood Cliffs, NJ: Prentice Hall.

Etzioni, Amitai (1988) *The Moral Dimension: Toward a New Economics*. New York: Free Press.

Freud, S. (1967) *Massenpsychologie und Ich – Analyse*. Frankfurt am Main and Hamburg: Fischer Verlag, Fischer Bucherei.

Fransman, M. (1994) Information, knowledge, vision and theories of the firm, *Industrial and Corporate Change*, 3(3): 713–57.

Giddens, A. (1984) *The Constitution of Society*. Cambridge: Polity Press.

Granovetter, Marc (1985) Economic action and social structure: the problem of embeddedness, *American Journal of Sociology*, 91(3): 481–510.

Gulati, R., Nohria, N. and Zaheer, A. (2000) Strategic networks, *Strategic Management Journal*, 21(3): 203–15.

Hayek, F.A. (1945) The use of knowledge in society, *American Economic Review*, 35, September: 519–30.

Heilbroner, R. (1991) *The Worldly Philosophers*, 6th edition. London: Penguin Books.

Hymer, S.H. (1979) The multinational corporation and the law of uneven development. In R.B. Cohen *et al.* (eds), *The Multinational Corporation*. Cambridge: Cambridge University Press.

Jensen, M.C. and Meckling, W. (1976) Theory of the firm: managerial behaviour, agency costs and ownership structure, *Journal of Financial Economics*, 3: 304–60.

Knight, F.H. (1921) *Risk, Uncertainty and Profit*. Boston: Houghton Mifflin.

Loasby, B.J. (1999) The significance of Penrose's theory for the development of economics, *Contributions to Political Economy*, 18: 31–45.

Marglin, S. (1974) What do bosses do? The origins and functions of hierarchy in capitalist production, *Review of Radical Political Economics*, 6 (winter): 60–112.

Marris, R. (1996) Managerial theories of the firm. In M. Warner *et al.*, *International Encyclopaedia of Business and Management*. London: Routledge.

Martin, R. and Sunley, P. (2003) Deconstructing clusters: chaotic concept or policy panacea?, *Journal of Economic Geography*, January 2003, 3(1): 5–35.

Nahapiet, J. and Ghoshal, S. (1998) Social capital, intellectual capital, and the organizational advantage, *Academy of Management Review*, 23(2): 242–66.

North, D.C. (1981) *Structure and Change in Economic History*. London and New York: Norton.

North, D.C. (1991) Institutions, *Journal of Economic Perspectives*, 5(1): 97–112.

Penrose, E.T. (1959/1995) *The Theory of the Growth of the Firm*, 3rd edn. Oxford: Oxford University Press.

Penrose, P. and Pitelis, C. (1999) Edith Elura Tilton Penrose: life, contribution and influence, *Contributions to Political Economy*, 18: 3–22.

Perrow, Charles (1986) *Complex Organizations*. New York: McGraw-Hill.

Pitelis, C.N. (1991) *Market and Non-Market Hierarchies*. Oxford: Basil Blackwell.

Pitelis, C.N. (ed.) (2002) *The Growth of the Firm – The Legacy of Edith Penrose*. Oxford: Oxford University Press.

Pitelis, C.N. and Wahl, M. (1998) Edith Penrose: pioneer of stakeholder theory, *Long Range Planning*, 31(2): 252–61.

Pitelis, C.N. and Pseiridis, A.N. (1999) Transaction costs versus resource value?, *Journal of Economic Studies*, 26(3): 221–40.

Powell, W.W. and DiMaggio, P.J. (eds) (1991) *The New Institutionalism in Organization Analisis*. Chicago, IL: University of Chicago Press.

Richardson, G. (1972) The organisation of industry, *Economic Journal*, 82: 883–96.

Slater, M. (1980) The managerial limitation to a firm's rate of growth, *Economic Journal*, 90: 520–8.

Schumpeter, J.A. (1942) *Capitalism, Socialism and Democracy*. New York: Harper and Row.

Turvani, M. (2002) Mismatching by design. In C.N. Pitelis (ed.), *The Growth of the Firm – the Legacy of Edith Penrose*. Oxford: Oxford University Press.

Williamson, O. (1975) *Markets and Hierarchies: Antitrust Analysis and Implications*. New York: The Free Press.

Young, A. (1928) Increasing returns and economic progress, *The Economic Journal*, xxviii(152): 527–42.

# 11
# The Role of Knowledge Quality in Firm Performance

*Christine W. Soo, Timothy M. Devinney and David F. Midgley*

## Introduction

The role of knowledge in firm strategy and performance is well documented in the literature. There are numerous theoretical and empirical studies examining the relationship between knowledge and firm performance. The essence of these studies is that the higher the level of knowledge acquired or accumulated, the greater the level of firm innovation and performance.

In this study, we examine an element of knowledge acquisition that is not addressed in previous studies – that of the quality of the acquired knowledge. We examine not only the frequency of knowledge acquisition, but also whether the knowledge being acquired is *useful* to the firm and *innovative* in terms of its newness and novelty. The study incorporates three components – first, we investigate the impact of knowledge quality on two measures of firm performance – innovation and financial performance. Second, we investigate the antecedents to knowledge quality, examining the impact of the formal and informal networks (building on the work of network and social capital theorists) and the concept of absorptive capacity. Third, our data allow us to investigate the specific sources of useful and innovative knowledge, which provides us with a richer understanding of the knowledge sourcing behaviours of organizations.

## Theoretical framework and hypotheses

There is an abundance of debate and dialogue in the literature on the role of knowledge in organizations. Researchers have investigated the phenomena from numerous angles – for example, inter-firm knowledge transfer (Simonin, 1999; Appleyard, 1996), intra-firm knowledge transfer (Szulanski, 1996; Zander and Kogut, 1995), learning from problem solving (Leonard-Barton, 1995), and learning from networks and collaborations (Liebeskind *et al.*, 1996; Powell *et al.*, 1996). The recent *Organization Science* special issue on 'Knowledge, Knowing and Organizations', contained articles addressing a variety of issues, ranging from knowledge sharing networks (Hansen, 2002) to the impact of knowledge characteristics on organizational structure (Birkinshaw *et al.*, 2002). Looking at the scope of the existing literature, issues of knowledge transfer and acquisition remain dominant. Organizations need to renew their knowledge base constantly in order to develop capabilities for flexibility, adaptation and innovation. Authors such as Argote and Ingram (2000) and Grant (1996) argue that the ability to integrate and co-ordinate different reservoirs of specialized knowledge residing within the firm constitutes an important organizational capability.

Building upon previous studies, this chapter investigates the nature of organizational knowledge acquisition and the impact on performance by incorporating various concepts such as social network theory (Liebeskind *et al.*, 1996), social capital (Nahapiet and Ghoshal, 1998) and absorptive capacity (Cohen and Levinthal, 1990). Where this study differs from previous work is in the development of the concept of knowledge quality – defined as the *usefulness and innovativeness* of acquired knowledge – and its impact on firm performance. Subsequent discussion will focus on the theoretical model and underlying constructs developed and tested here.

### The concept of 'knowledge quality'

Numerous studies have examined the process of knowledge acquisition and its impact on firm performance. For example, Appleyard (1996) examined inter-firm knowledge transfer, focussing on the method of transfer. In Mowery *et al.* (1996), Bierly and Chakrabarti (1996) and Almeida (1996), patent data was used to analyse the nature of knowledge transfer. In more recent studies (that is, Yli-Renko *et al.*, 2001; Lane *et al.*, 2001; Frost, 2001) knowledge transfer was investigated in the context of inter-organizational learning and innovation, and in Argote and Ingram (2000: 150), the authors argue that the creation and transfer of knowledge forms the basis of competitive advantage in organizations.

Despite the abundance of theoretical and empirical work in this area, a fundamental question that remains unanswered is – 'What is the nature of the knowledge being transferred?' In other words, we are interested in investigating not just the amount or frequency of knowledge transfer, but the quality of the acquired knowledge in terms of (1) its usefulness and importance to the firm and (2) the extent to which it is innovative, new or novel to the firm. The underlying motivation is that we are interested in whether the acquired knowledge adds value to, or makes an impact on the firm. In this study, the term 'knowledge quality' is defined as the acquisition of *useful and innovative* knowledge.

The rationale behind incorporating the dimensions of usefulness and innovativeness in our definition of 'knowledge quality' stems from two sources. The first source comes from our exploratory research which entailed interviews with managers from various industries. The objective of this interview research was to refine our study's model, and to ensure that we formulate appropriate measures for our constructs. However, the interviews also raise the issue of whether the acquired knowledge is useful and innovative. These managers were primarily interested in acquiring knowledge that allowed them to do things more efficiently in their organizations as well as more effectively, that is knowledge that added value to their organization. Details of the interviews are provided in the methodology section below. The second source comes from the work of Gilbert Ryle whose essay 'Knowing How and Knowing That' distinguishes between 'knowing that something is the case and knowing how to do things' (1945: 170). Ryle's statement below emphasizes that in order to effectively acquire a piece of knowledge one has to know how to use or apply it in problem solving and decision making.

> Effective possession of a piece of knowledge-that involves knowing how to use that knowledge, when required, for the solution of other theoretical or practical problems. There is a distinction between the museum-possession and the workshop-possession of knowledge. A silly person can be stocked with information, yet never know how to answer particular questions. (1945: 323)

Ryle's work leads us to consider whether knowledge acquisition involves the acquisition of knowledge that makes a difference. That is, when organizations (and its members) acquire knowledge from other parties (either internal or external), is that piece of knowledge useful in a way that it will assist in solving problems? Hence, we include the dimension of knowledge usefulness in our definition of knowledge quality. The specific items for measuring both knowledge usefulness and innovativeness will be discussed in a later section.

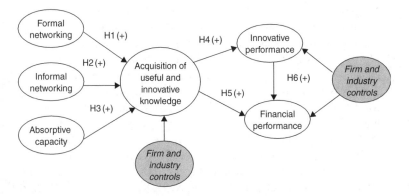

*Figure 11.1* Hypothesized model

*Note*: This is a simplified representation of the model; it does not show the control variables or the measures for each construct.

For the sake of simplicity, we make several qualifications in our conceptualization of knowledge quality. First, we acknowledge that there are several concepts in the knowledge literature which we do not include in our definitions – such as Teece's (1998) codified/tacit, observable/non-observable, positive/negative, and autonomous/systematic knowledge dimensions. This means that for the purpose of this study, we measure the nature of acquired knowledge in terms of its usefulness and innovativeness, but not along the tacit–explicit dimension. Second, for the purpose of this study, we limit our definition of knowledge quality to that of *acquired* knowledge, excluding knowledge that is generated or created within the firm.

In the following sections, we develop our model of knowledge quality, its antecedents, and its impact on firm performance, which is presented in Figure 11.1.

## Social capital and knowledge quality

The role of the firm's network ties as a valuable resource for learning and resource exchange is well documented in the literature. Nahapiet and Ghoshal's (1998) model of intellectual capital creation regards the role of social capital (in terms of network ties, shared language, trust, obligation, and so on) as the driving force behind the exchange of intellectual capital. Numerous studies have emphasized the important role played by network interactions in facilitating information and knowledge transfer. According to Powell *et al.* (1996: 118), 'a network serves as a locus of innovation because it provides timely access to knowledge and resources that are otherwise unavailable'. Henderson and Cockburn's study (1994: 67) showed that the firm's ability to 'encourage and maintain an extensive flow of information across the boundaries of the firm' was a significant contribution to research productivity.

Social network theorists advocate the importance of informal personal interactions as a source of resources and knowledge exchange. According to Granovetter (1992: 25), 'economic action (like all action) is embedded in ongoing networks of personal relationships rather than carried out by atomized actors'. Liebeskind *et al.*'s work on biotechnology firms (1996) found that knowledge exchange between firms occurred in the context of social networks, rather than being driven by a formal contractual agreement. Similarly, Yli-Renko *et al.*'s (2001) study found a positive relationship between social interaction and knowledge acquisition.

While social network theorists cite the importance of personal informal interaction, studies in the areas of joint ventures and strategic alliances have also investigated the issue of knowledge exchange between partners. Contractor and Lorange (1988: 9) assert that '... it is important that the partners have complementary strengths, that they together cover all relevant know-how dimensions needed ...'. In recent studies, both Stuart (2000) and Steensma and Lyles (2000) found that a major contributing factor to the growth, innovation rate and survival of inter-organizational alliances was the resources and knowledge flowing from the alliance partners. Building upon existing studies, we examine the role of both formal networking (governed by contractual arrangements such as strategic alliances and joint ventures) and informal networking (in the form of social networks) as sources of useful and innovative knowledge for organizations:

> *Hypothesis 1: There is a positive relationship between formal networking and knowledge quality*
> *Hypothesis 2: There is a positive relationship between informal networking and knowledge quality*

### Absorptive capacity and knowledge quality

Although the firm's formal and informal networks of interaction can be important sources of knowledge, the firm's own innate capacity to absorb and learn is also crucial. Cohen and Levinthal's (1990: 128) concept of absorptive capacity acknowledges that 'the ability of a firm to recognize the value of new, external information, assimilate it, and apply it to commercial ends' represents an important element in a firm's ability to innovate and learn. Many empirical studies have investigated the role of absorptive capacity in organizational learning and innovation. In their study of strategic alliances, Mowery *et al.* (1996) examined the role of absorptive capacity in the firm's ability to acquire its partner's capabilities and found that experience in an area related to the alliance partner's increased the chances of inter-firm knowledge transfer. Similarly, Pennings and Harianto (1992) found support for the hypothesis that prior accumulated experience in a certain technological area increased the likelihood of innovation adoption. In their study on international joint ventures, Lane *et al.* (2001) concluded that the ability to understand and apply external knowledge contributed to learning and performance.

Tsai's (2001) study found that the interaction of both network centrality and absorptive capacity contributed significantly to innovation and performance. This finding suggests that although an organization has access to knowledge sources through its network links, it may not have sufficient capacity to absorb the knowledge. In this study, we build on Tsai's (2001) work to investigate the role of absorptive capacity in the firm's ability to not only acquire knowledge, but to acquire knowledge that is both useful and innovative. At this stage, we are interested in the effects of absorptive capacity on the firm's ability to acquire knowledge, and will leave it to future research to test for effects on firm performance.

*Hypothesis 3: There is a positive relationship between absorptive capacity and knowledge quality*

It is important to note that our subsequent operationalization of absorptive capacity is both broader and more direct than previous empirical work where the emphasis has mainly been on the *proxies* of absorptive capacity. For example, Pennings and Harianto (1992) measure past accumulated technological experience as a proxy for absorptive capacity. In contrast, we employ a more direct approach by examining the extent to which a range of *actions* are taken to recognize, absorb and assimilate new external information and knowledge into the organization. We also go beyond the emphasis on R&D investment, recognizing that this may not be applicable across all industries.

## Knowledge quality and firm performance

Discussion thus far has centred on the various antecedents to knowledge acquisition, focussing on the role of formal and informal networks and absorptive capacity on the acquisition of knowledge that is useful and innovative (our definition of 'knowledge quality'). In this section, we focus the discussion of the impact of knowledge quality on firm performance – both innovative and financial performance.

There is a significant literature supporting the argument that organizational innovation is facilitated to a large extent by the continuous sourcing and renewal of knowledge. The need to overcome the various forms of uncertainty arising from innovation has led to the importance of sourcing new knowledge from both within and outside the organization. Work on social networks and inter-organizational relationships have argued that learning and knowledge transfer among firms are essential to the innovation process (for example, Powell *et al.*, 1996; Liebeskind *et al.*, 1996). Theories of 'dynamic capabilities' (Teece *et al.*, 1997) also emphasize the role of knowledge (particularly its constant renewal) as a source of innovation and competitive advantage. Similarly, the concept of 'knowledge integration' (Grant, 1996; Iansiti and Clark, 1994) emphasizes the ability to integrate different types of specialized knowledge to develop new innovation-enhancing capabilities. Henderson and Clark (1990) investigated the relationship between knowledge and innovation in their study of 'architectural innovation'. The basic premise of their argument is that firms need to develop and renew their architectural knowledge continually to prevent their knowledge from being obsolete in the event of radical innovation. As an illustration of the importance of accumulated knowledge stock for the firm's innovative capabilities, Helfat (1997) found that during periods of environmental instability, firms with greater amounts on accumulated knowledge undertook greater amounts of R&D. In a more recent study, Yli-Renko *et al.* (2001) found a significant positive relationship between knowledge acquisition and new product development.

Several studies have also investigated the impact of knowledge acquisition on firm performance. For example, Tsai (2001) concluded that the interaction between absorptive capacity and network centrality had a positive impact on business unit performance. Both Stuart (2000) and Lane *et al.* (2001) found evidence to support their hypotheses that knowledge acquired from alliance partners contributed significantly to alliance performance. In summary, we build upon previous studies to investigate whether the sourcing of useful and innovative knowledge by firms has an impact on the level of innovative and financial performance:

*Hypothesis 4: There is a positive relationship between knowledge quality and innovative performance*

*Hypothesis 5: There is a positive relationship between knowledge quality and financial performance*

## Innovation and financial performance

There is substantial empirical evidence in the literature pointing to a positive relationship between innovation and financial performance (at both the firm and industry levels). Banbury and Mitchell (1995) found that the introduction of incremental product innovations strongly influenced the market share and business survival of an industry incumbent. In other studies, innovative output has been attributed to improved stock price performance (Chaney and Devinney, 1992) and the persistent profitability of firms (Geroski *et al.*, 1993), after controlling for factors such as industry differences and the type of innovation. Soni *et al.* (1993) also found a significant positive relationship between innovation and sales growth. At the industry level, Chakrabarti (1990) found evidence to suggest that productivity growth in the chemical and textiles industries was associated, in part, with the rate of innovative output in those industries. Building on the positive relationship between innovation and financial performance established by numerous studies, a positive relationship is hypothesized between innovation and financial performance:

*Hypothesis 6: There is a positive relationship between innovation and financial performance*

## Methods

### Sampling

Our survey instrument was extensively pre-tested through interviews and a pilot sampling trial. A total of 16 interviews with managers from a variety of industries were conducted to refine the definitions, terminology and questions used in the survey. The revised survey was tested in a postal pilot study, which yielded a 20 per cent response rate from a total mail out to 120 managers. The main objectives of this pilot were to gauge the likely response rate, to further refine the questionnaire and to test the reliability of our measures.

The final version was then mailed to 2,137 organizations (with more than 20 employees) randomly selected from 17 manufacturing and service industries (based on two-digit SIC codes). The objectives of this procedure were to ensure generalizability of results across industries and to target industries where issues of knowledge acquisition and innovation are *important and relevant*. Specifically, we targeted industries facing dynamic and competitive environments with a consequent high need for knowledge acquisition and learning. The issue of relevance is also crucial to obtaining a reasonable response rate and high quality responses.

The questionnaire was addressed to the CEO or managing director of each organization. To minimize the limitations of using single inform-ant methodology, we took precautions to ensure informant compe-tency. First, the key objectives of the study and its central themes were outlined in a covering letter. If the CEO was unable to complete the sur-vey, they were asked to give it to a middle-senior-level manager with sufficient knowledge of the study's objectives. Second, we included cri-teria for assessing informant competency, such as tenure in the organi-zation, industry and current position.

The number of responses totalled 343 (yielding a 16 per cent response rate). After eliminating 26 surveys due to large proportions of missing data, the final 317 used in our analysis were fairly evenly distributed across manufacturing (44 per cent) and service (56 per cent) sectors as well as across the 17 industries (see Table 11.1). Firm size was also well distributed, with 40 per cent small firms (100 or less employees), 30 per cent medium-sized firms (100 to 400 employees) and 30 per cent large

*Table 11.1*   Distribution of survey respondents across industries

| Industries included in the study | Percentage of total responses | Percentage response within industry |
|---|---|---|
| Metal mining | 5 | 13 |
| Oil and gas extraction | 1 | 9 |
| Petroleum refining | 2 | 16 |
| Chemicals and allied products | 11 | 10 |
| Primary metal industries | 4 | 8 |
| Machinery, except electrical | 11 | 10 |
| Electrical and electronic machinery | 5 | 8 |
| Transportation equipment | 3 | 8 |
| Measuring instruments | 2 | 6 |
| Banking | 3 | 10 |
| Credit agencies | 3 | 8 |
| Security and commodity brokers | 2 | 5 |
| Insurance | 6 | 14 |
| Business services | 20 | 13 |
| Health services | 4 | 9 |
| Legal services | 5 | 10 |
| Miscellaneous services | 13 | 12 |
| *Total* | *100* | |
| *Total number of valid responses* | *317* | |

firms (more than 800 employees). The average and median sizes of these firms were 2,024 and 175 employees respectively. Tests of the distribution of returned surveys indicate that no industry or size bias existed in the responses received.

Analysis of respondent characteristics indicated that they had sufficient knowledge of the key issues of the study – all respondents occupied middle-senior management roles, and the average tenure at the organization, industry and current position were 12, 17 and 5 years respectively. Following the procedures of Armstrong and Overton (1976) we also tested for non-response bias by examining the construct means of early versus late respondents, and found no significant differences. On the assumption that late respondents are more similar to non-respondents this result suggests little non-response bias.

With surveys such as this there is always a concern about single respondent bias. In a related study, the survey was used in conjunction with six case studies (see Soo, Devinney, Midgley and Deering, 2002) and an identical model was estimated for each company. In this situation, as many as 120 responses were received from a single firm, hence we had both repeated measures of firm variables and estimates of the variance of individual measures. Although the models differed in the magnitude of various effects (as one would expect), the general form of the model and key conclusions remained valid.

Finally, to test for common method bias, we applied Harmann's *ex post* one-factor test (Podsakoff and Organ, 1986), which indicated that 19 distinct factors were needed to explain the 80 per cent of the variance in the measures used with the largest factor only accounting for 17 per cent of the variance. Hence, there was no 'general factor' in the data that would represent a common method bias.

## Measures

Our model and hypotheses were tested using data from a questionnaire survey. The questionnaire consists of both *formative* measures – that is, those observed indicators that cause or form the latent constructs – and *reflective* measures – that is, observed indicators that are caused or formed by the latent constructs (Bollen, 1989). Formal and informal networking, knowledge quality and innovation are measured by formative items as there are no pre-existing latent constructs. Absorptive capacity and financial performance are measured by reflective items as they represent effects of existing latent constructs. Each is discussed in detail in the sections below. All survey questions (except those pertaining to firm and industry demographics) use a seven-point Likert scale.

*Table 11.2*   Sources of formal and informal networking

| | Formal networking (Frequency) | | | Informal networking (Frequency) | |
|---|---|---|---|---|---|
| | Mean | Std Dev | | Mean | Std Dev |
| Parent/subsidiaries | 4.26 | 1.66 | Fellow colleagues | 5.99 | 1.15 |
| Customers | 3.90 | 1.76 | Customers | 5.34 | 1.28 |
| Suppliers | 3.75 | 1.58 | Parent/subsidiaries | 4.76 | 1.48 |
| Consultants | 3.53 | 1.40 | Suppliers | 4.63 | 1.28 |
| Research institutes | 2.75 | 1.25 | Consultants | 4.05 | 1.40 |
| Sales/marketing | 2.74 | 1.34 | Competitors | 3.58 | 1.27 |
| Competitors | 2.60 | 1.42 | Research institutes | 3.17 | 1.19 |
| | | | Sales/marketing | 2.97 | 1.26 |

*Note*: Mean scores are presented in decreasing order.

### Formal and informal networking (formative)

To measure formal networking activities, respondents were asked to rate the frequency of *formal* collaborations (such as joint ventures, strategic alliances, etc.) with a list of seven parties, namely customers, suppliers, competitors, research institutes, sales and marketing agencies, consultants, and parent company/subsidiaries. To measure informal networking activities, respondents were asked to rate the frequency of social interactions with a list of eight parties (the parties listed previously, plus fellow colleagues). The aim was to construct a comprehensive and 'generic' list of external and internal parties that can represent a *network of formal and informal interactions* for firms across a variety of industries. This approach is adopted from Appleyard's (1996) study on knowledge flows. Table 11.2 lists the parties of both formal and informal networking and their respective mean frequency scores. The latent constructs are formed by the frequency scores, for example, formal networking is formed by seven measures (made up of the frequency of formal collaboration with the seven parties listed in Table 11.2, which will be described in detail later in this chapter). Factor analysis was used to validate that these parties were independent sources (the results are not reported here for simplicity).

### Knowledge quality (formative)

To measure the construct of knowledge quality, a three-step approach was taken. First, respondents were asked to rate the frequency of acquiring knowledge[1] from a list of nine sources (these sources are listed in Table 11.3 and discussed later in the chapter). Second, respondents were

*Table 11.3*  Breakdown of knowledge sources and knowledge rating

| | Frequency | | | Usefulness | | | Innovativeness | |
|---|---|---|---|---|---|---|---|---|
| | *Mean* | *Std Dev* | | *Mean* | *Std Dev* | | *Mean* | *Std Dev* |
| Fellow colleagues | 5.36 | 1.33 | Fellow colleagues | 5.47 | 1.23 | Fellow colleagues | 4.83 | 1.34 |
| Parent/subsidiaries | 4.38 | 1.50 | Parent/subsidiaries | 4.83 | 1.41 | Consultants | 4.38 | 1.40 |
| Suppliers | 4.15 | 1.47 | Customers | 4.82 | 1.64 | Parent/subsidiaries | 4.18 | 1.41 |
| Published material | 4.11 | 1.54 | Suppliers | 4.79 | 1.40 | Published material | 4.10 | 1.36 |
| Customers | 3.94 | 1.70 | Consultants | 4.75 | 1.33 | Suppliers | 4.09 | 1.48 |
| Consultants | 3.81 | 1.47 | Published material | 4.57 | 1.41 | Competitors | 3.96 | 1.37 |
| Sales/marketing | 3.38 | 1.40 | Competitors | 4.43 | 1.47 | Customers | 3.69 | 1.50 |
| Competitors | 3.09 | 1.41 | Sales/marketing | 4.07 | 1.42 | Research institutes | 3.63 | 1.35 |
| Research institutes | 3.04 | 1.31 | Research institutes | 3.96 | 1.35 | Sales/marketing | 3.63 | 1.40 |

*Note*: Mean scores are presented in decreasing order.

asked to rate the usefulness and innovativeness of the knowledge that is acquired from each of the listed sources. Hence for each of the sources, a 'frequency', 'usefulness' and 'innovative' score are obtained. Preliminary analyses showed a strong correlation between the usefulness and innovative scores, and thus both are combined to form a 'quality' score. In the final step, both the 'frequency' and 'quality' scores are combined (multiplied together) to form the measure for knowledge quality. In essence, our knowledge quality construct encompasses dimensions of frequency and quality. That is, not only does it capture the frequency with which respondents acquire knowledge from a particular source (that is, customers), it captures the extent to which that knowledge is useful and innovative for them. The overall knowledge quality measure is estimated directly by the model with optimal weights estimated for each of the nine sources.

### Absorptive capacity (reflective)

We designed measures to capture two important aspects of absorptive capacity: first, *active information-seeking behaviors* – that is, the degree to which respondents actively seek external information, record it for future reference, use the acquired information in their work, and distribute the information to fellow colleagues. Second, we recognize that the development of absorptive capacity is a function of both past and ongoing *investments in knowledge accumulation*. To measure this, we investigated the degree to which respondents participate in academic/industry conferences, update their skills through training and self-learning, and keep abreast with the latest technology and knowledge related to their organization's business. Our measures are organizational – that is, they focus on the extent to which the firm has policies and procedures that encourage employees to seek external information and invest in knowledge accumulation.

### Innovative performance (formative)

To measure a firm's level of innovation, we compiled a list of 14 innovative outputs, incorporating new (and modified) products, services and processes (organizational, administrative and production), patents, licenses, publications and conference presentations. The aim was to construct measures that would be generic enough to be applicable to firms from multiple industries. Respondents were asked to rate their firm's frequency of producing these innovations compared to their

*Table 11.4* Measures of innovative performance

| Measures | Mean | Std Dev |
| --- | --- | --- |
| New product prototypes | 4.12 | 1.48 |
| New products or services introduced to the market which are new to the market | 3.89 | 1.58 |
| New products or services introduced to the market which are new to the firm | 4.40 | 1.42 |
| Significant modifications to existing products | 4.46 | 1.49 |
| Significant modifications to existing services | 4.45 | 1.42 |
| New or modified production/manufacturing techniques | 4.12 | 1.45 |
| New or modified administration/managerial practices | 4.44 | 1.27 |
| New or modified marketing techniques | 4.01 | 1.50 |
| Patents either applied for or ending | 2.70 | 1.70 |
| Patents obtained | 2.53 | 1.76 |
| Publications in academic, scientific or technical journals by your firm or its members | 2.98 | 1.63 |
| Formal presentations at conferences or seminars | 4.01 | 1.58 |
| Licenses or technology rights sold | 2.14 | 1.47 |
| Licenses or technology rights purchased | 2.49 | 1.70 |

competitors. Table 11.4 lists the measures used to form the construct of innovative performance.

### Financial performance (reflective)

Financial performance was measured using both market measures – market share and annual sales growth – and financial measures – after-tax return on investment and growth in total after-tax profits. These are commonly used in the strategy and marketing literatures (for example, Banbury and Mitchell, 1995) and reflect the multidimensional pressures managers face on a day-to-day basis. Following Johansson and Yip (1994) and Roth and Morrison (1990), these measures were treated as reflective indicators of an existing latent 'performance' construct.

### Control variables

We use firm and industry controls – that is, industry dummy variables, firm size, R&D intensity and ownership structure – to control for industry and firm effects that are known to exist with respect to innovation and performance (as shown, for example, in Acs and Audretsch, 1987), as well as knowledge quality. Controlling for these effects allows us to better identify the real impact of the model's focal constructs.

## Method of analysis

The data from the survey were analysed using partial least squares (PLS), a well-established technique for estimating path coefficients in causal models (for example, Johansson and Yip, 1994; Birkinshaw *et al.*, 1995). Its conceptual core is an iterative combination of *principal components analysis* relating measures to constructs, and *path analysis* permitting the construction of a system of constructs (Barclay *et al.*, 1995). The major advantages of PLS are that it: (1) accepts small sample sizes, (2) can deal with complex causal models and (3) does not require multivariate normality. It is especially suited to 'situations of high complexity but low theoretical information' (Barclay *et al.*, 1995: 288), a point that is particularly relevant here given that the field of organizational knowledge is relatively new with concepts and relationships still being developed.

## Results

### Descriptive data

Our primary interest is to investigate factors contributing to knowledge acquisition, the nature of acquired knowledge, and whether its level of frequency, usefulness and innovativeness contributes to firm performance. We are concerned with the impact of overall knowledge quality rather than the effects of different knowledge sources. Table 11.3 presents the breakdown of the frequency, usefulness and innovativeness scores according to the various sources of knowledge. An interesting point to note in relation to this is that fellow colleagues is rated the highest in terms of the most frequent, most useful, and most innovative source of knowledge, followed by parent company and other subsidiaries with the second highest frequency and usefulness ratings. External parties such as suppliers and customers rated reasonably high on frequency and usefulness, but lower on innovativeness. It is beyond the scope of this paper to investigate in detail the different sources of knowledge quality. These issues represent interesting future research questions.

For the PLS model, we are interested in two levels of analysis – the *measurement* model (that is, the reliability and validity of the measures used to operationalize the underlying constructs) and the *structural* model (that is, the relationships between the latent constructs). We present and discuss the results of the measurement model before proceeding to the latter.

## Measurement model

Examining the loadings and cross-loadings of each of the constructs' individual items assesses the reliability of the reflective measures. For an item to be reliable a minimum loading of 0.7 is required, indicating that more than 50 per cent of the variance of the measure is accounted for by the respective construct. In our study, all items had a loading with their respective constructs of greater than 0.7. Other measures of reliability are Cronbach's alpha and Werts, Linn and Joreskog's (1974) measure of internal consistency (IC). Table 11.5 lists the alpha and IC scores for the reflective constructs, indicating satisfactory reliability with the IC scores of 0.92 and 0.87 for absorptive capacity and financial performance respectively.

Finally, we assess the discriminant validity of the constructs by using Fornell and Larcker's (1981) measure of average variance extracted (AVE). The AVE measures the amount of variance captured by the construct (through its items) relative to the amount of variance due to measurement error. To satisfy the requirements of discriminant validity, the square root of a construct's AVE must be greater than the correlation between that construct and other constructs in the model. The correlation matrix in Table 11.5 shows that all the diagonal elements are

*Table 11.5* Measures of internal consistency and discriminant validity (correlations of latent constructs)

|  | Formal networking | Informal networking | Absorptive capacity | Knowledge quality | Innovative performance | Financial performance |
|---|---|---|---|---|---|---|
| Formal networking (F) | **1.00** | | | | | |
| Informal networking (F) | 0.50 | **1.00** | | | | |
| Absorptive capacity (R) | 0.32 | 0.35 | **0.82** | | | |
| Knowledge quality (F) | 0.32 | 0.44 | 0.41 | **1.00** | | |
| Innovative performance (F) | 0.32 | 0.38 | 0.38 | 0.42 | **1.00** | |
| Financial performance (R) | 0.03 | 0.09 | 0.13 | 0.10 | 0.28 | **0.80** |
| Cronbach's Alpha | N/A | N/A | 0.89 | N/A | N/A | 0.83 |
| Fornell's Internal Consistency | N/A | N/A | 0.92 | N/A | N/A | 0.87 |

*Note*: (F) indicates a formative measure; (R) indicates reflective measures; diagonal elements are square roots of average variance.

greater than the corresponding off-diagonal elements. The relatively high correlation between formal and informal networking might raise some concerns, however, at 0.50 this is well within commonly accepted benchmarks for discriminant validity.

## Structural model

The results of the structural model are presented in Table 11.6 and Figure 11.2. From these we can see that the constructs of knowledge quality and innovative performance are well explained (R-squares of 33 per cent and 23 per cent respectively) and that of financial performance reasonably well explained (R-square of 17 per cent). Four of the six paths estimated are significant at the 0.001 level, with the other two being not significant. Due to the significance of the paths and the reasonably high R-square values (both indicators of model fit for PLS), we can say that the model fits well overall and supports the majority of our hypotheses. Subsequent discussion will focus on the individual hypotheses and the results of the path estimations.

### Factors contributing to knowledge quality

Both informal networking and absorptive capacity have significant effects on knowledge quality but not formal networking, thus supporting Hypotheses 2 and 3 but not Hypothesis 1. The strength of the impact of informal networking (as compared to formal networking)[2] supports the proposition made by social network theorists that 'knowledge creation occurs in the context of a community, one that is fluid and evolving rather than tightly bound or static' (Powell *et al.*, 1996: 118). Our results indicate that firms source useful and innovative knowledge predominantly through social interactions among employees of the firms. This implies that the transfer of useful and innovative knowledge occurs through socialization, described by Nonaka and Takeuchi (1995: 62) as a 'process of sharing experiences and thereby creating tacit knowledge such as shared mental modes and technical skills'.

Absorptive capacity contributes significantly to the acquisition of useful and innovative knowledge by firms. This implies that the firm's propensity for sourcing useful and innovative knowledge is affected by its ability to absorb new knowledge (measured in terms of active knowledge seeking behaviours and investments in knowledge development and learning). These results support the findings of previous studies (see, for example, Pennings and Harianto, 1992; Lane and Lubatkin, 1998) where knowledge acquisition and learning were influenced by accumulated experience. The significance of both informal networking and absorptive capacity also supports Tsai's (2001) findings that although firms are

Table 11.6  Structural model results

| | Proposed effect | Path coefficient | t-value | Significance | Hypothesis supported? |
|---|---|---|---|---|---|
| **HYPOTHESIZED MODEL** | | | | | |
| **Effects on Knowledge Quality ($R^2 = 0.33$)** | | | | | |
| Formal networking | H1 (+) | 0.06 | 0.89 | n.s. | No |
| Informal networking | H2 (+) | **0.28** | **3.34** | *** | **Yes** |
| Absorptive capacity | H3 (+) | **0.32** | **3.35** | *** | **Yes** |
| Firm control: R&D intensity | | 0.16 | 2.41 | * | Control |
| **Effects on Innovative Performance ($R^2 = 0.23$)** | | | | | |
| Knowledge quality | H4 (+) | **0.43** | **4.39** | *** | **Yes** |
| Firm control: Local ownership | | 0.17 | 2.14 | * | Control |
| **Effects on Financial Performance ($R^2 = 0.17$)** | | | | | |
| Knowledge quality | H5 (+) | -0.02 | -0.23 | n.s. | No |
| Innovative Performance | H6 (+) | **0.28** | **4.10** | *** | **Yes** |
| Industry control: Transportation services | | 0.12 | 2.43 | * | Control |

Note: Control variables with significance levels below 0.05 are excluded. p-values: * $p < 0.05$; ** $p < 0.01$; *** $p < 0.001$; n.s. = not significant.

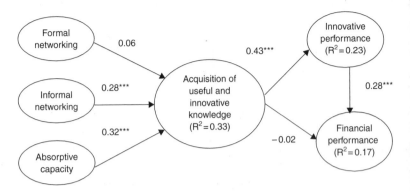

*Figure 11.2*   Structural model results

*Note*: Control variables are excluded; *** p < 0.001, ** p < 0.01, * p < 0.05.

$R^2$ are those obtained after controlling for (1) industry effects (industry dummy variables) and (2) firm effects – size, R&D intensity, and ownership structure.

exposed to sources of knowledge through their network links, they need to have the capabilities to understand and absorb such knowledge.

The descriptive data in Tables 11.2 and 11.4 suggest that firms engage in informal networking predominantly with colleagues and parent company/other subsidiaries, which are also regarded as important sources of useful and innovative knowledge. An interesting point to note is that although customers are rated highly as parties to informal networking, they are not generally regarded as sources of knowledge (and do not rate highly in terms of being sources of innovative knowledge). Future research will examine these results in greater detail. It will be interesting to examine different industries or types of firms and to investigate the patterns of networking and knowledge sourcing within these.

### Factors contributing to firm performance

Knowledge quality contributes significantly to innovative performance but not financial performance, supporting Hypothesis 4 but not 5. Innovative performance contributes significantly to financial performance, supporting Hypothesis 6. This set of results paints an interesting scenario – *organizations extract economic rents from knowledge only via innovative output*. In other words, when an organization absorbs or acquires new knowledge, this will impact its level of innovative output directly, which then contributes to financial performance. In essence, this supports previous research by Nonaka and Takeuchi (1995) and Leonard-Barton (1995) where knowledge creation and acquisition were seen as key elements to firm innovation, and also the work of Chaney and Devinney (1992) and Geroski *et al.* (1993) where innovation was found to have a significant contribution to financial performance.

This result echoes Ryle's (1945) proposition that effective possession of a piece of knowledge requires knowing how to use it to solve problems. Our findings show that the acquisition of useful and innovative knowledge is an important antecedent to innovation. This indicates that not only is knowledge acquisition important for organizations, but the application and utilization of knowledge within the context of problem-solving and innovation is equally important, thus suggesting that knowledge management can be viewed within the context of innovation management, as one cannot be separated from the other.

## Conclusions and implications

Firms are increasingly relying on acquiring knowledge from various sources to develop capabilities for learning and innovation. According to Argote and Ingram (2000: 165), 'the processes underlying knowledge transfer provide a basis for understanding the competitive advantage of firms'. Previous studies have looked at the impact of knowledge acquisition on firm performance – see, for example, Yli-Renko *et al.* (2001) and Lane *et al.* (2001). In this study, we investigate an aspect of knowledge acquisition that has not been addressed in previous work – that is, the quality of acquired knowledge in terms of its usefulness to the firm and its innovativeness.

Our results show that both informal networking and absorptive capacity contribute to knowledge quality, but not formal networking. This implies that social interactions (rather than formal structured interactions) are more conducive to knowledge transfer (particularly the transfer of useful and innovative knowledge), thus supporting the work of social network theorists (Liebeskind *et al.*, 1996; Powell *et al.*, 1996). The significant impact of absorptive capacity implies that not only is it important for firms to nurture informal networks, but their own ability to understand and absorb new knowledge is equally important. This 'dual necessity' is also suggested by Tsai (2001: 1003).

The impact of knowledge quality on innovative performance rather than financial performance also yields interesting implications. These results indicate that firms extract economic returns from acquired knowledge only through its impact on innovation, suggesting a mediating effect of innovation on the relationship between knowledge and financial performance. This implies that managers need to think about whether (and how) the knowledge they acquire is subsequently utilized in their firm's innovative activities. Acquired knowledge needs to be 'acted upon' in innovative activities, which will then impact on financial output.

A qualification to this conclusion is, however, that our data is cross-sectional, with innovative and financial performance measured at the same time. While it is logical that innovation precedes financial performance, longitudinal research is required to give us greater confidence in the causality of our results.[3]

With this qualification, our results have important theoretical and practical implications. Previous studies found that knowledge accumulation plays an important role in firm performance. In this study, we build upon these studies to show that the nature of the acquired knowledge contributes directly to firm innovation and, indirectly, to financial performance. Hence, we are able to develop and empirically validate a model linking the knowledge quality to firm performance, contributing to the work on social networks (Granovetter, 1992), social capital (Nahapiet and Ghoshal, 1998), and absorptive capacity (Cohen and Levinthal, 1990). In this chapter, we are interested in whether knowledge quality 'matters' and, hence, we are concerned with aggregate effects only. The next step in our research agenda is to examine the effects of knowledge sourced from different parties on different types of innovation. We will endeavour to answer questions such as 'Why are some parties more important sources of knowledge' and 'How does the knowledge acquired from different parties impact on different types of innovation?'

## Notes

1. In the survey, respondents were given a definition of knowledge which included both tacit and explicit knowledge, based on Machlup's (1980) definitions. At this stage, we are not investigating the effects or quality of different types of acquired knowledge.
2. Although formal networking has no significant effect on knowledge quality, it is correlated with informal networking (as indicated by Table 11.5). The relationships between these two constructs, in particular whether informal networking mediates formal networking, fall outside the scope of our study but are worthy of further investigation. We are grateful to a reviewer for making this point.
3. We are again grateful to a reviewer for making this point.

## References

Acs, Z.J. and Audretsch, D.B. (1987) Innovation, market structure and firm size, *Review of Economics and Statistics*, 71(4): 567–74.

Almeida, P. (1996) Knowledge sourcing by foreign multinationals: patent citation analysis in the US semiconductor industry, *Strategic Management Journal*, 17: 155–65.

Appleyard, M.M. (1996) How does knowledge flow? Interfirm patterns in the semiconductor industry, *Strategic Management Journal*, 17: 137–54.

Argote, L. and Ingram, P. (2000) Knowledge transfer: a basis for competitive advantage in firms, *Organizational Behavior and Human Decision Processes*, 82(1): 150–69.

Armstrong, J.S. and Overton, T. (1976) Estimating nonresponse bias in mail surveys, *Journal of Marketing Research*, 19: 396–402.

Banbury, C.M. and Mitchell, W. (1995) The effect of introducing important incremental innovations on market share and business survival, *Strategic Management Journal*, 16: 161–82.

Barclay, D., Higgins, C. and Thompson, R. (1995) The partial least squares (PLS) approach to causal modeling: personal computer adoption and use as an illustration, *Technology Studies*, 2(2): 285–324.

Bierly, P. and Chakrabarti, A. (1996) Generic knowledge strategies in the US pharmaceutical industry, *Strategic Management Journal*, 17: 123–35.

Birkinshaw, J., Morrison, A. and Hulland, J. (1995) Structural and competitive determinants of a global integration strategy, *Strategic Management Journal*, 16: 637–55.

Birkinshaw, J., Nobel, R. and Ridderstråle, J. (2002) Knowledge as a contingency variable: do the characteristics of knowledge predict organization structure?, *Organization Science*, 13(3): 274–89.

Bollen, K.A. (1989) *Structural Equations with Latent Variables*. New York: John Wiley & Sons, Inc.

Chakrabarti, A.K. (1990) Innovation and productivity: an analysis of the chemical, textiles and machine tool industries in the US, *Research Policy*, 19: 257–69.

Chaney, P.K. and Devinney, T.M. (1992) New product innovations and stock price performance, *Journal of Business Finance & Accounting*, 19(5): 677–94.

Cohen, W.M. and Levinthal, D.A. (1990) Absorptive capacity: a new perspective on learning and innovation, *Administrative Science Quarterly*, 35(1): 128–52.

Contractor, F.J. and Lorange, P. (1988) Why should firms co-operate? the strategy and economics basis for co-operative ventures. In F.J. Contractor and P. Lorange (eds), *Co-operative Strategies in International Business*. New York: Lexington Books.

Fornell, C. and Larcker, D.F. (1981) Evaluating structural equation models with unobservable variables and measurement error, *Journal of Marketing Research*, 18: 39–50.

Frost, T.S. (2001) The geographic sources of foreign subsidiaries' innovations, *Strategic Management Journal*, 22(2): 101–24.

Geroski, P., Machin, S. and Reenen, J.V. (1993) The profitability of innovating firms, *RAND Journal of Economics*, 24(2): 198–211.

Granovetter, M.S. (1992) Problems of explanation in economic sociology. In N. Nohria and R. G. Eccles (eds), *Networks and Organization: Structure, Form and Action*. Boston, MA: Harvard Business School.

Grant, R.M. (1996) Toward a knowledge based theory of the firm, *Strategic Management Journal*, 17: 109–22.

Hansen, M.T. (2002) Knowledge networks: explaining effective knowledge sharing in multiunit companies, *Organization Science*, 13(3): 232–48.

Helfat, C.E. (1997) Know-how and asset complementarity and dynamic capability accumulation: the case of R&D, *Strategic Management Journal*, 18(5): 339–60.

Henderson, R. and Clark, K. (1990) Architectural innovation: the reconfiguration of existing product technologies and the failure of established firms, *Administrative Science Quarterly*, 35: 9–30.

Henderson, R. and Cockburn, I. (1994) Measuring competence? exploring firm effects in pharmaceutical research, *Strategic Management Journal*, 15: 63–84.

Iansiti, M. and Clark, K.B. (1994) Integration and dynamic capability: evidence from product development in automobiles and mainframe computers, *Industrial and Corporate Change*, 3(3): 557–605.

Johansson, J.K. and Yip, G.S. (1994) Exploiting globalization potential: U.S. and Japanese strategies, *Strategic Management Journal*, 15(8): 579–601.

Lane, P.J. and Lubatkin, M. (1998) Relative absorptive capacity and interorganizational learning, *Strategic Management Journal*, 19: 461–77.

Lane, P.J., Salk, J.E. and Lyles, M.A. (2001) Absorptive capacity, learning, and performance in international joint ventures, *Strategic Management Journal*, 22(12): 1139–1162.

Leonard-Barton, D. (1995) *Wellsprings of Knowledge: Building and Sustaining the Sources of Innovation*. Boston, MA: Harvard Business School Press.

Liebeskind, J.P. (1996) Knowledge, strategy, and the theory of the firm, *Strategic Management Journal*, 17: 93–107.

Liebeskind, J.P., Oliver, A.L., Zucker, L. and Brewer, M. (1996) Social networks, learning, and flexibility: sourcing scientific knowledge in new biotechnology firms, *Organization Science*, 7(4): 428–43.

Machlup, F. (1980) *Knowledge: Its Creation, Distribution and Economic Significance* (Two Volumes). Princeton, NJ: Princeton University Press.

Miller, D. and Shamsie, J. (2001) Learning across the life cycle: experimentation and performance among Hollywood studio heads, *Strategic Management Journal*, 22(8): 725–46.

Mowery, D.C., Oxley, J.E. and Silverman, B.S. (1996) Strategic alliances and interfirm knowledge transfer, *Strategic Management Journal*, 17: 77–91.

Nahapiet, J. and Ghoshal, S. (1998) Social capital, intellectual capital, and the organizational advantages, *Academy of Management Review*, 23(2): 242–66.

Nonaka, I. and Takeuchi, H. (1995) *The Knowledge-Creating Company*. New York: Oxford University Press.

Pennings, J.M. and Harianto, F. (1992) The diffusion of technological innovation in the commercial banking industry, *Strategic Management Journal*, 13: 29–46.

Podsakoff, P. and Organ, D. (1986) Self reports in organizational research: problems and prospects, *Journal of Management*, 12(4): 531–44.

Powell, W., Kogut, K. and Smith-Doerr, L. (1996) Interorganizational collaboration and the locus of innovation: networks of learning in biotechnology, *Administrative Science Quarterly*, 41: 116–45.

Roth, K. and Morrison, A.J. (1990) An empirical analysis of the integration-responsiveness framework in global industries, *Journal of International Business Studies*, 21(4): 541–64.

Ryle, G. (1945) Knowing how and knowing that, *Proceedings of the Aristotelian Society*, 46 (1945–46): 1–16.

Simonin, B.L. (1999) Ambiguity and the process of knowledge transfer in strategic alliances, *Strategic Management Journal*, 20: 595–623.

Soni, P.K., Lilien, G.L. and Wilson, D.T. (1993) Industrial innovation and firm performance: a Re-conceptualization and exploratory structural equation analysis, *International Journal of Research in Marketing*, 10: 365–80.

Soo, C.W., Devinney, T.M., Midgley, D.F. and Deering, A. (2002) Knowledge management: philosophy, pitfalls and processes, *California Management Review*, 44(4): 129–50.

Steensma, H.K. and Lyles, M.A. (2000) Explaining IJV survival in a transitional economy through social exchange and knowledge-based perspectives, *Strategic Management Journal*, 21(8): 831–51.

Stuart, T.E. (2000) Interorganizational alliances and the performance of firms: a study of growth and innovation rates in a high-technology industry, *Strategic Management Journal*, 21: 791–811.

Szulanski, G. (1996) Exploring internal stickiness: impediments to the transfer of best practice within the firm, *Strategic Management Journal*, 17: 27–43.

Teece, D., Pisano, G. and Shuen, A. (1997) Dynamic capabilities and strategic management, *Strategic Management Journal*, 18(7): 509–33.

Teece, D.J. (1998) Capturing value from knowledge assets: the new economy, markets for know-how, and intangible assets, *California Management Review*, 40(3): 55–79.

Tsai, W. (2001) Knowledge transfer in intraorganizational networks: effects of network position and absorptive capacity on business unit innovation and performance, *Academy of Management Journal*, 44(5): 996–1004.

Werts, C.E., Linn, R.L. and Joreskog, K.G. (1974) Interclass reliability estimates: testing structural assumptions, *Educational and Psychological Measurement*, 34: 25–33.

Yli-Renko, H., Autio, E. and Sapienza, H.J. (2001) Social capital, knowledge acquisition, and knowledge exploitation in young technology-based firms, *Strategic Management Journal*, 22(6–7): 587–614.

Zander, U. and Kogut, B. (1995) Knowledge and the speed of the transfer and imitation of organizational capabilities: an empirical test, *Organization Science*, 6(1): 76–92.

# 12
## Making Sense of Customer Relationship Management Strategies in a Technology-Driven World

*V. Anyfioti, S. Dutta and T. Evgeniou*

In a world where rapid technological changes lead to continuously innovative forms of interactivity and connectivity among companies and customers, Customer Relationship Management (CRM) has emerged as a key managerial issue that companies increasingly need to master. The available CRM strategic options are now numerous. This chapter provides a framework that can enable managers to have a better understanding of the current status of CRM and future trends in their industry. We introduce a model that looks simultaneously at the two main levers of change in the market today: the increasing interactivity with customers and the networking effect among the market elements, namely customers and companies. Using examples from today's market we point out that scoring high in all CRM dimensions is not necessarily ideal for each and every company and we identify the key factors that should be taken into account in defining a successful CRM strategy.

### What is new in the market today

Since the days when Henry Ford gave customers a choice of any colour so long as it was black, companies in all industries have been increasingly parting from treating clients en masse with an 'I make it – you buy it' approach, to incorporating them in the design of their value propositions. Advanced communication and information technologies have led to high connectivity and rich interactivity among the 'market elements', namely customers and companies, triggering continuous changes in their roles and thereby leading to evolving CRM strategies.

We identify two key trends that include the majority of the issues a CEO is discussing with the CRM managers today:

- Customers are increasingly interactive, co-creating value and providing information to companies that use it effectively to define their value propositions.
- Companies and customers get connected in sophisticated information and relationship networks.

Firstly, the customers who have traditionally played a role as the 'passive receivers' of a firm's standard products are now becoming active value creators, often interacting closely with the companies. They are 'transmitting' their individual preferences collected in companies' databases, guiding the companies' value offerings, and expecting a product tailored to their individual needs. They now recognize that they have the opportunity to get 'exactly that' and not 'close to' what they want, by taking a step further from getting informed and knowledgeable on products and companies to actually interactively directing the companies explicitly – like in the case of surveys and after-sales services – or more and more often implicitly – for example, simply because now companies can track and store traces of customers' decisions processes easier – to make the perfect products for them.

High interactivity leads to a plethora of customer profile data that companies use to gain competitive advantage. Even though most initiatives are still concerned with collecting data in unified data warehouses – surprisingly even technology leaders like Microsoft had hundreds of customer databases until the mid-1990s (Seybold, 1998, 2001) – more and more often companies also analyse this data in various sophisticated ways with the help of widely available technologies to decide and often customize their value propositions. Amazon's 'collaborative filtering' technology is a well-known example, and similar technology is now used by a plethora of companies: using this clustering/profiling method companies provide useful recommendations to customers based on the combined preferences of groups of profiles with 'similar tastes', thereby increasing cross-selling opportunities. 'Cookies', tags that identify computers and can also be used to accurately identify geographical locations of users, are now widely used to track the navigation course of a web user in a website, providing information that is used, for example, to redesign the pages and information flow for maximum convenience or for targeted advertisement. Data mining techniques are increasingly being used to shed light on important issues such as which customers are interested in what, how to bundle products, or how to identify customers likely to leave.

The interactivity of customers with companies, however, goes further than information exchange: customers even participate more and more in the creation of the final products themselves! eBay, the internet auction site, provides an excellent example of co-creation (Friesen, 2001). Unlike traditional auctions, the customers provide the content of the auction catalogues, and also police the process by rating the products and the participants' credibility in each auction. eBay simply provides the platform and customers do the rest! The online bookseller Amazon offers another example: customers provide their book reviews and ratings, which become an essential source of value for future buyers. For information portals, such as AOL, Yahoo!, and Terra-Lycos, the customers provide a large part of the content of their sites – an impressive 65 per cent of Terra-Lycos' content (personal webpages, chatrooms, reviews and so on) (Terra-Lycos, 2001). The objective is not only to attract new customers but also to engage the existing ones in a constant interfacing process that will gradually build up their brand loyalty.[1] Nike provides a very good example of an offline company practising the same strategy through the Internet. On its website, Nike offers consumers the possibility to create their very own pair of shoes (or gloves or baseball bats) with their own choice of colours and their name or identity printed on the final product. The whole process is highly interactive, quick and playful, so that even if one doesn't end up purchasing 'personalized trainers', this process makes it very likely that these are the first products to catch the customer's attention the next time they enter a sports retail chain. At the same time this offers Nike the chance to learn directly from its customers about the new market trends. In this sense, Nike customers are also indirectly involved in new product development – an example of how deeply in the value chain the interaction with the customers reaches.

The second significant change, alongside increasing customer involvement and information exchange, is the extensive networking phenomenon among the market elements – namely customers and companies. This is not a brand new idea: companies have been forming partnerships and exchanging information with their suppliers and customers for many years. However, the development of technologies such as databases and the Internet has led to an explosion of information exchange between partnering companies and also among customers. As an SAP manager (SAP, 2001) put it, 'traditional CRM approaches would stop "at the doorstep" of the company's selling organisation. Today to be successful in CRM you have to extend your strategy to the company's back offices and also to external "ecosystems", suppliers, competitors, etc'. It is important to emphasize that this is a significant departure from traditional views of CRM (Seybold, 2001; Peppers and Rogers, 2001) that focus on the one-to-one relations of companies with customers: in this new process, CRM is also about how companies exploit the connectivity of the companies in their ecosystems and also the connectivity among their customers.

To begin with, with the help of the Internet it has become easy to link companies dynamically, in a sense creating partnerships 'on the fly', and giving customers the possibility to navigate seamlessly from one company to another. A company can easily refer to another's products on its website and, for example, if the customer follows the link and completes a purchase, this can lead to the payment of a pre-agreed commission fee. Affiliate programs are in this spirit. CD-Now, the online music retailer, was one of the first companies to implement such a program attracting most of the customers through it. By the mid-1990s Amazon had around 100,000 associates, a number that would have taken many years to reach without the easy links provided by the Internet. At the same time, new technologies further facilitate and enhance the benefits of these 'virtual partnerships on the fly'. For example technologies like the cookies-based DART of the online marketing company Doubleclick can be used to track customers' navigation routes for a network of partnering websites and then offer to the member companies better targeted online advertising. Microsoft Passport, which claims to offer consumers a relief from the usual hassle of entering their details in each and every website of a network of companies, is creating an integrated, seamless experience for the web surfers, while creating even more value to the participating companies in a form of invaluable information to refine their CRM strategies. Recent technological advances like XML-based CPExchange facilitate the exchange of customer information across companies and promise even deeper networking.

These are examples of a general trend, much broader and fundamental than information-based networking, that we have witnessed in the past few years both online and offline. It is the notion that companies – even competing ones – get together and, by using each other's products, supply chains, databases, and often customers, manage to extend their original offerings and move beyond their traditional target market segments. The philosophy 'I can't make it therefore I am not interested in it' is becoming obsolete. Through multidimensional partnerships companies can explore cross-selling opportunities, increase the number of 'touch points' with their customers, and offer complete solutions, thereby winning the customer's 'share of wallet' and increase customer loyalty. It doesn't really matter whether all the products a company sells carry the company's brand name. What is really important is that the customer has come to the company for ideas and has trusted the suggestions! British Airways offers one example of this. Their frequent flyer portfolio now includes several options, which are offered via a network of partners and often can lead to extra rewards. One can fly with BA Airways, but one can in addition organize one's holidays with BA Holidays, open an offshore bank account with Royal Bank of Canada, take out a new credit card with Visa – and even win loyalty air miles by doing home shopping at Sainsbury's. At the same time British Airways is a member of one of the pan-airline loyalty schemes, which includes other competing companies, such as Aer Lingus, American Airlines, Cathay Pacific and Iberia. Such alliances offer customers the possibility of winning interchangeable loyalty miles across the network of partners, thereby rewarding them for being 'loyal' to one of them. For the participating companies this means cross-selling and customer retention, but at the same time potential data sharing with some of their competitors – an example that shows how CRM has redrawn the line between business partners and competitors.

Customers also get together, interact, and consult each other more easily. The usual form of contact is through virtual communities of common interests, which are used as platforms to exchange ideas, share opinions, or make buying decisions. Many companies have already embraced the concept of communities, recognizing that it can be a powerful marketing and loyalty building tool. For example, the Wall Street Journal Interactive Edition creates forums where the readers can enter into discussions about 'hot' issues, returning to the same site often to check for responses, post something new, etc. Similarly, Microsoft's portal MSN and free e-mail service Hotmail, both a departure from Microsoft's core business in developing and selling software programs, provide Microsoft with a network of almost 100 million faithful consumers who use Hotmail to interact and in that way can be more easily lured to other services offered by MSN and to Microsoft products that are also linked with Hotmail, such as MS Outlook. In this way they, increase customer lock-in. Increasing customer interconnectivity is also used to create a customer community or forum for after-sales support. In a dedicated support 'chat forum' on the company's website, the customers offer advice to each other on common questions or simple problems encountered during the use of the products. For example, among other services Cisco operates the Open Forum, a database that researches quick answers to technical questions from a technical library or gives access to experts in the case of more complicated questions. By 1997, the Open Forum was already averaging 4,500 new technical questions per week.

## Introducing the Customer Integration–Market Integration matrix

To help managers to understand how the two identified trends (customer interactivity and market networking) have affected the dynamics of their industry so far and what are the anticipated moves in the future we have developed the Customer Integration and Market Integration matrix (see Exhibit 1 'The Customer Integration–Market Integration Matrix' at the end of this chapter). How a company scores in this framework reflects the breadth and depth of the CRM strategy followed, and the variety and effectiveness of the CRM tools used (see Exhibit 2 'CRM tools and strategies').

A company that scores low in both Customer and Market Integration is adopting a '*prêt-à-porter*' approach. It serves market segments rather than individual customers, typically does not aggregate and analyse customer data to target customers on a one-to-one basis, and its products and services follow directly from its own supply chain without getting into partnerships with companies that are not integral to that supply chain. This positioning may be more natural for some industries, such as the mass production consumer companies in food, healthcare, home care (companies such as Procter & Gamble, Colgate-Palmolive and Johnson & Johnson). These companies were set up to create, promote, and sell branded products to the mass consumer market. The level of complexity in their business in terms of number of products, customers, distribution channels and so on, and the massive economies of scale in manufacturing would not easily and cost-effectively support one-to-one marketing relationships and certain types of customization.

An industry or company that would score high in Customer Integration but low in Market Integration (occupying the top left-hand corner of the matrix) is instead like a '*tailor shop*'. Companies in this position would be expected to collect detailed information on their customers, beyond their purchase history and demographic data, from all available customer 'touch points' that is meeting points between company and customer. Then the data would be analysed and based on the findings the offerings would be adapted and customized for each individual customer or precise segment. Finally a company scoring high in Customer Integration would be expected to have a highly interactive communication front with the customers – it would provoke and then use their suggestions. At the same time, the low score in Market Integration would mean that the company does little in terms of partnering with others to extend its product range, or using customer communities to secure brand loyalty. Examples that would in general fit this positioning could be found in the heavy build-to-order industries – turbomachinery, shipbuilding, etc. In these cases the final product takes a long time to get to market and is extremely customer-specific (based on highly customized technical specifications). The company has therefore to know in great detail all the preferences of the customer and the latter is normally very much involved in the production process. In addition, in these industries, brand loyalty is usually built on the grounds of great expertise on a rather limited range of products and services, so downstream partnerships are unnecessary. In these industries, of course, because of the limited number of customers, a good CRM strategy may even be equivalent to simply good key account managers.

The lower right quadrant, characterized by high Market Integration, and low Customer Integration, features companies that offer a *'department store'* experience. These are very well connected and networked in the market, but target segments rather than individual customers. This translates to an extensive partnership web, horizontal and/or vertical, through which the company offers to the targeted customer segments a broad rather than a deep relationship. Market intermediaries, whose core capability is in extensive networking and aggregation of various goods and services, naturally fall in this quadrant. A familiar example of this concept is the 'shopping mall'. Its business model is not about offering customized solutions to individual buyers, but rather providing a huge variety of choices in an extremely convenient 'package' for some targeted customer clusters. Of course, for a company to be successful in the 'shopping mall' model, consumers have to regard its choices of third parties as having the same credibility as its own brand. To make a distinction here: we are not talking about one company extending its product range via brand extensions (even in unrelated product categories), as in the case of Virgin. We are talking here about a company that has partnered with other firms to expand to product categories that maybe have nothing to do with its core product offering. One example is the Sainsbury's partnership with Boots, which means that a grocery retailer will host beauty/pharmacy mini-stores in some of their outlets. Sainsbury's applies the same concept with Oddbins, opening 'in the store' wine stores. A high score in Market Integration would also mean some networking from the side of customers. The company would have created a community for customers (or potentials) with similar topics of interest, related to the products on offer.

This leaves us with the final quadrant in the matrix, characterized by high Customer Integration and high Market Integration. A company positioned there is like a *'personal shopper'*. It would be expected to combine: (a) extensive knowledge of the customer, (b) 'segment of one' customization possibilities, (c) a network of partners exploiting all available cross and up selling potential and (d) an interactive community of customers, who communicate and co-operate with the company to help create more value and who, in parallel, network with other customers and offer 'word-of-mouth' marketing. Is this an ideal situation? The truth is that benefits from a certain move – towards higher customer and/or market integration – can only be realized if the customers do need this extra value and are ready to pay for it. So, is the top right quadrant ideal for each and every industry? As we discuss below, it is not necessarily ideal for all companies to score in the top right quadrant of the proposed model. There are factors inherent in an industry or related to the specific market dynamics, which may predetermine the position of a certain industry on the matrix as well as the expected future evolution. To understand how the positioning of an industry or company would be defined as a result of any inherent characteristics of the industry, how it has evolved as a result of industry trends and dynamics, and how it is expected to change in the future depending on the CRM strategies to be applied, we now study some specific examples from different industries and then discuss some general principles to decide the ideal positioning in the proposed framework.

## Case studies

### Food retail industry

Although traditionally in the lower left 'Prêt-à-Porter' quadrant – retailers would offer mainly food products, display the merchandise on the shelves in a not-very-consumer-friendly fashion, and offer no possibility of customization of the shopping experience, this positioning has changed in the last few years – at least among the more advanced players – as new ideas in retailing and new technologies have made their impact (see Exhibit 3 'Example: Food Retailing Industry').

On the customer integration side we suggest that the shift so far was mainly the result of the implementation of category management programmes for positioning the products on the shelves according to shopping pattern indexes – revealed from the analysis of consumer spending data – and appointing one supplier in certain product categories as the 'category captain'. Although it is not often associated directly with CRM, the nature of the idea is very much related to customer integration – effectively changing the offerings based on information from the customers. Beyond category management, however, in the future we expect not only limited changes along the customer integration axis, but also that the focus will be on ideas that have, to some extent, already been tried and tested: loyalty cards and e-tailing.

Loyalty cards in food retailing started as a way to reward the higher spending customers while in parallel collecting valuable customer data in a non-intrusive way. The loyalty cards promised to offer personal information combined with transactional data that would help retailers to draw conclusions about several issues, such as which lines to continue, which lines to drop, which new products to introduce and so on. However, at the time of writing there is limited momentum in the industry towards that direction. In the UK, Safeway pulled out of the loyalty scheme in May 2002, announcing that it would rather return to the traditional price cut promotions, while saving about $50 million annually in costs. Asda, another big food retailer in the UK, tried the concept regionally but abandoned a nation-wide implementation. Sainsbury's and Tesco, on the other hand, are sticking with their loyalty schemes. They both claim that the data collected from the cards will help them to target customers better and increase their sales. It is hard to say which side is right. The truth is that loyalty cards request huge investment not only in installing software and hardware applications, but also in managing the data once it has been collected. Something similar is happening in e-tailing, which two years ago seemed to be about to start a new phase of evolution in grocery shopping. As with loyalty cards the concept has yet to take off. The initially forecasted numbers of customers that would do their grocery shopping online seem to have been overoptimistic.

On the other hand, we suggest that in future the major move of the industry will be focused on Market Integration rather than on Customer Integration initiatives. The key concept that will lead to higher Market Integration is the extension of the food retailers' partnership networks to non-core product categories, meaning non-food products, financial services, gas stations, car repairs and so on. This is a phenomenon that was initially used as a differentiating factor. However, today customers desire to do the grocery shopping and all other 'every-day' activities at the same location, to maximize convenience. Also, while the grocery market is mature, consumers' leisure spending has been increasing and offers better margin opportunities. This means that, in order, to continue profitable growth, food retailers will need to consider partnering with banks, petrol companies, travel agencies, printing shops, etc. to offer 'complementary' services to consumers, as in the example of Sainsbury's discussed above.

What does this mean in practice for a CRM manager of a food retail chain? In the view of a Partner at Roland Berger Strategy Consultants in Retail and Consumer Goods (Roland Berger, 2001):

> this increase in Market Integration is the next efficiency level step that all players, bigger or smaller will be required to take. This means that for those companies in the industry that have not yet made great advancements on their partnership and networking CRM approaches, some activation will be required sooner or later. This will not be about gaining competitive advantage but about staying afloat.

### Consumer electronics: Dell and HP

Dell is a company that was built around the concept of maximum Customer Integration – that is, it offers totally customized solutions to its customers, either consumers or businesses. It has separated its clients into clusters, and is currently in the process of redefining these cus-tomer segments into a total of 11 sub-groups (Peppers and Rogers, 2001), which helps to evaluate and pre-select products and services that would better suit each group. The customization process doesn't stop here. Once customers choose the type of computer they want to pur-chase, they can go ahead and configure the machine exactly in accor-dance with their needs or preferences, selecting from a series of options proposed by Dell. In a typical example more than 20 configu-ration possibilities will be offered, with multiple options on the key features: memory, hard drives, operating system, dock stations, key-board and so on. The details of each purchase are then stored by Dell under a unique customer and order or purchase number. This not only gives customers the ability to track the progress of a particular order at any time, but also gives Dell all the necessary historical data about each customer to offer ideas for future purchases and after-sales service. The extensive data collection and the comprehensive integration of information, complemented by Dell's next-day-on-site service support contracts (probably unique today for a large PC manufacturer), have repeatedly won Dell awards in customer satisfaction ratings, or service and reliability surveys.

PremierDell.com, directed at business customers (Peppers and Rogers, 2001), is one more example of a move along the customer integration axis. It is a web-based utility that gives customers the opportunity to manage their own business information and IT purchasing functions. More specifically, PremierDell.com is an extranet environment where customers can log on with the use of a password and have access to all of the information related to their business relationship with Dell – order tracking data, customized purchase orders, warranty deadlines, hardware inventory, purchase history and so on. The same extranet can also be used for the ordinary purchasing of new equipment, and even gives the possibility to the employees of the business customer to make their own purchases.

Dell is indisputably the highest scorer in Customer Integration in this industry and probably the only company that will manage to exploit the full competitive advantage of interacting with the customer at a truly one-to-one level. The reason is, of course, that since its inception the company has made customization and a direct one-to-one relationship with the customer its unique selling proposition. Thus, the infrastructure, the operations, the products and services, the kinds of people employed, everything about Dell is geared towards this concept. But what is Dell doing on the Market Integration side? Firstly, in their product catalogue they include a category called 'Software & Accessories', which offers various products – from printers, monitors and projectors to palm pilots and digital cameras. This part of the catalogue mainly features the products of other manufacturers and sometimes even competing ones, such as HP and Mitsubishi. In addition, Dell runs an affiliation program for those online companies that would like to refer customers to Dell and receive a commission upon completion of sale. In addition, on the Dell website one can find an after-sales service forum, where customers can ask for advice on technical or other issues and where they can get answers from other customers. Although very often a Dell representative ('talk moderator') intervenes in the customer exchanges, the structure of the site encourages the exchange of ideas and answers among the customers themselves. Finally Dell has business alliances with some software manufacturers – including Microsoft, WebMD, MedicaLogic – which target some of Dell's customer segments, for example Healthcare Public customers. Thus, Dell has made some strides on this axis, too.

Let us now take an example of a different business model in the same industry, Hewlett Packard. We wish to concentrate, in particular, on the B2C side of the HP business, which they call the Consumer Business Organization (CBO). In this case, the direct sales to consumers represent a very small percentage of the overall sales; the majority of the sales is made through wholesale and retail channels (at least on the B2C side of the business). Therefore, to begin with, HP doesn't control the relationship with the end users of their products, at least during the first stages of 'select and buy'. In the later phases of the customers' lifecycle (use, repurchase, recommendation), HP has the possibility to interact directly with at least a percentage of its customers. However, the initial contact is made through wholesalers and retailers. This creates an inherent difficulty in collecting and analysing customer data.

In order to initiate the direct customer relationship, given that they have no contact to the consumers at the moment of purchase, HP relies on registration cards that are included in the packaged final product and have to be filled in so that the warranty cover begins. After initiating the relationship with the consumers (at a later stage in the lifecycle of the product, when the registration cards are not filled), Hewlett Packard uses the information to conduct a segmentation exercise and subsequently targets consumer segments rather than individual users. As an HP Head of Customer Contact and Consumer Knowledge (HP, 2001) puts it:

> For us the one-to-one relationship is equivalent to mass customization. *For each business case there is a correct level of customization* ... If we tried in our consumer business organization to combine our present distribution model with a name-by-name relationship with our customers, we would end up with something complex and too expensive, for which customers would be unwilling to pay any premium.

Examples of such segments are the 'Proven Productivity' technology users that are looking for products and services to improve the efficiency and effectiveness of their work, or the 'Status seekers' that includes customers looking for a cutting-edge product, which at the same time is trendy and fashionable. HP will then try to strengthen the relationship with the consumers by sending them selected information on new products or services, special offers, tricks and tips, etc., all reflecting the needs and preferences of the segment in which they have been classified. So although HP does not have the fine-grained customer information that Dell can gather due to its distribution model, it can still have and use some information about its customers.

HP's decision to sell through wholesalers and retailers also creates different partnering choices and constraints along the Market Integration axis. The distribution chain (principally retailers) could be a major source of information about the end users. They know who bought HP products, when, and in conjunction with which other products – valuable customer behaviour data not only to drive even better customer segmentations, but also to find new cross-selling opportunities. If, in addition, the retailer operates some loyalty scheme (or similar), then they can even provide personal information about individual consumers. HP could collaborate with retailers to collect and analyse such broad customer data that would lead to better-targeted solutions and cross-selling for the different customer segments. In fact, HP is currently piloting a number of such collaboration programmes. Such partnerships, of course, take time because they require the building up of a certain level of trust with the retailers in order to make them feel comfortable that HP would not use such data to 'disintermediate' them. In exchange HP must be able to offer valuable information that would help retailers to achieve higher revenues per outlet, per product category and so on. The indirect sales channel also puts some further constraints on HP when it comes to pursuing *independent* alliances and cross-selling agreements, again for fear of channel conflict issues. Thanks to its business model, on the Market Integration axis HP faces a more complicated task in choosing and working with its partners. Despite these difficulties, there is a high likelihood that the value that could be created through such integration will be well worth the effort.

## The portals industry

The final example that we consider is the web portals industry, home to players such as AOL, Yahoo!, and MSN. This is an interesting industry for several reasons. Firstly, the offering to customers is content or information – a product that is easily customizable. Secondly, it is an industry owing its existence to the Internet and one that is built around the efficient and innovative use of technology. Concepts such as data collection, data integration and mining, and customer profiling are at the foundations of these businesses, and thus they have few of the difficulties in migrating to CRM-fluent organizations that more traditional businesses have. These factors indicate a high 'natural' Customer Integration positioning. Moreover, the initial business idea for portals was to create sites that would become 'reference points' for consumers.

The fundamental basis for that is to be able to aggregate about each topic of interest the maximum amount of reliable information, from the biggest possible set of 'partners', whether these are other companies or the consumers' community. In addition to the reference business, all the portals have quickly diversified into shopping, chat forums, hotel booking services etc. These two together position the portals' world in the high Market Integration, quadrant of the matrix.

Let's examine AOL as one example of how high Customer Integration and high Market Integration works in reality. For example, on the Customer Integration front, AOL has been very active in the development of a first-class customer support service. As early as 1993 they started a total revamping of their IT support infrastructure. They offer several different support channels to their clients: toll-free telephone, online, fax link and bulletin boards. On the online channel, the customer can choose between live conference, e-mail responses from AOL support representatives, and online messaging board where members would respond to one another. However, what gives AOL a high score in Customer Integration is the fact that they have built an IT infrastructure, which monitors all calls, e-mails, etc., to the support centers. This information is then used to analyze the causes of technical questions, as well as the offered resolutions and to make relevant improvements to the newer versions of the software. The IT system also gives the possibility to the support staff to view all client information and history when answering a technical question. But more important, AOL also uses the analysis of customer data as a tool to decide on new services or upgrades of its software. For example the personal calendar and personal stock portfolio tracking were included in the site when AOL discovered that customers were more likely to renew subscriptions and maintain accounts when AOL was part of their daily routines. Still on the customer integration axis, other examples include MyAOL which allows users to personalize the AOL web pages that they usually navigate, on-line customer support through real-time personal interaction at Shop@AOL, and the list goes on.

AOL also provides plenty of Market Integration examples. When navigating the Shop@AOL pages, the user effectively enters a gigantic shopping centre with numerous product categories and merchandising partners. At the moment more than 300 AOL Certified Merchants are featured on the site. AOL guarantees to consumers that these partners comply with some criteria preset by AOL and provides tools that help customers browse, get informed, and choose products. For example users can sort requests for products by category, relevance, price, popularity, name or brand, can call on a 24 × 7 basis to a member of the AOL support staff to ask for navigation and other details, or can use the AOL clearance house for great bargains.

But AOL has extended its partnership network to areas other than shopping. The most famous content-driven partnership came from the merger of AOL with the media giant Time Warner. Some recent initiatives resulting from this merger: pre-listening to music singles, sneak previews of video clips, behind-the-scenes footage before new songs debut, and a subscription music service serving up thousands of songs from selected music labels. Another partnership is that with CitiGroup for the provision of a payments infrastructure for ecommerce transactions and for moving money easily on the Internet. The technology is embedded throughout AOL's numerous affiliates, such as CompuServe, Digital Cities and AOL.com. Citigroup's family of products, including brokerage and insurance services from subsidiaries Salomon Smith Barney Inc. and Travelers Group Inc., are the preferred financial services brands on AOL.

However, the concept that probably creates the highest percentage of value for AOL on the Market Integration axis, is the company's focus on the use of customer communities as integral part of their business model. As in 1995 the *New York Times* were quoting 'Wherever it goes, AOL's focus is on fostering interest-based communities on-line. The service's members spend 60% of their time communicating with each other'. Applications such as the Instant Messaging (or ICQ as many people know it) have put AOL at the top of the list of the 'least intimidating' Internet Service Providers and have won the loyalty of many online amateurs, who use the Internet mostly as a communication tool.

If we look in detail at the activities of other portals we find similar initiatives that target either the customization of the information (often with the customer's intervention) or the aggregation of cross-selling opportunities through a network of commercial partners. Not all companies necessarily score the same along the two axes but they are typically found in the top right quadrant, with the trend to move to even higher Customer and Market Integration.

## Managerial implications

It is quite clear from the previous analysis that CRM does not and should not mean the same for every company. The High–High quadrant is not the ultimate aspiration, and equally the positioning of a company in the Low–Low quadrant should not be regarded as equivalent to a 'grey' future. A company's CRM strategy should be based on the inherent characteristics of the industry, the actions expected of the other players, and the internal operational/cultural obstacles that the company has to overcome. In the final section of this chapter we will try to summarize some observations drawn from our previous analysis, which can be used to determine the appropriate level of Customer or Market Integration for a given industry (see exhibit 'Managerial Decision Factors').

## Customer integration decision factors

● *Some customers are more valuable than others*

As we discussed in the HP example, one way to determine the optimal degree of interaction between a company and its customers is to profile the customer base by value. In other words, if 20 per cent of the customers provide 80 per cent of the revenues and/or profits, then it may be worthwhile to invest time and money in establishing personal and highly tailored relationships with each one of these customers – especially where the absolute value of each customer's business is substantial. Such industries include banking, heavy build-to-order industries like shipbuilding, the aerospace and defence industry, real estate, etc. If, however, the value per customer is evenly distributed among the customer base (a situation that is frequently the case in mass-produced, low-ticket items) the costs of high Customer Integration may not be justified in economic terms. Moreover, two further obstacles stand in the way of Customer Integration for these companies: the operational difficulties involved in mass-customizing mass-produced products, and the reliance on third-party distribution channels. These third parties often tightly control access to customer data and may refuse to stock too wide a variety of any one manufacturer's products.

Take as an example a manufacturer of personal healthcare products like Colgate Palmolive. Their most loyal customer that never uses any other toothpaste but Colgate during her entire life would, overall, contribute less than $1,000 in 60 years of use. Even if we add all of the other product categories of Colgate Palmolive (personal care, household care, fabric care and pet nutrition) and assume the same 100 per cent loyalty, we still would not achieve much more than $5,000 over 60 years of use. This would be something like the maximum customer lifetime value in revenues that Colgate Palmolive could achieve with a single customer. It is easy to imagine how much money would be justifiable for this same customer in CRM!

- *Variability/uncertainty in customer needs/demand vs easy product differentiation*

Another decisive factor is the variability and the uncertainty in the customers' needs. If we use the same example of Palmolive, the company can have a high degree of certainty that by conducting conventional market research they can more or less direct their product development to cover most of the consumer's needs. The variability in tastes, preferences and buying patterns in toothpaste and healthcare products are not extremely diverse and in the final purchase decision, the functional – that is, cleaning teeth – outweighs the discretionary (whether there is a toothpaste with, for example, sweet & sour taste). This means that engaging in a one-to-one dialogue with the consumers and allowing them to create their own product would drive up complexity without necessarily creating the kind of extra value for the customer for which they would be prepared to pay an adequate premium. On the other hand, the example of AOL shows that when product differentiation is cheap – as in the case of information goods – then satisfying high variability of customer needs is economically feasible and promising.

## Market integration decision factors

- *Complexity of the value chain*

When looking at the Market Integration side and the examples from our analysis, one characteristic that should be taken into account is the complexity and fragmentation of the value chain in the industry. The more complex is choosing, buying, and using a product or service, the more necessary it will be for the customer to establish a relationship with an 'aggregator' of products, services and information.

Customers do not want to maintain many 'best friend' relationships with companies. Each of these commercial relationships requires time to provide information and interact with the company, and the customer will not offer this privilege unless they can see a clear benefit in the increase in convenience and comfort that this relationship will offer. Such a close contact is often necessary when the selection–purchase–use cycle involves many steps, numerous companies and a great deal of information. In such cases, customers may seek help in one company that can reliably aggregate all the necessary data and suggest the right overall solution. An industry that provides such an example is construction engineering in heavy industries, for example refinery, petrochemicals, etc. When a company like BP wants to build a new facility it will hire a construction engineering company, such as Fluor Corporation, or Bechtel Group, and this company will have the responsibility to aggregate all the necessary information and resources to define, buy and implement the project in conjunction with numerous external contractors.

- *Share of customer relationship*

Another factor that influences the extent of a company's investment in Market Integration initiatives is the share of the customer relationship that this company can assume given its position in the industry value chain. Consumers and business customers are not interested in having an endless number of CRM relationships. Within a given value chain, they typically prefer to have a relationship with a company that aggregates for them all the relevant information, services, products, etc. and thus increases the efficiency and convenience of purchase. Let's refer to this as 'breadth of trust'. At the same time the customers will accept suggestions and use a company's partnership network, only if they have a minimum 'level of trust' in the information aggregator. The combination of level of trust and breadth of trust will define the share of the customer relationship that a given company can get.

Imagine the following example: after a new car rolls off the production line, multiple providers of services or equipment position themselves between the car manufacturer and the end user: car retailers, insurance companies, leasing companies, repair shops, gas and car wash stations, telematics companies, consumer electronics companies and so on. Owning a car covers much more 'breadth of trust' than just choosing a car brand, which is mainly a 'level of trust' decision in the car manufacturer. This means that if a car manufacturer wants to establish and maintain a one-to-one relationship with the consumer, enhance brand loyalty and capture most of their lifetime value, they have to integrate those downstream steps in the value chain that would give them enough 'breadth of trust'. It is only a good combination of 'level of trust' with 'breadth of trust' that will make a relationship meaningful for a customer to build her loyalty upon!

The factors discussed above are not the only ones that should be involved in a decision of what level of Customer Integration and Market Integration a company should choose. After defining the characteristics that point to a certain 'natural' positioning of an industry in the matrix, as well as the anticipated trends that will change this positioning in the future, a company should focus on its internal strategy and dynamics. It is true that in some cases certain moves on the horizontal or the vertical axis will be necessary to remain competitive. One such example we analysed was in the food retailing industry, where a shift towards higher Market Integration is expected as the new 'efficiency level' for the whole industry. In this new situation, most players will have to follow or stay out of the game. However, there are other cases where a move away from the industry average can provide a major competitive advantage if designed and executed well – like the Tesco.com example. A successful shift demands a well-through-out strategy, an organizational structure and a company culture that support the changes and the choice of the right technologies.

## Exhibits

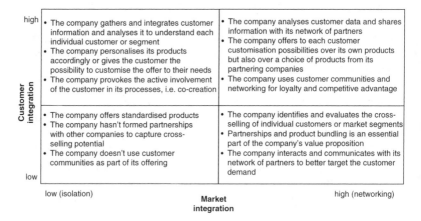

Exhibit 1   The Customer Integration–Market Integration Matrix

*CUSTOMER INTEGRATION measures*:

1. *Amount and quality of information exchanged between the customer and a company*
   Information here refers mainly to data transferred from the customer to the company (preferences, personal information, complaints, suggestions, etc.) or vice versa (that is in the form of customer service, etc.) rather than publicly released data on the company and its products (that is annual reports, etc.)
2. *Proactiveness of the customer in providing the company with the above information*
   Measures the degree of proactive interactivity between the customer and the company. Are there mechanisms that proactively guide the

customer to direct the company to the 'right' solutions? that is Are there mechanisms for the customers to provide all the relevant information – for example, through cookies – and also extra information – for example, reviews and ratings at Amazon and eBay – or co-create value – for example, the catalogues' content of eBay – if they wish to?

3. *Effective use of the collected information by the company*

Refers to the methods used within companies to analyse customer data (conjoint analysis, data mining, etc.) and consequently adapt their products or include new services that better satisfy individual customers or market segments. For example 1-800-flowers.com, the online shop for flowers and other gifts, stores the information provided by their corporate customers or consumers while buying gifts for different occasions and then uses this information for their 'reminder' service, where they send personalized e-mails to remind customers of an occasion for which they may need a present, and also suggest a present. Also, is the company proactively communicating with the customers, based on the information the latter have provided? For example, BankOne alerts customers to new bills as soon as they log on to online banking, and Juniper Bank alerts customers via e-mail, pager cell phone or PDA when a balance runs low or bills are due.

*MARKET INTEGRATION measures*:

1. *Connectivity among companies*

Refers to the extent and the quality (level of information exchange and the data integration between the company and its partners) of the partnership network of a company – either on the supply or on the demand side. Looks at the methods that a company employs to recognize and evaluate the cross-selling potential of individual customers or market segments and how well it captures this potential via a network of partnering companies. Connectivity among companies can also include the 'supply' side – that is, the networking between a company and its suppliers, which leads to better demands prediction and therefore more effective customer response.

2. *Connectivity among customers*

Looks at the role of customer communities within a certain industry and how effectively a company is using the existence and effects of customer networking as part of its business model. It measures the ability of a company to create value from the interactions between its customers – that is, increasing customer satisfaction by giving customers access to other customers' expertise.

296

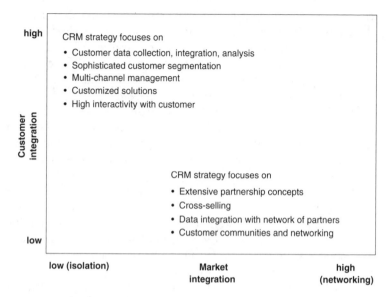

*Exhibit 2*   CRM Tools and Strategies

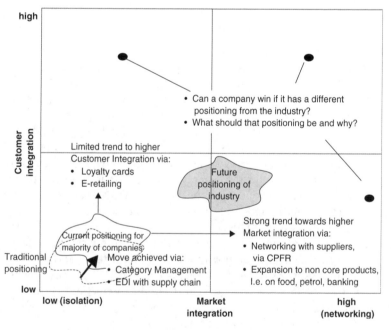

*Exhibit 3*   Example: Food Retailing Industry

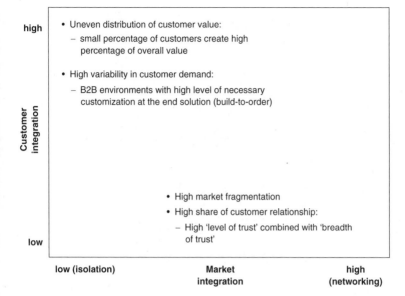

*Exhibit 4*   Managerial Decision Factors

## Note

1. With the cost of winning new customers being estimated at 4 or 5 times that of retaining the existing ones, it is no wonder that companies are constantly seeking novel ways to ensure loyalty.

## References

Friesen, B. (2001) Co-creation, When 1 and 1 make 11, *Consulting for Management*, March.
HP (2001) Private communication.
Peppers, D. and Rogers, M. (2001) *One to One B2B*. Doubleday.
Roland Berger Strategy Consultants (2001) Private communication.
SAP (2001) Private communication.
Seybold, P. (1998) *Customers.com*. Century Business Books, Random House, London.
Seybold, P. (2001) *The Customer Revolution*. Crown Pub. Century Business Books, Random House, London.
Terra-Lycos (2001) Private communication.

# Index